OXFORD HISTORICAL MONOGRAPHS

Editors

BARBARA HARVEY   A. D. MACINTYRE
R. W. SOUTHERN   A. F. THOMPSON
H. R. TREVOR-ROPER

THE ORIGINS OF
THE SECOND
REPUBLIC IN SPAIN

by

SHLOMO BEN-AMI

OXFORD UNIVERSITY PRESS
1978

Oxford University Press, Walton Street, Oxford OX2 6DP

OXFORD LONDON GLASGOW NEW YORK

TORONTO MELBOURNE WELLINGTON CAPE TOWN

IBADAN NAIROBI DAR ES SALAAM LUSAKA

KUALA LUMPUR SINGAPORE JAKARTA HONG KONG TOKYO

DELHI BOMBAY CALCUTTA MADRAS KARACHI

British Library Cataloguing in Publication Data
Ben-Ami, Shlomo
    The origins of the Second Republic in Spain—(Oxford historical monographs).
    1. Republicanism in Spain—History—20th century
    2. Spain—History—Dictatorship, 1923–1930
    3. Spain—Politics and government—1923–1930
    4. Spain—History—Revolution, 1931
    I. Title II. Series
    322.4'2'0946   DP247   78–40079

ISBN 0–19–821871–0

*Printed in Great Britain by
William Clowes & Sons Limited
London, Beccles and Colchester*

To
Ronen and Yotham

PREFACE

The Second Spanish Republic and the Civil War have excited students of history and have been the subject of important and pioneering studies. This understandable fascination with the 1930s has, however, helped to perpetuate the lack of scholarly attention directed towards the 1920s. This study seeks to help fill this historiographic lacuna and to aid an understanding of the roots of the Republic.

This book is not a narrative history of the years 1923–31, but is a study of Spain's political transformation from Dictatorship to Republic. The ephemeral and chaotic life of the First Spanish Republic (1873–74) discredited republicanism in Spain for years to come. It is thus of special interest to study the resurrection of republicanism in Spain during the 1920s and the beginning of the 1930s, as this was of crucial importance to the elaboration of a solid democratic alternative to arbitrary autocracy. Of similar importance was the growth of a well-organized, confident, and 'responsible' social democratic move-ment in Spain during the 1920s. The emphasis is on an examination of the democratic and 'modernizing' processes which were unleashed by Primo de Rivera's dictatorship and which culminated in the declaration of the Second Republic on 14 April 1931. Considerable attention is also focused on the first six months of Republican government. This is done in order to examine the transition from Monarchy to Republic at the national as well as at the local level, and to explain the origins of the Republic's drift towards a more accentuated radical posture after October 1931, a drift which has now become the issue of a heated historiographical controversy.

It is a special pleasure to me to acknowledge my debt to those persons and institutions who have helped me in the accomplish-ment of this book. Raymond Carr, Warden of St. Antony's College, Oxford, has used his vast knowledge, his experience in guiding research students, his endless patience and his warm personality to lead me into a fascinating and unexplored chapter of Spain's modern history. His help in bringing this book to print was invaluable. I am also indebted to Dr. Joaquín Romero Maura for being kindly available for frequent discussions during his directorship of the Iberian Centre at St. Antony's College. The present Director of the Centre, Dr. Juan Pablo Fusi and Dr. José Varela Ortega have both illuminated my way with their critical comments. I should also like to thank Mr. Adrian Lyttelton and Professor Hugh Thomas, who were my examiners when the thesis version of the present book was submitted for a D.Phil. degree, and who have subsequently encouraged me in undertaking its publication. The editors of the Oxford Historical Monographs Series, Dr. Angus Macintyre and Mr. A. F. Thompson have both made great efforts to overcome the technical difficulties which sometimes made the prospects of publishing this book look very gloomy.

I should like also to express my gratitude for the help given by the staffs of the following institutions: in Madrid, the Archivo Historico Nacional, the Biblioteca Nacional, the Ateneo Library, the Hemeroteca Nacional, and the Hemeroteca Municipal; in Salamanca, the Archivo de Salamanca; in London, the British Museum Reading Room, and the British Museum Newspaper Library at Colindale; and in Oxford, the Bodleian Library. I want to offer special appreciation to those people in Spain who opened their families' private papers to me: Doña Soledad Ortega, Doña Felica Unamuno, the Marquis of Santo Floro, the widow of Don Santiago Alba, and Dr. Romero Maura.

It is a pleasant duty to thank the authorities of the University of Tel-Aviv whose unfailing assistance has supported me throughout the preparation of this study. Professor Zvi Yaavetz, under whose guidance the Tel-Aviv University Department of History has become a congenial and stimulating focal point for students of history, has given continuous inspiration and encouragement. Finally, I am happy to acknowledge my gratitude to my wife who, in addition to providing secretarial assistance, has carried with devotion the burden of family responsibilities during my absences in Spain.

1977   SHLOMO BEN-AMI

CONTENTS

ABBREVIATIONS

I. SOURCES

ACM	*Acción Católica de la Mujer*
AHN	Archivo Histórico Nacional, Sección de Gobernación, Serie A
Alianza	*Boletín de Alianza Republicana*
BEO	*Boletín Eclesiástico del Obispado de . . .*
BOEA	*Boletín Oficial Eclesiástico del Arzobispado de . . .*
BOEO	*Boletín Oficial Eclesiástico del Obispado de . . .*
BOO	*Boletín Oficial del Obispado de . . .*
BUGT	*Boletín de la Unión General de Trabajadores*
DSCC	*Diario de Sesiones de las Cortes Constitutuyentes*
EC	*El Crisol*
ED	*El Debate*
EI	*El Imparcial*
EP	*El Progreso*
ES	*El Socialista*
F.O.	Foreign Office papers in the Public Record Office, London
HL	*Hojas Libres*
HMM	Hemeroteca Municipal de Madrid
LE	*La Epoca*
LV	*La Vanguardia*
MA	Maura Archive
NE	*Nueva España*
OA	Ortega Archive
RA	Romanones Archive
SA	Archivo de Salamanca, Jefatura, Servicio Documental. Sección Politico-Social
SAA	Santiago Alba Archive
SO	*Solidaridad Obrera*
UA	Unamuno Archive

II. INSTITUTIONS

AC	Acció Catalana
ACR	Acció Catalana Republicana
AR	Acción Republicana
ASR	Agrupación al Servicio de la Republica
CEDA	Confederación Española de Derechas Autónomas
CG	Comisión Gestora
CNT	Confederación Nacional de Trabajadores
CONCA	Confederación Nacional Católico-Agraria
CP	Comité Paritario
DP	Diputación Provisional
DR	Derecha Republicana
FAI	Federación Anarquista Ibérica
FNTT	Federación Nacional de Trabajadores de la Tierra
FRG	Federación Republicana Gallega
IRS	Instituto de Reformas Sociales
ORGA	Organización Republicana Gallega Autónoma
PRLD	Partido Republicano Liberal Demócrata
PRRS	Partido Republicano Radical Socialista
PSOE	Partido Socialista Obrero Español
UA	Unión Agraria
UGT	Unión General de Trabajadores
UM	Unión Monárquica
UP	Unión Patriótica

NOTE ON TERMINOLOGY

The main terminological problem a book on Spain presents is that of the anglicization of Spanish terms. This has been approached in this work in an arbitrary but consistent way.

I. The names of parties and institutions are used according to their most familiar sound. Thus 'Derecha Republicana' is preferred to the English 'Republican Right', and 'Accion Republicana' is preferred to 'Republican Action'. But, the 'Conservative Party' is preferred to the official Spanish name 'Partido Liberal-Conservador'. Institutions like *Ayuntamiento* (city council) and *Diputacion Provincial* (Provincial Council) are best known in their Spanish form, and have, consequently, been used in that form. As for place-names, only four have been anglicized: Catalonia for Cataluña, Biscay for Vizcaya, Seville for Sevilla, Castile for Castilla.

II. The following usage of capital letters has been adopted:
1. For the official name of institutions and corporate bodies.
2. For denoting the institutional aspect of a term. Therefore, 'Conservative', 'Republican', and 'Socialist' determine an organization or the affiliation to a body, whereas the same words with small letters denote the abstract concept of the terms.

III. Full details of books cited in the references will be found in the bibliography.

INTRODUCTION: FROM CONSTITUTIONAL MONARCHY TO POLITICAL VACUUM

In the years between 1868 and 1874 Spain had experienced political instability: a revolution against Queen Isabel II, a foreign king, the perpetual Carlist rebellions, a Republic, a cantonalist insurrection, a monarchist pronunciamiento, and the restoration of the Bourbons in the person of Alfonso XII. The political architect of the restored Monarchy, Cánovas del Castillo, laid the foundations of the so-called 'Restoration system', according to which the country was ruled until 1923, when Primo de Rivera 'pronounced' against the system, then in the words of its enemies 'exhausted'.

The message preached by Cánovas was that of conciliation within the Monarchy as the common institution which should embrace 'all Spaniards without any distinction whatsoever'. The constitution of 1876 was intended to be the major instrument of Cánovas in pursuing these aims. It provided for the co-sovereignty of the king and the parliament, and gave to the monarch the exclusive right both to appoint governments and to dissolve the Cortes. It was in the corridors of the Palacio de Oriente, the king's residence, rather than by an appeal to public opinion or to the electorate, that parties and politicians were expected to look for power. This involved the king in the pettiness of day-to-day politics and party intrigues, exposing him as well as the Monarchy to public criticism.

Cánovas was determined that a change of government should neither be caused nor followed by violent political upheavals in the nineteenth-century tradition. A 'pacific rotation'—the *turno pacífico*—between two major parties—Cánovas' Conservatives and Sagasta's Liberals—was, therefore, established. Both parties were expected to make this practice widely acceptable by attracting to the dynastic parties political forces on the extreme right and on the revolutionary and democratic left.[1] Foreign observers familiar with the European parliamentary system

[1] For the formation of the parties and the origins of the *turno* see R. Carr, *Spain 1808–1939*, pp. 357–60.

could not understand this artificial rotation of governments. 'The government here is not overthrown by a vote of no confidence in parliament nor by the defeat of a project of law nor because of the opposition of public opinion.'[2] This could not be otherwise, because the government designated by the king was always given the opportunity to 'make' new elections the results of which were 'prepared' by an electoral machine directed from the Ministry of Interior with the help of patronage and the manipulation of local political bosses, the *caciques*. The ruling party would then have a majority in parliament, and His Majesty's Opposition be granted a respectable share of seats. A government never lost an election. *Caciquismo*, a combination of manipulation by politicians, of administrative patronage—a natural growth in a politically illiterate electorate, became the essence of the system. 'The overturning of voting urns, the resurrection of the dead for voting lists, bribery and intimidation' in backward rural districts, combined with a massive abstentionism in the big cities, enabled the system to work relatively smoothly for years.[3]

By the turn of the century, however, the rotative system entered a process of disintegration, as the traditional parties were torn by dissidence. The Cuban disaster (1898), in which Spain lost the remnants of its old empire to the United States, forced many to think in terms of 'regeneration'. In politics, Silvela and Maura were the outstanding protagonists of regeneration by means of a political 'revolution from above' which would purify the system and would encourage public involvement in politics. Both failed. And in 1909 Maura managed to arouse against himself the 'revolution from below', a wave of popular protests against the Moroccan war, which culminated in the anti-clerical manifestations of the so-called 'Tragic Week' in Barcelona. This could have been treated by Maura simply as a problem of public order had not the Liberals joined a circumstantial alliance with the anti-dynastic left to bring about his downfall. The Liberals' adherence to the cry of 'Maura, No!' was a manifestation of the disintegration of

---

[2] *Le Figaro* 5 July 1890.
[3] For the quotation see G. de Azcárate, *El Régimen Parlamentario en la Práctica*, p. 79. For caciquismo see J. Costa, *Oligarquía y Caciquismo Como la Forma Actual de Gobierno en España, Urgencia y Modo de Cambiarla, passim.*

the *turno*.[4] Subsequently Maura split the Conservative Party and refused to play a role in the 'rotation', while the Liberals, though in power until late in 1913, were far from being a coherent team.

The disintegration of the traditional parties and the uneasy existence of the *turno*, both substantial threats to the Canovist system, came together with a growing menace from the anti-dynastic left, Catalan particularism, the army's renewed interference in politics and a disastrous involvement in Morocco. In the crisis of 1917 all these elements combined in a circumstantial alliance aimed at bringing about political reform; but the basic discrepancies between such a heterogeneous conglomeration enabled the regime to overcome the crisis by exploiting its differences.[5]

In the aftermath of 1917, the various Liberal and Conservative factions were unable to offer to the king coherent governments. The Liberals were split between *Romanonistas*, *Garcíaprietistas*, and *Albistas*—personalistic factions named after their leaders—while the Conservatives were torn by the uncompromising hostility between Dato and Maura; the former was the party's official leader, the latter unofficially patronizing a *Maurista* movement on the fringe of parliamentary politics. The postwar economic crisis also contributed to the exhaustion of the regime by stimulating an increasingly militant workers' movement, which in Catalonia was reflected in the anarcho-syndicalist campaign of terrorism to which the government reacted by counter-terrorism.[6]

To add to these difficulties, in July 1921 the already unpopular war in Morocco produced a shameful and disastrous defeat. Thousands of soldiers lay dead around Annual when an army of tribesmen had overrun their positions.[7] The fashionable slogan in politics was from now on the demand for an

[4] Carr, *Spain*, pp. 477–89. For a special study of the events of 1909 see J. Conelly Ullman, *La Semana Trágica*.

[5] For a detailed study see J. A. Lacomba, *La Crisis Española de 1917*. The issue is synthesized in Carr's *Spain*, pp. 500–6.

[6] For governments after 1917 see Carr, *Spain*, pp. 506–8. For the post-war economic crisis and social unrest see F. Romeu, *Les Clases Trabajadoras en España 1898–1930*, pp. 123–64.

[7] For Spain's wars in Morocco see D. Woolman, *Rebels in the Riff*. For Annual see especially pp. 80–102.

investigation into 'responsibilities' for the disaster. The fact that the king himself was believed to be behind General Silvestre's precipitate advance into the trap of Annual made the issue more sensitive. Neither the Conservative government that was in office when the 'disaster' occurred nor two subsequent Conservative governments (Maura's and Sánchez Guerra's) felt anxious to investigate the political, as opposed to the military 'responsibilities'. They would not give the liberals and the anti-dynastic left satisfaction on this score. And on 7 December 1922 a heterogeneous liberal coalition, presided over by García Prieto came to power in response to the cry for 'responsibilities'.[8]

Though vested interests might have been seriously alarmed by the advanced programmes of the government (these included a mild agrarian reform, taxation of excess war profits and of religious property, and the abolition of obligatory religious education), it was the issue of responsibilities for the Moroccan war, the Catalan question, and public order that created the ambiance which 'justified' Primo de Rivera's *coup d'état*.

By mid-July an investigating committee concerned with 'responsibilities' was appointed by the Cortes, which then dispersed for the summer vacation. On 1 October, parliament was to be reopened probably with a debate on the conclusions of the committee, in which Republicans and Socialists were also represented. *ABC* forecasted 'grave difficulties' for the regime in the course of the inquiry.[9] The Socialists meanwhile led a vociferous campaign against the Moroccan war and in favour of investigation of 'responsibilities'. The army and politicians, interested in whitewashing their respective faults, were publicly denigrated.[10]

On the other hand, military set-backs in Morocco during the summer and the government's lack of a coherent attitude towards the war invited criticism also from the right. The military were leading an unrestrained campaign against both the Liberal coalition and 'politicians' as a whole during the

---

[8] For the governments after Annual and 'responsibilities' see Vizconde de Eza, *Mi Responsibilidad en el Desastre de Melilla como Ministro de la Guerra*, pp. 5–16; Carr, *Spain*, pp. 521–22.

[9] *ABC* 11 July 1923.

[10] *ES* 31 July 1923; 1, 3, 9 September 1923. See also M. Cordero, *Los Socialistas y la Revolución*, pp. 40–1. Besteiro pointed to this campaign as the principal motive of the *coup d'état*: see A. Saborit, *J. Besteiro*, pp. 244–5.

months that preceded the *coup d'état*. Alba, the Minister of Foreign Affairs, was singled out for his pacifist policy in Morocco, and for depriving the army of the post of High Commissioner in the protectorate, a post which he gave to a politician, Luis Silvela. At the beginning of August a group of generals, including Primo de Rivera, met at the Casino Militar in Madrid to launch an open attack on the 'civilian criteria' held by Alba, and to point out the growing rift between the minister and 'the military family'.[11] The government was warned against pursuing Alba's advice, because the army 'would no longer tolerate being a toy in the hands of opportunistic politicians'.[12]

At the beginning of September, however, the government made a substantial step towards meeting the demands of the army by endorsing the recommendations of the General Staff, i.e. not to withdraw from the present lines in Morocco. This caused the resignation of the ministers Chapaprieta, Gasset, and Villanueva, who advocated economies in Morocco.[13] *Ejército Español* welcomed this development, and even had words of praise for the Minister of Foreign Affairs: 'Alba is now more conscious than ever of his duties as a statesman. He has abandoned for the moment projects which he had previously defended. He has demonstrated that he possesses the political understanding lacking in his dissident colleagues.'[14]

But, although the situation in Morocco was 'cleared of obstacles',[15] the government was not granted a truce by its opponents. Armed robberies in Barcelona and Gijón, terrorism and separatist demonstrations in Catalonia, and the 'extreme criteria' that seemed to be prevailing in the 'Committee of Responsibilities' combined to motivate a hysterical press campaign against the government. *ABC* deplored the 'sad impression' created by the disorientation in the coalition. *La Vanguardia* regarded the lack of coherence in the coalition as 'the collapse of the whole system' of the Restoration, and attacked the 'criminal lack of patriotism' of the ministers. *Ejército Español*,

[11] *Ejército y Armada* 2 Aug. 1923.
[12] Ibid. 14 Aug. 1923; and *El Ejército Español*, 21 Aug. 1923.
[13] *ABC* 1 Sept. 1923. For this governmental crisis see also J. Chapaprieta, *La Paz Fué Posible*, pp. 135–44.
[14] 3 Sept. 1923.
[15] *Ejército Español* 4 Sept. 1923.

which a few days earlier praised the government, warned now that 'if its feebleness goes on, it will be necessary to put upon *good Spaniards* the task of correcting so many insults'.[16] The 'good Spaniards' were available in the army, and circumstantial evidence indicates that the king himself was not ignorant of their programme of overthrowing the parliamentarian regime. But Primo's *coup* played a central role in undermining the constitutional position of the king and, consequently, in the republican propaganda that led to the Republic; so whence comes the belief that Alfonso XIII had foreknowledge of that *coup*?

Since 1921 the king had exhibited signs of impatience with the parliamentarian regime, which, he believed, seriously obstructed the material development of the country, and was responsible, by cutting the army budget, for the shortcomings in Morocco. In July 1923, he told a minister, Salvatella, that 'the setting up of a military government is becoming inevitable', and at the beginning of August he openly confessed to Maura his readiness to lead a *coup* personally.[17]

Meanwhile, the 'military family' was becoming increasingly alienated from the politicians. This was reflected in a parliamentary incident at the beginning of July, when Sánchez Guerra slapped General Aguilera, the most senior officer in the army, for insulting the honour of civilians. The incident electrified the higher command, and rumours about an imminent *coup* started to spread.[18] This incident, however, eliminated Aguilera's candidature as commander of a military uprising. A 'strong' general was available in Barcelona: Primo de Rivera, the local

---

[16] For terrorism and separatism see daily reports in *LV* 2–13 Sept. 1923. For a separatist congress two days before the *coup d'état* see R. Xuriguera, *Els Exiliats Acusen*, pp. 155–8. For responsibilities see *Ejército Español* 6 Sept. 1923. For the attacks of the press see *ABC* 1 Sept. 1923; *LV* 6, 9 Sept. 1923; and *Ejército Español* 12 Sept. 1923. For a good account of the period that preceded the *coup d'état* with an emphasis on the irresponsible attitude of the press, which virtually invited a *coup*, see José and Luis Armiñan Oriozola, *Francia, el Dictador y el Moro. Páginas Históricas*, pp. 27–42, and F. Hernandez Mir, *Un Crimen de Lesa Patria. La Dictadura ante la Historia*, pp. 15–17.

[17] See the king's speech in Cordoba, May 1921 in A. Lerroux, *Al Servicio de la República*, pp. 255–6; See a survey of the absolutist tendencies of the king in Burgos y Mazo, *De la República a . . . ?*, pp. 20–30, his 'confession' in J. Cortés-Cavanillas, *Alfonso XIII, Vida, Confesiones y Muerte*, pp. 286–7. For Salvatella see *ABC* 19 Sept. 1930. For Maura see G. Maura, *Bosquejo Histórico de la Dictadura*, pp. 20–1, 27.

[18] *ABC* 4–6 July 1923. Romanones, *Notas de Una Vida 1912–1931*, p. 210.

captain general. He had won the support of the Catalan
bourgeoisie for his tough attitude against terrorism. This viceroy
of Barcelona, as the Socialist Prieto called him in parliament,
was constantly attacking the government for its soft approach
on the issue of public order. By the end of June he had met in
Madrid the king and Generals Saro, Daban, F. Berenguer and
Cavalcanti who were then still hoping that Aguilera would
lead them. In July Primo approached General Sanjurjo who
promised to support him should he attempt a *coup d'état*. In
subsequent visits to Madrid, he strengthened his links with the
'four generals', though he did not manage to enlist Aguilera;
and on 9 September, when he returned to Barcelona from his
last visit to Madrid, he made the final preparations.[19]

He managed to enlist generals with commands in Catalonia,
like Barrera and López de Ochoa, as well as General Mercader,
a personal friend of the king. These, in addition to Sanjurjo in
Zaragoza and 'the four' in Madrid, were the only officers fully
committed. At last he decided to 'pronounce' on the morning of
the thirteenth, thus advancing his plan by twenty-four hours:
the conspiracy was no longer a secret, and the Minister of War,
Aizpuru, had tried to dissuade him in a telephone call, while
another minister, Portela Valladares, was on his way to
Barcelona. Aizpuru did not make any serious effort to curb
Primo's activities. Furthermore, he seemed to have deliberately
provided the 'pronouncers' with arguments against the government by recommending an amnesty for Corporal Barroso, who
had led a soldiers' mutiny against the Moroccan campaign.
Yet, during the thirteenth and the first hours of 14 September,
Primo was fully aware of his military isolation. Apart from
Catalonia and Zaragoza, he had no support. Muñoz Cobos, the
captain general of Madrid, hesitated, and not until the king
had made clear his position did he join the movement. Zabalza,
the captain general of Valencia refused to support the *coup*,
though Gil Dolz, the local military governor and García Tryo,

---

[19] For the 'elimination' of Aguilera see Burgos y Mazo, *La Dictadura y los
Constitucionalistas*, i, 56–7; Prieto in *ABC* 4 July 1923. For Primo's relations with the
government see M. García Venero, *Santiago Alba, Monárquico de Razón*, p. 179. For
Primo's meetings in June see ibid., p. 177; and for a survey of his contacts see Primo de
Rivera, 'The Last Four Articles', *The Times* 20 March 1930. For Sanjurjo see José and
Luis Armiñan, *Epistolario del Dictador*, p. 364.

8 INTRODUCTION

his colleague in Castellón, managed to take over strategic points in what amounted to a mini *coup* against Zabalza.[20] Yet Primo de Rivera's bluff succeeded. Firstly, he managed to create the impression that he was the master of the situation. On the thirteenth, when everything was unclear, he was giving a confident interview to the press tracing a detailed programme of his future government; he inaugurated a furniture exhibition in Barcelona as if he was the representative of the legal government and not a rebellious general. In an order of the day to his soldiers he warned the 'ex-government' of a military confrontation, and made clear his intention to fight to the end. Secondly, the first reaction of the press and public opinion was favourable or indifferent to this 'attempt at a national regeneration', as *La Vanguardia* put it. *ABC* spoke of the 'calm expectation' of the public, and *El Sol* was convinced that the pronouncers would maintain their positions 'at any risk'. Finally, the paralysis of the government was total. Alba's insistence that Primo should be dismissed was disregarded, and he resigned before the *coup*. No serious attempt was made to mobilize the loyal military. Indeed, the government adopted a stoical attitude, maintaining that it could only be dissolved by force; meanwhile it waited for the *deus ex machina*, the king, to arrive from San Sebastián and to solve an issue that the government had complete authority but no confidence to deal with alone.[21]

[20] For an account of the participants see E. López de Ochoa, *De la Dictadura a la República*, pp. 24–32, Primo in *The Times* 20 Mar. 1931; and J. Milego, *El General Barrera*, pp. 15–18. For Aizpuru see Chapaprieta, *La Paz*, pp. 133–4. Primo later promoted him, see Armiñan, *Epistolario*, p. 115. For Muñoz Cobos see ibid., pp. 220–1, 241. (Primo's letters to Magaz and Tetuan, 20 and 23 June 1925). For Sanjurjo's role see E. Ayensa, *De Teniente-General a Recluso 52*, pp. 30–2. See also Muñoz Cobos's telegram to Primo on the evening of 13 Sept. in Martínez de la Riva, *Las Jornadas Triunfales de Un Golpe de Estado*, p. 49. For Valencia see V. Marco Miranda, *Las Conspiraciones Contra la Dictadura*, pp. 11–18. The findings of the 'Committee of Responsibilities' of the Republic support this view concerning Aizpuru's involvement, Primo's lack of support in the army, and the King's previous knowledge: see Cordero, *Los Socialistas*, pp. 166–79. The best general account of the *coup* is in Hernandez Mir, *La Dictadura*, pp. 47–106.

[21] Primo's interview to the press in *LV* 14 Sept. 1923. His order of the day in Martínez, *La Jornadas*, pp. 44–5. For the exhibition see ibid., pp. 45–9. For the attitude of the press see Martínez, op. cit. 101–9. For the public's reaction see F. Villanueva, *La Dictadura Militar*, pp. 31–2; F. O. 371/9490: E. Howard to Curzon, 15 Sept. 1923. For the government see *Ejército Español* 13, 14 Sept. 1923; and García Venero, *Alba*, pp. 179–84. For Alba see his *Para la Historia de España* (artículos publicados en Mayo 1930 por *El Sol*), pp. 1–9.

With Primo lacking the unanimous support of the army and with a paralysed government in office, it was for the king to make the fatal and final decision. The military movement was something that he had been anxiously expecting for some time and the last conspiracy was not a secret from him. Ten days before the uprising, the conspirators briefed him on their plan, and about a week later the Spanish ambassadors abroad were briefed by Primo himself. It is inconceivable that a personal friend of the king like Quiñones de León, the ambassador in Paris, would have let Alfonso be surprised by a military *coup*. When Primo published his manifesto with the cry of 'Long live the King' and with a ruthless attack on politicians for whom the king had no sympathy, Alfonso's position as the master of the situation was reaffirmed. In his long and deliberately slow journey from San Sebastián to Madrid, he 'compared the data and clarified his doubts', and when he arrived in the capital on the morning of the, fourteenth he was already convinced that most of the garrisons in Spain were ready to obey his decision, and that no civilian or military movement on behalf of the government had emerged. He therefore rejected the government's demand that he should dismiss the 'pronouncers', who, on the other hand, were pressing him to make a quick decision in order to avoid use of force by the conspirators. The government consequently resigned, and Primo was summoned to form a new one. Primo's enterprise thus succeeded both because of lack of opposition (Royo Villanova called it 'a *coup* by Article 29'—this article provided for the automatic election of unopposed candidates) and the king's support.[22]

By his adherence to rebellion against constitutional legality, the king had helped to create the myth of his 'responsibility' for the Dictatorship and, consequently, had put himself in an unconstitutional position. His opponents blamed him for preparing the *coup* in order to avoid the debate on the responsibilities of Annual precisely when the Cortes was about

---

[22] For the decisive role of the king see E. Aunós, *Primo de Rivera Soldado y Gobernante*, pp. 56-7; his conversation with Austen Chamberlain in F.O. 371/15093: Rumbold to MacDonald, 28 Mar. 1924. For the ambassadors see Primo in *The Times* 20 Mar. 1930; Armiñan, *Francia, el Dictador*, p. 62. For the king's behaviour see his 'confessions' in Cortés-Cavanillas, *Alfonso XIII*, pp. 131, 288-9. For pressure from the pronouncers, see Primo's telegram to Muñoz Cobos in J. Arrarás, *Historia de la Cruzada Española*, i, 143-144. For Royo see García Venero, *Alba*, p. 196.

to act as a genuine parliament. The king's defenders insisted that, in accepting a *fait accompli* that was acclaimed by public opinion, he was the true interpreter of the national will. And even if he had violated the constitution, *salus populi* was more important than any written law. He had sacrificed himself, it was alleged, to prevent a civil war.[23] Whatever the truth, the myth prevailed. The fate of the king and the Monarchy was from now on inextricably bound up with that of the Dictatorship. Alfonso had deprived himself of the alternative of ever ruling again under the Cánovas constitution.[24]

The kind of regime created by Primo de Rivera was neither a Mussolinian fascism nor a bloodthirsty tyranny. Essentially Primo's uprising was deeply rooted in the tradition of an army which 'in one hundred years had carried out one hundred pronunciamientos', while fascism was a purely civilian movement. The *Somatén*, a civilian militia, which he re-established, was a Catalan traditional institution, rather than an imitation of the *Fascio*. Once in power Primo kept insisting, as if his was a Roman dictatorship, that he would soon 'return the country to normality'. Meanwhile, he abolished 'politics' and parliamentarism which he despised. He suspended the constitution and ruled by decree, constantly coercing the king to consent to his arbitrary measures. Primo interfered with the independence of the judiciary, he subjected politicians to administrative persecution and he defamed them constantly in a press that was open to his daily notes but closed to his opponents' replies.[25]

During the first two years, Primo de Rivera ruled with the

---

[23] For his opponents see M. Domingo, *Que Espera el Rey?*, p. 129; Azaña, *Obras Completas*, i, 543–4; Saborit, *Besteiro*, p. 247; R. Pérez de Ayala, *Escritos Políticos*, p. 176; I. Prieto, *Palabras al Viento*, p. 233; A. Lerroux, *Al Servicio*, p. 211. See also the editorial of *La Libertad* 13 Sept. 1923. For his defenders see some examples of a large apologetic literature: Salvador Canals, *Spain, the Monarchy and the Constitution*, pp. 10–16; Manuel Bueno, *España y la Monarquía*, pp. 95–8; J. M. Pemán, *El Hecho y la Idea de la Unión Patriótica*, pp. 15–17; 'Un Español Neutral', *Réplica al Conde de Romanones*, pp. 284–8.

[24] The king was fully aware of his delicate position, and made efforts to deny any participation in the *coup*, see his conversations with the Italian ambassador in *I Documenti Diplomatici Italiani* 7° serie 1922–1935 vol. ii no. 382, Paulucci de Calboli to Mussolini, 18 Sept. 1923, and with the British ambassador in F.O. 371/9490: Howard to Curzon, 20 Sept. 1923.

[25] For Primo comparing himself with Prim and rejecting the analogy with fascism see *LV* 14 Sept. 1923. For the Somatén see J. M. March, *El Somatén, Su Origen y Su Naturaleza*, pp. 10–30. For his attitude to parliamentarism see his declarations in Révész

assistance of a Military Directory; in this team he was the only member with the status of minister, personally responsible to the king. This obviously singled them both out as responsible for unconstitutional rule.[26] Though Primo promised that as soon as he found 'pure men' uncorrupted by 'old politics', he would give up his 'parenthetic' rule,[27] it took him seven years to give up, and then without enthroning any 'new' men or any new regime. By the end of 1925 he set up a Civil Directory which meant that, officially, the army was taken out of politics. But the essence of the system did not change. Primo himself referred to the new government as 'the replacement of a military dictatorship by a civil and economic dictatorship; a more adequate dictatorship, though not less vigorous'.[28] But though he continued to maintain the fiction that the constitution, to which the new Directory swore loyalty was only suspended and not abolished,[29] the king had emphasized his 'responsibility' by renewing his confidence in the Dictatorship.[30]

An attempt both to create a substitute for the old parties and to give a popular, civilian aspect to the Dictatorship had already begun in September 1924 with the creation of the *Unión Patriótica*. It was sponsored by Primo and organized from above, not as a political party but as 'an association of all men of good will' who opposed a return to the old regime, and who respected the figure of the Chief of State. With the values of 'Monarchy, Religion, and Fatherland' as its ideological basis, the UP was conceived by Primo as the 'European avant-garde' against the menace to 'Christian society', and as the successor of the Dictatorship. For Pemán, the UP ideologue, this organization provided the regime with 'a constant expression of public acceptance'. But, being essentially an imposition from above, the UP was a futile experiment. It was joined by 'new men' but

---

Andrés, *Frente al Dictador*, pp. 99–102. For his arbitrariness and the defamation of politicians see López de Ochoa, *De la Dictadura*, pp. 67–77; and *ABC* (editorials) 13 Sept. 1924, 5 Jan. 1929.

[26] See the testimony given by the members of the Directory to the Committee of Responsibilities in RA Legajo 36 no. 40.

[27] *El Sol* 16 Sept. 1923.

[28] Quoted in J. Pabón, *Cambó* ii, part ii, p. 523. See also Calvo Sotelo, *Mis Servicios al Estado, Seis Años de Gestión*, pp. 98–105.

[29] *El Sol* 3 Dec. 1925.

[30] Pabón, op. cit. 534; G. Maura, *Bosquejo*, pp. 138–43.

also by many caciques and by the detritus of the old parties. Many joined it to get posts in the *Ayuntamientos* and *Diputaciones*, and in 1929 *ABC* noticed that though under an *Upetista* denomination, the same caciques were running the local administration. A plebiscite 'organized' by the UP in 1926 provided 7,506,468 'adherents' to the dictator. But the way by which it was done meant that it was far from indicating the existence of spontaneous support either for the UP or for Primo.[31]

Having abolished 'politics', Primo had only the 'concrete achievements' of his rule to justify the Dictatorship. Some of his opponents even recognized that the solution of the Moroccan problem was enough to justify it.[32] However, he started in 1924 by advocating withdrawal from advanced lines, adopting a purely diplomatic approach and an abandonist policy, a policy for which the military had always attacked the *políticos*. However, favourable circumstances enabled him to co-ordinate a common operation with the French, which culminated in the successful landing at Alhucemas. Primo's confidence increased, so much so that he asked that Spain should have a permanent seat in the Security Council of the League of Nations.

This spectacular victory as well as other achievements like that of bringing 'an end to separatism', to terrorism, to strikes, and to the 'communist threat' were, according to the panegyrists of the regime, an indication that the Dictatorship should continue and that corrupt politics should be banned for ever. Primo was described as the 'saviour of the Fatherland', promoter of a new 'pax Octaviana'. He was compared to Hannibal and Napoleon. He was 'a Christ', 'a genius', the new El Cid. His human virtues were also emphasized: he was simple, hard-working, modest, and generous. The nationalists pointed even at a daring flight to South America, not only as the reflection of the revival of Hispano-americanism under the Dictatorship, but also as a scientific victory for the 'Iberian race', which was possible only under Primo's 'regenerationist' rule.[33]

[31] For Primo's definition of the UP see Révész, *Frente*, pp. 89–98; and *Unión Patriótica* 15 Jan., 15 Sept., 15 Nov. 1927, 1 Jan. 1928. For Pemán see his *El Hecho*, pp. 11–115. For ways of recruiting members see a manifesto of a government delegate in RA Leg. 75 no. 6: *La UP de Sacedon al Pueblo* 19 Sept. 1924. For the composition see Maura, *Bosquejo*, pp. 134–6; C. Sotelo, *Seis Años*, pp. 331–4. For the plebiscite see RA Leg. 2 no. 28: *Plebiscito Nacional*.

[32] Villanueva, *La Dictadura*, p. 185.

[33] For examples of a vast panegyric literature on 'achievements' see E. Diaz-Retg,

However, the discontent of politicians because of the prolonged suspension of the constitution, the constant clandestine agitation of the republicans and extreme left, an increasing dissatisfaction in the army, and the alienation of both students and intellectuals combined to produce a series of conspiracies and embarrassing demonstrations which, though incapable of overthrowing the regime, contributed to its exhaustion. As early as in July 1924 Primo faced a conspiracy of the same four generals who in Madrid supported his *coup*.[34] In November anarchists whose official organizations had been banned by the dictator made an unsuccessful attempt to incite the troops in the Atarazanas barracks in Barcelona to mutiny.[35] One month later three 'communists' were executed for leading an armed incursion into Spain near Vera de Bidasoa, though it was later proved that the whole affair was fabricated by *agents provocateurs* of the Spanish police.[36]

Catalan extremism, which was stimulated by Primo's reversal of previous commitments to respect the cultural and regional aspirations of Catalonia, became a serious nuisance for the dictator. Maciá, the leader of *Estat Catalá*, led attempts against the regime from his exile in France. In June 1925 his men attempted unsuccessfully to blow up the royal train. In November 1926 Maciá led an incursion into Spain in person. Though the French police arrested the whole group near Perpignan, the Catalan cause as well as attacks on the Spanish Dictatorship received worldwide publicity.[37]

In June 1926 the first serious attempt to overthrow the regime took place. A group of prestigious officers conspired

---

España Bajo el Nuevo Régimen; Cortes-Cavanillas, *La Dictadura y el Dictador*; M. Jover Mira, *La España Inmortal*; José Pemartin, *Los Valores Históricos de la Dictadura Española*; For Primo's virtues and personality see Cortes-Cavanillas, op. cit. 303–34; E. Tarduchy, *Psicología del Dictador*; Révész, *Frente*; and J. Capella, *La Verdad de Primo de Rivera*, pp. 27–33, 79–85. For the flight see *Glorias de la Raza. La Voz del Pueblo y el Raid Huelva-Buenos Aires*, especially pp. 5–8.

[34] F.O. 371/10593: Gurney to MacDonald, 2 Aug. 1924.

[35] G. Maura, *Bosquejo*, p. 96.

[36] J. Cueto, *Cuentos al Nuncio. Sobre Derivaciones Republicanas de los Sucesos de Vera*, pp. 79–87. For official reports see *El Sol* 11–15 Nov. 1924.

[37] For anti-Catalanist measures see A. Joaniquet, *Alfonso Sala Conde de Argemí*, pp. 267–314; C. Sotelo, *Seis Años*, pp. 66–7; and A. Peers, *Catalonia Infelix*, pp. 179–86. See also Primo in *El Sol* 21 Mar. 1925. For the various attempts see Fernandez Almagro, *Historia del Reinado de Alfonso XIII*, p. 437; M. Tuñon de Lara, *La España*, pp. 158–9; and *El Sol* 5 Nov. 1925.

together with a heterogeneous conglomeration of anarchosynd-
icalists, politicians and republicans in order to restore 'constitutional legality'. The *coup*, nicknamed the *Sanjuanada*, failed; yet
Primo's confidence was shaken: 'I believe that I am not isolated,
but if I am to perish, I'll go down fighting'.[38]
Malaise in the army increased. Primo's control of promotions
and dissatisfaction among officers with the way the dictator
involved the army in local politics through the *Delegados
Gubernativos* led to discontent. Agitation was mainly concentrated
in the artillery corps, since Primo abolished in June 1926 their
privileged status which allowed them promotion by seniority
rather than by merit. After three months of sporadic rebellion,
the corps was subdued in September 1926. But it was a Pyrrhic
victory for the regime. The artillery removed its support from
both the Dictatorship and the Monarchy.[39]
In fact, artillery units were the central military elements
involved in the most spectacular attempt against the regime in
January 1929. It was led by Sánchez Guerra, a Conservative
ex-premier. Though only the artillery in Ciudad Real fulfilled
its commitment and the movement was easily suppressed in
Valencia because of the confusion of its leaders, Primo de
Rivera was disappointed at the lack of spontaneous reaction by
the UP and the *Somatén*. Sánchez Guerra was acquitted by a
military tribunal in what amounted to a recognition that a
rebellion against an unconstitutional government was not
punishable. The trial was regarded as an uprising of the army
against the regime, and this further shook Primo's confidence as
well as the regime's prestige. He reacted by dissolving the
whole artillery corps, and by declaring 'a halt in the march
towards normalization'.[40]

[38] For the Sanjuanada see Almagro, op. cit. 478–84; and Romanones, *Notas*, pp.
224–5. The quotation is in Armiñan, *Epistolario*, p. 366.
[39] For Primo's arbitrariness in matters of promotion and the alienation of officers see
Queipo de Llano, *El General Queipo de Llano Perseguido por la Dictadura*, pp. 62–75; López
de Ochoa, *De la Dictadura*, pp. 94–102; E. Mola, *Obras Completas*, pp. 1024–5; Armiñan,
Epistolario, pp. 77, 88–9, 241–4, 250. For 'Delegados' see Gen. J. García Benitez, *Tres
Meses de Dictadura Obrero-Ateneista*, pp. 20–2; C. Sotelo, *Seis Años*, pp. 24–27; and a
favourable account in 'E.T.L.', *Por Pueblos y Aldeas; De las Memorias de un Delegado
Gubernativo*, see especially pp. 7–10. For the artillery see E. Benzo, *Al Servicio de Ejército*,
pp. 158–86.
[40] For the conspiracy see Rafael Sánchez Guerra, *El Movimiento Revolucionario de
Valencia*; For the trial see Emilio Ayensa, *Vista de la Causa Seguida Contra el S. Sánchez*

But 'normalization' did not depend only on the dictator's will. 1929 was also the year of an acute financial crisis. Economic prosperity had been the regime's strongest staff, drawing public attention from politics. Ambitious investments in public works provided jobs and created an atmosphere of prosperity. These schemes were financed by an inflationary extraordinary budget, through large issues of public bonds, which were bought enthusiastically by both big and small savers. Calvo Sotelo, the Finance Minister, explained the reason for the policy: 'A dictatorship cannot embark upon a programme of slow development because the country must profit immediately from the new regime.'[41] A high tariff policy, state-controlled monopolies and an excessive interventionism created an autarkic 'national economy' which gradually became a burden on the state and increasingly unacceptable to businessmen and consumers alike: the rise in prices in Spain was the highest in Europe. Capitalists who had profited in the prosperous years now considered the regime no longer of service to them. Heavy taxes on industry and commerce were bitterly opposed by business circles, as were interventionism and protectionism, both seen an unbearable 'tutelage' especially by those who, like some agriculturalists and small businessmen who suffered from the excessive favouritism shown by the government towards big monopolistic companies, did not benefit directly. 'The government,' they said, 'invades a terrain, that for the sake of economic prosperity should be closed to all official obstruction.'[42]

Guerra. For the dissolution of the artillery: *El Sol* 20 Feb. 1929. For the two quotations see F. Villanueva, *Que ha Pasado Aquí?*, pp. 20–2, 60.

[41] C. Sotelo, *Seis Años*, pp. 394–5.

[42] For the economic policy see surveys in *The Economist* 15 Mar. 1924, 29 Oct., 26 Nov. 1927; R. Perpiñá, *De Estructura Económica y Economía Hispana*, pp. 317–19: a list of 46 Committees to control the economy. Velarde Fuertes, *Política Económica de la Dictadura*. For a critical approach see F. Benitez de Lugo, *Obra Económica, Financiera y Monetaria de la Dictadura*. For prices see *The Economist* 4 July 1925; 16 Apr., 29 Oct., 26 Nov. 1927, 28 Dec. 1929; *Boletín del Banco Urquijo* Feb. 1930. For opposition to taxation see E. Aunós, *Calvo Sotelo y la Política de su Tiempo*, pp. 81–2; and C. Sotelo *Seis Años*, pp. 126–8. For capitalists see L. Araquistáin, *El Ocaso de un Régimen*, pp. 250–3; and Department of Overseas Trade, *Economic Conditions in Spain*, p. 13. G. Maura, *Bosquejo*, pp. 302, 306, 315, 334–5 emphasized the role of the economic crisis in the fall of the regime. For opposition to interventionism and protectionism, see *El* 26 May 1929; and *Boletín de la Cámara Oficial de Comercio Industria y Navegación de Malaga* Feb. 1929. Agriculturists also attacked the high tariffs for industry while their products were exposed to competition, see *Boletín de la Asociación de Agricultores de España* Oct. 1929.

The depreciation of the peseta during the last months of the regime increased difficulties. The rise in internal prices, the trade deficit, political uncertainty and international speculation combined to explain the phenomenon. The confidence of businessmen was shaken, prices on the stock exchange dropped, and in December Primo publicly admitted the bankruptcy of the government's monetary policy. *ABC* blamed the lack of constitutional legality for all misfortunes. The regime's whole success had been based on lavish expenditure, and now retrenchment was necessary. By mid-January 1930 the peseta dropped from thirty-seven to forty to the pound. Industrialists dependent on raw material from abroad ran into difficulties. Calvo Sotelo resigned amid the resentment of the capitalists and rumours about a national government with Cambó, the Catalan financial expert, as premier.[43]

It is, however, necessary to stress that the economic crisis of 1929 in Spain does not seem to have been a catastrophic 'crash', as it was in some other countries. Neither on the eve of the fall of the Dictatorship, nor on the eve of the proclamation of the Republic, in April 1931, was this crisis reflected in an avalanche of unemployment, massive bankruptcies, and economically motivated popular unrest.

The year 1929 was rather the 'culminating point of an ascendant movement of economic expansionism',[44] a point after which a *gradual* crisis, whose gravest manifestations would develop from 1932 onwards,[45] would evolve. This 'culminating point' was achieved in several sectors of the economy. Bank shares reached their highest value, and a record number of bank branches was established all over the country. The production of electric energy and the number of new power stations installed during 1929 increased considerably in comparison with previous years. The mining industry had also witnessed

[43] For a survey of the peseta crisis see *The Economist* 28 Dec. 1929, *Banco Urquijo* Feb. 1930. For the stock exchange see *Banco de Crédito Local de España, Memoria de 1929*; and *B. Urquijo* Nov., Dec. 1929. Primo's confession is quoted in Tuñón de Lara, *La España del Siglo XX*, p. 178. For the influence of political uncertainty see C. Sotelo, op. cit. 286–287. For the effect on industrialists and their resentment see *Boletín . . . de Malaga*, June 1929; F. Villanueva, *Que Ha Pasado . . .?*, pp. 124–5; and C. Sotelo, op. cit. 291. *ABC* 30 Dec. 1928 and 29 Dec. 1929.

[44] *El Financiero*, no. extraordinario dedicado a 1929. Nov. 1930, p. 10.

[45] A. Balcells, *Crisis Económica y Agitación Social en Cataluña 1930–1936*, p. 8.

a boom: 163,367 workers were employed in all the ramifications of the industry, 5,847 more than in 1928; while the value of output increased by 199 million pesetas. A further reduction of imports, by 268 million pesetas in comparison to the previous year, had contributed to narrow the chronic trade balance deficit; and, though exports decreased slightly, they still were the second highest since 1910. In comparison with other countries, the number of bankruptcies in Spain in 1929 was tiny: an average of nine per month comparing with 821 in Germany, 1,642 in the U.S.A., 684 in France, and 345 in England.[46]

Symptoms of crisis, however, there were. The abolition of the extraordinary budget reflected 'a complete change of policy'. Political uncertainty, as well as the psychological effect of the Wall Street crash caused a sharp drop in share prices on the main stock exchanges of Spain. The depreciation of the peseta had increased the price of raw material and imported machinery; but the drop of 447,797 pesetas' worth of imported machinery was not yet an indication of a deep crisis in Spanish industry. In the agriculture there was in 1929 a moderate crisis of over-production. The wheat harvest in central Spain was optimal. This contributed to lower prices in the local market, hitting Castilian farmers. A similar fate was shared by growers of rye, barley, and oats because of considerable importation of maize. The crisis became especially acute for olive growers because of over-production (the index of production rose from 65 in 1928—a year of frost—to 224 in 1929) and a decrease of 50 per cent in exports compared with 1928. The wine industry also ran into difficulties when the French imposed a ban on the import of foreign wines. There was also a drop of nineteen million pesetas in the export of oranges. But the facilities for export arising from the depreciation of the peseta, and an increase in the export of other agricultural products, such as fruits and vegetables, contributed to moderate the crisis.

---

[46] For banks see Ildefonso Cuesta Garrigos, 'Los grandes bancos españoles. Su evolución (1922–1943)' in *Moneda y Crédito* Dec. 1944 no. 11. For electric energy see *El Financiero*, p. 51; For the mining industry see statistics and articles in *Anuario Estadístico* 1929; *Boletín del Banco Urquijo* Feb. 1930; *El Financiero*, pp. 22–3; and a very optimistic survey in *Economic Conditions in Spain*, pp. 22–3. For the trade balance see *El Financiero*, p. 92; and *Anuario Estadístico*, 1929.

Otherwise the drop of sixty million pesetas in the export of agricultural products in 1929 (eighty-five per cent of the total drop in exports that year) might have reached the figure of 145 million.[47] Though a crisis in agricultural Spain, the natural market of Spanish industry, was likely to have a damaging effect on industry, it is evident that no sudden and spectacular deterioration in the conditions of the popular classes was taking place on the eve of the fall of the Dictatorship. Small investors, businessmen and capitalists were the main embittered elements who removed their support from the dictator. It was not until the closing months of 1929 that the shadow of unemployment fell over Spain, because of the adverse effect of the depreciation of the peseta on some industries. But, although there are no official figures, observers noticed that

the unemployment question is not a vital one in Spain. It may be safely asserted that there is very little, if any, unemployment in the country normally. And even agricultural unemployment is eased by the recruiting of labourers under contract for South America, France and the West Indies.[48]

It is true that wages, mainly those of unskilled workers, showed a slight fall after 1925. But the damaging effect that this trend was likely to have on workers was partly neutralized by a drop in the cost of living. The index of the cost of living of a working-class family, which in October 1923 was 167·6 and which reached its highest average point in the period October 1925–March 1926 (180·8), was by the end of 1929 at the relatively low point of 165·5. There was a clear tendency towards a depreciation in the price of basic food, while the price of industrial products had a slight tendency to increase.[49]

---

[47] For the stock exchange see *El Financiero*, p. 55 and 'Crónicas Bursatiles' in *Boletín del Banco Urquijo* Nov.–Dec. 1929; Jan. 1930. For the extraordinary budget see *El Financiero*, p. 51. For machinery, indexes of production and export see *Anuario Estadístico*, 1929. For agriculture see José Vásquez Trigo, 'La Agricultura y la Ganadería españolas en 1929' in *El Financiero*, pp. 109–19. For an optimistic analysis of the agriculture see *Economic Conditions* June 1930. For complaints of agriculturists see *Boletín de la Asociación de Agricultores de España* Oct. 1929, Jan. 1930.

[48] Department of Overseas Trade, *Economic Conditions in Spain*, June 1930, pp. 23, 45.

[49] 'Coste de Vida del Obrero', *Anuario Estadístico* 1929, and *El Financiero*, p. 78. For wages see data in M. Tuñón de Lara, *El Movimiento Obrero en la Historia de España*, pp. 755–67.

However, unfortunately for the dictator, the financial crisis came simultaneously with the collapse of his experiment in transforming his provisional rule into a permanent regime. He destroyed old politics without becoming himself a political architect. In September 1926 he announced the formation of a National Assembly in which 'all classes and interests' would be represented to assist the government, and to provide the king with prominent figures whom he could consult when the government fell. The king, however, was reluctant to approve such a step which could be interpreted as abrogating the 1876 constitution. But he seemed to have been convinced by the 'consultative' rather than 'constituent' character of the Assembly; and in September 1927 he signed the appropriate decree, creating a body designated from representatives of the local and provincial administration, the UP, and cultural and economic organizations. This enraged politicians as well as the Socialists who boycotted the new body, though some like Gabriel Maura and La Cierva were conspicuous in their collaboration.[50]

Primo hoped that the constitutional draft that was to be elaborated by the Assembly would be submitted to a plebiscite, and that then the UP would take over the reins of government.[51] But the draft which was presented both to the Assembly and to a free debate in the press, in July 1929, did not satisfy the dictator, while the press rejected it out of hand, and the public treated it with indifference. Primo de Rivera himself, as early as January 1928, had serious reservations about the excessively 'monarchist' orientation in the constitutional committee, and he warned them against granting the king too much authority. 'One of the errors of old politics', he wrote to Gabriel Maura, 'was to let the king play too big a role.' Primo was impressed by Mussolini's objections to the draft and stressed his opposition to the prerogatives of the king, who, as he said to the Duce, 'unlike the cautious and wise Italian king, has a tendency to act on his own initiative, and, therefore, his independence of action should

---

[50] For the king see G. Maura, *Dolores de España*; and F.O. 371/12717: Rumbold to Austen Chamberlain, 14 Sept. 1929. Maura and La Cierva in their respective *Recuerdos de Mi Vida*, pp. 184–6, and *Notas de Mi Vida*, pp. 301–5.
[51] *Unión Patriótica* 15 June 1928, 1 Mar. 1929.

be limited.' The politicians longed for a simple return to the 1876 constitution, and the left pointed to the absolutist content of the new constitution and to its undemocratic origin. The dictator's attempt by the end of July to increase his manœuvrability by inviting the ex-premiers and the Socialists to the Assembly failed in what became a manifestation of no confidence in the regime.[52] Stuck with a constitution that no one really wanted, Primo de Rivera declared by mid-December that he had given up his intentions of promulgating a constitution.[53] And by the end of the month he submitted to the king another programme. It consisted of the designation in September 1930 of a transitional government which, though preserving the policies of the Dictatorship, the UP, the *Somatén* and even the Assembly, would lead the country back to constitutional normality. At the same time, he conducted a campaign for the reorganization of the UP. Both this fact and the 'programme' were a clear indication that Primo saw the end of his rule approaching, and the only thing that he had in mind was to defend his collaborators as well as his achievements from future political upheavals. But the king rejected the 'programme'. This was the 'death sentence' of Dictatorship, according to Calvo Sotelo, a view shared by the dictator.[54]

However, a couple of days later Primo agreed with the king on another programme: a partial renovation, by election, of Ayuntamientos and Diputaciones, while the Assembly would continue until its term expired, and then it would be replaced by a more 'constitutional' body.[55] Primo's colleagues in the cabinet rejected the proposal, and suggested that he should preside personally over the transition to another regime by

---

[52] The draft is in *Boletín de la Asamblea Nacional* 1929, vol. iii, pp. 1–136. For the press and the public see C. Sotelo, op. cit. 338; and *EI* 24 Oct. 1929. For leftist criticism see Martí Jara, *El Rey y el Pueblo, passim* and *El Sol* 6–30 July 1929. For Primo's views see *ED* 13 Sept. 1929; and J. M. Pemán, *Mis Almuerzos Con Gente Importante*, pp. 33–6. For Primo's view on the king's prerogatives see MA Leg. 86: Primo de Rivera to Gabriel Maura, 21 Jan. 1928. For Mussolini and Primo's remark on the king see *I Documenti Diplomatici Italiani*, vol. viii, no. 156, Medici to Grandi, 15 Nov. 1929.

[53] *Unión Patriótica* 15 Dec. 1929.

[54] For the programme see C. Sotelo, *Seis Años*, pp. 342–9, and Aunós, *Primo de Rivera*, pp. 184–7, 193–8. For reorganization of the UP see *Unión Patriótica* 1, 18 Jan. 1930. C. Sotelo's reaction to the king's rejection is in C. Sotelo, op. cit. 351; and Primo's in *Unión Patriótica* 4 Feb. 1930.

[55] *ABC* 3 Jan. 1930.

running the elections that would reveal his popular support. Elections were something that he despised, and he ruled this alternative out.[56] It could not be otherwise when he himself declared on 31 December: 'The aristocrats hate me ... the conservatives refuse to adhere to the Dictatorship ... nor am I assisted by the elements of the Church ... Bankers and industrialists ... employers ... functionaries ... the press ... and other sectors ... do not support the Dictatorship.'[57] In addition to these difficulties, rumours about a new plot were common knowledge. Its centre was in Andalucía where 'Constitutionalists' like the Andalucian cacique Burgos Mazo, liberals like Miguel Maura and Miguel Villanueva, whose rebellion reflected the profound crisis of confidence now undergone by conservatives, the republican Martínez Barrios and the revolutionary aviator Ramón Franco conspired with General Goded to overthrow the dictator. The *coup* was scheduled for 24 January; but it was postponed because of rumours of an imminent change of government, this time with Generals Berenguer and Saro as a new Military Directory. Primo de Rivera asked for the dismissal of Don Carlos, the captain general of Andalucía and a member of the royal family, who seemed to support the conspiracy as far as it was aimed against the dictator and not against the king. The king rejected the demand. This was a new manifestation of lack of confidence in his premier.[58]

The threat of a new *coup* that might develop into an anti-monarchist movement obviously encouraged the king to get rid of Primo and to return to solid 'constitutional' soil. On the other hand, Primo, faced with total isolation and with a focus of rebellion in Andalucía, on 26 January made a public appeal to the captains general to grant him a vote of confidence.[59] Within the pseudo-legal framework of the Dictatorship, this was an attempt at a new *coup d'état* by Primo, this time against the king, on whose will rather than on that of the people or of

---

[56] C. Sotelo, op. cit. 353-4.

[57] Quoted in E. Aunós, *España en Crisis*, pp. 309-10. See also Aunós, *Primo de Rivera*, pp. 187-93: a survey of the overwhelming opposition.

[58] For the plot see Villanueva, *Que ...?*, p. 178; M. Maura, *Así cayó Alfonso XIII*, pp. 29-31; Hernandez Mir, *La Dictadura*, pp. 346-60.

[59] Quoted in Tuñón de Lara, *La España*, p. 181.

the army the regime was dependent. But the response of most of the generals was critical. Even his friend Barrera rebuked him for inviting an already agitated and increasingly anti-Primo army to interfere in politics. Barrera and others reiterated their subordination to the king and to any government enjoying his support. Once again the king could claim to represent the national will, and he 'bourbonized' his dictator, as he had done so many premiers in the past, compelling him to resign on 28 January 1930. Next day, Primo published his swan-song, a note apologizing for his tactless appeal to the army, and spreading the fearful message that in Spain 'true freedom ... must be accompanied by the Civil Guard'.[60]

The task of leading the transition to a constitutional regime was given by the king to General Berenguer. Berenguer became the defender of a precarious Monarchy, which from now on was attacked constantly by its enemies for patronizing a dictatorship. An appeal to the 'old' politicians was ruled out for the moment. But the Conservative predominance in the new government indicated that a return to the *turno* was expected. Furthermore, the solutions suggested by this cabinet reflected a policy which conceived 'normalization' as a step backward rather than forward: a complete restoration of the 1876 constitution, a revival of the traditional parties, the summoning of an ordinary rather than of a Constituent Cortes, and the automatic designation of pre-1923 councillors to Ayuntamientos and Diputaciones. Berenguer refused to consider the demands of the left that municipal and provincial elections should precede the general election because the composition of these organizations provided him with a monarchist majority which was 'a guarantee for the future and the only element of equilibrium and stability that we possess'. Berenguer strove to maintain the monarchist predominance in a country that still expected to be asked whether it was really monarchist. He

[60] For an evaluation of the note to the generals see Villanueva *Que ...?*, pp. 172–175; Ossorio y Gallardo, *Mis Memorias*, pp. 153–4. For the answers see D. Berenguer, *De la Dictadura a la República*, p. 17; J. Milego, *El General Barrera*, pp. 97–101. Pabón, *Cambó*, ii, part i, 592 claims that only Sanjurjo and Marzo supported Primo. For 'Bourbonizing' see Salvador Canals, *La Caída de la Monarquía*, p. 39. The last note is in *LE* 29 Jan. 1930. A further proof that Primo was 'bourbonized' is his attempt to return to power a week later by means of another *coup*: see Berenguer, *De la Dictadura*, pp. 78–79, and J. Capella, *La Verdad*, pp. 87–8.

therefore urged the new civil governors to defend the regime 'from the enemies of the Monarchy, who are our common enemies'.[61] This policy of 'nothing has happened' proved to be inadequate. Spain was about to enter one of the most politically intense periods in its history, and a return to the past was the exact opposite of what the public expected. The country was in an agitated mood, and Berenguer himself said that he assumed power when Spain was like 'a bottle of champagne about to blow its cork'. Furthermore, the fact that the new premier was among those 'responsible' for the disaster of Annual was unlikely to appease those who understood 'normalization' also as an investigation of 'responsibilities'.[62]

In order both to appease agitated elements and to disassociate the Monarchy from its harmful identification with the Dictatorship, Berenguer led a campaign of demolition against the legacy of the Dictatorship: Primo's collaborators were not given ministerial posts; the statutes of the FUE—a left-wing student organization banned by the dictator—were ratified; exiled professors were allowed to return, professional organizations recovered their autonomy, a general amnesty was conceded, the anti-Catalanist decrees were abrogated, and a general revision of the dictatorial legislation was started. Many of these steps were obviously welcomed; but the fact that they were carried out by decree and not in an elected parliament made them not less arbitrary. Furthermore, the abolition of dictatorial legislation which carried the king's signature was likely to be interpreted as a public denunciation of the king's support for the dictator.[63]

Perhaps Berenguer's gravest blunder was the slowness of his pace towards 'normalization'. It took him almost a year to

[61] For the government and its programme see *ABC* 29, 30 Jan. 1930; Berenguer, op. cit. 30–9, 40–8, 58–63. For the Ayuntamientos see J. M. Hoyos y Vinent, *Mi Testimonio*, p. 23. The quotation is in Berenguer, op. cit. 136. For the governors: *ABC* 19 Feb. 1930.

[62] For the ambiance in the country see Mola, *Obras*, pp. 246–51, 1037. Berenguer is quoted in pabón, *Cambó*, ii, part ii, 12. For an attack on the nomination of the man responsible for Annual, Berenguer, as Premier, see E. Ayensa, *Del Desastre de Annual a la Presidencia del Gobierno, passim.*

[63] For the revision see Berenguer, *De la Dictadura*, pp. 68–9; *ABC* 1, 2, 6 Feb. 1930. For Catalonia see *ABC* 27 June 1930; and J. Milego, *El general Barrera*, pp. 128–37. For the last statement see Alcalá Galiano, *The Fall of a Throne*, p. 79, and Cortés-Cavanillas, *Alfonso XIII*, pp. 195–6.

decide on a precise date for the elections, a date which he constantly postponed under the pretext that a new electoral register had to be prepared. Even the rightist *El Debate* finally warned him of the disastrous effects of his dilatory tactics, which created the impression that the Monarchy was afraid to face the electorate.[64] Meanwhile the republican and anti-monarchist movement was gaining momentum, and when by the end of the year the elections were finally announced, the left was in the middle of preparations for a revolution and had, anyway, no intention of taking part in any election other than that to a Constituent Cortes empowered to reform the constitution, nor in a general election held before the municipal elections. Berenguer, on the other hand, refused to reverse the order of the elections.[65] That the government was drifting into a position where the first concern of ministers was the defence of the throne, even if that meant a reversion to dictatorial methods, further undermined its position.

In addition, the Berenguer government had to face an economic crisis, which was to reach its climax later during the Republic. In 1930 the signs of depression that appeared in 1929 were accentuated, and, though less influenced by the world crisis than other countries, Spain did not escape industrial maladies altogether. The figures of production for 1930 showed a clear reduction as compared with 1929. This was especially so in the mining and iron and steel industries, though only during the Republic would secondary industries be affected, thus creating large-scale unemployment. A decrease of thirty-three per cent in the import of raw materials in 1932 in comparison with 1930, and a drop of prices on the stock exchange from 100 in 1930 to 78·5 in 1931 and 62·69 in 1932 are indications that the main crisis still lay ahead. Exports of agricultural products also declined after 1930. Thus after 1930 industry had to struggle against the reduced purchasing power of that part of the population engaged in mining, and that dependent on agriculture. Moreover, unemployment both in industrial Catalonia and in the agrarian south was after late 1930 becoming

[64] *ED* 23 Oct. 1930.
[65] For the issue of the elections, see Berenguer, op. cit. 121–4. For the 'revolutionary spirit' by the end of the year, see Mola, *Obras*, p. 480. For the order of the elections, see Berenguer in *ABC* 27 Sept. 1930.

an increasing problem, though still confined to reasonable dimensions. In addition, the cost of living for a working-class family had increased considerably during the last months of 1930 and the first months of 1931. A policy of economy failed to curb the depreciation of the peseta. Nor was a renewed intervention in the foreign exchange market, with the help of foreign credits, successful. In mid-August the peseta reached a record level of 47·80 to the pound and Arguelles, the Minister of Finance, abdicated in despair. Financial experts could see nothing wrong in the economy itself that could justify the depreciation and the fall in share prices. They pointed to political uncertainty, strikes, and public agitation. Industry continued to be affected by the monetary crisis, but seemed to welcome the abolition of excessive state intervention in the economy; agriculture on the other hand was going through a serious crisis with the price of wheat at a very low level, and wine producers complaining loudly of the burden of taxation.[66]

With no spectacular successes either in politics or in economics, the *Dictablanda*, as Berenguer's rule was nicknamed, lasted only a year. The electoral abstention of the left backed by that of some monarchists, brought about Berenguer's resignation on 14 February 1931. The mission of 'returning' to constitutional rule under the Monarchy proved to be impossible.

[66] For a survey of the economic situation in 1930–1 see *Economic Conditions in Spain* Jan. 1933, May 1952. For data on production see *Anuario Estadístico* 1931. For unemployment and cost of living see below, p. 131–2. For the peseta see *The Economist* 5 July, 23 Aug. 1930, Berenguer, *De la Dictadura*, pp. 76–8. For the reasons, levels of depreciation and the crisis in the stock exchange see *Banco Urquijo* June–Dec. 1930, Jan.–March 1931; *El* 3 July 1930. For abolition of state intervention see Perpiñá, *De Estructura*, pp. 319–20. For the agricultural crisis see *Boletín de la Asociación de Agricultares de España* Feb., Mar., June, July, Dec. 1930; *Boletín Oficial del Fenix Agrícola* Feb., May 1930.

I

REPUBLICANISM AND REPUBLICANS UNDER THE 'DICTADURA' AND THE 'DICTABLANDA'

I. A REPUBLICAN AMBIANCE

Spanish society reached a turning point during the 1920s. Population increased by about ten per cent and, though still an essentially agrarian-based society, Spain was increasingly acquiring urban features. Towns of over 10,000 inhabitants increased their population by about two million and those of over 100,000 by about one million. On the other hand, towns of less than 10,000 inhabitants remained virtually at a standstill. People travelled more than ever before; the number of commuters per year using the rail system increased by 3·5 million in the first three years of the regime. It dropped to lower figures later only because the number of cars almost quadrupled during the Dictatorship and a network of modern roads was established. Other important symptoms were the number of telephones (doubled during the Dictatorship), the increasing popularity of the radio, and a spectacular drop in the rate of illiteracy in the 1920s, a drop which was the highest of the century up to 1960: 8·57 per cent for men and 9·15 per cent for women.[1]

Furthermore, the Dictator's expansionist economic policy expanded the Spanish middle classes. For example, the number of taxpayers registered as industrialists and merchants rose by about 62 per cent. Though part of this sudden build up of the Spanish bourgeoisie might have been only in appearance and attributable to more effective measures against tax evasion, the existing evidence points to substantial real growth. The proportion of the industrial proletariat in the working population increased from 21·94 per cent to 26·51 per cent while that of

[1] *Anuario Estadistico de España* 1929, 1931; *Radio Tecnica* 1929; *Radio y Luz* 1931; *Boletín de la Camara de Transportes Mecanicos* Apr. 1928; J. Diez-Nicolas, *Tamaño, Densidad y Crecimiento de la Poblacion en España*, p. 19.

workers in the service sector increased from 20·81 per cent to 27·98 per cent at the expense of agricultural manpower. The influx of students to business schools in unprecedented proportions was also a genuine reflection of the proliferation of opportunities in banking, industry, commerce and in the administration of public works. With the growth of prosperity came a greater capacity to save. Private savings more than doubled during the Dictatorship, and the new savers belonged mostly to the rising petty bourgeoisie, though workers, artisans, and maidservants also shared this propensity to save.[2]

However, small entrepreneurs and members of the liberal professions saw with alarm, after 1929, how their position was threatened by political uncertainties, by the continuing depreciation of the peseta, and by clear signs of economic recession; moreover, many small businessmen were unable to compete with the large monopolistic companies created and favoured by the dictator. It was not Cobden or Bright who wrote the manifesto addressed to the dictator by the country's Chambers of Commerce and Industry in support of the 'sacred' principle of free enterprise: 'The government is brutally repressing the sacred principle of the free concert of wills and interests. It is about time that everyone can produce whatever he likes, sell whatever he can, buy whatever he needs as the market for his products allows him.' Berenguer's Dictablanda was not to bring salvation to embittered business circles, and they joined, on the eve of the proclamation of the Republic, in the chorus of protests against a regime responsible, in the words of Mahou, the famous brewer who was also the president of the Madrid Chamber of Industry, for 'the breakdown of business'.[3]

The coming of the second Spanish Republic was to be, in a way, the culminating point of a process of social evolution that

[2] *Anuario Estadístico* 1929, 1931; Tuñon de Lara, *La España*, pp. 134–5; *El Movimiento Obrero*, pp. 145–8.

[3] For the increasing opposition of business circles see *Boletín de la Camara Oficial de Comercio e Industria de Sabadell* 1928–9; *Boletín de la Camara Oficial de Comercio e Industria de Lérida y su Provincia* Jan.–May 1926, Jan.–Feb. 1930; *Boletín de la Camara Oficial de Comercio, Industria y Navegación de Málaga* Feb., June 1929, Feb. 1930; *Boletín de la Camara de Comercio de Madrid* Jan.–Apr; *Boletín de la Camara Oficial de Industria de la Provincia de Madrid* Apr. 1931. As for the professional classes, especially in provincial capitals, there were indications that, as one provincial organ put it, 'the physician, the engineer and the lawyer simply do not earn enough to make a living.' See *La Voz de Galicia* 25 Apr. 1931 as well as the frequent protests in *Boletín del Colegio de Abogados de Madrid* 1930–1.

had gained momentum in the twenties. An increasingly urban society was now attracted by the material and political temptations of 'Europeanization', and considerable portions of the middle classes, especially their lower strata, were now ready to imitate more advanced political models than that represented by an 'arbitrary', 'degrading', paternalistic Dictatorship whose economic achievements had moreover been exhausted, and by an unrepresentative monarchy in a painful process of decline. The frustrated middle classes 'threw themselves', to use the expression of a contemporary, into the Republic as an outlet for their vague expectations for change, and as the best available means of securing their position at a time when the disintegrating regime was creating a dangerous vacuum of power. The republican 'revolution' was for many a conservative solution.[4]

The dictatorial rule of Primo de Rivera and the anti-constitutional behaviour of the king in supporting such a rule were evidently major causes of republican and anti-monarchist sentiments that spread during the Dictatorship and its aftermath among an increasingly politically-aware community. The middle class Republican parties, which in 1923 were deep in a process of disintegration and in a mood of frustration because of their failure to change the political system either through conspiracies or by legal means, were stimulated by the blunders of the Monarchy to revise their doctrines and to increase their following. The 'neutral mass', generally considered as politically indifferent, was tempted by an increasingly anti-monarchist ambiance to be more politically aware. The liberal intelligentsia, whose human and civil dignity was trampled underfoot by the dictator, woke up to become the ideological axis of the republican revival. This, and the evident erosion of monarchist feelings even in the traditional Monarchist parties, joined together to undermine the Monarchy's position.

The paralysis of political activities during the Dictatorship meant that this trend was not reflected in any substantial growth of the existing Republican parties. It was, therefore, a

[4] Gil Robles, *No Fué Posible la Paz*, p. 33; M. Maura, *Así Cayo Alfonso XIII*, p. 145; H. Maura, *Tras el Sentido Común*, pp. 104–5; Ossorio y Gallardo, *La Crisis del Sentido Conservador*; 'La República: El Sentido de Una Evolución Social' in *La Voz de Galicia* 25 Apr. 1931; *El Debate* (editorial) 14 Apr. 1931.

consciousness developing independently of the Republican organizations.[5] However, given the existence of the sentiment, it was believed that parties would spontaneously emerge once liberties were restored.[6] This trend was also noticed by worried monarchist observers. Both the Infanta Eulalia and Gabriel Maura pointed to the miraculous belief of many people in the Republic or in 'something new'. Others spoke about the growing conviction that justice and progress were incompatible with the rule of a dictator and a perjured king.[7] Some monarchists passed to republicanism as an immediate reaction to the *coup d'état*. Such was the case of many among the rank and file of the Reformist party; and Romanones, the leader of the Liberal party, was afraid that unless a constitutional regime was immediately established many in his party would follow suit. His fear materialized when the king refused to reassemble parliament after three months of adjournment, thus formally violating the constitution. An open attack by Romanones on the Moroccan policy of Primo made an anonymous opponent of the regime believe that he *also* had become republican. And, when a republican leaflet reputedly signed by Gabriel Maura was circulated, it was making a joke supported by the fashion of 'going over' to the Republic even in 'zones traditionally loyal'.[8]

This 'divorce between general opinion and the crown'[9] was not the result of a republican campaign, but republicans cultivated it and made political capital out of it. Sánchez Guerra's dramatic protests against the king's intention to summon the notorious Assembly is an example. It was published by the republican *Hojas Libres* in 10,000 copies and circulated in the streets clandestinely. Though Sánchez Guerra did not aim at creating a republican reaction, the people who applauded

[5] L. Jiménez de Asua, *Política, Figuras, Paisajes*, p. 32; Pérez de Ayala, *Escritos*, p. 216.
[6] RA Leg. 89 no. 8; a censored article from *La Voz Valenciana*.
[7] Eulalia de Borbón, *Memorias*, pp. 251–2; G. Maura, *Bosquejo*, p. 377; SAA: Antonio Zozaya to Alba, 23 July 1927.
[8] F.O. 371/9490: E. Howard to Curzon, 20 Sept., 22 Nov. 1923 reporting a conversation with Romanones. The anonymous letter to Romanones is in RA Leg. 28 no. 3: Anticoaba to Romanones, 25 July 1925. For G. Maura see *ES*, 10 Apr. 1929. For the move of 'conservative' elements towards republicanism see Elias Fite, *Política Republicana, la Obra de un Partido*, p. 251; *The Times* 13 Mar. 1929; and a letter to the editor from a Spanish reader in *El Republicano*, Rosario de Santa Fe, 5 Sept. 1928.
[9] RA Leg. 63 no. 31; Romanones to the king, n.d.

him when he came to a bullfight in September 1926, those like
Arturo Casanuevas who was expatriated for supporting him
openly, and the underground literature that mushroomed all
over the country in his support, were pointing at a republican
solution. Republicans exploited the atmosphere to launch
attacks on the Monarchy under the cover of 'theoretical'
articles in which a biblical anti-monarchist text was reproduced
and in which the immunity of 'heads of states' was questioned
on juridical grounds.[10]

The growing interest in politics, which in 1929 crystallized
around the public debate on the constitution proposed by the
Assembly, and around a liberal constitution suggested by *El Sol*,
had in these circumstances a discernible leftist nuance. Most of
the speakers who discussed in the Academy of Jurisprudence
Roig Ibáñez's lecture on 'the constitution Spain needs' (a
programme for a transition from absolutism to a republic),
exposed republican ideas; while the immense crowd that
attended the sessions demonstrated a deep interest in politics.
Simultaneously what *La Epoca* called 'a renaissance of political
literature' was taking place. According to an inquiry made by
La Noche the best-sellers were books dealing with contemporary
history, revolutions, and democracy versus absolutism. It was a
bad year for dealers in belles-lettres. What a frustrated
monarchist like Alcalá Galiano considered a simple loss of
affection for the Monarchy, was seen by a republican like
Marañón as the introduction to 'the great battle between
Spain's past and its future'. Not even Primo de Rivera could
disregard the 'growing republican opinion', a phenomenon also
lamented by the Liberal monarchist *El Imparcial*.[11]

The fall of the Dictatorship and subsequent relative liberali-
zation obviously enabled leftist opinion to mobilize more

[10] Sánchez Guerra's manifesto in his *Al Servicio de España*. For their circulation see *HL*
June 1927. For underground literature see *Ya es tarde (sobre Sánchez Guerra y la
monarquía)*; *Noticiero del lunes (sobre Sánchez Guerra y Primo de Rivera)*; and *A los nietos de los
héroes de 1808* in HMM, A/1730, A/1711, A/1723. See the theoretical articles in *El
Presidencialista*, May 1928. The biblical text 1 Sam. 8: 11-12.

[11] Roig Ibáñez, *La Constitución que Precisa España*, pp. 241-53. For the debates see
Ossorio y Gallardo, *La España de Mi Vida*, p. 105. The programme of *El Sol* and the
reactions to it are surveyed in ibid. 23, 26, 27 Mar., and 2, 3, 9 Apr. 1929. For political
literature see *LE* 1 July 1929; *EP* 12 Mar. 1929; and an illuminating survey in
Emiliano Aguado, *Don Manuel Azaña Díaz*, pp. 168-73. Alcalá Galiano, *The Fall of a
Throne*, p. 22. Marañón in *ES* 16 Dec. 1928. Primo in ibid. 14 Mar. 1929. *El* 5 Sept. 1929.

vigorously. It was now expected that 'politics would be given top priority by the public'.[12] Two months after the dictator's resignation, *ABC* described the atmosphere in the country:

> There is internal agitation in Spain, agitation that cannot be calmed by the methods of traditional politics. A considerable section of youth is becoming alienated from the institutions, and the neutral classes are starting to face the unknown without apprehension. It is the same spirit that could be remarked in France on the eve of the revolution . . . For the first time in our history, vested interests have lost the fear that audacious ideas generally inspire in them.[13]

Foreign observers as well as Spaniards were impressed by the sudden upsurge of republicanism and anti-monarchism, as a movement of protest against the Dictatorship. Both republicans and monarchists recognized that this was indeed the major origin of the movement. All agreed that Primo de Rivera had created more republicans than the fathers of Spanish republicanism—Salmerón, Sol y Ortega, and Lerroux[14]—put together. In this 'deluge of republicans' confessions of republicanism became commonplace.[15] Republicans appeared where they were least expected: in royal academies, convents, in Jesuit and Augustinian communities, among the lower clergy and 'even under the stones'.[16] Children's games now included fights between 'republicans' and 'monarchists', and in Ossorio y Gallardo's house 'even the cat' had become republican. Romero Otazo, a professor of canon law, made a public republican confession; and two republican councillors in the Madrid *Ayuntamiento* managed to convert to republicanism two monarchist councillors. A leader of the upper middle class and Monarchist *Lliga*, Vallés i Pujals, shocked his hearers when he declared that 90 per cent of the members of his party were actually republicans. In order

---

[12] *Política, Revista mensual de doctrina y crítica*, 31 Jan. 1930.

[13] *ABC* 4 Apr. 1930.

[14] For observers see *The Times* 30 Jan., 4–5 Mar. 1930; *The Economist* 8, 22 Feb. 1930; *New Statesman* 17 Feb. 1930; F.O. 371/15041: Grahame to Austen Chamberlain, 30 May, 7 June 1930; Mola, *Obras*, pp. 245–51; *El* 9, 21 Feb. 1930. For monarchists see Romanones in García Venero, *Alba*, p. 286; and Benigno Varela, *Cartas de un Aragonés al Rey Alfonso XIII*, pp. ix–x. For republicans see Marcelino Domingo, *Adonde Va España?*, p. 266; Jiménez de Asua, *Política*, p. 33; and *NE* 30 Jan. 1930.

[15] *El Presidencialista*, April 1930.

[16] Roberto Castrovido in *EP* 25 June 1930; and for the lower clergy see ibid. 30 Oct. 1930.

to behave according to the latest fashion, even a beauty queen made a republican confession and an unsuccessful bullfighter was booed by the crowd as 'monarchist'. People of the liberal professions, especially teachers who resented clerical hegemony in the educational system, and lawyers who were shocked by the lawless procedures of the dictator, saw the Republic as the natural consequence of an oppressive regime which made them fall in love, more than ever, with freedom; and many businessmen who suffered from the high-tariff policy of Calvo Sotelo now saw the Republic as a conservative solution.[17] The Republicans did not fail to exploit the tense anti-monarchist ambiance. The year 1930 was recorded in the Ministry of the Interior's Archive as highly agitated, and the left was credited with most of the meetings that took place.[18] *La Epoca* noticed with dismay how 'republican meetings are multiplying, professional agitators are alarming rudimentary consciences, and newspapers financed by *conservative capital* are opening their columns to republican propaganda'.[19] At the 'meetings of republican affirmation' the speakers, though insisting on the same issue manipulated by non-republican liberals like Ossorio y Gallardo (that of the king's violation of the constitution), did so as the best possible tactic for both bringing down the Monarchy and mobilizing public opinion.[20] Furthermore, an anti-monarchist campaign had better prospects of cementing the solidarity between Republicans whose political and social conceptions differed very much from each other.[21] It is significant, therefore, that an alliance between young Republicans of different parties should be called 'League For Union and Anti-Monarchist Action'.[22] A stronger Monarchy

[17] For Romero Otazo see *El Sol* 22 May 1930. For the councillors and the beauty queen see *EP* 25 June 1930. Vallés i Pujals in *EI* 27 Mar. 1930; and later in *ABC* 6 July 1930. For the bullfighter see J. García Benitez, *Tres Meses de Dictadura*, p. 13. For children see J. Tusquets, *Orígenes de la Revolución Española*, pp. 84–5. For the cat see J. A. Balbontín, *La España de Mi Experiencia*, pp. 206–7. For liberal professions and merchants see J. Felix Huerta, *Sobre la Dictadura*, p. 75; and the growing resentment against the Monarchy and 'old politics' in *El Mercantil Patronal* May–Sept. 1930, Feb. 1931. See also *NE* 14 Nov. 1930.

[18] AHN Leg. 51: 'Mitines 1930'.

[19] *LE* 28 Apr. 1930.

[20] Indalecio Prieto, *Convulsiones de España*, ii, 351.

[21] See the credos of the republican parties below pp. 47–67.

[22] *El Presidencialista* Apr. 1930.

than that of Alfonso XIII, Romanones claimed, would not be able to resist for long attacks like that launched by Prieto at a lecture in the Ateneo. Indeed Alfonso was the best weapon in the hands of the republicans, and his abdication was seen by Ossorio as the only way to save the Monarchy. The republicans' propaganda provided the public with abundant information on the corrupt business deals of the king and his absolutist tendencies. They managed to put the king in the dock, so that people blamed him 'even for the injuries of footballers and bullfighters'. Leftist meetings had greater prospect of attracting an audience than monarchist gatherings. 'Like the spectator in a bullfight' they looked for 'the biting sentence, the injurious comment'. The public received such a dose of political lectures that José Ortega y Gasset had to be asked kindly not to speak on politics in the Ateneo Guipuzcoano 'because people are fed up with political lectures'.[23]

The first half of 1930 was also the period of clear cut definitions by politicians. In such a moment of transition and confusion in which anything was expected;[24] when ideals which were for decades the foundation of society appeared as senile and useless;[25] and when political anxiety and effervescence was apparent even among sectors that had always been disgusted by politics,[26] no wonder that the public was asking the leaders to define themselves, and to trace a clear line of conduct. The first 'definition' was that of Sánchez Guerra. The huge sum of 1,000 pesetas for a ticket was paid for his lecture. The speaker, though not defining himself as a republican, launched such a violent attack on the king that Marañón considered it 'a great step towards the Republic', and Prieto claimed that 'one more blow' would be sufficient to bring down the Monarchy. Young

[23] See Prieto, *El Momento Político* 25 Apr. 1930 in HMM, A/1644; and Romanones' comment in J. Pabón, *Cambó*, ii, part ii, 26. Ossorio y Gallardo *Incompatibilidad*, pp. 28–37. For republican anti-Alfonso propaganda see *El Republicano. Aparecera Cuando Quiera* in HMM A/1310; and *La Gaceta de la Revolución* 28 Jan., 5 Feb. 1931. See comments of foreign observers in F.O. 371/15041: Grahame to Leeper, 7 Aug. 1930; and *Journal de Genève* 16 Dec. 1930. For 'injuries' see *NE* 14 Nov. 1930. For 'spectator in a bullfight' see *Vanguardia*, Badajoz, 2 Mar. 1931. For the crowd in 'leftist' gatherings see Rafael Sánchez Guerra, *Dictadura, Indiferencia, República*, pp. 84–5. For Ortega see OA: José Mugica to Ortega, 9 July 1930.

[24] Don Jaime de Borbón in *Estampa* 29 Apr. 1930.

[25] Ossorio, *Incompatibilidad*, p. 6. See also Aunós in *ABC* 24 July 1930.

[26] *La Ciencia Tomista* Mar.–Apr. 1931.

republicans could now see 'the beginning of the end of the Monarchy', and monarchist speakers were shocked by the damage inflicted on their cause, as well as by the fact that 'leaders of the nobility, culture, capital, labour, politics, the arts and even the army ... mingled that night with the people'. The public seemed to be mainly interested in the 'definition' of those who were not yet republicans. Therefore a speech by Melquiades Alvarez raised a higher degree of expectation than that of Marcelino Domingo in Zaragoza, who as a republican was out of the game. But, when the first did not 'define' himself as a republican the audience was bitterly disappointed.[27]

The left, however, brought under attack not only the Monarchy as an institution, but also other fundamentals of the system. The demand for abolition of the Monarchy was inextricably bound up with a quest for human emancipation, civil rights, and an end to clericalism. A feminist summed up all these aspirations in one word: 'Europeanization'. Jiménez de Asua, a republican professor, blamed Catholicism for 'the dryness of the Spanish soul, the intolerance, the horror of nudity and hygiene, the consideration of sexual intercourse as a sin ... all the sad characteristics of the Spaniard'. By March 1930 a Lay League had been set up by Luis Araquistáin and other socialists and republicans, who thus found their common denominator in anti-clericalism. An intensive campaign was started to protect 'the persecuted dissidents, Protestants and Spanish Jews', and the foundation of Associations of Ex-Pupils of Lay Schools was encouraged. Catholics were so alarmed that they saw the whole campaign as an 'instrument of international Freemasonry directed against Spain'.[28]

---

[27] *NE* 14 Nov. 1930 on the anxiousness for definitions. For public excitement over the speech see Federico De Magriña, *Impresiones Políticas del Momento*, pp. 99–103; and *EI* (editorial) 26 Feb. 1930. For 1,000 pesetas see *EP* 1 Mar. 1930. Two newspapers advanced the date of their first appearance in order to cover the exciting event, see *Cartel Político* 27 Feb. 1930; and *Comentario* 3 Mar. 1930. The speech is in Emilio Ayansa, '*Yo No Merezco Ser Ministro del Rey ni Gobernante en España*', pp. 90–113. Marañón and Prieto in *LV* 28 Feb. 1930. Young republicans in *Juventud*, Alicante, 2 Mar. 1930. For monarchist comments see *EI, LE* (editorials) 28 Feb. 1930; *ABC* 28 Feb. 1930 (Romanones); and the quotation in *The Times* 26 Apr. 1930. For Melquiades and M. Domingo see Pabón, *Cambó*, ii, part ii, 27.

[28] The feminist and Jiménez de Asua in *Juventud* 5 Jan., 23 Feb. 1930. For the League see *Agrupación Socialista Madrileña*, I Semester 1930. For Araquistáin's views see *El Presidencialista* Nov. 1928. For activities and propaganda see *Alianza* Mar. 1930; *NE*

Equally alarming was the identification of women of unorthodox opinions with the 'new wave'. When a women's Ateneo was opened in Seville, its president declared that 'militant middle-class women are prepared to fight for a more open society'. The National Association of Spanish Women campaigned for women's suffrage, and supported those Republican parties which included political rights for women in their platforms. In February a Women's Republican Association was set up to propagate 'the most regenerative modern ideas' as well as the belief that 'whatever is healthy and intelligent today, can be nothing but republican'. The feminists hoped that a Republic would fulfil their aspirations, while republicans encouraged the movement for its 'republican' significance.[29]

Another symptom of the mobilization of the left in 1930 was the upsurge of political literature and permissive literature and customs. Cheap editions of political novels were available in any kiosk; and 'red' literature became a source of disquiet for Mola, the Police Chief. Many young people showed that 'they have the high spirit of the hero of La Mancha' by reading these books, and Marañón, who had himself produced translations of some political novels, saw with delight how this reflected a growing civic and republican awareness. Pornographic literature together with the Tango, the Charleston, and the cinema, which in the early years of the Dictatorship were reaching the most backward and remote villages, were already accentuating there the struggle between 'old' and 'new'. People in cities and towns seemed to be more curious, ashamed to confess their ignorance. An increasing number of periodicals and newspapers were making their first appearance since the fall of the Dictatorship, creating the impression that a 'leftist crusade' was being launched. The efficiency of this crusade increased when, in December 1930, the editors of eighty republican newspapers all

---

15 June 1930; *EP* 3 July 1930; *ES* 23 July, 4 Nov. 1930. For the right's reaction see *ED* 30 May 1930; and *La Ciencia Tomista* Jan.–Feb. 1931.

[29] For the Ateneo see *Estampa* 27 Feb. 1930. For the National Association's campaigns see *Mundo Femenino* Oct., Dec. 1930, Jan., Mar. 1931; and *Juventud* 23 Mar. 1930. For the republican organization see *Mujeres Españolas* 23 Feb. 1930. For the upsurge of feminism on the eve of the Republic see María Oñate del Pilar, *El Feminismo en la Literatura Española*, pp. 237–46; and María Martínez Sierra, *La Mujer Española ante la República*. Jiménez de Asua recognized both the social and political significance of the movement, see his *Juventud*, pp. 81–97; and *Al Servicio de la Nueva Generación, passim.*

over the country met in Madrid to decide on a common front
and to set up the Association of Leftist Journalists.[30]

In conclusion one might say that 1930 was a highly political
year, in which even the right recognized that all public issues
had focused in one central dilemma: Republic versus
Monarchy.[31]

2. THE REBELLION OF STUDENTS AND INTELLECTUALS

The years 1924–31 witnessed a spectacular upsurge of political
awareness in Spanish universities. Leftist students and intellectuals played a major role in fomenting opposition to the
Dictatorship and to the Monarchy, and in creating the
nationwide protest that finally brought about the downfall of
both.

Primo de Rivera, by not trying seriously to enlist the support
of the intellectuals, who were not great supporters of the old
regime either, and by making martyrs out of their leading
figures, had provoked students to rise up against his regime.
Until then they lacked any spirit of association, enjoying sport
and what Gabriel Alomar alluded to as 'panem et circenses'.[32]
Unamuno's exile for protesting against the intervention of the
dictator in the trial of a prostitute produced 'an enormous
excitement' among liberals;[33] it stimulated the *Unión Liberal de
Estudiantes*, which until then had directed its activities against
Catholic students, to demonstrate against the dictator. One year

[30] See a collection of eleven novels in *Colección Novela Política* (Publicación de Prensa
Gráfica, Madrid 1930); and *Colección Novela Roja* in HMM, Carp./18. For young people
see *EP* 14 May 1930. Marañón in *El Sol* 23 May 1930. For alarm see Mola, *Obras*, p. 584;
and *ABC* 20 Mar. 1931. For pornography see a collection of 13 weekly novels: *FRU FRU*
in HMM; governor's reports in AHN Leg. 48: 'Pornografía'; and the manifesto *Católicos
A Defenderse!* in RA Leg. 28 no. 33. For the cinema see Rafael Sánchez Guerra in *Komedias
y Komediantes* 26 Jan. 1930. For 'new winds' in a backward village see Angel Samblancat,
El Aire Podrido; El Ambiente Social de España Durante la Dictadura, pp. 42–50. For curiosity
and a demand for a more 'European Spain' see *El Cruzado Español* 25 Oct. 1929; *Heraldo
de Chamartin* 10 Jan. 1930 (this was a borough of workers); *NE* 8 Nov. 1930. For the press
see the lists of new publications in *Alianza* Jan.–Oct. 1930. For the crusade see Alcalá
Galiano, *The Fall*, pp. 39–51, 91–2. For the 'press front' see *NE* 5 Dec. 1930; and *ES* 12
Dec. 1930.
[31] *LV* 3 July 1930; *La Región*, Alcazar de San Juan, 18 Jan. 1931.
[32] For students early political indifference see Emilio Gonzalez López, *El Espíritu
Universitario*, pp. 19–25. Sport, especially soccer, was blamed for this: see *El Presidencialista*
Aug. 1928, Feb. 1929; *ES* 28 Oct. 1925; and Pedro Rico, *El 'Sport' en España, passim.
Alomar in *EP* 8 May 1929.
[33] UA: Prieto to Unamuno, 20 Feb. 1924.

later, with the blessing of a clandestine letter by Unamuno, they transformed Ganivet's funeral into a manifestation with shouts of 'Down with the King' and 'Long live the Republic'.[34] When a militant student, José Maria Sbert, was exiled for attacking the dictator in public in May 1925, Marañón rejoiced at 'the liberal reaction' of students, in whom he had previously no faith.[35] In October, incited by Unamuno, whose manifesto was spread by republican elements,[36] they broke up the inauguration ceremony of the academic year presided over by a member of the Directory. And when Unamuno's chair was officially declared vacant in April 1926, a professor, Jiménez de Asua, and a student were exiled to the Chafarinas for raising their voices in protest. The dictator's abortive attempt to absorb militant students in the *Unión Patriótica* indicated how they were becoming a nuisance to him.[37]

These sporadic protests started to be canalized into a nationwide movement with the collaboration of leftist intellectuals and republican militants, when, in January 1927, the *Federación Universitaria Escolar* (FUE) was founded. It immediately became the predominant force in most of the campuses, at a time when even Maurista and conservative professors were adhering to a manifestation of anti-monarchism by the senate of Madrid university, which defeated a motion to concede a doctorate *honoris causa* to the king. Though the FUE insisted on its apolitical character, some of its leading members together with republican professors like Giral, Marañón, and Jiménez de Asua were among the founders of the *Liga de Educación Social*, which strove to mobilize workers, feminists and youth in 'a new attitude of the individual towards himself and towards society'.[38]

Student radicalism was to flourish along with the process of economic and social modernization unleashed by the dictator, a

[34] Gonzalez, *El Espíritu*, pp. 72–93; J. López-Rey, *Los Estudiantes Frente a la Dictadura*, pp. 20–5, 68–70.

[35] *NE* 18 Oct. 1930: an interview with Sbert; Marino Gómez-Santos, *Vida de Gregorio Marañón*, p. 234.

[36] UA: Eduardo Ortega to Unamuno, 31 Oct. 1925.

[37] Marco Miranda, *Las Conspiraciones*, p. 99; David Jato, *La Rebelión de los Estudiantes*, p. 33; Gonzalez, op cit. 61–4.

[38] For FUE see López-Rey, *Los Estudiantes*, p. 27. For the Senate see *HL* May 1927; and F.O. 371/12719: Rumbold to Austen Chamberlain, 4, 12 May 1927. For the L.E.S. see López-Rey, op. cit. 50, 54–5; and its manifesto in E. Comin Colomer, *Unamuno, Libelista*, pp. 80–1.

process reflected also in the sudden expansion of the educational system. The number of students in teachers' colleges, for example, increased within the first four years of the regime by 80 per cent. There was a spectacular increase, especially in the last three years of the regime, in the population of the twelve Spanish universities: the number of students more than doubled during the Dictatorship (27,800 in 1923, about 60,000 in 1929–30) while in the decade prior to 1923 the increase had hardly approached 8 per cent. The campuses were being invaded by an influx of middle-class students who, conservatives warned hysterically, 'took their instructions from Moscow'. The sudden emergence of large student populations in urban capitals at a time of rapid economic growth and urbanization has been everywhere a contributory factor to student activism; Primo de Rivera's Spain was no exception. The rebellious attitude of the FUE reflected the unrest of the younger generation of the bourgeoisie confronted by the contrast between a paternalistic dictatorship and the 'values of university life'. Conservatives lamented with dismay that student activism in the Spain of the late twenties and early thirties was the reflection of 'European' influences, and of the young generation's 'moral breakdown' at a time when 'paternal authority, especially in urban society' was collapsing.[39]

It was indeed around an unorthodox vision of society and morality that student dissent was to concentrate. After launching its first strike in March 1928 in support of a lecture by Jiménez de Asua on sexual matters, the FUE embarked upon a struggle against another Church-sponsored measure: Article 53 of the Callejo reform, which allowed Catholic colleges to give academic degrees. This struggle developed gradually into a political issue. After a series of peaceful petitions from both students and professors failed to dissuade the dictator from enacting the decree, most of the country's universities went on strike in March 1929. The dictator's residence and the offices of *El*

---

[39] For the statistical data see *Anuario Estadístico* 1929, 1931. For the social origin and the moral profile of the new student see 'El Estudiante Como Fuerza Social' in *Nueva España* 2 Jan. 1931; *La Voz de Galicia* 25 Apr. 1931. Seymour Lipset, 'Students and Politics in Comparative Studies' in S. Lipset and Philip Altbach, *Students in Revolt*, stresses the connection between student activism and a sudden growth in university population. For a more comprehensive study of the FUE's rebellion see S. Ben-Ami, 'Los Estudiantes contra el Rey' in *Historia-16*, Oct. 1976.

Debate and *ABC* were stoned, 'for hire' was written on the façade of the royal palace, a network of clandestine leaflets ridiculing Primo de Rivera was established, and street demonstrations became commonplace in many provincial universities. *El Debate*, supported by the rightist press, called hysterically for the suppression of the 'politically motivated' movement, claiming that 'Spain does not need the universities, and can better manage without them'. On 17 March all the universities were indeed closed by decree, and government delegates were appointed to administer them. Professors circulated manifestos attacking the 'bureaucratization' of the universities, and upholding the student cause. Menéndez Pidal's personal protest was supported by forty outstanding figures of the Spanish intelligentsia, some of whom, including Fernando de los Ríos, Sánchez Román, J. Ortega y Gasset, and Jiménez de Asua resigned from their chairs. To the accusation that they were manipulated by politicians, the students responded with an attack on clericalism, and on 'Alfonso Africanus', the king. They declared solidarity with their professors, promising to struggle together with them 'until the tyrant is overthrown'. It was finally the government that gave up. Anxious to impress the members of the League of Nations holding their meeting in Madrid, and worried at possible damage to the economy from student disturbances, the dictator decreed the opening of the universities on 20 May, released Sbert from prison, and, on 24 September, capitulated totally by suspending Article 53.[40]

The struggle of the universities, however, went on precisely because it was aimed against the regime, rather than against any of its measures. The FUE now demonstrated, with the

[40] For the strike of March 1928 see *HL* March 1928. For the peaceful struggle see López-Rey, op. cit. 38–48. For the course of the strike and the disturbances all over the country see ibid. 56–142; *El Sol* 10–15 March 1929 (on Madrid); *LV* 13–23 March 1929 (on Barcelona); E. Esperabe de Arteaga, *La Universidad de Salamanca de 1923 a 1930. Contestando a Unamuno*, pp. 33–4 (on Salamanca). For the right's attitude see *ED* 15, 17 Mar. 1929; *ABC* 13 Mar. 1929; *LV* 21 Mar. 1929. For the professors see López-Rey, op. cit. 159–70; *El Sol* 2 Apr. 1929; and RA Leg. 63 no. 53: *Escrito de J. de Asua Renunciado a la Cátedra de Derecho Penal* 24 May 1929. For examples of clandestine leaflets see *Escrito de los Estudiantes* in RA Leg. 63 no. 49; Antonio Gascón, *Los Estudiantes*, pp. 41–44; British Museum Library 1865C 19(98): 'A collection of tracts attacking the Monarchy', 17 May 1929. For the economic damage see *LV* 23 Mar., 14 Apr. 1929; *El* 20 Mar. 1929; and *The Economist* 23 Mar. 1929. For Primo's capitulation see *The Times* 21, 23 May 1929.

support of the senate of Madrid university, on behalf of a 'rehabilitiation' of Sbert, and the restitution of the professors who had resigned. On 20 January 1930 most of the universities were again on strike. The literary clandestine war against the 'alcoholic general' was intensified, and the demand for his resignation put forward.[41]

Primo de Rivera abdicated with the noise of students' shouts still echoing in his ears. When a dictator announces every day that he is rejuvenating and regenerating a country, he obviously faces a great dilemma when the young generation rise up against him and the kind of state he is creating. 'The future', predicted the new organ *Política*, 'will be that which youth now vigorously entering politics will mould'. But, the Dictatorship, according to the FUE militant López-Rey, failed to acquire even 'a parody of juvenile acquiescence'.[42]

Whether it confessed it or not, the FUE's movement was both 'political' and 'leftist'. Students were identified with and encouraged by people like Marañón, Unamuno, and Jiménez de Asua, who preached a Republic. The latter told them how the professors 'are contemplating your rebellion with emotion'; and confessed his delight with the republican character of the movement; and Fernando de los Ríos followed suit with a similar declaration. López-Rey openly referred in 1929 to the Republic as the 'only open door'.[43] Others recognized that the movement was the consequence of 'a strong orientation towards extreme democracy' coming from the campuses.[44] This 'orientation' was inextricably tied up with the rejection of old moralities and traditional values, sympathy towards occasional demands for free love and praise for nudism, a greater interest in politics and a growing literary sensitiveness at a period when 'rebellious' authors like García Lorca, Salinas, and Albertí were

---

[41] López-Rey, op. cit. 271–310. For how the strike spread in the country see *Nota Oficiosa, Ultimas Noticias del Movimiento Escolar, 24 Jan. 1930* in RA Leg. 2 no. 44.

[42] Jiménez de Asua, *Juventud*, p. 149. *Política*, 31 Jan. 1930.

[43] For Unamuno's interest in the movement see UA: Marañón to Unamuno, n.d. Arturo Soria, a member of the FUE's Junta, pointed out to me, in a private conversation in Madrid, June 1972, the close contacts with these elements. For López-Rey and Jiménez de Asua see Jiménez de Asua, op. cit. 13–116, 159; F. de los Ríos in *El Sol* 5 Nov. 1929.

[44] *El Presidencialista* Aug., Dec. 1928; and Castrovido in *EP* 12 Mar. 1929.

making their appearance and Ortega's *Revista de Occidente* was sponsoring the 'new wave'.[45] If a proof were needed that the FUE's rebellion was not exclusively anti-Primo, but also republican and anti-monarchist, it was provided by the students' refusal to concede a truce to the Berenguer government, despite the latter's conciliatory initiatives. They were ready 'to kick the crown as if kicking a ball'.[46] When the *Unión de Estudiantes Hispanos* (the central organization of the provincial FUEs) made an impressive show of power in its annual congress, *El Debate* saw it as a branch of the republican offensive. Indeed, two months earlier, many members of the FUE started to join the new Association of Republican Students under the blessing of *Alianza Republicana*.[47] López-Rey represented the FUE in the commemoration of the first Republic, and Republicans courted the students asking them to join their parties, and promising to include their aspirations in their platforms.[48]

The FUE's agitation was now an integral part of the anti-monarchist effervescence. Such was the case of the demonstration and strike that developed in several universities following an enthusiastic reception given to Unamuno on May Day in Madrid by workers, republicans, and students, all of whom were said to be united in the battle against the 'crowned robber'. When in Barcelona a monarchist student was called on 1 October to inaugurate the academic year, the gathering was broken up with shouts of 'Long live the Republic'; and, when the Republican leader, Maciá, was expelled, the students protested in the streets of many cities for several days, giving to a foreign observer the impression that '90 per cent of the students in this country are anti-monarchists'. The strikes of the Socialists and the Anarcho-Syndicalists in mid-November in Madrid and Barcelona, were also followed with solidarity demonstrations by the FUE. In January 1931 a minor clash

[45] See López-Rey's lecture in Jiménez's *Juventud*, pp. 129–43; An inquiry of *El Sol* (7, 9, 24 Jan., 7, 11 Feb. 1930) on 'What does the young generation think?'; *ES* 11 Apr. 1929 (F. de los Ríos, 27 Mar. 1930 (Louis de Brouckere). For the authors see Tuñón de Lara, *Medio Siglo de Cultura Española*, pp. 237–58.
[46] Unamuno in *Juventud* 23 Feb. 1930.
[47] *ED* 29 Apr. 1930; *El Presidencialista* and *Alianza*, Mar. 1930. For Alianza Republicana see below, pp. 68–76.
[48] *Alianza* Feb. 1930; *NE* 15 Mar., 1 May 1930.

with monarchist militants resulted in a strike followed by riots in many provincial universities aimed at bringing down 'the king and Berenguer, his amnestied general' (an allusion to his responsibility for Annual). As always 'spiritual support' was provided by Unamuno, and now also by the Socialist Fernando de los Ríos. The recent frustrated republican revolution of December[49] led the government to assume that it was now witnessing its continuance. It decreed, therefore, on 5 February the closing of all the universities in the country. It was only a few days later that the government itself fell without much glory.[50]

Leftist intellectuals, stimulated by the atmosphere created by the students' rebellion and by the agitated mood of the country, tried to canalize this movement of protest into an intellectual Republican organization: the *Agrupación Al Servicio de la República*, founded on 10 February 1931 by Marañón, R. Pérez de Ayala, and J. Ortega y Gasset. This 'triumvirate' had been in confrontation with the regime throughout its last years. Marañón was arrested in 1926 for his alleged participation in the 'Sanjuanada', and for being a 'revolutionary figure' according to the dictator, and when he was released, he launched an open attack on the king in *Hojas Libres*. In October 1929, he considered republicanism as part of his natural being, 'just like breathing and walking'. After the fall of the Dictatorship, he accentuated his republican attitude, and at the end of January 1931, he wrote confidently to Unamuno: 'All is going well, we are all pushing faithfully towards a better Spain'.[51] Pérez de Ayala, who was a member of Alianza Republicana since its foundation in 1926, bitterly attacked the praetorian character of the Dictatorship, while recognizing its tremendous impact on

---

[49] See below pp. 94–99, 147–151.

[50] For the May events, see *Rebelión* 14 June, 19 July 1930; 'A tract accusing the King as responsible for the shooting of students' 8 May 1930, in British Museum Library 1865 C. 19(98); *ABC* 6–9 May 1930. For October in Barcelona, and other cities see *SO* 2–3 Oct. 1930; *LV* 4 Oct. 1930; and *ABC* 28, 30 Oct. 1930. The foreign observer: F.O. 371/150 41: Grahame to Henderson, 17 Oct. 1930. For the strikes see Gascón, *Los Estudiantes*, pp. 84–5, 88; and *El Noticiero de la Huelga Escolar 29 Jan. 1931* in HMM A/1673. For Unamuno see UA: Marañón to Unamuno, 31 Jan. 1931. For de los Ríos' message to the students from prison see *BUGT* Feb. 1931. The government's measures are in *ABC* 5 Feb. 1931.

[51] The dictator in *The Times* 1 July 1926; Marañón in *HL* May 1927; *EP* 1 Oct. 1929; UA: Marañón to Unamuno, 31 Jan. 1931.

the republicanization of many people, a republicanization which, in 1929, he tried unsuccessfully, together with Jiménez de Asua, Marañón, and Sánchez Román to consolidate into a 'new' Republican Party.[52]

The prestigious philosopher Ortega y Gasset was more hesitant than his colleagues in joining the republican wave. In April 1929, after he resigned his chair, many young people, both rightist and leftist, referred to him as to the potential leader of a movement of renovation, and a group of young intellectuals, among them Federico García Lorca, asked him to lead their movement of rebellion against political indifference (*apoliticismo*) and on behalf of a 'modern' and 'intellectual' orientation towards freedom. He refused, unwilling to define himself in the traditional terms of 'left' and 'right', thus disappointing some republicans. When at the beginning of 1930 everyone was expecting him to 'define' himself in those terms, he was calling for the 'nationalization' of the state, social transformation and active involvement in politics. It was a neo-Maurista ideology rather than 'pure' republicanism. Even when on 15 November 1930 he launched a violent attack on the 'Berenguer error' (the attempt to return to normality as if nothing had happened) ending with a Catonian *delenda est monarchia*, he was still looking at a Maura as the real prophet of Spain's reconstruction, criticizing republican romanticism and its melodramatic revolutionarism.[53]

However, in the dogmatic ambiance of the period, Ortega was classified as leftist, and he himself finally understood that it was under the auspices of a vigorous republicanism rather than under the decadent Monarchy that his ideas about nationalizing the state could materialize. In February 1931 he therefore joined Marañón and Pérez de Ayala in founding the ASR in whose initial manifesto they all agreed that only a Republic

[52] Perez de Ayala, *Escritos*, pp. 146–7, 162–4, 177–8, 216–7; and his long letter to Unamuno, 17 Dec. 1925 in UA.

[53] For young people see OA: letters from Angel Vega y Goldom, from José Diaz García, 26, 27 May 1929, and from Confederación de Estudiantes Católicos, 6 Dec. 1929. For the group of young intellectuals see ibid: letters from F. Soler Fando and Teofilo Ortega (an Albista) 4, 10 May 1929; and J. Ortega y Gasset, *Obras Completas*, xi, pp. 102–5. Republicans' disappointment in *EP* 11 May 1929. For a call to 'define' himself see OA: Ossorio to Ortega, 5 Apr. 1930. For 'nationalization' see *El Sol* 5 Feb. 1930; and for the 'error' see his *Obras*, pp. 274–9. The last statement is based on his article in *El Sol* 6 Dec. 1930.

could accomplish the 'gigantic work' of modernizing the nation, both technically and socially. The ASR appealed mainly to students and intellectuals, but the fact that it was conceived as a 'levy-*en masse* against the Monarchy' rather than as a 'party' in the strict sense of the term, enabled many people who already belonged to other parties to join it. The response of the public was impressive. A fortnight after its foundation, the ASR had 15,000 members, a figure which in April had risen to 25,000.[54]

3. THE UPSURGE OF REPUBLICAN ORGANIZATIONS

a. Inertia and clandestinity

In spite of limitations imposed by Primo de Rivera on political propaganda, Republican centres and organizations preserved their historical framework during the Dictatorship, in order to be ready to absorb, when the time came, what Pérez de Ayala called 'the ideology and republican sentiments diffused throughout the country'.[55]

Their activities, however, were limited. Intimate meetings, commemorations, and even forbidden games, which were used as a substitute for political activities, reflected a languorous existence. Those, like Alejandro Lerroux, who missed the good old days of mass demonstrations and inflaming oratory, had now to keep silent and prepare their forces 'for the necessary heroism'. Mass rallies like those intended by Marcelino Domingo and Emiliano Iglesias were forbidden, and newspapers had to coexist with the censor or vanish, like Eduardo Ortega y Gasset's *Justicia.*[56]

---

[54] Ortega was already considered 'republican' in February 1930 (OA: letter from Luis Velasco, 10 Feb. 1930). For the ASR see Ortega, *Obras*, pp. 125–8; and Marino Gómez-Santos, *Marañón*, pp. 287–90. For response see OA: letters from Modesto Cuadrillero, a group of people, Juan Rosillo and Publio Suarez 21, 26, 27, 29 Mar. 1931; *LV* (editorial) 20 March 1931; *The Times* 25 Feb. 1931 and *EC* 25 Apr. 1931.

[55] Pérez de Ayala, *Escritos*, p. 217.

[56] For activities see *The Times* 14 Feb. 1928; *República, Semanario de Inteligencia Republicana* 11 Feb. 1926; AHN Leg. 45: reports from Alicante 8 Feb. 1928, no. 126, and from Barcelona 26 Oct. 1928, no. 526; and *ES* 24 Apr. 1927, 16 June 1928. See how the centre in La Coruña disintegrated in Domingo Quiroga Ríos, *Quien Es y Adonde Va Santiago Casares?*, pp. 26–8. Lerroux in *Mis Memorias*, p. 538. For Domingo and Iglesias see AHN Leg. 51: from the Ministry of the Interior to Governor Alava, 26 Feb. 1926; Leg. 42: circular to the Governors of Galicia, 2 Dec. 1924, no. 30. For 'Justicia' see UA: E. Ortega to Unamuno, 3 Dec. 1923.

It was, therefore, all the more impressive when the commemoration of the anniversary of the first Republic in February 1926 demonstrated how 450 clubs, casinos, and centres all over the country responded to a central initiative, and celebrated nostalgic gatherings with the 'Marseillaise' as a substitution for forbidden political speeches. This response was a source of confidence for the organizers at the *Escuela Nueva* in Madrid, who were brought to believe that they had under their control a 'legion, sufficient to organize a new state'. Even monarchists were impressed by what was 'no longer a mere nostalgic manifestation, but a prophetic prediction of a possible Republic'.[57]

The fact, however, was that political paths were closed, and conspiracy, which was a tradition, became a necessity.[58] Already in October 1923, Lerroux wrote to Blasco Ibáñez that he expected that 'a new military *coup d'état*, but not a militarist one, would bring us to power'. This flamboyant and unrealistic assertion which circulated clandestinely helped to maintain the 'sacred fire' in many hearts, avoiding desertions and rejuvenating republican veterans.[59]

It is, however, evident that republican participation in the conspiracies against the Dictatorship was very often a case of individuals improvising rather than a significant organized civilian movement. Moreover, in all the cases the republicans were one of the many and different elements committed. Consequently, the overthrow of the Dictatorship rather than of the Monarchy was the major aim. In September 1924, Lerroux and other republicans were in contact with General Cavalcanti and monarchist figures who led an abortive anti-Primo coup.[60] In the 'Sanjuanada' Alianza Republicana contented itself with a secondary role, leaving the leadership to General Aguilera, monarchist, and 'constitutionalist' elements. Lerroux, after making initial contacts, disappeared from the scene leaving it to secondary republican figures in Valencia, and to Federals

[57] The reports from the meetings in the provinces were concentrated in a clandestinely published book: Alianza Republicana, *El 11 de Febrero 1926*, pp. 21–173. For the monarchists see a censored article of *El Diario Universal* in RA Leg. 78 no. 5.

[58] Azaña, *Obras*, iii, 877.

[59] Lerroux, *Al Servicio*, pp. 245–7; Villanueva, *La Dictadura*, p. 67.

[60] Lerroux, *Memorias*, p. 541; RA Leg. 63 no. 66: Tomas Benet to Romanones, 12 Sept. 1924.

and Anarcho-Syndicalists, 'because' he said, 'it was below my dignity'. The dictator, however, by arresting republicans like Marcelino Domingo, Barriobero, and Marañón, the first and the last on groundless accusations, tried to overemphasize the republican aspect of the movement, in order to distract the public's attention from 'the real military character of the conspiracy which was exclusively directed against him'.[61]

Republican participation was more substantial in Sánchez Guerra's coup. When Sánchez Guerra went into exile, Eduardo Ortega believed that 'the case of Spanish freedom has now a prestigious and authoritative leader'. And by the end of 1927 a 'united front' was established between him and republicans, with Marcelino Domingo strongly believing that Sánchez Guerra was the Spanish Thiers, who might give way to the Republic in due course. However, all that was agreed in meetings between representatives of Alianza Republicana and Sánchez Guerra was the concession of 'freedom of organization and for the spreading of ideas', and the summoning of a Constituent Cortes. Catalan Republicans, who were also approached to join the movement, set up a revolutionary committee headed by Companys and consisting of every leftist force in the region from the Radical Republicans to underground cells of Anarcho-Syndicalists and Communists. On the day of the *coup*, Republican leaders were at their posts. In Murcia there were Alvaro de Albornoz, Angel Galarza and Artigas Arpón; in Alcoy Juan Botella was to preside over a four-day strike; Lerroux was in Barcelona; while republican Valencia was supposed to play a leading role by taking over municipal councils in the province. However, all these forces were condemned to inactivity when the army failed to act. Nevertheless, republicans continued to manifest their 'conspiratorial vocation' and in the last 'constitutional' conspiracy that coincided with the fall of the Dictatorship, the Radical Republican leader, Martínez Barrio, and Miguel Maura were trying to add

[61] Antonio Marsá Bragado and others, *Libro de Oro del Partido Republicano Radical 1868–1934*, p. 162; Lerroux, op. cit. 541. For Marañón see Romanones, *Notas*, p. 224. For Domingo see his interview in *NE* 8 Nov. 1930. The last quotation in RA Leg. 5 no. 29: 'R.' to Romanones, n.d. For an emphasis on republicans' role see Marco Miranda, *Las Conspiraciones*, pp. 23–5, 57, 78. For Barriobero see Ramiro Gómez Fernández, *La Dictadura me Honró Encarcelándome*, pp. 37–43.

a republican content to the *coup*'s platform while Ramón Franco, was pressing for an even more leftist orientation.[62] No less effective than any republican conspiracy was the libellous campaign against both the Dictatorship and the Monarchy. Unamuno, who refused to write in Spain because of the censorship,[63] collaborated in France with Blasco Ibáñez in *España con Honra*, and with Eduardo Ortega in the publication of *Hojas Libres*, a monthly collection of censored information and violent attacks on the regime, that circulated clandestinely like 'sacred bread', and which was financed by Spanish republicans abroad. Even Unamuno's wife was used to infiltrate libels into Spain. When the French authorities expelled E. Ortega from Bayonne, he started in Paris the publication of *España* with a similar content. Blasco Ibáñez's *Alfonso XIII Unmasked*, a libel against the king, was published in many languages, and thousands of copies were infiltrated into Spain by republican activists. It forced the Monarchy into a defensive position; monarchist propagandists alleged an 'international campaign' against Spain, and mobilized panegyrists to refute Blasco's accusations, showing thereby how serious was the damage caused to the king's prestige.[64]

b. Reorganization and doctrinal 'ventilation'

The turning point in the evolution of republicanism from clandestinity to open reorganization came in July 1929. The authorization given by the dictator to a free discussion of the

[62] For E. Ortega and the united front see *HL* Nov. 1927, Feb. 1928; López de Ochoa, *De la Dictadura*, p. 138. For Alianza see M. Burgos y Mazo, *La Dictadura y Los Constitucionalistas*, ii, pp. 31–2; Marco Miranda, *Las Conspiraciones*, pp. 58–9, 114; and E. Iglesias in *EP* 7 Aug. 1930. For the constitutionalist character see R. Sánchez Guerra, *El Movimiento*, p. 137. For Catalan republicans see A. Ossorio y Gallardo, *Vida Y Sacrificio de Companys*, pp. 62–4. For republicans in the movement see Marco Miranda op. cit. 124, 144, 149–152; R. Gomez Fernandez, *La Dictadura*, pp. 80, 94, 101–6, 242–7. *EP* 27 Jan. 1929 (Lerroux); *NE* 8 Nov, 1930 (M. Domingo). For the last conspiracy see Burgos y Mazo, op. cit. 182–3; Maura in *Estampa* 6 June 1931; and Ramón Franco, *Madrid Bajo las Bombas*, pp. 95–7.

[63] UA: Prieto to Unamuno, 2 June 1926, 30 Mar. 1928.

[64] For *HL* see Maura, *Bosquejo*, pp. 235–6; *El Republicano* 5 Oct. 1928; private conversation with Felisa Unamuno 8 Mar. 1974. See *España* 18 Nov. 1929. For *España con Honra* see Marco Miranda, op. cit. 33. For Blasco see his *Alfonso XIII Unmasked, The Military Terror in Spain*. For infiltration and extraordinary circulation see R. Xuriguera, *Els Exiliats*, pp. 198–200; and the Monarchy's response in *La Monarquía* 20, 27 Dec. 1924; Alfonso De Grijalba, *Los Enemigos del Rey*; and an attempt to win over Antonio Maura 'in support of the sovereign against the traitor' in MA: Juan Mata to Maura, n.d.

constitutional draft elaborated by the Assembly stimulated the political forces to a clearer expression, and the Republicans were the first to awake.[65]

During the preceding period, the Radical Party, with its historical centre in Barcelona, manifested its existence through humble gatherings, sporting events, and intimate acts of homage to its leader, Lerroux.[66] In such circumstances, and with no political meetings to mobilize the party, the 'sacred fire' was preserved by pathetic editorials:

The Radical Party stands firm, concentrated in its centres, gathered around its co-operatives, dedicated to the improvement of its schools by which it contributes ... to the amelioration of the race ... Who would dare to say that the Radical Party has finished its mission? It is alive, assembled in its tents ... Like the veteran soldiers of Napoleon, we who follow Lerroux can say: 'The guard dies, but never surrenders'.[67]

But in July more tangible expressions of existence were becoming evident. Doctrinal articles and political affirmations started to appear. The constitution of the Assembly was rejected by Lerroux and Emiliano Iglesias for disregarding the 'national sovereignty', and for making impossible the creation of a federal state, possible only under a democratic flexible constitution. 'Structural reorganization' of the party and 'doctrinal ventilation' was advocated to cope with the political opportunities about to appear once the Dictatorship was over. An appeal was therefore made to a wide public. Workers were supposed to be attracted by a slogan on 'distribution of wealth', Catalan autonomists were approached with the banner of a 'federal Republic', anti-clericalism was preached as 'likely to excite everybody', the anti-protectionist credo was put forward on behalf of both a cheaper food-basket for the working class as well as free trade for those commercial sectors which supported it, and the 'Republic of virtues' was advocated for everyone.[68]

[65] *The Times* 22 July 1929.
[66] *ES* 26 Sept. 1924; *LV* 10 Mar. 1928; *EP* 17 Jan., 20 Feb., 26 Apr. 1929; SA Leg. 1161: Simón Beltrán and staff of *El Progreso* to Lerroux 8, 25 Oct. 1928.
[67] *EP* 27 Apr. 1929.
[68] Lerroux in *EI* 10 July 1929, and *EP* 11–12 July 1929. E. Iglesias in ibid. 14 July 1929. For the appeals see ibid. 9, 13, 16, 18, 20, 21 Aug., 3 Oct. 1929; 1 Jan. 1930.

In spite of personal rivalries between party activists, 'indiscipline', 'gossip', the withdrawal of some centres from the party, and financial difficulties throughout the last year,[69] the Radicals were able to initiate a process of structural reorganization, a process which culminated in regional assemblies at the end of the year and the beginning of 1930 in Barcelona, Madrid, Huelva, Valencia, and La Coruña. When only the preparatory contacts of this reorganization were being made, *El Progreso* was confidently exclaiming: 'Which opposition party in Spain ... could offer such a number of branches maintaining one ideal?'[70]

In the subsequent period of relative political freedom conceded by the Berenguer government, the Radicals, whose main tradition and power lay in Catalonia, laid stress on their historical mission of harmonizing the Catalans' particularistic aspirations with Spain's national unity. Their propaganda was, therefore, directed against both the Monarchist *Lliga* on the right and the Catalan nationalists of *Acció Catalana* and *Estat Català* on the left, while trying to attract their bourgeois and working-class following. Lerroux, however, dictated a cautious line of conduct towards the left, whose collaboration might be needed for political alliances.[71] The Lliga's regionalism was attacked as false, because it supported any central government, including the Dictatorship, that promised to protect the economic interest of the Lliga magnates. An attempt by the *Diputación Provincial*, under the presidency of the *Lliguista* Maluquer i Viladot, to draw up a project of autonomy was rejected as a caciquista and undemocratic procedure. Only a federal Republic and an elected Constituent Cortes, it was argued, could fulfil Catalan aspirations. On the social level, the Radicals presented themselves as the defenders of the small companies against the expansionism of big business sponsored by the Lliga and encouraged by the Dictatorship's economic policy. On the other hand the Catalan left[72] was accused of being excessively

---

[69] SA Leg. 1161: Emeterio Palma and Ignacio Elevia to Lerroux, 7 Nov. 1929.

[70] SA Leg. 1709: *Asamblea Regional del Partido Republicano Radical de Cataluña*; Leg. 1161: the Valencia branch to Lerroux, 3 Nov. 1929; *EP* 8 Mar.; *LV* 23 Feb. 1930 (Huelva); *EP* 4 Mar. 1930 (La Coruña); *Alianza* Apr.; and *El Sol* 29 Apr. 1930 (Madrid); *EP* 25 Oct., 6, 8, 10 Nov. 1929 (Barcelona). The quotation is in *EP* 24 Aug. 1929.

[71] Lerroux in *EP* 11 Jan. 1930.

[72] For the Lliga see below, pp. 162–165. For the Catalan left see below pp. 60–66.

nationalistic and reluctant to compromise with a federal Republic with its centre in Madrid. Emiliano Iglesias warned that 'these damned Catalanists' might create a cantonalist movement that would destroy the prospects of a viable federal Republic. At the same time, efforts were made to attract the working class, which otherwise might join the Catalanist left. A campaign was launched on behalf of 'social' prisoners, cheaper bread, and against income tax on workers' wages. A demand for a 'new social order' and a public admission of 'the philosophy of Karl Marx' before an audience of workers reflected the demagogic aspect of the effort. Rafael Guerra del Río was more sincere, and indeed represented more accurately the social and political views of his party, when he declared:

We should not lead the Syndicalists astray. When the Republic comes we shall defend it against both the right and the left ... We must avoid a situation in which the Republic could be born in the midst of street uprisings against the social order, because this would mean condemning it to death by another sword.

Meanwhile, in spite of their campaign to undermine their rivals' position, the Radicals were committed to the principle of unifying all the Catalan left, and subsequently the Spanish left, as a *conditio sine qua non* for 'bringing about the Republic'. For the sake of union Lerroux, though recognizing that his party had special 'historical rights', was even ready to withdraw his candidature in future elections in Catalonia in order not to alienate those in the Catalanist parties who opposed him.[73]

Lerroux was, indeed, throughout the Dictatorship and its aftermath undergoing a personal metamorphosis; the street demagogue of the past was becoming a 'responsible' and 'governmental' politician. And his absolutist rule over the party meant that his ideas were automatically those of the party, though a democratic façade was always maintained. He was the 'iron surgeon', the 'caudillo, the jefe, the guide, the counsellor and the soul of the party'. The ultimate decision on

[73] *El Progreso* is a mine of information on the Radical Party in this period, see selected references: on the Lliga, 25 June, 5, 10–12 July 1930; on the Catalan left, 5, 16 March, 5, 7, 9, 14, 19 Aug. 1930; on workers, 18, 19 Feb., 4, 23 Mar., 27 June, 12 Aug., 12 Oct. 1930. The quotation in 2 Nov. 1930; on union 6, 8, 11, 13 Feb. (Lerroux), 25 Mar., 26 Apr., 1 May, 11 June 1930. For social and political affirmations see also Rocha in *ABC* 27 Feb.; *LV* 27, 28 Feb. 1930; and a meeting in ibid. 29 Apr. 1930.

the most minor issues lay with him, and his instructions started with 'my desire is . . .'[74] In matters of doctrine, his 'desire' already in 1924 was for a moderate Republic in which 'discipline, law, and authority' would prevail. In 1926 he called upon the rich, landlords, industrialists, merchants, and bankers 'to co-operate in order to create a new situation, in which it will be possible to make reforms which will disarm the demagogy, and which will calm down, satisfying as far as possible, the just and legitimate aspirations of the needy classes.'[75] In January 1929 he was openly advocating a Constituent Cortes, and claiming that should it decide against a republican regime, the republicans 'would have no right to implant their ideal by revolutionary means'. Later in the year he called for an 'institutionalized evolution', a 'national government of all the political groups' both to avoid a 'soviet' alternative and to summon the Constituent Cortes.[76] During the Berenguer period Lerroux, 'the only caudillo with the capacity to dominate the masses', according to *El Imparcial*, put his talents in the service of the conservative Republic. For its sake he continued to appeal both to the conservative classes to rally behind 'a non-violent political transformation', and to the union of the left. This should include 'disappointed ex-monarchists' as well as the extreme left, adherence to the principle of 'national sovereignty', not 'Republic', being their common denominator. Once the Republic was established—either by a controlled revolution or in a Cortes—it should be ruled by 'radical ideas implemented in a conservative way'. Moderation and evolution was Lerroux's message. Even when he warned of a 'total revolution which would spread from the fields of Andalucía to the great cities, and would kick out the king', it was in order to avoid rather than to encourage it.[77]

[74] For expressions of personality cult see Elias Fite, *Política Republicana*, p. 260 and *EP* 26 June 1929, 19 Mar., 23 Apr., 5 June 1930. For minor issues see SA Leg. 1161: J. Colominas Maseras and Antonio Pons to Lerroux, 11, 13 Nov. 1929. For 'my desire' see *EP* 6 Sept. 1929.

[75] RA Leg. 2 no. 32: Lerroux to an unidentified correspondent 2 Oct. 1926. For the conservative Republic earlier see E. Fite, op. cit. 259–60.

[76] *La Rioja*, Logroño, 14 Jan. 1929; and A. Lerroux, *Para un Periódico de America, Colaboración o Revolución* in HMM, A/1685.

[77] *EI* 12 Apr. 1930. For Lerroux's ideas on the Republic and unity see his articles in *EP* 22, 23 Feb., 26 Apr., 7 June, 18 July, 3 Oct., 1930; *NE* 15 Sept. 1930; his speech in

The revolutionary oratory Lerroux condemned had been, since 1929, more characteristic of the new *Partido Republicano Radical Socialista*. Its main founders, Alvaro de Albornoz and Marcelino Domingo, though adopting the old republican formulae of anti-clericalism and laicism, were throughout the Dictatorship appealing for the creation of republican parties disassociated both from the petrified dogmas of 'historical republicanism' and from its attachment to *Caudillismo*. They both preached for the politicization of the working class, and for a mass party with press, money, and discipline, 'like Herriot's Radical-Socialists in France'. 'Old republicanism', they said, failed to attract the working class to its ranks, and was thus never able to become a mass movement. Their major concern was, therefore, to put forward social programmes in an effort to unify socialism and republicanism into a both politically and socially leftist mass movement. Only such a mobilization of public opinion could produce radical governments, and could change the face of Spanish traditional politics, of which 'old republicanism' was an integral part.[78]

In July 1929, they broke officially with old republicanism (since 1919 they had been in dissidence with their original party, the Radicals) to found the PRRS in whose programme they introduced their basic views together with a mixture of revisionist socialism which did not recognize the class struggle, a jacobin oratory, a sympathetic approach to Catalan autonomist aspirations, and an appeal for agrarian reform.[79]

The explicit anti-*Lerrouxista* orientation of the PRRS and its manifest openness towards *Obrerismo*, while criticized by the Radicals as a 'French imitation', opened wide prospects of

---

Alianza Apr. 1930; his appeal for unity as early as in 1924 in SA Leg. 1161: Marcelino Domingo to Lerroux, 9 June 1924; and *La Zarpa*, Orense, 27 Dec. 1924. The last quotation is from his leaflet *Responsabilidad, Inmunidad, Inpunidad*, July 1930 in AHN Leg. 45: Governor of Madrid to Gobernación, 12 July 1930.

[78] Alvaro de Albornoz, *La Tragedia del Estado Español*, pp. 108–11, 119–21; *Intelectuales y Hombres de Acción*, pp. 59–68; *El Temperamento Español*, pp. 120–3; his introduction to Gabriel Morón, *El Partido Socialista ante la Realidad Política de España*, pp. 13–26; and his *El Peligro del Caudillaje en el Régimen Presidencial* in RA Leg. 54, no. 3. Marcelino Domingo, *Autocracia y Democracia*, pp. 273–5, 299–302; *Que Espera?*, pp. 177–81; and his articles in *EP* 11 Apr., 4, 19 May 1929; and *NE* 15 Apr. 1930. See also the political biography: A. Garcitoral, *La Ruta de Marcelino Domingo*, pp. 166–70.

[79] *Manifiesto del PRRS A La Democracia Republicana*, Dec. 1929 in HMM A/1674; a meeting in *El Sol* 5 Nov. 1929; and Garcitoral, op. cit. 180–5, 226–7.

success among urban 'intellectuals' and working-class elements. Already in February 1930, the Republicans of the working-class district of Chamartin joined the PRRS 'because of the need to advocate social and radical conceptions'. Party propagandists held meetings all over the country. New centres and branches were inaugurated in provincial towns like Puente de Tocinos, Medina de Rioseco, Monteagudo, Quitapellejos (all in Murcia), Lalueza (Huesca), Callosa de Segura, Murla (Alicante), and Almonacid de la Sierra (Zaragoza), to mention only a few examples. Simultaneously, preparations for the first national congress of the party were started. In preparatory manifestos, special appeals were made to 'socialists who do not belong to the Socialist party', to Anarcho-Syndicalists and to small and middle-class peasants, whose land tenure the Radical Socialists promised to protect from both 'red' demagogy and the big landowners' 'appetite'. As a culmination of this intensive labour of propaganda and organization, the national congress, held during the last days of September, elected the governing bodies of the party and ratified its programme, emphasizing the need to nationalize the Bank of Spain, land and railways and to separate Church and state.[80]

The fate of the Federal party, which was throughout this period a 'shadow' of the historical party,[81] reflected the danger of extinction that threatened those political organizations unable to 'ventilate' their doctrines and to launch a great campaign of propaganda. To hold a federalist credo and to possess an anti-clerical passion was not to have a peculiar platform when most of the Republican groups were advancing federalist formulae and were anti-clerical. Some steps of reorganization, however, were taken early in 1929. In the old strongholds of Mallorca even some deserters of the Monarchist Liberal party were absorbed. In November 1929, the Madrid branch launched the

[80] For criticism from Radicals see Lerroux, *Memorias*, p. 557, and *EP* 5, 13 Nov. 1929. For acclamation by 'new republicans' see Gabriel Alomar in *El Sol* 26 Oct. 1929. *Heraldo de Chamartin* 20 Feb. 1930. For meetings see E. Ortega in *LV* 25 Feb., 22 Mar., 1930; *Alianza* Apr. 1930; *EP* 1 May 1930. M. Domingo in *LV* 20 Apr.; *EP* 13 Apr.; and *El Sol* 3 Aug. 1930. For a meeting of 900 propagandists in Bilbao see AHN Leg. 29: Governor of Bilbao to Gobernación, 1 Dec. 1930. For centres see reports in *El Sol* 7, 9 May, 16, 28 Aug., 3, 9 Sept. 1930. For manifestos and congress see *NE* 15 Apr., 1 July 1930; SA Leg. 2613: *PRRS Ideario Aprobado por Unanimidad en el Congreso Nacional Celebrado los dias 25–27 de Septiembre de 1930*; and *El Sol* 25–28 Sept. 1930.
[81] E. Aunós, *España*, p. 355.

initiative of summoning a national assembly of all the regional organizations of the party in order to elaborate a common attitude towards propaganda, party structures, and political alliances. But the assembly did not materialize, nor did the appeal 'to neglect those opinions which had hitherto proved fruitless' release the party from its stagnant existence. The national committee called in December 1929 for an end to the 'intransigence of the past' and for collaboration with other republican parties towards 'common goals'. But the autonomy of each branch and Hilario Ayuso's 'intransigence' against 'rightist republicanism' prevented a coherent effort of the whole party to exploit the political opportunities. In September 1930 a breach was evident when different branches like those of Jaén and Madrid were forging their own separate alliances with other parties, regardless of 'party decisions' and defying 'historical intransigence'.[82]

It was by a similar defiance of 'historical' frameworks that *Acción Republicana* attempted to win a place on the map of Spanish republicanism. Manuel Azaña, the founder of the group, moved in the first days of the Dictatorship from an 'accidentalist' approach towards the form of regime to categorical republicanism. From the pages of the review *España*, he made a mockery of the pathetic republicanism of Lerroux and Blasco Ibáñez, stressing his quest for more realistic formulae. Although his violent anti-clericalism recalled traditional *Lerrouxismo*, it was a rooted intellectual conviction rather than a superficial imitation. Foreseeing the political confusion that would develop after the Dictatorship, he called for the creation of 'new' republican parties to exploit it. In early 1925 he helped to found *Acción Política*, a 'nucleus of intellectuals' striving for a Republic. It consisted, among others, of Jiménez de Asua, José Giral, Pérez de Ayala, Luis Araquistáin, Martí Jara, and Honorato de Castro. In May of that same year the group developed into Acción Republicana, when Azaña wrote its foundation manifesto. In it the group was defined not as a political party, but as 'the embryo of a party, a centre of organization, an agent of liaison' that would absorb 'the new

---

[82] See information and articles in *EP* 18 Jan., 1, 28 May, 28 Dec. 1929, 4, 8, 10 Jan. 1930; *LV* 23 Feb., 16 Sept. 1930; *ABC* 28 Oct. 1930; *NE* 18 Oct. 1930; *Alianza* Apr. 1930 (Ayuso); For the breach see *El Sol* 16 Aug., 20 Sept. 1930; and *ABC* 14 Sept. 1930.

republican sentiment' which emerged from the harsh experiences of the Dictatorship.[83]

It was, however, only after the restrictions of the Dictatorship were removed at the beginning of 1930, that Acción Republicana appealed again to the public, in order to exploit an ambiance which was in itself a 'great propagandist of the Republic'. Provincial sections were set up in Granada, Palencia, Salamanca, Zaragoza, Huelva, Barcelona, Murcia, and Segovia. A central committee was elected under Azaña's leadership, in spite of claims that they did not have a *jefe* like 'old republicans'; and a campaign of propaganda was started. The group, however, still refused to be a 'party', leaving its members to hold 'their particular points of view within or outside the group, so long as they stay within a republican affirmation'.[84]

But, in the more precise terms put forward by Azaña and other propagandists, the 'republican affirmation' that Acción Republicana stood for was a radical conception. He warned the great wave of new republicans against 'a negative republicanism born out of the corruptions of another regime'. Republican consciousness should be carefully cultivated in order that a 'republican Republic' rather than a 'Monarchy without king' could be set up. In addition, the Catalan left should be encouraged by genuine support for Catalan autonomist aspirations, even if it decided 'to embark upon a separate destiny'. AR sent for that purpose its representative Antonio Vilanova to sponsor the creation of a group for 'Republican Solidarity in Catalonia'. Azaña preached a Republic 'as radical as the most radical among the republicans would like it to be'. And the groups' representative in Almería, Antonio Campoy, told a working-class crowd that for them this meant the curbing of rising prices and taxes, an improvement of wages, and an end to *latifundismo*. For a middle-class public, Azaña put forward the

[83] Azaña, *Obras*, i, 475–6, 498–9, 500–1. For his conversion to republicanism see J. Marichal, *La Vocación de Manuel Azaña*, p. 138. For 'Acción Política' see *El 11 de Febrero*, pp. 139–40; and Jiménez de Asua, *Anecdotas de las Constituyentes*, pp. 10–11. The manifesto in Azaña, op. cit. ii, 4–5.

[84] See the manifesto of January 1930 in *Libro de Oro*, pp. 153–4. For organization and sections see *EP* 9 Mar. 1930; *El Sol* 17, 20 Apr. 1930; *EI* 14 Mar. 1930; *El Luchador*, Alicante, 10 Apr. 1930.

more mild and general terms of 'federalism', 'anti-clericalism', 'anti-militarism', and a 'parliamentary bourgeois Republic'.[85]

The 'negative republicanism' which Azaña warned against was precisely the kind of republicanism represented by the *Derecha Republicana*. It was born 'out of the corruptions' of the Monarchy, when outstanding ex-monarchist figures rose up both to create a movement of protest, and to canalize the overwhelming republican wave into respecting the fundamental principles and the material interests of conservatives.

This conception was reflected in the political transformation of Alcalá Zamora. An ex-minister of the Monarchy and a great cacique in his fief of Priego (Córdoba), he became an enemy of the Dictatorship, which had persecuted him and deprived him of his political fief. But even when he urged the dictator in a private letter to abdicate, he expressed his 'deep appreciation of the monarchist sentiment', and his anxiety to save 'whatever is possible to save of the monarchist principle and the dynastic interest'. With the fall of the Dictatorship, he regained his private following and set out to enlarge it making use of the popular demand for a Constituent Cortes. But it was an unequivocal commitment either to the Monarchy or to the Republic that the expectant public asked of the leaders; and Alcalá Zamora had to move from constitutionalism to overt republicanism. On 11 April 1930 he promised never to set foot again in the palace 'so long as its owner was there'. A couple of days later he told a crowd of 4,000 people in Valencia that monarchist ex-ministers had a duty to serve the Republic, because an exclusively 'republican Republic' was condemned to death. Only conservative figures like Hindenburg and Thiers, he said, had made possible the Republics in their countries. He himself hoped that even more rightist elements than himself would join his conservative 'Republic of order'. In subsequent speeches all over the country he set upon enlisting the 'conservative classes' to join the Republic, and to form 'a barrier against sovietism', in order to save both themselves and the nation. It was, indeed, to the instinct of self-preservation of

[85] Azaña, *Obras*, ii, 7–11 (speech, 11 Feb. 1930); ibid. iii, 537–76 (speech, March 1930 in Barcelona); ibid. ii, 13–17 (speech, 28 Sept. 1930). Azaña also in *El Sol* 1 Apr. 1930; *EP* 14 Aug. 1930. Antonio Vilanova in ibid. 23 July 1930; Antonio Campoy in *NE* 14 Nov. 1930.

the well-to-do that Alcalá Zamora appealed, rather than to a mature republican consciousness. Alcalá Zamora was in fact calling upon his fellow conservatives to assume the leading role in Spain's political revolution, so as to be in a position to prevent it from 'degenerating' into a social catastrophe. Nevertheless, the impact of the conversion of a monarchist ex-minister to the Republic was tremendous. Left republicans welcomed it as a 'successful manœuvre' to attract the bougeoisie. It 'increased in geometrical progression enthusiasm for the Republic'. For alarmed monarchists who rejected Alcalá Zamora as a traitor, his campaign was a gigantic effort to sink the Monarchy. *ABC* expressed this almost hysterically: 'He has already travelled many kilometres over the country, sowing salt and curses in order to uproot monarchism. Wherever his devastating oratory passes, the monarchist plant withers.'[86]

The conversion of Miguel Maura to republicanism was the result of a somewhat different personal evolution. As a young *Maurista*, he had already belonged to a movement of protest against both caciquismo and the old political system. When in 1928 he toured the country it was in order to examine 'what was left of monarchist feelings'. He noticed that many Mauristas were becoming hostile to the Monarchy. In June 1928 he already spoke of the Republic as 'the perfect regime', though he still advocated a transitional 'bridge' of constitutional Monarchy. But in the 'constitutionalist' conspiracy of January 1930 he was acting as a republican; and a month later, he clearly 'defined' himself as a rightist republican. In subsequent speeches in Zamora, Pamplona, Salamanca, and Madrid, he reiterated his belief in a conservative Republic that would respect religion, property, as well as the 'administrative' (not political) individuality of the regions within 'Spanish unity'. He hoped that the

---

[86] *ABC* 1 June 1930. For his persecution by the Dictatorship see S. De Madariaga, *España, Ensayo de Historia Contemporánea*, p. 383. His letter to the dictator is in *HL* Feb. 1928. For his political following see *LV* 1 Feb. 1930; and J. Tomas Valverde, *Memorias de un Alcalde*, pp. 79–86. For early constitutionalism see *ABC* 10 Jan., *LV* 7 Feb. 1930. Declaration of 11 April in *EP* 11 Apr. 1930; the speech of Valencia is in *El Sol* 15 Apr. 1930. For subsequent speeches see ibid. 30 Apr. 1930 (San Sebastián); *ABC* 2, 21, 31 May 1930 (Zamora, Malaga, Madrid). Reaction of left republicans in *NE* 1 Sept., 18 Oct. 1930. The monarchist reaction in *LV* 20 Apr. 1930; *ABC* 2 May 1930; *NE* 1 Sept. 1930; *El* 4 May 1930. General impact in Miguel Maura, *Así*, p. 57; and F. Villanueva, *No Pasa Nada!*, pp. 29–35.

Monarchy would give way peacefully to avoid a 'violent revolution'. The adherence of a son of Antonio Maura, a symbol of conservative and monarchist Spain, to the campaign against a perjured king and an 'undiscussed institution' (the Monarchy), made him anathema among the right, a traitor to his name and his class. Even a republican audience questioned the republicanism of a Maura whose father was responsible for the 'crimes' of 1909.[87]

Maura's and Alcalá Zamora's ideas were incorporated in the Derecha Republicana, when it was founded officially on 14 July 1930. It sought to be the 'centre' of a broadly conservative Republic based upon 'law and authority', with a president as the new *poder moderador*, and a bicameral system that would 'reflect faithfully the Spanish social structure'. Religion was to be defended from the excesses of both republican anti-clericalism and traditional clericalism, and regionalism was to be prevented from disintegrating the nation. However, the new party showed a certain capacity to adapt itself to regional and local conditions. Maura had been earlier encouraging the embryonic Catalan branch under Solá Cañizares to have a 'frankly Catalanist orientation' which later developed into a mild middle way between the Lliga's and the left's extremism; and in Alicante, the party's section, in contrast with official declarations against 'state interventionism', campaigned against the importation of French wines, which hit local agricultural interests.[88]

Against the background of republican effervescence that overtook the country in 1929–30, and stimulated by a sense of 'citizenship' and by the desire 'to multiply their individual efficiency', many republican autonomous groups also emerged

[87] For Maurismo see J. Gutierrez-Ravé, *Yo Fuí un Joven Maurista*, pp. 187–206. For Maura's 'tour' in 1928 see his *Así*, pp. 19–25. His declaration in June is in *El Presidencialista* June 1928. For the conspiracy see Burgos y Mazo, *Los Constitucionalistas*, iii, 10–11. His speeches are in *ABC* 21 Feb., 8, 29 Apr. 1930; *LV* 29 July 1930; *El Sol* 17 Oct. 1930; See also his leaflet *Contestando a Don Gabriel Maura. 1930* in HMM A/1709. For the reaction of right and left see Honorio Maura, *Tras el Sentido Común*, pp. 9–10; *ABC* 5 July 1930.

[88] See the manifesto of foundation *Carta Circular de la Derecha Republicana*, 14 July 1930 in RA Leg. 2 no. 25. The views on the religious issues are best summed up by J. Torrubiano Ripoll, *Rebeldías*, pp. 5–21 who later joined the party. For Catalonia see *El Sol* 7 May 1930; and F. De Solá Cañizares, *El Moviment Revolucionari a Catalunya*, pp. 138–41. For Alicante see *El Luchador* 16 Oct. 1930.

in the provinces after years of lethargy.[89] These regional and local sections did not always define themselves as belonging to any of the national parties, though most of them were absorbed by Alianza Republicana. However, their essentially local character brought them often to identify the Republic with precise answers to particular regional issues. Such was the case of the *Partido Republicano Autónomo de Córdoba*. In May 1930 it held its first regional congress after many years with representatives of elected juntas from all over the area. After paying lip-service to the theoretical principles of republicanism, it concentrated the debates on agrarian demands: stability of tenancies, co-operatives, abolition of *latifundios*, the curbing of unemployment and rural education.[90] The republicans of Palencia and Burgos, both wheat-growing areas, emphasized in their first public manifesto, in June 1930, that though they would like cheap bread for the workers, they opposed massive importation of wheat as likely to ruin Castilian farmers, and in Almansa, 'Bread, Land and Freedom' was chosen as the most suitable slogan by local Republicans. The *Agrupación Republicana de la Provincia de Zamora*, however, chose to express itself, in its first manifesto in the general terms of the 'civic awakening of the nation'.[91]

A particularly strong party was the *Unión Republicana Autonomista de Valencia* with its organ, *El Pueblo* and with historical branches in towns like Alcira, Jatiba, and Gandia. During the Dictatorship it attracted Valencianist elements, who were alienated by Primo's anti-regionalist policy. Being essentially a bourgeois party, it came to an agreement by the end of 1929 with Lerrouxismo, in order to create a bourgeois leftist bloc as a fitting culmination of the historical affinity of its late leader, Blasco Ibáñez, with Lerroux. At the beginning of 1930 the party dominated the city council of Valencia; and Julio Just, one of its leaders, appealed for an accentuation of the Valencianist nature of the party, emphasizing its interest in the export of oranges, and relations with the increasing working-class population in the area. In contrast to the much smaller

---

[89] SA Leg. 39: Lerroux to Pareja Yevenes, n.d.
[90] *Alianza* May 1930.
[91] *El Norte de Castilla* 12 June 1930; *Alianza* June–July 1930; *NE* 11 Dec, 1930 (Almansa); *Alianza* Apr. 1930 (Zamora).

and more radical *Agrupació Valencianista Republicana*, the Unión Republicana seemed to be deeply rooted in the region. Nine hundred and fifty delegates of 112 branches made its regional congress a manifestation of power under Sigfrido Blasco's leadership.[92] After the fall of the Dictatorship, an upsurge of republicanism took place also in Galicia. Its main feature was autonomist and *Gallegista*. In March 1930 various local groups were merged in a regional organization, the *Organización Republicana Gallega Autónoma* (ORGA), under the leadership of Santiago Casares Quiroga and the nationalist Antonio Villar Ponte. Its main concern were issues peculiar to Galicia: the abolition of the *Foro* (a *minifundista* land tenure), the struggle against caciquismo, and the cultural and administrative autonomy of the area. Its new-found strength enabled the party to organize protests against the ex-collaborators of the the dictator as well as against the caciques of the Monarchist ex-minister, Bugallal.[93]

Catalan republicanism profited both from the general anti-monarchist reaction in the country, and from an upsurge in separatist feelings as a response to the anti-Catalanist measures of the dictator. The teaching of Catalan and its literature was intensified. Separatist slogans, clandestine nationalist celebrations, and agitation among the youth induced an observer to claim in 1927 that 90 per cent of the Catalans were becoming separatists. Separatism, as Romanones noted, was a manifestation of anti-monarchism.[94] With the fall of the Dictatorship, this process was accentuated. The Monarchist and 'españolista' *Lliga* was losing ground; the captain general of Barcelona, Despujols, became alarmed by the leftist trend. A visit of

[92] See articles and information in *EP* 8 Jan., 13 Apr., 28 May, 6 Sept. 1930. For the city council see *ABC* 19, 27 Feb. 1930; Julio Just in *NE* 1 Mar. 1930. The congress in *Alianza* June–July 1930. See also the study by Alfons Cucó, *El Valencianisme Polític 1874–1936*, pp. 183–96. See the Valencianism of Ricardo Samper in *La Voz Valenciana* 17 Feb. 1930.

[93] For the labour of reorganization see *LV* 8 Feb. 1930; *Alianza* Apr., June–July 1930. For confrontation with Bugallalistas see *NE* 28 Nov. 1930; and Domingo Quiroga Ríos, *Quien Es. . .?*, pp. 31–2. For a survey see also ibid. 28–30; and Vicente Risco, *El Problema Político de Galicia*, pp. 189–90, 229–30.

[94] For the various aspects of the upsurge of Catalanism see M. García Venero, *Historia del Nacionalismo Catalan*, ii, 329–31; Aymani i Baudina, *Maciá, Trenta Anys de Política Catalanista*, pp. 116–19; *The Times* 12 Sept., 10 Nov. 1924, 22 June 1925. For the observer see F.O. 371/12717: Rumbold to Austen Chamberlain, 17 Feb. 1927; and ibid. 11936 7 Apr. 1926 (quoting Romanones). See also *HL* Sept. 1927.

Castillian intellectuals to an excited Barcelona, in March 1930, originally planned as a mutual cultural homage, became an act of solidarity with leftist Catalonia, or, as Rafael Campalans put it, 'the San Sebastián pact of the intellectuals'.[95] The growing anti-monarchist feelings in Barcelona even caused the local British consul to suggest that the crowd that applauded the king on his visit to the city in May must have been paid to do so.[96]

The Catalan party which most contributed to the republicanization of the region, and which finally profited most from it was *Estat Català*. Founded in 1922 by Francesc Maciá as a reaction against the mild Catalan statute elaborated by the Lliga, and in order to propagate the principle of self-determination, it went underground with the rise of the Dictatorship. Its activists started to spread clandestine nationalistic propaganda, and were able to attract to their ranks many young people and workers. These were impressed by Estat Catala's emphasis on social issues, a feature attractive to an industrial province like Barcelona, and by its Marxist interpretation of Catalonia's history. No more stories about kings and their distinguished vassals, but the class struggle between exploited and exploiters. Many, it seems, were 'marching to Russia through Catalonia'.[97]

Estat Catala's popularity in Catalonia was enhanced by the revolutionary activities of Maciá. From his exile in France he ran a nationalistic campaign on behalf of a leftist Catalan Republic, attractive to lower-middle-class republicans, to romantic Catalanists, and to the working class. After abortive attempts to form a revolutionary front with other sections of Catalan nationalism represented by Rovira i Virgili and Nicolau d'Olwer, he started to work on his own with the support of Anarcho-Syndicalists.[98]

---

[95] For the San Sebastián pact see below, pp. 80–84.

[96] For the republican trends see A. Hurtado, *Quaranta Anys d'Advocat*, iii, 30; Despujols in Mola, *Obras*, p. 259. For the intellectuals see *El Sol* 22 Mar. 1930. *ABC* 27 Mar. 1930 lamented the leftist character of the meeting; and R. Campalans, *Hacia la España de Todos*, p. 48. The consul in F.O. 371/15041: Peterson to Arthur Henderson, 23 May 1930.

[97] For the origins of the party see Alfons Maseras, *La Nostra Gent. Francesc Maciá*, pp. 31–4. For activities and development during the Dictatorship see J. Aiguader, *Cataluña y la Revolución*, pp. 44–52.

[98] For the propaganda see *L'Éveil Catalan*, Perpignan, 15 Sept. 1924, and the manifesto of Candido Rey, *Hermanos! Trabajadors Españoles de Francia!* in AHN Leg. 42:

Though all of Maciá's conspiracies ended in Quixotic failures, he managed to become a popular martyr and the champion of socially and politically leftist Catalanism. His close contacts with the Anarcho-Syndicalists and left republicans like Rodrigo Soriano put the Spanish authorities on constant alert. His tours of propaganda among Catalan communities all over the world, his public trial in Paris after the failure of the 'invasion' that he led near Prats de Molló in November 1926, and the public nationalistic gatherings over which he presided (one of which elaborated a constitution for the 'Catalan State') gave worldwide publicity to the Catalan cause. This was from now on more identified with the figure of Maciá than with that of Cambó, the *Lliga* leader.[99]

With the fall of the Dictatorship, Estat Catalá accentuated its *obrerismo*, and directed its campaigns against both the Monarchy and the tendency of the Lliga to reassume the monopoly of Catalan politics. A statute of autonomy elaborated by a non-elected and predominantly 'Lliguista' *Diputación Provincial*, was rejected for a statute that would recognize Catalonia's right to enact advanced social reforms, the champion of which Maciá consistently endeavoured to be. Furthermore, Catalan freedom was incompatible with the Monarchy that had trampled underfoot its particular character for years, and with the social regime that enabled the 'big business circles' supporting the Lliga to exploit the Catalan working class and to drive out of business smaller entrepreneurs, whose interests Estat Catalá tried to uphold. Estat Catalá joined the campaign on behalf of amnesty for social and political prisoners, as a means of mobilizing leftist opinion against both the Monarchy and the Lliga. When at the end of September 1930, Maciá was expelled

---

Direccion General de Seguridad 7 Oct. 1924, no. 72174. For the front see Xuriguera, *Els Exiliats*, pp. 162–7.

[99] For the conspiracies and the trial see Maseras, *Francesc Maciá*, pp. 35–49; F. Madrid, *Els Exiliats de la Dictadura*, pp. 160–204. For relations with Anarcho-Syndicalists see AHN Leg. 42: a report from the Spanish consul in Toulouse, 7 Nov. 1924, no. 1857, and from the Spanish ambassador in Paris, 27 Oct. 1924, no. 1742. For relations with Soriano and other left republicans see SAA: Rodrigo Soriano to Alba, 7 Feb. 1925. For his propaganda and fund raising among Catalan communities see Aymani i Baudina, *Maciá*, pp. 143–51; and *Constitució Provisional de la Republica Catalana, Aprovada per l'Assamblea Constituent del Separatism Catalá, Reunida a L'Havana 30 Sept.–2 Oct. 1928*, Havana, 1928.

for his illegal entry into Spain, which the Anarcho-Syndicalist *Solidaridad Obrera* called a 'manly gesture', his men blamed the Lliga even for that. But the wave of sympathy for the old man that excited Catalan opinion, mainly the extreme left, was an indication that the propaganda aims were achieved. When, in February 1931 he finally returned home, he was acclaimed by a nationalist euphoria, which he further encouraged when he declared: 'I return more separatist, if possible, than when I left.'[1]

The apotheosis of Maciá by the Catalan left enabled him, three weeks after his return to Spain, to preside over a large 'conference of the left', in which the *Esquerra Catalana* was founded. The existence of numerous petty-bourgeois Republican autonomous groups and workers' centres like the *Ateneo Republicá de Barcelona, Casa del Pueblo de Blanes, Izquierda Universitaria, Partit Republicá Catalá* under Companys, *Izquierda Catalana* under Lluhi Vallesca, *Unió Socialista de Catalunya* under Gabriel Alomar, and dozens of other centres scattered all over the region,[2] brought Luis Companys and Lluhí Vallescá, by the end of November 1930, to suggest their unification, in view of the fact that they did not differ in their basic principles. One week before Maciá's return they published a manifesto calling for the 'setting up of an organization of pure Catalanism within a common discipline', an appeal which Maciá later reiterated when he called for an end of the 'monopoly of the conservatives over Catalan aspirations'. On 14 March, the representatives of 120 local and provincial centres from all over the region met to decide on the agenda of the *conferencia d'esquerres*, which was finally inaugurated on 18 March. The conference agreed on the foundation of a large party, the *Esquerra Catalana*, whose basic programme consisted of anti-clericalist and anti-militarist affirmations, a social platform that, though stressing the necessity to introduce insurance against unemployment, a problem which was becoming acute in Catalonia, was considered too mild and bourgeois-

---

[1] For the statute and 'obrerismo' see *EP* 20 June 1930, and Maciá's public manifesto in *ABC* 20 July 1930. For amnesty see *La Rambla de Catalunya* 24 Feb. 1930 and subsequent numbers. For the expulsion and sympathy see *LV* 26, 27, 30 Sept. 1930; *SO* 1 Oct. 1930; *La Batalla* 3 Oct. 1930; and Aiguader, *Cataluña*, pp. 103–9. For his return see Aymani, *Maciá*, pp. 156–60; and *The Times* 24 Feb. 1931.

[2] Accounts of the foundation of increasingly numerous centres and their activities can be found in abundance in the Barcelona newspapers *La Vanguardia* and *El Progreso* throughout the years 1929–31.

oriented by the extreme left. The decisions on the Catalan issue were very much in accordance with the line of Estat Català: 'too much Catalanism for a party that must share the destiny of other leftist parties from Spain', according to *Solidaridad Obrera*.[3]

Though less committed to the social demagogy of the Esquerra, *Acció Catalana* represented the same 'excess' of Catalanism. It was founded in 1922 as a splinter group from the Lliga, in protest against the latter's acceptance of the 'fiction of the Spanish state'. They substituted for the Lliga conception of 'Catalunya enfora' (active interventionism in Spanish politics) that of 'Catalunya endins' (exclusive Catalanism), and rejected the term 'Regionalists' for that of 'Nationalists'.[4]

During the Dictatorship, Acció Catalana did not go underground because it did not engage in any serious political activity. But, though its leaders Rovira i Virgili and Nicolau d'Olwer went into exile, other representatives of the party took up a position of open rebellion against the regime. They criticized the anti-Catalanist measures of the dictator whether in the *mancomunidad* or in the Bar Association of Barcelona, where Durand i Balada and Carrasco Formiguera, both party members, became the leaders of the nationalist faction. Party members were also active in protesting to the League of Nations on behalf of the 'rights of oppressed minorites', as well as in cultural activities. Furthermore, motivated by the harsh experiences of the Dictatorship, Acció Catalana moved to a republican position, and in August 1929 Nicolau d'Olwer gave a first public confession of republicanism.[5]

The fall of the Dictatorship enabled Acció Catalana both to accentuate its new republican significance and to look for a

[3] For Macià's apotheosis and his triumphal march throughout the region see *SO* 11 Mar. 1931. For preliminary contacts and response see *LV* 29 Nov. 1930, 18 Feb., 12, 13, 15, 17 Mar. 1931; and Macià's appeal in *LV* 14 Mar. 1931. For the conference see *LV* and *SO* 19, 20 Mar. 1931. For the Esquerra and unemployment see Balcells, *Crisis Económica*, p. 18.

[4] Jaume Bofill i Mates, *Una Política Catalanista*, pp. 7–14, 40–2; García Venero, *Vida de Cambó*, pp. 317–21.

[5] For the party's reaction to the Dictatorship see A. Perucho, *Catalunya Sota la Dictadura*, pp. 56–9; in the Mancomunidad: Santiago Alba, *Para la Historia*, p. 24. International and cultural activities in Bofill i Mates, op. cit. 17–18. For the Bar Association see Hurtado, *Quaranta Anys*, ii, 170–71, 179–80. For republican declaration see N. d'Olwer in *EP* 18 Aug. 1929.

place of its own in Catalan politics between the Lliga and Estat
Catalá. In a public and 'subversive' manifesto at the beginning
of March, it stated that only those Catalanists who were
'liberals, democrats and republicans' could join the party. The
federal Republic was put forward as the most suitable regime
for Catalonia, because 'popular sovereignty is incompatible
with hereditary institutions and irresponsibility'. In an extraordinary congress of the party in June, while it rejected the
Lliga's undemocratic attempt to elaborate a statute, neither did
it endorse Estat Catalá's appeal for democratic self-determination. However, in a public speech Carrasco Formiguera used
what the authorities called an 'extremely separatist' language.
This was so because of the need to compete with both the
Catalan left and right, the split from which had constantly to
be justified. The Lliga was aware of the fact that Acció
Catalana's moderate social conceptions and its aggressive
Catalanism were likely to deprive the Lliga of its traditional
middle-class following; and there is evidence of efforts being
made by the Lliga to put some of its men on electoral lists
outside Catalonia, to guard against a future defeat at the polls
in the region. It seemed, however, that the Lliga's fears were
exaggerated, and that Acció Catalana's attempt to answer the
challenge of Estat Catalá by making use of an extreme
nationalist language, and by presenting itself as the champion
of worker's aspirations, threatened to alienate from the party
the basically Catholic and conservative elements without
attracting the extreme left, whose natural home was Estat
Catalá.[6]

The foundation of *Acció Republicana*, at the beginning of
January 1930 only complicated the labyrinth of Catalan politics.
The new party stood for a greater emphasis on cultural
Catalanism rather than any new and vigorous political effort.
It was initated by Rovira i Virgili after he split from Acció
Catalana in 1929 to found the *Fundació Valentí Almirall*. This
organization was strictly cultural and nationalist. But its

---

[6] *LV* 5 Mar. (the manifesto), 25 May (the authorities) 1930; *EP* 20 June 1930
(d'Olwer on the Federal Republic); Carrasco in *ABC* 31 Aug. 1930. For the congress
see *LV* 27 June 1930. For elections see *NE* 1 June 1930. For A.C.'s dilemma between
extreme left and right see articles in *EI* 7 Nov; and *ED* 11 Dec. 1930. For ideological
orientation of the party in 1930 see Bofill i Mates, *Una Política*, pp. 32–5, 45–6, 57.

emphasis on the need to become a 'popular organization that will unite in brotherhood the liberal and leftist forces of Catalonia' and on a 'catalunya endins' orientation, both clear political affirmations, resulted in its developing into a party, Acció Republicana.[7] Its 'liberal, democratic and republican' credo, and its adherence to the principles of a federal Republic and to the 'Catalanization of Catalan politics' in public manifestos and propaganda meetings during the Berenguer period, showed that it did not have any specific contribution to make that was not already made by Acció Catalana.[8]

The realization by both parties of their common ground and of the futility of a separate existence brought them by the end of February 1931 to unite their forces in a common party, the *Acció Catalana Republicana-Partit Catalanista Republicá*. After preliminary contacts had pointed out 'the complete coincidence' in their views, and after having overcome a minor dissidence in the right wing of Acció Catalana opposing the union, a common programme was elaborated. This endorsed the demands for autonomy, individual, civic, and religious freedom, and the determination to keep 'Spanish parties' (a clear allusion to the Radicals) out of Catalan politics. The programme, however, also manifested that the ACR was ready to collaborate with such parties for the establishment of the Republic in the 'Spanish state'. Nevertheless, its first public meeting on 22 March as well as other statements by its protagonists, made clear that the new party stood for Catalanism above anything else. Its republican affirmations were the consequence of a pragmatic conviction that not only were their nationalist aspirations compatible with the Republic, but also that, in the present political circumstances, republicanism represented a practical way of fulfilling them. As far as its place in Catalan politics was concerned, the ACR was conceived as 'a genuine attempt to unite, in a centre position, the great mass of Catalans who are displeased by the Lliga's "españolismo" and by its defence of the regime, as well as by Estat Catalá's drive towards communism'.[9]

[7] *EP* 25 Sept. 1929, 3 Jan. 1930.

[8] *EP* 30 Jan. (Rovira), 16 Mar. 1930; and *ABC* 16 Mar. 1930 (manifesto); *LV* 18, 19 Sept., 19 Oct. 1930 (declarations and meetings). Aiguader, *Cataluña*, p. 137.

[9] For preliminary contacts, foundation, and programme see *LV* 31 Jan., 1, 12, 14

Nor was the republican wave all over Spain always a positive movement, as we have seen. The fact is, however, that whether for regionalist considerations, anti-monarchist feelings, or deeply rooted republicanism, an overwhelming demand for a Republic was being put forward and was gradually gaining momentum during both the *Dictadura* and the *Dictablanda*.

Mar. 1931. For the dissidence in AC see *El Correo Catalan* 26 Feb. 1931. For the meeting see *LV* 24 Mar. 1931. See also how Bofill i Mates, one of the leaders, evaluated the doctrines of the party in his *Una Política*, pp. 27–31, 46, 55–6, 68–72. The last quotation is from Ferran Soldevila's article in *Revista de Catalunya* Mar. 1931.

II

REPUBLICANS: THE QUEST FOR UNITY AND THE CONFRONTATION WITH THE REGIME

During the years 1926–31, the scattered centres of the Republican parties had consistently manifested an urgent desire for unity that would enable them to launch an anti-monarchist offensive, more effective than that represented by their diffuse existence. Their capacity to do so by overcoming fundamental differences between themselves reflected a sincere devotion to the republican cause as well as a certain quality of statesmanship in their leaders. It was after all the coalition which was established as a result of these contacts and the political platform that it elaborated which became the 'soft mattress', to use Miguel Maura's expression, on which the Republic was finally born. However, both a lack of confidence in its competence to establish a Republic by legal means, and its constant aim of harassing the Monarchy, brought the Republican coalition after August 1930 to make use of the weapon of civilian and military conspiracies. These failed to 'bring about the Republic', but there is little doubt that they helped to exhaust the Monarchy and its defenders.

I. ALIANZA REPUBLICANA

The first substantial step towards unity was made in February 1926 with the foundation of Alianza Republicana. It was initiated by republican intellectuals from the *Escuela Nueva*, a leftist club whose propaganda and educational activities constantly enraged the authorities. After 1925 Giral, Martí Jara, and Graco Marsá exerted their influence on Republicans, Socialists, Reformists, and even anti-Primo Monarchists with the aim of converting them to unity. A positive response, however, came only from Lerroux's Radicals, Hilario Ayuso's Federals and Marcelino Domingo's Catalan Republicans. To celebrate their agreement they organized on 11 February an anniversary of the first Republic, considering all adherents to the commemoration automatically as affiliates of the new Republican alignment, the Alianza Republicana.[1] The response of Republican organizations all over the country was overwhelming. The 450 centres and organizations, claiming a total membership of 99,043, which adhered to the initiative, made Alianza Republicana a manifestation of naïve faith as well as a promising factor for the future. In Catalonia, Luis Companys stimulated the *Unió de Rabassaires* (a tenants' association) with its 14,000 members, seven syndicates and three newspapers (*La Terra, L'Avenir, La Lluita*) to join Alianza. The Republicans of Igualada, with the aim of 'giving an example to the Spanish left', started to organize local joint committees for separate clubs, and the veteran Republican ex-Deputy Marceliano Isabal presided in Zaragoza over the union of provincial forces. From Valencia the ex-Deputy Fernando Gasset reported the enthusiasm of the 19,657 registered members in the region. 'We want to shorten the distances between us and to strengthen the ties until a league of the left, as wide as possible, is made. The masses will be satisfied if those who think as *correligionarios*, treat each other as brothers.' The Republicans of Alhama de Almería followed suit with a similar desire, a desire which those of Córdoba considered as 'the only guarantee for a Republic'. The Republicans of Moclinejo (Malaga) claimed that the idea of unity created such an excitement among them, that they felt as if they had won the 'biggest prize in the national lottery on Christmas day'. Though not republican, the *Izquierda Liberal* of Seville was also stimulated by this enthusiasm to support the initiative, pointing out that its minimum programme was 'the restoration of legal normality as a step towards full and free expression of the national sovereignty'. It was clear, therefore, that Alianza had opened wide options of union, as the Marquis of Carvajal wrote to Lerroux. 'From now on', he added, 'no one has the right to be silent. The responsibilities for activity or inactivity will soon become obvious. Nothing and no one could justify our abstention.' Not without reason was the

---

[1] For 'Escuela Nueva' see *Alianza* Apr. 1930. For the preliminary contacts see *Libro de Oro*, p. 152; and *El 11 de Febrero*, pp. 5–6.

Governor of Barcelona alarmed by this sudden movement of the 'republican confraternity'.[2]

The principles upon which Alianza was set up reflected both an attempt to elaborate a common denominator between Republicans, and an endeavour to forge an ad-hoc 'possibilist' alliance with non-republican liberals for bringing the country back to 'constitutional normality'. Azaña's *Acción Política* brought into the programme the federalist conception of the 'Iberian United States', as likely to appease regionalist Republicans, as well as committed Federals, and those still attached to the legacy of the first Republic. The spirit of 'new' republicanism was incorporated into the platform by a disassociation from archaic slogans on behalf of a concrete programme of education, development and social reforms, a programme to be worked out by a special commission. The fact that a directive *Junta* rather than a single *Jefe* was elected, and the recognition of the complete autonomy of each group that joined Alianza, which thus became a federation of parties rather than a unitary body, were pointed out as a novel experiment in getting rid of old *Caudillismo*. A romantic aspect was introduced by Marcelino Domingo when he wrote in to the foundation manifesto that the components of Alianza had sworn not to separate until the foundation of the Republic (an allusion to the 'Jeux de Paume oath'). Meanwhile, however, a milder programme was suggested to other 'democratic forces' who had in common with the Republicans disagreement with the present regime. In this programme Alianza did not commit itself by making any extreme affirmations on state and Church relations or Morocco. This was so because, as it confessed, 'we are well aware of the limits imposed on us by reality.' This 'realism', indeed, made Alianza an acceptable partner for monarchist-led conspiracies,[3] but it did not placate observers from the left who, like Luis Araquistáin, remarked how Alianza was even prepared to act like 'H.M.'s opposition'.[4]

---

[2] For the reports from the provinces see letters and information scattered in *El 11 de Febrero*. For Igualada see *EP* 27 Feb. 1926; For the Izquierda Liberal see *El Liberal, Sevilla* 12 Feb. 1926; and Demófilo de Buen's (one of the leaders) evolution to republicanism during the Dictatorship in *LV* 26 Feb. 1930. For the Governor of Barcelona, see his report in AHN Leg. 45; 18 Aug. 1926 no. 437.

[3] See above, pp. 45–47.

[4] See Alianza's manifesto in HMM A/1690; and programmatic affirmations in *El 11*

Despite the political restrictions imposed by the regime, Alianza developed a certain degree of activity, which, though far from spectacular, kept the organization alive. The Junta, consisting among others of Lerroux, Azaña, and Marcelino Domingo, co-ordinated local and provincial committees all over the country. Its members travelled to settle disputes between local leaders, to get into personal contact with the Barcelona Revolutionary Committee, and the Republican strongholds in Valencia, or to cultivate their relations with republican army officers and sympathetic trade unions, like that of the telegraphists. The Junta met once a week in Lerroux's house to discuss current events, rather than to plan a republican movement. When Primo de Rivera announced the convocation of the National Assembly, it was Alianza which exerted pressure upon Monarchist leaders to elaborate a common protest.[5]

However, political restrictions and personal differences gave Alianza the image of a paralysed and divided organization. Members and centres complained that no contact had been maintained with them concerning matters of doctrine and organization. Moreover, not even another enthusiastic commemoration of the anniversary of the first Republic in 1928 could conceal the growing breach between the 'old' and 'new' republicanism within Alianza. A young member of the Federal party called indignantly for the burial, once and for all, together with the old dynastic parties, of the remnants of the corpse that constituted the old Spanish republicanism. Marcelino Domingo, Alvaro de Albornoz, and Azaña accentuated their hostility to Lerroux on the same grounds. Azaña was especially irritated by some patriotic and imperialist expressions of Lerroux. The 'new' Republicans were able to attract into the ranks of Alianza many who strove to introduce a change in the

---

de Febrero pp. 138–41, a circular to the branches pp. 201–4. For the greater openness of republicanism see *Republica* 11 Feb. 1926; and Blasco Ibáñez's 'Los Hombres que Gobernarán Nuestra Republica' in *El 11 de Febrero*, pp. 178–87. For Araquistáin see his critical articles in *El Sol* 3, 4, 15, 26 Apr. 1926.

[5] For activities see 'Memoria de la Secretaría de la Junta Nacional Interina que Alianza Republicana presenta a la Asamblea Nacional', Madrid, 29 Sept. 1930 in *Libro de Oro*, pp. 171–5. See also ibid. 160; Azaña, *Obras* iii, 881, 885–7; and Lerroux, *La Pequeña Historia*, pp. 51–2. For the Assembly see RA Leg. 54 no. 21: Junta Provisional de Alianza Republicana to Romanones, n.d.

stagnant conceptions of the past. However, the incapacity of Alianza to move from the petty conspiratorial contacts with 'discredited' politicians into an open mobilization of opinion, brought the 'new' elements to attempt a major breakthrough.[6] July 1929, the month that witnessed the awakening of Spanish republicanism, also saw the breach in Alianza brought into the open. Motivated by the same hostility to 'old politics' in Alianza, Marañón, Pérez de Ayala, and Jiménez de Asua declared their separation from it.[7] Marcelino Domingo, who said in the junta meeting of 25 June 1929 that Alianza must be maintained 'by all means', changed his mind a couple of weeks later when he realized that the idea that he had put forward in the press—of setting up 'a new party'—was enthusiastically welcomed by many. And when it was announced that a national assembly of Alianza would discuss whether Alianza should continue to exist, his followers approached various provincial branches to vote against the continuation of Alianza, and thus to pave the way for the creation of a 'large party to which workers could belong'. Neither Marcelino Domingo nor Alvaro de Albornoz took part in the assembly on 14 July, at which representatives of thirty-five provinces were present. Salmerón, their colleague, was there only in order to press for the liquidation of Alianza which, according to the dissidents, had no *raison d'être* after having failed to bring about the Republic. The Radical representatives, however, managed to persuade most of the delegations not to split; and in the final vote only Soria supported the dissidents, while Alicante, Guipúzcoa, Logroño, and Valencia abstained. However, the conspicuous absence of the Federals Ayuso and Pi y Arsuaga indicated that they, too, might soon follow the Radical-Socialists.[8]

The change of attitude of Marcelino Domingo between June

[6] For paralysis see *El Republicano* 20 Aug., 5 Sept. 1928. For the anniversary see *El Sol* 12 Feb. 1928. For tensions between 'old' and 'new' see the declaration in *El Presidencialista* May 1928; *ES* 16 June 1928; Azaña, *Obras* iii, 894; *El Republicano* 5 Sept. 1928; and SA Leg. 1161; Martin Salvador to Lerroux, 14 Nov. 1928 on the reflection of this tension even in Spanish Republican centres abroad.

[7] Jiménez de Asua, *Anecdotas*, p. 11.

[8] For Domingo's change of attitude between June and July see *EP* 19 July, 4 Sept. 1930; and *ES* 2 Oct. 1929. For the Assembly see *EP* 5 Sept. 1929, 36, 31 July 1929; *ES* 2 Aug. (an official note of Alianza) and 6 Aug. 1929 (an account by the Alicante representative).

and July indicates that he and the Radical-Socialist Party which he subsequently founded, were not opposed in principle to the unity of Republicans. His main concern was to profit from the republican ambiance in the streets by building a new party, and then to return to Alianza with a more powerful following. To stay in a common junta with Lerroux, who in his recently published pamphlet 'collaboration and Revolution' had said, among other things, that a country might sometimes need to be ruled by a Dictatorship, would have meant jeopardizing the prospects of building such a 'new' party. Marcelino Domingo was increasingly aware of the variety of republicanism from the extreme left to the extreme right, and he suggested that all these should be united only after each had been canalized into different parties in free contact with a mobilized public opinion. A premature unity, in his conception, would only suppress this spectacular upsurge of republican sentiment, rather than encourage it. Furthermore, the 'bureaucratic' character of Alianza under the predominance of the 'conservative' Lerroux was incompatible with the revolutionary temperament of the Radical-Socialists. According to Salmerón, it lacked the 'moral capacity' to enlist army support. Alvaro de Albornoz perceived it as 'an amalgam without ideals and without nerves for action', while Domingo attacked it as a 'clumsy' organization at a time in which 'guerrilla' tactics were needed.[9]

However, the coincidence of the split with the relaxation of political restrictions enabled Alianza to overcome the crisis. Its activities increased rather than diminished. A register of members was started, the autonomous parties of Valencia, Córdoba, Castellón, and Zaragoza reiterated their support, and that of Alicante dismissed its delegate to the national assembly for abstaining from supporting the majority. Demonstrations of loyalty continued to pour in from all over the country, and on

[9] For Domingo's motives for leaving Alianza see *EP* 28 July 1929; Lerroux's article is in HMM A/1685. Both he (*EP* 26 July 1929) and Domingo (*ES* 17 Jan. 1930) recognized that this article was one of the reasons for the split. See also articles and declarations by Domingo in *ES* 2 June, 6 Aug., 4, 29 Sept. 1929. For Salmerón see *Libro de Oro*, p. 149. For Albornoz see *ES* 10, 14 Aug. 1929. See an endorsement of the dissident's views in *El Diluvio* 1 Aug. 1929.

14 August Alianza's secretary, Marsá Bragado, could claim a membership of 150,000. A new constitution was elaborated encouraging the setting up of regional, provincial, and local committees of Alianza; and the links between the branches were strengthened. Furthermore, attempts were made to cope with the demands for 'modern' ideas. Antonio Montaner called in a meeting of Alianza for the end of the emotional attachment to 'the programme of 1884', and for a widening of the social and ideological basis of the movement. Articles were published claiming that the Socialists had in fact absorbed the basic social ideology of the fathers of Spanish republicanism; and Lerroux's participation in the assembly of the *Confederación Hidrográfica del Ebro* was interpreted as a growing interest of Alianza in agrarian issues.[10]

Though the split of the intellectuals was certainly harmful because of their prestige, Marañón had made it clear that he had no intentions of gathering a political following. The fact that the Federals followed the dissidence of the Radical-Socialists did not seem to have a disastrous effect either. Ayuso claimed that the 'federalist content' of his party's platform, had been 'overshadowed and neglected' by Alianza. But precisely the 'federalist' structure of his party enabled autonomous branches, like those of Galicia, Baleares, Huelva, Madrid, and Linares to remain in Alianza regardless of the national leadership's attitude. Ayuso himself continued to maintain that dissidence had not shaken Lerroux's position as the 'axis of Spanish republicanism'. The latter, however, though expressing satisfaction with the dissidence ('I prefer a small group of devoted friends rather than a mass of the "lukewarm" and "irresolute"'), suggested that the dissidents should not be insulted, in order to encourage their return. Unity stood above any other consideration, and he was ready to sacrifice even his dignity for its sake. If Alianza should decide that he would have to join Primo's Assembly, he would do even

---

[10] For register see SA Leg. 1161: Bruno Centich to Lerroux, 26 Nov. 1929. For reiteration of adherence see *ES* 4, 8, 9 Aug. 1929 (Málaga, Alicante, San Sebastián); *EP* 19, 21, 31 July (Córdoba, Castellón, Zaragoza), 27 Aug. (Seville), 3 Aug., 1 Sept. (Valencia, Menorca); 8, 18 Aug., 10 Sept. (Galicia). See also SA 1161: Radicals of Valencia to Lerroux, 3 Nov. 1929. Even Acció Catalana was said to be interested in joining Alianza, see *El Sol* 7 Aug. 1929. For structural reorganization see *EP* 23 Aug., 20, 29 Oct., 6, 12, 24 Nov. 1929, 7 Jan. 1930. Montaner, and articles in *Alianza* Jan., Mar. 1930; and *EP* 11 Dec. 1929.

that, he said. He was convinced that without unity no Republic was possible.[11] With the fall of the Dictatorship Alianza embarked upon an extensive campaign of propaganda, intensifying its reorganization. After February 1930 local, regional and provincial juntas of Alianza were elected in hundreds of towns and cities throughout the country. The anniversary of the First Republic of 1873 was, for the first time since 1923, celebrated with political gatherings. New branches of Alianza were set up in rural areas like Almería, Cáceres, Badajoz, Ciudad Real, and old Castile; and leaders like Lerroux and Azaña attended their meetings and endorsed their demands whether against caciquismo and latifundismo or on behalf of the interests of small landowners.[12]

The strength of Alianza was enhanced further when a change of tactics by the PRRS brought the dissidents back to the fold. Since the fall of the Dictatorship, and after he had built up the skeleton of a party, Marcelino Domingo propagated the idea that only a co-ordinated effort of the whole left under a minimum programme of 'Republic and parliament' could bring about the Republic. He realized that a wider programme would only narrow the coalition. Furthermore, the revolutionary figure of July 1929 was now preaching as a tactical device an alliance whose image would have to be one of 'order' and 'responsibility'. Its prestige should lie 'not in creating tumults but in avoiding them; not in becoming an opposition but in being a government; not in being a menace to, but a guarantee of, security'. As a 'circumstantial necessity', he would even accept a Republic governed by conservatives like Sánchez Guerra.[13] With these concepts in mind the PRRS signed an

[11] Marañón in *EP* 25 July 1929. For the damage of the intellectuals' withdrawal see Martínez Barrios in *ES* 17 Aug. 1929. Marsá in ibid. 14 Aug. 1929. For the Federals see Ayuso in *EP* 11 Aug. 1929; and in SA Leg. 1161: Pedro Martínez Orozco to Lerroux, 8 Nov. 1929. For those who remained see *Alianza* Jan., Sept.–Oct. 1930. Lerroux's declarations on the dissidents and on union are in *EP* 3 Sept. (the quotation), 21, 25, 28 Aug., 3 Sept. 1929. *El* 23, 26 Feb. 1930 recognized Lerroux's sacrifices on behalf of unity.

[12] For the Anniversary see *ABC, El Sol* 12 Feb. 1930; and detailed reports in AHN Leg. 45: *Actos celebrados en Provincias por .Republicanos en 11 Febrero*. Reports on local reorganization can be found in abundance in *Alianza* Feb.–Oct. 1930. For Lerroux in Ciudad Real and Azaña in Salamanca see ibid. Mar., Apr. 1930.

[13] See Domingo's ideas in his *Que Espera el Rey?*, pp. 172–7; *LV* 13, 26 Feb., 21 Mar. 1930; *ABC* 14 Feb. 1930; *ES* 11 Feb. 1930; and *El Pueblo*, Tortosa, 24 May 1930.

alliance with Alianza in mid-May. The agreement, however, did not provide for the dissidents' joining Alianza, but for a 'co-ordination' between both organizations. Their co-operation, it was stated, would not be automatic and would be considered according to 'the immediate needs of political action'. This agreement was also subscribed by Casares Quiroga on behalf of the ORGA so that by the end of May 1930, apart from the Socialists and Catalans, virtually the whole of Spanish organized republicanism was embraced in a tactical, if not ideological, alliance.[14]

2. TOWARDS THE SAN SEBASTIÁN COALITION

The next tactical step which culminated in the San Sebastián pact was to forge an alliance with the Catalans, by bringing Spanish Republicans to subscribe to the basic autonomist demands of the Catalan left.

This alliance, however, was preceded by a consistent attempt of the Catalans to create a coherent bloc of their own, a bloc which could exert a stronger pressure in negotiations with any 'Spanish' government. Though the 'Catalan Alianza Republicana' did not materialize officially, the abortive attempt to set it up certainly proved one important thing. Although the Catalans were mainly interested in their own liberties, their republicanism was part of a general Spanish process. Even the most extreme separatists were not moving within an exclusively Catalan field, but within the larger orbit (Monarchy versus Republic) of Spanish politics. Federalism, not separatism, was definitely the magic word for Catalans; and salvation was therefore looked for through political agreements with the Spanish left rather than through a separatist insurrection or a fanatic 'Catalunya endins'.

The quest for unity of the Catalan Republicans was constantly jeopardized by mutual suspicions between left and right, as well as by differences over the issue of 'endins' and 'enfora'. Acció Catalana had refused during the two last years of the Dictatorship to take part in the 'Catalan Revolutionary Committee', in which Estat Catalá, Communists, and Anarcho-Syndicalists represented an extreme left tendency, while the Radicals were

---

[14] For the agreement see *Libro de Oro*, pp. 149–50; and *Alianza* May 1930.

expelled because of their 'behaviour on the day of Sánchez Guerra's coup'.[15] In February 1930 the division between left and right was emphasized by the creation of *Izquierda Republicana*, a coalition of *Acció Republicana*, the Federals, and Luis Companys' *Partit Republicá Catalá*. This conglomeration accepted in principle the 1919 statute suggested to Catalonia by the Monarchy, and kept cordial relations with the Radicals. Neither Estat Catalá nor any other extremist group was invited to join their common committee, which, in any case, did not become a clear political alliance.[16]

Even the initially encouraging manifesto of the *Inteligencia Republicana* in March 1930 did not develop into a Catalan political bloc. It was a minimum programme consisting of social reforms, a federal Republic and political liberties subscribed to by practially all the political forces of the region including the Radicals and *Acció Catalana* to the right and Communists and Anarcho-Syndicalists to the left. It was significant, however, that the manifesto clearly called for a co-ordinated effort of 'men of good will both in Catalonia and *Spain*' for the implantation of a 'democratic Republic'. But Inteligencia Republicana failed also to produce the longed-for Catalan 'Alianza'. The common activities of its members, despite the setting up in June of a *Comité de Inteligencia*, were very sparse. Both Acció Catalana and Acció Republicana considered the others as excessively 'españolista' and 'anarchist', while the Radicals alleged that these two parties 'wanted everything for Catalonia', thus alienating the Catalan working class and other republicans looking for an understanding with Spain. *Estat Catalá*, despite its militancy, stood for a more realistic formula, convinced that only by making out of Catalonia a revolutionary force in the all-Spanish revolution could it reach its aspirations. On 20 July Maciá called for the establishment of a federation in friendly relation with 'brothers from Spain'. But, this, he added, must be preceded by a 'Catalan united front'. Lluhí Vallescá, speaking on behalf of a socially leftist Catalanism, criticized the 'Catalunya endins' of both Acciós and called for a struggle for a Spanish federal

---

[15] Aiguader, *Cataluña*, pp. 75–6.
[16] See current information on 'Izquierda' in *LV* 8, 20, 28 Feb., 23 May 1930; and relations with Radicals in *EP* 12 Feb. 1930.

Republic which would automatically mean recognition of Catalonia's rights. The fact however was that on the eve of the San Sebastián pact, Inteligencia Republicana did not exist, mainly because of the refusal of both Acció Catalana and Acció Republicana to subordinate themselves to the decisions of a predominantly leftist joint committee.[17] The same line of division in the Catalan left could be noticed in the negotiations for an alliance with Spanish Republicans. The latter, since the Alianza–PRRS–ORGA agreement in mid-May, were engaged in a tireless attempt to 'unify all the Republican Parties for a revolutionary movement'.[18] The first approach was made that same month to the Izquierda Republicana alignment. A clear negative answer was given only by Acció Republicana, which was bitterly disappointed with the 'Spanish' proposition that mentioned neither the 'federal Republic' nor 'autonomy'. The Federals and the Partit Republicá Catalá gave evasive answers.[19] In July Marcelino Domingo came personally to Barcelona to propose 'a revolutionary movement' for the establishment of a 'federal Republic'. 'A Republic in Spain', he added, 'means autonomy for Catalonia;' and those who refused to collaborate for the creation of a Spanish Republic were consequently jeopardizing the prospects for Catalan autonomy. Moreover, he claimed, they were thus jeopardizing the possibility that the Socialists, who stipulated a Socialist-Republican alliance with 'a complete unity between republicans', might ever join the revolutionary movement. Estat Catalá responded affirmatively to the proposition, though Aiguader claimed to have previously drawn a commitment from Domingo that 'the revolution should recognize from the first moment the personality of Catalonia'.[20]

Acció Catalana and Acció Republicana continued to be the

[17] Inteligencia Republicana's manifesto is in J. Peirats, *Los Anarquistas en la Crísis Política Española*, pp. 24–5. For the Radicals' views and allegations see *EP* 4, 24 July 1930. Acció's views are in ibid. 8 July 1930 (quoting 'La Nau'), 11 July 1930 (Bofill i Mates); and *El Sol* 17 Aug. 1930 (a declaration by Bofill.) For Estat Catalá see Aiguader, *Cataluña*, p. 145; Aymani i Baudina, *Maciá*, p. 167, and Maciá's manifesto in *ABC* 20 July 1930. See Lluhí Vallescá's article in *Alianza* Aug. 1930.
[18] This was one of the clauses in Alianza–PRRS–ORGA agreement; see *Alianza* May 1930.
[19] *LV* 23 May 1930.
[20] For Domingo's mission see *El Sol* 8, 16, 1930; and Aiguader, *Cataluña*, pp. 75–8.

main obstacle to unity. Rovira i Virgili refused to be in alliance with the Radicals, whom he referred to as 'federals only in name'. He pointed at the opposition of Rocha, their representative in the city council of Barcelona, to the Catalanization of the university, as a manifestation of anti-Catalanism. Bofill i Mates had more practical reservations. An alliance with 'Spanish' republicans, he argued, might enable them to develop electoral strongholds in Catalonia.[21] In both cases, what was implicit in the term 'Spanish' Republicans was a basic mistrust of Lerroux and his Radicals, as Marcelino Domingo and others indeed pointed out.[22] By the end of July Giral, a member of Alianza's junta, renewed the appeal to the parties of Izquierda Republicana. He explained that the affirmation of a 'federal Republic' was omitted from the previous bases of the agreement between Spanish Republicans, an agreement that now included the *Derecha Republicana* as well, because it was considered unnecessary, since virtually all the Republicans included federalism in their programme. Now, however, this had been explicitly introduced into the bases, in order to please the Catalans. Acció Republicana still refused to be persuaded, while the Federals and the Partit Republicá Catalá claimed that they were anyway represented in the alliance, the first through their autonomous branches, and the latter through their president, Marcelino Domingo. Acció Catalana followed in Acció Republicana's footsteps, claiming that a pact must be based on 'common ideals' and 'mutual confidence', which it did not feel towards 'some of the elements who have signed the pact'.[23]

Nevertheless, the attempts to overcome the opposition of the Catalanists went on until they resulted, on the eve of the San Sebastián meeting, in a surprising change of attitude by the Catalans. This was the consequence of their conviction that the alliance might be set up with their rivals of the Estat Catalá as the sole representatives of Catalan republicanism. This, together with pressure from their rank and file, and the public and secret assurances that they had received during the first two weeks of August, may help to explain the reversal in their

---

[21] Rovira in *La Nau* 15 July; and Bofill in *La Publicitat* 16 July 1930.
[22] See *Alianza* Aug. 1930; *EP* 25, 27 July 1930.
[23] *LV* 26, 30 July 1930; *Alianza* June–July 1930.

attitude. They were about to betray the ideal of non-involvement in Spanish politics, an ideal on which the whole existence of their parties, as splinter groups of the Lliga, was based. But they seemed to be assured of getting far-reaching concessions for Catalonia in exchange. In a public speech in Barcelona on 2 August, Marcelino Domingo assured them that the 'Catalan factor' was the predominant issue in the Republican pact, and that all Spanish Republicans had adopted the idea of 'an autonomous and particular regime' for Catalonia. 'Once we arrive at the Cortes of the Republic,' he added, 'Catalonia will be allowed to present itself with its full individuality before the different peninsular regions.' The adherence of the Catalan Derecha Republicana to these affirmations and the attempt to blame them for any future failures of the republican movement threatened to isolate further the two Acciós should they still refuse. Nevertheless, on 12 August Rovira and Nicolau d'Olwer rejected a last minute attempt by Salmerón to break the deadlock. But two days later the broader forum of their parties' directive juntas, more genuinely representative of the rank and file, put them in the minority by adhering overwhelmingly to the 'Spanish' proposals.[24]

The San Sebastián meeting on 17 August was designed for forging the agreement with the Catalans and for making preliminary arrangements for a revolutionary movement. No programmatic discussions were held, because the representatives of the parties assembled there[25] differed on any issue that was not a vague affirmation of the need to establish a Republic. The heterogeneity of this conglomeration was an impediment to elaborating decisions which might alienate any of its components. Moreover, in their subsequent struggle against the Monarchy

[24] Marcelino Domingo in *El Sol* and *LV* 3 Aug. 1930. For an example of how the Acció's were 'blamed' see Artigas Arpón in *NE* 1 Sept. 1930 (article written before 'San Sebastián'). Solá Cañizares speaking on behalf of Derecha Republicana in *LV* 14 Aug. 1930. For Salmerón see ibid. 13 Aug., and *EP* 14 Aug. 1930. For the directive junta see *ABC* 15 Aug. 1930. See a discussion of Acciós' attitude in Aiguader, *Cataluña*, pp. 138–9; and *EP* 16 Aug. 1930.
[25] Azaña and Lerroux (Alianza Republicana); Domingo, Albornoz, and Galarza (PRRS); Alcalá Zamora and Maura (DR); Casares Quiroga (ORGA); Aiguader (Estat Catalá); Carrasco Formiguera (Acció Catalana); Matías Mallol (Acció Republicana); Felipe Sánchez Román, Eduardo Ortega, and Prieto as individuals and Sasiaín, the president of the local Republican centre.

they were interested, above all else, in closing their ranks.[26] The fact that the Federal party was not invited to the meeting illustrated the pragmatic character of the gathering. It was much more practical to agree on specific concessions to the Catalans, concessions which were anyway open to various interpretations, than to commit the future Republic to a clear-cut federal constitution. It is obvious, however, that the weakness of the Federals, and the fact that many of their branches were incorporated within Alianza Republicana, contributed to make a compromise with the Federal party, and hence with a federalist doctrine, simply unnecessary.[27]

At the meeting the Catalans presented their case in an uncompromising manner. Aiguader said bluntly that Catalonia was more interested in its 'national freedom' than in a Spanish Republic, and that the victory of the revolution should 'automatically' mean the recognition of Catalonia's right 'to organize its liberties according to its own will'. Carrasco Formiguera followed suit with a doctrine of 'autodetermination', which would have to prevail from the very moment of the declaration of the Republic. He added that Catalonia should be politically independent of Spain with 'neighbourly relations' as the only connection between the two states.

The 'Spanish' reaction was mixed. Maura, representing his party's commitment to the unity of Spain, maintained that a more modest minimum basis must be agreed upon 'without mortgaging the future with compromises'. The Radical-Socialists represented different views. Alvaro de Albornoz was excitedly critical of the egoism of the Catalans, who wanted to exploit the Spanish revolution for their own narrow ends. But Marcelino Domingo, whose links with Catalan autonomism were reflected in his relations with Companys' Partit Republicá Catalá, supported the Catalan view. Alcalá Zamora was, surprisingly, also sympathetic, thus differing from his colleague Maura. He even confessed that his 'centralism' in the past was unjustified.

---

[26] See the article of the Radical-Socialist Botella Asensi in *NE* 1 Aug. 1930.

[27] See *Alianza* Sept.–Oct. 1930 claiming that the Federals were not invited because they were 'waiting for a decision of their national congress'. García Venero, the secretary of the Federal Party of Santander, as well as representatives of other branches, refuted this argument: see M. García Venero, *Historia del Nacionalismo Vasco*, pp. 468–9.

Lerroux, who later claimed that this was the only way to calm down 'these wild beasts' from Catalonia, said emotionally that he 'fully subscribed' to the Catalan aspirations. At that stage Casares Quiroga asked for Galicia and the Basque provinces the same rights as those proposed to Catalonia. As far as Galicia was concerned, there were no reservations. But Prieto, the Socialist leader of Biscay, opposed 'reactionary' Basque nationalists, who might stand against the whole leftist spirit of the Republic. The Catalans then suggested that all the statutes, including their own, 'could not deny the liberal and democratic spirit of the revolution . . . The particular statute could not contradict the work in its totality'. This, having satisfied both Prieto and Sasiaín, brought an end to the debate on the 'Iberian nationalities'.

The issue of 'revolution' was dealt with briefly. A Revolutionary Committee was elected, and commissions were appointed to negotiate with the Socialists, the Communists, the Anarcho-Syndicalists and with military elements, for their adherence to a revolutionary movement aimed at overthrowing the Monarchy.[28]

Since no written minute of the meeting had been made, different interpretations of the San Sebastián pact have been put forward by both sides. The Spaniards emphasized the authority of the future Constituent Cortes either to approve or to reject the statute that would be elaborated by the Catalans. The latter, on the other hand, minimized the role of the Cortes, and emphasized the recognition of the 'automatic' right of Catalonia for self-determination, once the revolution had won. In an official note given to the press by the Catalan delegates they said that the pact had recognized the 'living reality of the Catalan problem', and that 'the triumph of the revolution is *per se* the recognition of the personality of Catalonia'. The autonomous constitution of Catalonia, they added, would be elaborated by the Catalans themselves, who would also have to approve it in a plebiscite. Then, 'only those parts of the statute

[28] See accounts on the meeting in Aiguider, *Cataluña*, pp. 78–85; M. Maura, *Así*, pp. 70–2; *El Pueblo Vasco*'s and *La Voz de Guipúzcoa*'s accounts are in M. Fernández Almagro, *Catalanismo y Republica*, pp. 143–6; F.O. 371/15041: Grahame to Henderson, 19 Aug. 1930 stressing Maura's and Prieto's tough attitude; Lerroux, *La Pequeña*, pp. 54–5. For Alcalá Zamora see an interview with 'one of the participants' in *Estampa* 15 Aug. 1931.

concerning the definition of powers between the central and the autonomous government of Catalonia would be presented to the approval of the Constituent Cortes'. Estat Catalá went even further by claiming that 'the Catalan personality should be proclaimed *by a revolution* and should not be the product of a debate in the Cortes, nor of any "foreign intervention"'. This revolutionary thesis was designed probably for the consumption of the anarcho-syndicalist public to whom Estat Catalá constantly appealed. Carrasco Formiguerra seemed to be not less radical in his Catalanist interpretation, though his remarks about the revolution were more cautious.[29]

In spite of basic discrepancies over the interpretation of this 'authentic pact between gentlemen', as Maura called it, neither the Catalans nor the Spaniards were now ready for a confrontation. So long as the Republic was only a dream and the struggle with the Monarchy a tangible reality, the existence of a revolutionary alliance and the determination to widen the anti-monarchist front by the inclusion in it of the army and the working class, were both more exciting and more urgent issues to deal with. Not until the 'proclamation of the Catalan Republic' on 14 April 1931 would Spanish Republicans really worry about the correct interpretation of the San Sebastián pact. Furthermore, the emphasis of the Catalan delegates on the victory of their tactics over those of the Monarchist Lliga, which had never been able to assure a satisfactory autonomy for Catalonia,[30] was perfectly compatible with the republican campaign to undermine monarchism wherever possible. Put in its true context, the San Sebastián pact, rather than a spectacular turning-point, was a step in the long process of tactical unification of the left, a process which started on 11 February 1926, and which would culminate only when, two months

---

[29] For the Spanish version see Maura, *Así*, pp. 71–2; *EP* 19, 21, 30 Aug. 1930; see an endorsement of this version by the Governor of Guipúzcoa in his telegram to the Ministry of the Interior, 18 Aug. 1930 in AHN Leg. 45, no. 504; and Alcalá Zamora's speech on 22 Aug. 1931, quoted in Bofill i Mates, *Una Política Catalanista*, pp. 112–13. The Catalan official note is in *La Publicitat* 19 Aug. 1930. For Estat Catalá's version see *La Rambla de Catalunya* 25 Aug., 1 Sept. 1930. For the less extreme version of Acció Catalana and Acció Republicana see Rovira i Virgili, *Catalunya i la Republica*, pp. 29–32, 48–53, 57; *LV* 21 Aug. 1929; and a comparison of both in J. Estelrich, *El Moment Politic*, pp. 51–3.

[30] *La Rambla de Catalunya* 1 Sept. 1930.

later, an agreement would be reached with the Socialists.[31] However, the significance of the pact should not be minimized. The Catalan Republican movement had at last been induced to collaborate with an all-Spanish revolution. This not only had added strength to the movement, but, at the same time, had 'neutralized' the Catalans by avoiding the possibility that they might obstruct the revolution, a possibility had not an agreement been reached with them.[32] Now, all the Republican parties in the country had subscribed to a common determination to co-ordinate their efforts against the Monarchy. This determination was, according to a confident Alvaro de Albornoz, 'the instrument of steel, which would cut the Gordian knot of Spanish politics'.[33]

3. PROPAGANDA, CONSPIRACY, AND *RETRAIMIENTO*

The San Sebastián pact and the imminence of a close agreement with the organized working class stimulated the Republican alignment to intensify its activities on two levels: open propaganda and conspiratorial action.

The gathering of a crowd of 20,000 in the Madrid bullring on 28 September, and the subsequent national assembly of Alianza two days later, marked the culmination of a nationwide campaign of republican affirmation that started at the beginning of the year. The Ministry of the Interior was throughout the year practically inundated with republican petitions for holding meetings all over the country. This campaign, however, was frequently stymied by governmental restrictions on 'meetings of propaganda with a republican character', until June 1930.[34]

Nevertheless, since early April preparations had been under way for the bullring meeting to which were invited 'all the factions, parties, and groups which compose the anti-monarchist Spanish democracy'. Lists of trains and reduced fares to Madrid

---

[31] See below, pp. 145–147.
[32] See Aiguader, op. cit. 77.
[33] *El Sol* 9 Sept. 1930.
[34] For petitions see AHN Leg. 45: 'Republicanos 1930'. For restrictions see ibid., a circular to the Governors no. 1240 25 Feb. 1930; from the Ministry to the Governor of Logroño no. 962, 10 Mar. 1930 (forbidding republican meetings in Cervera Río Alhama, Alfaro, Cenicero, and Calahorra); Leg. 51: circular no. 1, 3 Apr. 1930. Student riots also initiated restrictions, and on 16 May and 5 June 1930 *El Progreso* still protested against them.

were published, tickets were distributed to the centres, and delegations were designated. The gathering itself was a tremendous success. Republicanism, which used to be identified with underground committees and tiny cells, emerged from this meeting, according to observers, as a massive movement excellently disciplined and confident of its capacity to govern the country. *El Imparcial*, which on the eve of the meeting alluded to the 'lack of force' of the Republicans, referred three days later to the leftist ambiance reflected in it as the reason why a Liberal government should rule the country. Speeches by representatives of practically every sector of Spanish republicanism, brought the Monarchy under violent attacks, which culminated in Alcalá Zamora's eloquent denigration of 'the most treacherous and illegitimate power that exists in the world'. The speech of Lerroux, the old emperor of working-class Barcelona, was a combination of well-measured assertions about a moderate Republic and a demagagical approach that 'magnetized the crowd'. 'Had he preached rebellion', *La Libertad* wrote, '20,000 souls would have followed him'. The main contribution of the gathering, however, was in increasing the republicans' feeling of self-confidence. They referred to their manifestation of power as an example of genuine 'European' mass politics, that indicated that 'the Republic is knocking at the door'.[35]

This confidence was enhanced by the national assembly of Alianza opened two days later with the presence of 700 delegates from all over the country, and by subsequent meetings. Its final resolutions referred to the Republic as a tangible reality. A 'Spanish Republican Saving' fund was established as the 'first public debt of the republican state', and appeals were made to other anti-monarchist parties and to the students, 'who had given the *coup de grace* to the first Dictatorship', to join Alianza in its victorious march towards the Republic. Subsequent mass gatherings like that of the bullring of Valencia crowded

[35] For the preparations for the gathering see *El Sol* 29 Mar., 25, 26, 27 Sept. 1930; *ABC* 11 Apr. 1930; *Alianza* Apr., May, Aug. 1930; and *EP* 1, 10–12 Apr., 18, 28 May; 19, 21, 25 Sept. 1930. For observers see *The Times* 29 Sept. 1930; *The Economist* 4 Oct. 1930; and Romanones and Berenguer in *ABC* 30 Sept. 1930; *EI* 27, 30 Sept. 1930. The full text of the speeches is in *EP* 1 Oct. 1930. *La Libertad* 30 Sept. 1930. For confidence see *Heraldo de Chamartín* 1, 20 Oct. 1930; *EP* 2 Oct. 1930; and messages of solidarity from the provinces in *El Sol* 7, 9 Oct. 1930.

with 25,000 people, that of Alicante with 4,000, the huge meetings in favour of an amnesty organized in Catalonia by a 'Committee for Liberty' of all the Catalan left, a committee that represented a 'Catalan Popular Front', and smaller meetings held all over the country, were not considered any more as simple acts of propaganda. Attended by speakers from all the San Sebastián parties, they were in Lerroux's and Pedro Rico's words 'last minute appeals' to those who had not yet joined the republican wave; or, as the propagandist Torreblanca put it in Alicante, 'a muster parade which enabled the *caudillos* to survey their armies on the eve of the proclamation of the Republic'.[36]

Simultaneously with these civilian 'muster parades' the Republican coalition embarked upon clandestine revolutionary activity. It is, however, noteworthy that the heterogeneity of the coalition, the central role allocated to the conservative Alcalá Zamora within it, the participation of socially moderate *Lerrouxismo*, and the social-democratic features of the Spanish Socialist movement, later to be absorbed into the coalition, combined to give a cautious and 'unrevolutionary' character to the attempts against the Monarchy. These were conspiracies aimed at creating a Republic, rather than a revolution aimed at mobilizing the man in the street for an armed insurrection. The attempts to enlist both Communists and Anarcho-Syndicalists seem to have been made not only in order to add strength to the general effort, but in order to impose on them the compromising commitments of a bourgeois republican conspiracy aimed at a political rather than at a social revolution.[37]

The compromising and moderate features of the movement were reflected already in the preliminary deliberations of the Revolutionary Committee. When in October the Provisional Government was designated, the key posts of Premier and Minister of the Interior were allocated to the two conservatives

---

[36] For the national assembly see *Alianza* Sept.–Oct. 1930. For the meetings of Valencia, Alicante, and Albacete see *Rebelión* 25 Oct. 1930; *EP* 23, 25 Oct. 1930; and *El Sol* 21 Oct. 1930. For massive mobilization in Catalonia under a 'pro-amnesty' pretext see *LV* 16 Sept., 3 Oct. 1930; Solá Cañizares, *El Moviment*, p. 13; Aiguader, *Cataluña*, pp. 113–19. For the predominance of republican meetings during Sept.–Dec. see AHN Leg. 51: '1930, Mitines'.

[37] This was recognized both by the critics of the movement and by its protagonists; see Cesar Falcón, *Crítica de la Revolución Española* pp. 22–50; Graco Marsá, *Lucha de Clases*, pp. 7–8; and Alcalá-Zamora in *La Batalla* 5 Mar. 1931.

Alcalá Zamora and Maura, though they represented a party created only three months previously. An obvious appeal to conservative opinion not to fear the Republic, it certainly reflected a determination not to push, at that stage at least, too much to the left. The attempts to minimize the share of the Radicals in the government, by allocating to them fewer ministries than they expected, given their strength as a party, were a manifestation of personal mistrust of Lerroux, rather than of an opposition to the social and political moderation that he stood for. The programmatic issues dealt with were either solved in a compromising manner or postponed until the Constituent Cortes of the Republic had been summoned, all being determined to avoid a 'governmental crisis' until then. The sensitive issue of the relations between state and Church was, therefore, left for a later stage. But general principles, like the need to abolish illiteracy, to reduce the army cadres, to maintain cordial relations with the League of Nations and to carry out an agrarian reform, were broadly agreed upon.[38]

In its preparations for the revolution, the Provisional Government pursued a similar line of both enlisting heterogeneous partners and bringing them to agree on a minimum programme for the Republic, by exploiting their grievances against the Monarchy.

Such grievances had been developing among certain corps and officers since the arbitrariness of the dictator had put them in the anti-monarchist camp. The artillery that in 1926 had been deprived of its prerogatives as a corps and humiliated by the dictator, turned its anger against the 'treacherous king'. Groups of artillery officers organized in clandestine cells called for 'a liberal, constitutional and parliamentarian regime' that would recognize 'the sovereignty of the people'. Cadets in the Military Academy of Segovia chanted the 'Marseillaise' and destroyed statues of the king. In Ciudad Real, in January 1929, the military rebels fraternized with the republicans who considered them as 'loyal collaborators of the Republic'. Some

---

[38] For the designation of the Goverment see Maura, *Así*, pp. 83–5, 92–3; Lerroux, *Mis Memorias*, pp. 547–8; *Pequeña Historia*, pp. 59–61; I. Prieto, *Convulsiones* ii, 323–4. For the programmatic deliberations see Maura, op. cit. 81–3; Alcalá-Zamora, *Los Defectos de la Constitución de 1931*, pp. 11, 87; Prieto in *La Gaceta de la Revolución*, 28 Jan. 1931; and Marcelino Domingo in *Vanguardia*, Badajoz, 23 Mar. 1931.

infantry generals, such as Queipo de Llano and López de Ochoa, also became republican because they were discriminated against by the dictator in matters of promotion. In Barcelona a *Junta de Defensa* of embittered officers called for an end to the rule of 'the degenerate Bourbon family' and to establish a Republic that would put the army back in its barracks. Even in the navy there were signs of anti-monarchist agitation when its General Staff was abolished by Primo de Rivera. And, by the end of the Dictatorship, a Revolutionary Military Association was set up to collaborate with republicans and other elements of the opposition.[39]

During the first months of the Berenguer government, the 'Association' continued to absorb exasperated officers from the air force, where the 'revolutionary' Ramón Franco was a popular idol, and among artillery officers, many of whom were embittered by the decree of 15 February 1930 restoring the system of promotion abolished by the dictator, and thus destroying the career of those who had been promoted by him. The authorities were becoming aware of the 'contamination' of the military. Berenguer had to warn officers against taking part in political meetings; while Mola was increasingly alarmed by the 'republicanization' of many garrisons in the country, of *Carabineros*, engineers and Civil Guards as well as of the navy. If not from 'republicanism', the army certainly suffered from 'confusion' and from lack of monarchist coherence.[40]

These conditions invited the Provisional Government to cultivate them. Mola noticed that by the end of November there was hardly any corps, centre, or military dependency whose staff had not been explored by the Revolutionary Committee. He had a list of one hundred officers clearly committed to the revolutionary movement already by mid-

[39] For the artillery see RA Leg. 2 no. 36: *A Nuestros Compañeros del Ejército y al País*: 24 Nov. 1926; Leg. 2 No. 45: 'Carta Dirigida por Lerroux a F. Morayta de Ciudad Real', n.d.; *HL* Apr. 1927, Sept. 1928, Jan. 1929 (articles written by artillery officers); for Queipo see his *El General*, pp. 7–21; also his *El Movimiento Reivindicativo de Cuatro Vientos*, pp. 21–2. For the Junta de Defensa see RA Leg. 2 no. 25; *Las Juntas de Defensa. A los Pocos Lectores de 'La Nación'* Aug. 1929. For the navy see ibid. Leg. 63 no. 44; 'Anónimo del Comité de la Armada Dirigido a Sánchez de Toca con Motivo de la Supresión del Estado Mayor Central', n.d. For the Revolutionary Association see Ramón Franco, *Madrid*, pp. 87–8, 93.

[40] Berenguer in *ABC* 13 Feb. 1930; Mola in *Obras*, pp. 273–5, 291, 348–50, 369.

September; while the navy in El Ferrol was constantly giving signs of support to the movement. In September Queipo de Llano had set up a Military Revolutionary Committee with representatives of virtually every corps in the army. This committee was in close contact with the civilian committee presided over by Alcalá Zamora, and, though it consisted of officers up to the rank of colonel, it was engaged in confidential contacts with Generals Villabrille and Nuñez de Prado.[41] A similar rapprochement with republicanism was taking place in the Anarcho-Syndicalist CNT. Already in 1926 Alianza Republicana was in contact with the CNT in an attempt to mobilize it on behalf of a republican movement. The CNT's subsequent participation in practically all the conspiracies that took place against the Dictatorship, in close contact with politicians, indicated that doctrinal apoliticism was overcome when the temptation of getting freedom of organization under a bourgeois liberal regime was put forward.[42] This 'reformist' attitude was reiterated when, in April 1930, the National Committee of the CNT manifested in public its 'circumstantial solidarity with other social and political forces', and when Pestaña, the Cenetista leader, told Mola that the CNT 'would sympathize with that regime which would place it nearer to its ideals'.[43]

The Republican alignment made efforts to exploit this trend in the CNT, a difficult task given the fact that it refused to stage a popular revolution. At the beginning of June 1930 a commission of the 'Revolutionary Committee of the Radical-Socialist Federation' approached CNT members and suggested a collaboration. Though this was rejected on the ground that only the CNT's National Committee was entitled to decide on such a matter, unofficial contacts went on. The *Cenetistas* Progreso Alfarache and Rafael Vidiella were in San Sebastián

---

[41] Mola, op. cit. 394, 1039–41. Berenguer minimized the volume of army involvement, but recognized the navy's agitation, see his *De la Dictadura*, pp. 221, 228–30. For the navy see also Franco, *Madrid*, p. 112; and *The Times* 15 Oct., 18 Nov. 1930. For the Committee see Queipo de Llano, *El Movimiento*, pp. 54–5; and Prieto, *Convulsiones* i, 62.
[42] For Alianza see A. Marsá Bragado and others, *El Republicanismo Histórico*, pp. 45–6. For collaboration with the bourgeoisie against the Dictatorship, see Angel Pestaña, *Lo que Aprendí en la Vida*, pp. 103–5; and J. Peirats, *Los Anarquistas*, p. 23. The communist *L'Humanité* Paris, 23 Sept. 1924 wrote on 'anarchists and bourgeois in Spain hand in hand'.
[43] *Alianza* Apr. 1930; Mola, *Obras*, p. 284.

on the day of the famous pact, a curious coincidence precisely when the republicans made their decision to contact the CNT. In September, the National Committee of the CNT, without the approval of its Regional Committees, was negotiating with republican and military elements, through its delegates Mauro Bajatierra and Salvador Quemades. At the beginning of October the CNT organ, *Solidaridad Obrera*, flirted openly with the republicans, when it praised the Madrid bullring gathering, adding that: 'The workers, although proclaiming their apoliticism . . . are on the side of the republicans. A Republic which would offer certain social achievements would be preferred to the Monarchy.' The balance between left and right in the Provisional Government was, according to the same organ, 'a guarantee of revolutionary seriousness'.

Contacts were continued between Rafael Sánchez Guerra, the Provisional Government's representative in Barcelona, and Cenetista leaders like Pestaña, Peiró, Pou, and Magriñá. These agreed to launch a revolutionary strike in support of the republican movement, arguing that the only compensation they asked was that the Republic should concede them syndical freedom. But the refusal of the Provisional Government to deliver weapons to them was a serious obstacle to a clear-cut commitment by the CNT. It felt that the Republicans were trying to stage a *Militarada* rather than organize mass popular movements. That is why *Cenetista* elements, though they collaborated with the Provisional Government, maintained a more revolutionary option by cultivating their relations with a Revolutionary Committee of young radical officers. This consisted of figures like Ramón Franco, Alejandro Sancho, and Captain Medrano. It was, indeed, a confused situation in which two simultaneous movements were planned, the CNT being in touch with both, though officially with none.[44]

Nevertheless, preparations for a military *coup* supported by a general strike and scheduled for late October were being made

[44] For information on CNT-republican contacts see Mola, *Obras*, pp. 351–2, 389, 405; Rafael Sánchez Guerra, *Proceso de Un Cambio de Régimen*, pp. 21–5; Peirats, *Los Anarquistas*, p. 65; and *La Batalla* 11 July 1930. For the 'flirtation' see *SO* 1, 11, 15 Oct. 1930. For the 'two movements' see Peirats, op. cit. 61–2; Maura, *Así*, p. 100; and Mola, op. cit. 334, 362–4, 381, 389–90. For the Anarcho-Syndicalists' resentment of a 'Militarada' see *SO* 21 Oct. 1930.

throughout that month. Queipo de Llano had a detailed military plan which consisted of the seizure of key institutions in Madrid with the support of students and telegraph workers. The authorities had been on the alert since early in the month, noticing military ramifications of the movement in Bilbao and Valencia, and how students were being approached by professors committed to the revolution, like Sánchez Román, Honorato de Castro and Jiménez de Asua. Simultaneously the Catalan Committee For Amnesty was transformed into a Revolutionary Committee composed of representatives of all the Republican parties in the region, and in close contact with the Regional Committee of the CNT and even with members of the Anarchist FAI. Rafael Sánchez Guerra was the liaison man between the Committees of Madrid and Barcelona, and he contributed not only to co-ordinate their activities, but also to settle disputes between such opposing elements in the Catalan coalition as the Radicals and Estat Catalá.[45]

It was precisely this kind of tension between left and right, and the Provisional Government's hesitations, which jeopardized the 'October revolution'. Early in October Ramón Franco and Captain Sancho gave an ultimatum to the Republicans that if the revolution did not start before 19 October, they would act alone with their allies from the CNT. In the Catalan Committee, both Estat Catalá and the *Cenetistas* Pou and Magriñá shared this revolutionary impatience of Franco and a doubt about the Provisional Government's revolutionary intentions. On the other hand, the conservative Alcalá Zamora was reluctant to bet on a *coup* whose main civilian support was that of the Anarcho-Syndicalists. Hence the constant attempts to enlist the more moderate and politically minded Socialist movement and its disciplined following as a potential buffer against the uncontrolled revolutionism of the CNT. This was achieved officially only on 20 October.[46] Meanwhile, Alcalá Zamora claimed that the main impediment to launching the *coup* was the refusal of the millionaire Juan March to finance the

---

[45] For the military plan see Queipo de Llano, *El Movimiento*, pp. 63–4; and Mola, *Obras*, pp. 434–5, 454. For the alert of the Government in October see ibid. 392–3, 406–8; and Berenguer, *De la Dictadura*, pp. 202, 232–3. For the Catalan Committee see Solá Cañizares, *El Moviment*, pp. 13–14, 45–6; and Rafael Sánchez Guerra, *Proceso*, pp. 16–17.

[46] For the Socialists in the republican movement see below, pp. 145–151.

revolution. In these circumstances of uncertainty, members of the Catalan Revolutionary Committee, CNT militants and Franco were arrested on 11 October by a vigilant Mola, who thus indicated that he had at least some knowledge of what was being prepared. This was enough to jeopardize the whole October movement, and the Provisional Government urged the CNT not to launch its scheduled general strike. The Socialists, who had instructions for a general strike later in October, did not act once they realized that the military were also paralysed.[47]

Despite the failure to produce a co-ordinated and coherent coup, October was a month of agitation and disorder, which caused the liberal monarchist Santiago Alba to predict a 'Republic of chaos', and the conservative *La Vanguardia* to allege that 'Russian money' was at work behind the scenes. The Provisional Government was, however, officially alien to the wave of strikes and demonstrations, a fact that irritated leftist republicans. The strikes that took place throughout September and October all over the country were sponsored by the Communists and the CNT, while the Catalan FUE demonstrated on behalf of the arrested members of the local Revolutionary Committee, and the youth of Alianza Republicana manifested their solidarity with the rioters.[48]

These 'revolutionary gymnastics', in which the CNT played the main role, blackmailed the republicans into official negotiations on 29 October. A week earlier *Solidaridad Obrera* attacked the Provisional Government violently for avoiding official commitments with the CNT, so that its aspirations could be later disregarded.[49] Now the same organ claimed that the CNT had never made an agreement with the Provisional Government,

---

[47] For the tensions between extremism in Barcelona and moderation in Madrid see R. Franco, *Madrid*, pp. 111–12; Solá Cañizares, *El Moviment*, pp. 30–1. For J. March see Queipo de Llano, *El Movimiento*, pp. 66–7; and Lerroux, *Pequeña Historia*, pp. 62–65. For the arrests and their impact on the suspension of the movement see *ABC* 12, 14 Oct. 1930; Mola, op. cit. 411–14; Queipo, op. cit. 58–9; R. Franco, op. cit. 117–120. For the Socialists see Saborit, *Besteiro*, 265–6.

[48] SAA: Alba to Amos Salvador, 30 Oct. 1930. For 'Russian money' see *LV* 16 Oct. 1930. Maura, *Así*, p. 101 on the alienation from this movement. For the irritation of leftist republicans see *NE* 25 Oct., 1 Nov. 1930. For the strikes of September and October see practically every number of *The Times* and *ABC* during both months. For the students see *SO* 19 Oct.; *LV* 17 Oct.; *EP* 14, 15 Oct. 1930. For Alianza see ibid. 19 Oct. 1930.

[49] *SO* 21 Oct. 1930.

and that the last chain of strikes was motivated by economic rather than political reasons. This might have reflected, as a member of the local Revolutionary Committee claimed, discrepancies within the CNT over the issue of collaboration with the Republicans. However, it seemed also to be an appeal both to Mola to release from prison their 'innocent' colleagues, and to the Provisional Government to come to terms with the CNT. The prospect of militant unions carrying on their separate revolution was not a very attractive alternative for the Republicans, and on 29 October they sent Maura and Galarza to Barcelona to co-ordinate the so called 'Maura Plan' that officially included the CNT as well as the local Revolutionary Committee. Maura promised that in a future revolution the Socialists would strike *en masse*. He asked the CNT to launch a strike, but a 'pacific' one, in order to avoid a confrontation with the army, the bulk of the local garrison being alien to the conspiracy. However, Maura's insistence on a 'pacific' strike was, according to other participants in the meeting, motivated by a fear that the CNT leaders might not otherwise be able to control the revolutionary dynamics of a non-pacific strike. In his short visit Maura also managed to patch up the quarrel between the Catalanists and the Radicals in the local Revolutionary Committee. A fortnight after his visit the *Pleno de Regionales* of the CNT approved the agreement 'with the political elements in order to make a revolutionary movement', while insisting paradoxically that the political purity of the CNT had been maintained.[50]

However, despite the fresh unity between the military, the unions and the Republicans, an abortive coup in November reflected again the basic discrepancies between the cautious Republicans, the impatient military, and the extremists in Catalonia. Mola was getting alarmed when reports came in of alleged infiltration of weapons from France and of a high level of agitation in some garrisons and among workers in Andalucía.

[50] For the denials of the CNT see *SO* 12, 14, 15, 17, 18 Oct. 1930; and a special letter from Pestaña in prison in ibid. 23 Oct. 1930. For discrepancies in the CNT see Solá Cañizares, *El Moviment*, pp. 56–8. For Maura's plan and his meeting with the Revolutionary Committee see the testimony of the participants, in ibid. 16–25, 19–22 (quoting Rovira i Virgili in *La Nau* 7 July 1931). The CNT's decision in Peirats, *Los Anarquistas*, pp. 27–31 (quoting Peiró).

A *coup* was indeed being prepared for 18 November. But an apolitical strike of the UGT on 15 November,[51] a strike which put the government on full alert, made it obligatory to postpone the *coup*. The Catalan Revolutionary Committee, however, under the pressure of the *Cenetistas* Pou and Magriñá, was tempted to launch its own coup, and the CNT went on a revolutionary strike from 17 November up to the twentieth, thus causing the arrest of hundreds of its militants. Only after a personal intervention of Maura and Rafael Sánchez Guerra did the CNT stop its strike, in order to give a chance to a more carefully planned *coup* in December. These constant delays caused many officers to desert the whole movement, and, in order to curb the desertions, Queipo de Llano's Military Committee was tempted to stage a separate *coup* on 26 November, without even consulting the Provisional Government. However, the sudden escape of Franco from prison the day before jeopardized the plan, by putting the authorities on the alert once more.[52]

The reluctance of the Provisional Government to be pushed by extremist elements, and its feeble co-ordination with the military and the unions, combined to produce the tragedy of Jaca. This consequently contributed to the failure of the official movement planned for 15 December. Throughout the last days of November and the beginning of December, garrisons in Madrid, Valencia, Logroño, Huesca, and Jaca were said to be engaged in last-minute preparations. Members of the Provisional Government were appointed to lead and supervise the *coup* in the provinces, and the unions were committed to a general strike. But then the garrison of the northern town of Jaca acted precipitately. Captain Galán, the allegedly extremist leader of the local Revolutionary Committee, had been exerting pressure on the Provisional Government since October to make up its mind on a definite zero hour, arguing that weather conditions in the north might jeopardize a military action if it was not

[51] See below, pp. 132-133.
[52] Mola's report on agitation in his *Obras*, pp. 429-32; Queipo, *El Movimiento*, p. 80, on the postponement of the *coup* because of the Socialist strike. For the movement in Catalonia and Maura's intervention see *LV* 18-22 Nov. 1930; R. Sánchez Guerra, *Proceso*, pp. 27-31; Solá Cañizares, *El Moviment*, pp. 64-71; and Peirats, *Los Anarquistas*, pp. 65-6. For Franco's escape and the military *coup* of 26 Nov. see R. Franco, *Madrid*, pp. 139-46.

carried out before the winter snow. On 11 December Galán informed Madrid that he was to strike on the next day. This reflected the flimsiness of the revolutionary machine. It is hardly conceivable that he would have done so had he known that the whole movement was scheduled for the fifteenth. Therefore, on the same night of the eleventh, Casares Quiroga and Graco Marsá were sent to Jaca to dissuade him. Though Casares rushed to sleep in a local hotel, Graco Marsá displayed a greater sense of responsibility by trying, that same night, to convince Galán to postpone his own rising to the fifteenth, warning him that the Provisional Government was determined neither to support him directly, nor to follow in his footsteps, but rather to isolate his excessively revolutionary zeal. The radical members of the FUE who were in Jaca to participate in the rising did not represent anyone but themselves. But Galán's feelings that the Captain General of Aragon was preparing measures to crush his plot, and his claim about an agreement that he had with the workers in Zaragoza that they should launch a strike simultaneously with his *coup*, made his decision unshakable. On the twelfth, Galán's regiment took over the town, declared the Republic and embarked upon an ill-organized march towards the provincial capital, Huesca. But the fact that Zaragoza's railway workers did not go on strike, and that the Provisional Government did not try to force the Government to scatter its efforts by advancing the nationwide movement, enabled the authorities to move troops from Zaragoza. In a bloody encounter, Galán's regiment was dispersed, and he surrendered together with his lieutenant Captain García Hernández.[53]

Though the rebellion of Jaca was a failure, the execution of Galán and García Hernández one day later, contributed, in Lerroux's words, 'to strengthen the revolutionary architecture'.

[53] For preparations of the movement of 15 December see Mola, *Obras*, pp. 471–5; Queipo, *El Movimiento*, pp. 81–2; Prieto, *Convulsiones* i, 62, ii, 323–4. For Galán see Graco Marsá, *La Sublevación de Jaca. Relato de un Rebelde*, pp. 37–42, 43–51, 57–9, 70–71, 79–80, 93–199 and *La Gaceta de la Revolución* 12 Feb. 1931. For the alienation between Galán's 'anarchism' and the Provisional Government's moderation see M. Maura, *Así*, pp. 111–12; and Cesar Falcón, *Crítica de la Revolución*, pp. 54–9. For the tremendous impact of the failure to strike in Zaragoza see Queipo, op. cit. 127; Berenguer, *De la Dictadura*, pp. 242–3. For the FUE see *ABC* 16 Dec. 1930; and a private conversation with Arturo Soria.

The true nature of Galán either as an opportunist or as a utopian communist became irrelevant, once the republicans decided to cultivate his myth. Songs were composed and spread in the streets, the king was blamed for refusing an amnesty, and the most minor details of the execution were put before the public. This campaign was so harmful to the cause of the Monarchy that Cortés Cavanillas, a monarchist panegyrist, alleged that the judge in Galán's trial was a mason who decided deliberately to stimulate the anti-monarchist campaign, by sentencing the captains to death. The judge's version of the story does not imply either this or the personal responsibility of the king. But the myth was there. And the monarchist press, by distorting and exaggerating Galán's revolutionism, only contributed to make a martyr out of him, as in the case of Ferrer in 1909.[54]

However, once Galán had failed, the 'official' movement was condemned to a similar fate. On 14 December, most of the members of the Provisional Government were arrested, and many officers started to desert, especially when they realized that the Socialists did not intend to launch their promised strike in Madrid on the next day. They were probably, as Mola alleged, deterred by Galán's execution. Others were arrested in the provinces, and some went abroad with members of the Provisional Government like Prieto and Marcelino Domingo. A decree at the beginning of December, meeting the professional demands of the artillery, might also help to explain the desertions. In such circumstances, the taking over of the Cuatro Vientos military airfield by Ramón Franco and Queipo de Llano on 15 December, could hardly have saved the movement, though it did save their 'honour'. Franco flew over the capital, but was reluctant to bombard the royal palace and to kill innocent children. The republican leaflets that he threw out instead did not seem to have any great effect on the population once the leadership of the movement vanished; both Queipo

<hr />

[54] Lerroux in his *Pequeña Historia*, pp. 87–8. For the myth see *El Republicano, Detalles Rigurosamente exactos del Fusilamiento del Capitán Galán in HMM A/1310; La Gaceta de la Revolución* 12 Feb. 1931; and the hymns in Balbontín, *Romancero del Pueblo Español*, pp. 83–108. J. Cortés-Cavanillas, *Alfonso XIII*, p. 189. The version of the judge is in José Casado García, *Porqué Condené a los Capitanes Galán y García Hernández?*, especially pp. 16, 28. For the monarchists' embarrassment see Benigno Varela, *Cartas*, pp. xiv–xv.

and Franco rushed to find shelter in Portugal when loyal troops came to take over the airfield.[55]

In Barcelona, the 'December revolution' was no less a failure. The constant delays and the lack of coherence in the conglomeration that composed the Revolutionary Committee made it a farce. The Catalans opposed the 'españolista' style of the manifesto written by Lerroux for the occasion. They formulated their own, emphasizing that 'the Republic would mean the recognition of the San Sebastián pact', and calling on the CNT not to exceed the peaceful limits of the revolution. But, in a separate manifesto, the CNT claimed that its members were committed 'to carry out the political transformation of the Spanish state by revolutionary means', though it promised to make a 'pacific' revolution. In any case there was very little concrete action. A column that was supposed to depart from Lérida to assist the Jaca mutineers failed to materialize. On 14 December, an attempt by Anarcho-Syndicalists and a handful of soldiers to take over an armament store in Prat de Llobregat ended in a Quixotic failure and in the arrest of the two local CNT leaders, Pou and Magriñá. Moreover, on the next day only the small Socialist unions in Barcelona went on strike, while the massive CNT hesitated to do so once it realized that the Socialists in Madrid had not fulfilled their promises. However, neither the strike that finally started on the sixteenth, nor an abortive attempt to carry out a 'Catalan Cuatro Vientos' by occupying the airfield of Prat de Llobregat, saved the movement from failure. The authorities were on full alert, and the Civil Guard and the *Somatén* fully mobilized. Without serious military assistance and a determined leadership, it was hardly possible to succeed in such circumstances. And on 18 December the demoralized Revolutionary Committee of Catalonia was dissolved.[56]

[55] For the Socialists see below, pp. 148–151. For arrests and desertions see Queipo, *El Movimiento*, pp. 121–2, 126; Mola, *Obras*, 518, 544–5, 618–19; Prieto, *De Mi Vida* i, 102–5; Marcelino Domingo in *Vanguardia*, Badajoz, 23 Mar. 1931; Azaña in *Estampa* 6 May 1931; and R. Sánchez Guerra, *Proceso*, pp. 42–3. For the decree see *ABC* 2 Dec. 1930. For Cuatro Vientos see Queipo, op. cit. 91–113; Franco, *Madrid*, pp. 163–175. For the normal aspect of the town see F.O. 371/15042: Grahame to Henderson, 16 Dec. 1930.

[56] See the detailed accounts of the participants: Solá Cañizares, *El Moviment*, pp. 75–80, 84–5, 88, 91–3, 97–104, 107–8, 111–13; R. Sánchez Guerra, *Proceso*, pp. 49–53, 66–8, 76–84, 91–3; see also *The Times* 18 Dec. 1930. For the authorities' precautions see AHN Leg. 42: telephone conferences between the Minister of the Interior and the Governor of Barcelona, 15 Dec. 1930, nos. 1057, 1097.

The provinces, however, responded more faithfully than Madrid and Barcelona, creating the impression that the less controlled and less 'bureaucratized' movements were more genuinely revolutionary. *Cenetista* and Communist strikes that had been taking place since early December gained momentum once the Socialist UGT joined in on 15 December. The extension of the strikes alarmed the government, and in Alicante it was necessary to use the Foreign Legion, especially brought from Morocco, in order to crush what threatened to become a popular uprising. Disturbances and bloody confrontations took place in several villages of that province as well as in the province of Valencia, in San Sebastián, and in Gijón. Telegraphic communications were interrupted, and railways were destroyed in Elche, Elda, Monovar and Novelda. Conservative opinion was hysterically alarmed. *ABC* alluded to the Kerenskian role of Alcalá Zamora, when it claimed that the conservative Republic was not possible in Spain. Berenguer publicly accused 'international communism' as the main factor behind the scenes. Indeed, Trotsky was fascinated by the 'revolutionary symptoms' of the December incidents, precisely because they were not controlled by the Provisional Government, then in prison. The attempt of the republicans to credit themselves with the 'overwhelming republican character' of the movement was true only in the sense that republicanism was understood as any public protest against the Monarchy.[57]

In spite of its failure, the December movement made manifest that

The revolutionary spirit has invaded everything, absolutely everything, from the humblest up to the highest social classes. Workers, students, civil servants, industrialists, merchants, rentiers, men of liberal professions, the military, and even priests were represented in the

[57] For the strikes in the provinces since early December see Mola, *Obras*, p. 480; *ABC* 6 Dec. 1930; *SO* 10–13 Dec. 1930. For the revolutionary strikes since the fifteenth see *ABC* 17–20 Dec. 1930; and AHN Leg. 42: circular 15/853, 19 Dec. 1930 providing a map of the strikes. For the incidents in the provinces see Berenguer, *De la Dictadura*, pp. 255–7; Mola, op. cit. 558–63; *The Times* 16, 20 Dec. 1930; *ABC* 18, 20 Dec. 1930. For a detailed report on Alicante see *EC 7, 14 Apr. 1931*. For the right's reaction see *El* 19 Dec. 1930; *ABC* 24 Dec. 1930; and Berenguer in ibid. 30 Dec. 1930. Leon Trotsky, *Escritos Sobre España*, p. 25. For a similar line of analysis see C. Falcón, *Crítica de la Revolución*, pp. 73–4; and J. Maurín, *La Revolución Española*, pp. 73–4. The republican claim is in *El Republicano* in HMM A/1310; and *La Gaceta de la Revolución*, 13, 28 Jan. 1931.

December uprising, which was the beginning of the end of the Monarchy.[58]

It was the remarkably energetic reaction of the authorities that suppressed the movement at the start, scattered its leaders, and isolated its main centres of rebellion. Despite the fact that the clumsiness and the divisions within the republican movement had contributed considerably to the failure, a mood of optimism dominated republican circles. This optimism, according to Marañón, derived from 'contemplating how the tide is rising'. The spontaneous uprising in small *pueblos*, it was argued, contradicted the thesis about lack of 'public spirit' in such places. The government, a republican clandestine publication added, had won a Pyrrhic victory 'because a discredited regime is a defeated one'.[59]

To cultivate this image of the regime, rather than to bring it down was the aim of the constant conspiratorial activity led by an isolated Lerroux since mid-December. It could hardly be otherwise when the CNT manifested a clear distrust of the Republicans, and bitterly criticized their consistent unwillingness to support a popular movement. The CNT was now mainly interested in legalizing its syndicates, and in releasing its militants from prison. Both, it felt, could not be achieved by adhering to more abortive attempts. Neither were the Socialists a very reliable partner for revolutions. Their pro-collaborationist leaders were either in exile or in prison. And the decision of the Executives of their movement, at the beginning of February, to collaborate with 'anti-monarchist elements' was unlikely to be interpreted by anti-collaborationist leaders like Besteiro and Saborit as leading to an involvement in another revolution. Lerroux's pathetic manifesto applying for unity among the 'forces of December' and praising them for fulfilling their commitment—an attempt to attract the Socialists who failed to

---

[58] Mola, op. cit. 480.

[59] For the authorities' reaction see a few of many examples in *AHN* Leg. 42: 'El Movimiento Revolucionario 1930', circulars no. 126, 728, 745, 764, 773, 765, 13–15 Dec. 1930 (orders to mobilize loyal forces, Civil Guard etc., occupation of strategic points, key buildings etc.). For the crucial role of the Civil Guard in Valencia see ibid.: Chief of the Civil Guard in Valencia to the Minister of the Interior, 20 Dec. 1930 no. 1176. Marañón to Unamuno, 17 Dec. 1930 in UA. The clandestine publication is *La Gaceta de la Revolución*, 13 Jan. 1931.

strike in Madrid—did not diminish his isolation. Neither did he seem to have any substantial support in the army. Furthermore, Lerroux who, conspicuously enough, was not arrested like other members of the Provisional Government because of a certain sympathy towards him among the authorities, was not trusted by his colleagues. Alcalá Zamora, from his cell in the Model Prison, refused to deliver 'secret' information to Lerroux; and he was left to conspire mainly with a limited circle of friends from the Radical party. The Model Prison, rather than the revolution, was since December the 'palace of Spanish honour' to which a heterogeneous crowd came to pay daily homage to the new martyrs of the cause, the members of the Provisional Government.[60]

Nevertheless, Lerroux's Revolutionary Committee was active in harassing the authorities and the regime. He appealed from the pages of *La Gaceta de la Revolución* to the army and to the Civil Guard to join the republican movement, promising them better material conditions. He even met General Sanjurjo, the commander of that corps, in an attempt to enlist him—an amazing meeting, considering that Lerroux was then 'wanted' for conspiracy. In his contacts with the provincial Revolutionary Committees, Lerroux urged them constantly not to give the Monarchy a moment of truce, in order to push it into the dilemma of having to choose between a new dictatorship or a Constituent Cortes, 'both steps towards the Republic'. Rumours about imaginary or real *coups* spread constantly. To such a rumour was attributed a sharp drop in the value of the peseta, at the beginning of January. At the middle of February another coup was said to be imminent. Sánchez Román, Jiménez de Asua, and Rafael Sánchez Guerra were in a conspiracy, which involved also the air force in Getafe. It seemed, however, that this obscure plot was not fully supported by Lerroux. The clandestine manifesto of the conspirators did not even mention the word 'Republic', but only the 'red flag of revolution'. In a

[60] For the CNT see Mola, op. cit. 632–3; *SO* 17, 19, 21 Feb. 1931. For the Socialists see *BUGT* Feb. 1931; Lerroux's manifesto is in Villanueva, *No Pasa Nada!*, pp. 151–4. For the army see Mola, op. cit. 604–9, 634–5; and Berenguer, *De la Dictadura*, pp. 350–1. For not arresting Lerroux see Mola, op. cit. 518; Hoyos y Vinent, *Mi Testimonio*, pp. 59, 60–2. For Lerroux's isolation see his *Pequeña Historia*, pp. 80–2. For the Model see *La Gaceta de la Revolución* 9, 21 Jan. 1931; Maura, *Así*, pp. 107–8, 117; Largo Caballero, *Mis Recuerdos*, p. 114.

'message from the Spanish republicans to the French people' Lerroux stressed that he preferred to transform the regime by constituent elections. Meanwhile, the greatest contribution of his Revolutionary Committee to the anti-monarchist effort was perhaps its clandestine literary campaign. Mola could never know 'where the hell' were printed *El Murciélago*, *El Republicano*, and *La Gaceta de la Revolución*, in which the Monarchy, the 'half bred Cuban' and 'amnestied General' Berenguer, and the 'corrupt Gutierrez', the king, were constantly defamed.[61]

The failure of the attempts against the regime and the clandestinity into which the republican movement had been thrown, paved the way to its abstentionism in the elections summoned by the government. It was both a consequence of lack of political liberties and a means to bring down the Berenguer government, which they had failed to overthrow by conspiracies.

It is evident that a clear-cut abstentionist attitude was adopted only by the end of 1930. Electoral preparations were being made by Republican parties throughout that year. The Radical party was constantly urging its members to check whether they were included in the electoral census, as it had 'a tremendous importance for the political future of the country'. It even supported the idea of holding a general election before the municipal elections, claiming that the Cortes would amend the Municipal Statute, and then the municipal elections could be held more democratically. Electoral abstention was, anyway, dismissed as leading nowhere. A similar attitude was adopted by all the Republican parties in Catalonia. In mid-September, all these parties even set up a common committee to discuss electoral matters and to press for larger parliamentary representation for Catalonia. By the end of that month, the electoral tension in Barcelona was so great, that the *Ateneo Barcelonés* decided not to allow any more political meetings. The national assembly of Alianza Republicana rejected on 30 September a

---

[61] For the appeal to the army and the Civil Guard see *La Gaceta de la Revolución* 28 Jan., 12 Feb. 1931; and Lerroux, *Pequeña Historia*, pp. 83–4 on his conversation with Sanjurjo. Lerroux's message to the Provincial Committees is in Mola, *Obras*, pp. 579–580. For the Peseta see *The Times* 7 Jan. 1931. For the conspiracy of mid-February see R. Sánchez Guerra, *Proceso* pp. 130–2; Mola, op. cit. 667–9; and *LV* 18 Feb. 1931. Lerroux's message to the French is in *La Gaceta de la Revolución* 5 Feb. 1931. For the clandestine press see Mola, op. cit. 631.

motion declaring 'an absolute boycott of the monarchist state'. Indeed, it suggested that each party should separately and independently elaborate its attitude towards the elections. In that same meeting, Pedro Rico attacked electoral *retraimiento* as the legacy of a lack of civic education. He was aware that the next parliament would be 'illegal' and would neglect the issue of 'responsibility'. Yet, he believed that a Republican parliamentary opposition could run a very effective campaign against the Monarchy.[62]

However, after late September, when Republicans started to concentrate their energies in conspiracies, electoral activities were limited, and, after the failure of the 'December revolution' *retraimiento* was finally used as the last weapon against the government. In the national congress of the PRRS at the end of September abstention was adopted unanimously, amid a revolutionary euphoria. A 'party of struggle' was bound to be tamed by parliamentary routine, some members argued; while others suggested anarcho-syndicalist 'direct action' as the only appropriate means of struggle against the regime. Marcelino Domingo who in February 1930 claimed that whatever parliament was summoned, constituent or ordinary, would be bound to have a constituent character, now supported *retraimiento*. 'The new Cortes', he said, 'would be exactly like Primo's Assembly'.

Nor did the other parties engage in any electoral preparations during the autumn and the winter. The Radical Puig de Asprer rejected elections that would be held on the basis of the present Ayuntamientos dominated by Monarchists, and alleged that they would, anyway, be 'made' by the authorities. The left republican *Nueva España* claimed that, 'since there is no constitution', by participating in ordinary elections, Republicans would recognize *de jure* the constitutional personality of the regime. And Rafael Sánchez Guerra, a rightist Republican, could not but agree that 'lack of sincerity' and 'illegality' would be the predominating features of the coming elections. It was

---

[62] For the Radicals see *EP* 29 Mar., 1, 6 Apr., 3, 8 June, 27 July 1930. For the Catalan parties see *LV* 31 Aug., 16, 19, 24, 28 Sept. 1930. For Alianza see *Alianza* Sept.–Oct. 1930 (Pedro Rico's and also Rafael Guerra del Rio's speeches). See also Zugazagoitia in *NE* 11 Oct. 1930.

conspicuous that neither Alianza Republicana nor the Provisional Government elaborated a common electoral strategy, though the elections were imminent. By the end of December, the governors could provide the Ministry of Interior with hardly any information on Republican electoral activities, but only with 'rumours' about Republican candidates here and there. A month later most of the Republican parties signed a common declaration of abstention. Acció Catalana and Acció Republicana followed suit with a declaration that this 'illegal' parliament would be unable to give 'a constitutional solution to Catalan desires for autonomy'. Now, the *Junta Nacional* of Alianza Republicana called officially to its members to abstain, and *La Gaceta de la Revolución* clearly stressed the revolutionary aspect of the move. This was recognized with dismay by the monarchist *La Vanguardia*.[63]

The Berenguer government, which survived military *coups* and strikes, was finally brought down by this revolutionary abstentionism. It was against the background of the overwhelming *retraimiento* of the left, that the Monarchist Liberals decided to strike a final blow at the government.[64] By their abstention the Republicans had taken away the *raison d'être* of Berenguer's government: to bring the country back to 'normality' by means of ordinary elections.

[63] For the Radical Socialists see *EP* 28 Sept. 1930 (the congress); *El Sol* 3 Sept. 1930 (Albornoz); *El Liberal* 13 Feb.; *LV* 3 Aug.; *El Sol* 22 Oct. 1930 (Marcelino Domingo); Puig in *LV* 1 Nov. 1930; *NE* 11 Oct. 1930. See articles of R. Sánchez Guerra on 30 Jan., 9 Feb. 1931 in his *Un Año Histórico, España 1931*, pp. 39-45, 59-65. For the governors see reports in AHN Leg. 29: from Las Palmas, Córdoba, Alicante, Pontevedra, Tarragona, and Barcelona, 30 Dec. 1930 nos. 1580, 1594, 1558, 1596, 1588, 1559. The common abstention in *ABC* 31 Jan. 1931. The Catalans in *LV* 10 Feb. 1931; Alianza in *La Gaceta de la Revolución* 28 Jan., 12 Feb. 1931. The last reference is in *LV* 13 Feb. 1931.

[64] See below, pp. 204-205.

III

A DECISIVE REINFORCEMENT: REFORMIST SOCIALISM

Spanish Socialists were among the main beneficiaries of the Dictatorship. Both their party, the *Partido Socialista Obrero Español* (PSOE), and their union, the *Unión General de Trabajadores* (UGT), were relatively free to develop their regular activities. This enabled them to preserve their framework and even to increase their following. Being a well-organized and well-disciplined movement with an essentially social-democratic ideology, the Socialists became the main axis upon which the whole republican movement was to rest. It is evident, however, that the favours of the dictator made the Socialists reluctant to collaborate with a republican movement or with any oppositional trend. It was the weakness of the regime by mid-1929, a weakness which in the economic field threatened to undermine the social achievements of the last years, that brought the Socialists to join the choir of protest which gave the *coup de grace* to the exhausted Primo de Rivera. An emphasis on trade union issues, and a doctrinal 'anti-collaborationism' with bourgeois parties inherited from the past combined both during the Dictatorship and its aftermath, to jeopardize the Republicans' attempts to harness the Socialist movement to the anti-monarchist effort. Only when it became evident that the republican movement was 'serious' and that Socialist abstentionism might enable the extreme left to push the movement towards an uncontrolled revolution, did the Socialists join the Republican coalition. This was not done, however, without creating a breach between collaborationists and their opponents. This breach was, among other things, a struggle between rival factions for the leadership of the Socialist movement, a struggle which would continue throughout the Republic.

1. COLLABORATION WITH THE DICTATORSHIP, AND ISOLATION FROM THE LEFT

It was to be expected that, when Primo de Rivera rose in arms to end the reign of political parties, the Socialists, as strong opponents of the old regime, would not mourn. However, the military rising which, according to a common manifesto of the UGT and the PSOE, probably did not come as a surprise to the king, did not give rise to great satisfaction among Socialists. They expressed their fear that the military regime might intensify the war effort in Morocco. 'The people, therefore', they concluded in the same manifesto, 'should not support the military. The attitude of the working class should be to isolate the movement rather than to enlarge it'.[1] But the passive attitude of both the UGT and the PSOE, which would soon develop into collaboration with the Dictatorship, did not help to 'isolate' the uprising. The sporadic strikes of Communists and Syndicalists died out without creating an ambiance of resistance. The Socialists rejected an invitation from these elements to set up a 'committee of action against the war and the Dictatorship'. The Executives of both Socialist bodies warned their members against joining any initiative which they might be invited to join by 'well-intentioned but impatient people or by those who want to throw the proletariat into sterile movements which can only serve as a pretext for repression'.[2] The lessons of the 1917 abortive revolution in which the Socialists exposed their painfully cultivated organization to governmental repression, seemed to be fresh in the memory of Socialist leaders. Now they opted for opportunism.

The cautious reaction of the Socialists to the *coup d'état* was a manifestation of their lack of confidence in their capacity to carry on a revolutionary strike from which the working class would benefit. At most, they believed, it would result in a return to power of old politicians over the corpses of workers. The opportunistic conclusion was, therefore, to make the best of a bad bargain by exploiting the new situation for the sake of their organizations. This brought them to recommend a policy of dialogue with the new regime. They urged their representatives to intervene in any institution, such as the *Ayuntamientos* and *Diputaciones*, in which questions concerning the working class

[1] *ES* 13 Sept. 1923.
[2] *ES* 14, 18 Sept., 4 Oct. 1923; F.O. 371/9490: Howard to Curzon, 14 Sept. 1923 reporting on the lack of revolutionary ambiance. See for the rejection of extreme left appeals: J. Maurín, *Los Hombres de la Dictadura*, pp. 154-5.

might be discussed, instead of following the paths of 'false revolutionarism'. The proposals of the extreme left for a revolutionary proletarian front were thus rejected; and a sober decision was made to cultivate Socialist strength under Primo's protection at the expense of both the Anarcho-Syndicalists and the Communists. An appeal to Melquiades Alvarez by the ex-deputies of the Socialist minority to take measures, as president of the Congress, in order to establish 'a new civilian regime of effective liberty', was an indication of the lack of any revolutionary intention.[3]

The readiness of the Socialists to establish a dialogue with the Dictatorship corresponded with the aims of the dictator who affirmed that:

We are fundamentally concerned with the well-being of the working class; we strive to achieve a Christian and just equilibrium between the haves and the have nots who aspire by honest and legal means to become haves ... until a complete and harmonious association (between Capital and Labour) is achieved, there can be no social peace, nor maximization of output.

He called upon employers to sacrifice part of their profits in order to improve the cultural and economic standards of their workers, whom he urged to follow the teachings of 'the most patriotic and intelligent of Spanish Socialists, Pablo Iglesias ... who had never ... approved of violent actions'. Primo de Rivera believed that socialism should not be a political organization, but a socio-economic association which, so long as it acted within peaceful trade unionist lines, should enjoy all the freedom required for its development. He was determined to attract the Socialists to a *modus vivendi* with the state both because it isolated the violent Anarcho-Syndicalists, and because he considered them as a responsible element which could help him to lead the country towards economic progress—the major enterprise of the new regime—without the vicissitudes of violence and strikes.[4]

---

[3] M. Cordero, *Los Socialistas* pp. 54–5, 60–4 on Melquiades and the tactic decided upon. For this see also Arquistáin, *El Ocaso*, pp. 222–3; *ES* 22, 27 Sept. 1923. The Socialists' moderation was acclaimed by the bourgeois left: *El Sol* 27, 29 Sept. 1923.

[4] For the quotations from Primo's declarations see Révész, *Frente al Dictador*, pp. 104–10; *ES* 28 Sept. 1923; 27 June 1928; Calvo Sotelo, *Seis Años*, p. 330; and E. Aunós, *La Política Social de la Dictadura* pp. 31–3.

Asked by the dictator to be essentially *Pablistas*, the Socialists had no difficulty in adapting themselves to the new situation, while the Anarcho-Syndicalists went underground. Thus were opened the years of collaboration. The first overt step was made by Primo when he invited Llaneza, the Asturian miners' leader, with the approval of the Executives of both the UGT and the PSOE, to discuss workers' demands in two successive meetings. Llaneza came out from the meetings with the belief that 'none of the legitimate achievements of the workers is in danger'. A visit of the Duque de Tetuan, captain general of Madrid, to the *Casa del Pueblo* of Madrid ended in mutual praise and relations of confidence. And when the old Ayuntamientos and Diputaciones were dissolved, Primo de Rivera invited the Socialists to send their own representatives to the new bodies that replaced them, which they agreed to do as long as they were themselves allowed to designate their delegates.[5]

A greater participation was open to and was required from Socialists, as social legislation developed. In June 1924, the old *Instituto de Reformas Sociales* was abolished to be replaced by the *Consejo de Trabajo* in which a representation of the UGT similar to that on the old IRS was necessary: the Socialist members were Largo Caballero, Nuñez Tomas, Lucio Martínez, and Santiago Pérez Infante. The UGT found no reason to reject the invitation to the Consejo de Trabajo, since it only ratified an existing situation. But when on 13 September 1924 there appeared the decree creating the *Consejo de Estado* as a consultative body of ex-ministers and prominent personalities', and inviting a member of the Consejo de Trabajo to join it, it became a controversial question whether to agree to the designation of Largo Caballero by the Consejo de Trabajo as its representative in the Consejo de Estado. The Executive of the UGT unanimously approved Largo's designation, but in the Executive of the party, Fernando de los Ríos and Prieto considered this a deviation from a previous decision that the Socialists should themselves elect their representatives as well as the reflection of an excessive tendency to collaborate with the Dictatorship—a

---

[5] For Llaneza see *ES* 2, 5 Oct. 1923. For the Duque de Tetuan see Largo Caballero, *Mis Recuerdos*, p. 85. For city councillors see *ES* 14 Apr., 10 Nov. 1924. The Madrid Socialists vetoed a governmental designation of Arteaga, one of their members, as councillor: *ES* 10 Jan. 1928.

collaboration that now appeared political rather than social. The Executive of the PSOE refused to discuss the matter, claiming that it belonged to the jurisdiction of the UGT; this was a weak pretext, since the composition of both Executives was almost identical. And when, in December 1924, the National Committee of the party approved the *fait accompli*, Prieto announced his resignation from the Executive. Largo Caballero himself recognized that the Consejo de Estado was an undemocratically elected body, but he considered it as significant 'political advance' for the working class to be represented on so important a body.[6]

The extensive social legislation carried out by Aunós, the Minister of Labour, brought Socialist functionaries into other bodies on which both employers and the state were likewise represented. Such were the *Consejo de Administración y de Información Telegráfica*, the *Consejo Interventor de Cuentas de España* and the *Junta de Abastos*. Yet, in an effort to 'preserve the dignity' of Spanish socialism, Socialists withdrew from the *Junta de Subsistencias*, when it became dependent of Martínez Anido, the Minister of the Interior, with whom they refused to collaborate because of his image as the oppressor of the Barcelona Syndicalists; they likewise withdrew from the *Consejo de Economía Nacional* because of the participation of Catholic syndicates.[7]

The climax of Aunós' policies, and one which the Socialists considered as their major achievement, was the corporative organization established in November 1926 to deal with labour conflicts and social legislation, through joint committees of workers and employers, from the local and professional level up to the regional and national. This was the greatest contribution of the Dictatorship to the strengthening of Socialist organizations. The decree creating the *Comités Paritarios*—as these arbitration boards were called—stated that only the

[6] A. Ramos Oliveira, *Historia de España* ii, 476; Saborit, *Besteiro*, pp. 237–8; Largo Caballero, *Mis Recuerdos*, pp. 91–4—all of whom give a survey of the question. For a strongly favourable attitude to the participation in the Consejo de Estado see E. Santiago, *La UGT ante la Revolución*, pp. 40–4; and M. Cordero, *Los Socialistas*, pp. 65–67. See also *ES* 11 Dec. 1924; *El Sol* 12 Dec. 1924.

[7] For the social legislation and Socialists' participation in the various bodies, see full details in Aunós, *La Política Social*, pp. 33–83. For the withdrawal see E. Santiago, *La UGT*, pp. 39–40. For a criticism of the excessively bureaucratical features which the Socialist movement was acquiring through its participation in these bodies, see J. Andrade: *La Burocracia Reformista en el Movimiento Obrero*, p. 242.

organized proletariat should be represented in them. The Anarcho-Syndicalists, whose organizations were dissolved, rejected the C.P.s as opposed to the principle of 'direct action' against the employers; and the Catholic syndicates could hope to have a substantial representation only in their strongholds in Barcelona, Navarra, and the north. Thus the Socialists acquired the lion's share of working-class representation in the corporative organization, and, as if by royal decree, workers in the big cities joined the UGT, so that they could be represented in the committees.[8]

The most bitter opposition to the C.P.s came from the employers. At first, they welcomed the committees as 'elements of concord between the two antagonistic factors of production'; but they soon realized that most of the labour disputes were being decided in favour of the workers, mainly through the intervention of the state delegate. They complained that, whereas they had no choice but to accept the committees' decisions, the workers could always use the strike weapon, which they occasionally did when they disapproved of the decision of the committees. This agitated the employers who, in addition, alone bore the burden of financing the C.P.s. Furthermore, the C.P.s acquired legislative and executive functions which, so long as workers' hegemony was protected by the state delegate and there was no parliament in which the employers could present their grievances, became intolerable from the employers' point of view. Employers' organizations, therefore, opened a systematic campaign on behalf of a reform in the regulations of the C.P.s. In order to curb Socialist hegemony in them, the *Asociación de Estudios Sociales y Económicos*, essentially an employers' organization, suggested that the elections for the committees should be direct and individual

[8] For details of the corporative system see Aunós' *La política Social*, pp. 57–77; and his *La Reforma Corporativa del Estado*, pp. 129–39. See also Giuseppe Bottai, *Esperienza Corporativa*, pp. 419–30: The main difference from the Italian system was that in Spain it was voluntary, while in Italy obligatory. See *The Times* 25 July 1927 for the Syndicalists' attitude. For the Catholic syndicates' complaints against Socialists being preferred in the C.P.s see *Boletín del Sindicato Católico de Tipógragos y Similares*, Madrid Nov. 1928, Jan. 1929; and *El Dependiente Español. Organo de la Federación Nacional de Dependientes de Comercio, Industria y Banca*, Nov. 1928, on the complete victory of the UGT over the Catholic syndicates in the elections for C.P.s in Madrid and Bilbao. For an increase of 17,000 members due to the corporative system, see E. Santiago, *La UGT*, p. 45.

rather than on corporative lines, so that unorganized workers could also be elected. Employers also asked that the presidents and secretaries of the C.P.s should be elected by the committees themselves rather than appointed by the government, that the state should share the financial burden of the committees, and that they should deal exclusively with questions of arbitration and conciliation rather than legislation. None of these demands was met by Aunós, who was proud of the corporative organization as it was originally promulgated. On more than one occasion he reassured workers' leaders of his determination to keep the system intact. Neither were the attempts of some employers to delay the formation of the C.P.s in their industries successful.[9]

The Socialists were the most fervent defenders of the C.P.s. As soon as the decree was promulgated, they started a widespread campaign aimed at urging the workers to join in committees through UGT representatives, to fight the employers' opposition, and to justify their acceptance of the C.P.s on doctrinal grounds as against their critics from the left. To the workers they explained that by joining the C.P.s they would pursue 'the same norms of tolerance and equanimity' which both the UGT and the PSOE had maintained ever since their foundation. Largo Caballero tried to reassure those purists who feared that the acceptance of the corporative organization meant the abandonment of the class struggle. 'We have only canalized it into legal channels,' he said, and added, 'this is an aspect of economic democracy which will save the national economy from upheavals by meeting the just demands which are the minimum programme of the UGT and the PSOE.' In a speech in Zaragoza, he called for the 'humanization of the class struggle', claiming that the

---

[9] For employers' attitude to the C.P.s, see *Industria, Organo de la Cámara oficial de Industria de Madrid* Dec. 1926, Oct. 1928; *LE* 12, 21 Jan. 1929; *ED* 22 Jan. 1929, on the strike in the Barcelona exhibition as an example of workers' reaction to an adverse verdict of the C.P. For Aunós' unshaken stand in front of employers' demands see *Boletín de la Cámara oficial de Comercio e Industria de Lérida y su Provincia* Jan.–Mar. 1929; *España Comercial* July 1928; *BUGT* Mar. 29; and *ES* 13 Feb. 1929, 12 Jan. 1930. The *Boletín oficial de la Sociedad General de Obreros Gasistas, Electricistas, Teléfonos, Aguas y Similares de Madrid* June 1928 complained that dilatory tactics of employers had prevented the establishment of C.P.s in their industries, but a few months later they had to give up, and the C.P.s were finally set up; for this see *La Turbina. Revista de la Federación Nacional de Obreros de la Industria de Gas, electricidad y similares de España*, Madrid, Mar. 1929.

systematic use of the strike weapon was no longer adequate when workers could achieve almost all their aspirations by peaceful means. Largo Caballero, Wenceslao Carrillo, and Saborit made it clear that they would have accepted the C.P.s even if they had known that no material gains would come out of them for the workers, because a Socialist abstention would have given the hegemony in the C.P.s to their enemies; all the more so when so many concrete achievements, such as favourable collective contracts and the recognition of the UGT as the main workers' organization in the country with a clear juridical personality, were involved. The mere fact that the employers were bitter opponents of the C.P.s was, according to Saborit, an indication that 'they were a substantial advance in social legislation'.[10]

Moreover, under the pretext of spreading the idea of the C.P.s among workers, hundreds of meetings were held by Socialist propagandists all over the country to consolidate and enlarge their organizations. This is the more striking when it is compared with the frequent restrictions imposed on socialist propaganda before the creation of the C.P.s. Local branches had been forced to organize propaganda under the pretext of 'too frequent' administrative meetings, and national leaders were prevented from attending even May Day gatherings in the provinces. After the promulgation of the decree on corporative organization, propaganda became free, both on a regional and national scale.[11]

[10] For an exposition of the advantages of the C.P.s and Socialist attitude towards them see *ES* 27 Jan., 12 Nov. 1927; Largo's speeches in ibid. 4 Mar. 1927, 3, 17 Jan., 12 Apr. 1929 and his articles in 9–15 Mar. 1929; and *BUGT* Oct. 1929. See the speeches of W. Carillo and Saborit in *La Turbina* Mar. 1929; Saborit's speeches in Bilbao and Teruel in *ES* 20 Nov. 1927, 31 Mar. 1929; de los Ríos in Bilbao *ES* 12 Jan. 1929. See the editorials in *ES* 31 Oct., 22 Sept. 1928 against *El Debate's* favourable attitude to the employers' point of view. For a brief defence on the C.P.s see also E. Santiago, *La UGT*, pp. 25–6, 31–5, 44; and M. Cordero, *Los Socialistas*, pp. 64–5.

[11] For restrictions before November 1926 see AHN Leg. 45: circulars nos. 142, 278, 9 Mar., 14 Apr. 1926; Leg. 50: circulars nos. 741, 1063, 24 Apr. 1924, 28 Apr. 1925. For administrative meetings see ibid. Leg. 51: Governor Alicante to Ministry of the Interior, 4 Oct. 1926 no. 624. For the upsurge of propaganda after November 1926 see Maurín, *Los Hombres*, p. 189; Araquistáin in S. Canals, *La Caída de la Monarquía*, p. 33. See also Governors' reports on unrestricted campaigns of propaganda in AHN Leg. 45: Governor Alicante to the Ministry of the Interior 7, 8 Oct. 1928 nos. 4342, 4354, 4363; Governor of Málaga to the Ministry of the Interior 7 June 1927 no. 176 on six meetings organized by Saborit in four days.

However, Socialist organs and speakers were in a constant defensive stance when confronted by criticism from politicians, republicans, and from their own ranks. They rejected the derogatory term 'collaborationism' given to what they chose to call 'interventionism', an old Socialist norm of conduct. 'We do not like to be', argued an editorial, 'cannon fodder in the struggle of the bourgeoisie and the old regime against the Dictatorship. We have a revolution of our own which we will carry out when the time comes.' Meanwhile, neglect of the 'material needs' of the working class because of lack of political liberties would be folly both because it would not advance the struggle against the Dictatorship, and because Socialists had continued to fight on behalf of the working class throughout the Restoration period despite frequent suspensions of the constitutional guarantees. Furthermore, the Dictatorship was, according to Besteiro, more favourable to the workers' cause than the old regime. 'Therefore', he concluded, 'we are ready to suffer all the inevitable criticisms provided that Spain be freed from . . . the traditional obstacles.' Legalist scruples were rejected by Saborit and Federico Androve, when they claimed that the old regime was also established by a *coup d'état*—that of Sagunto in 1874—while the system of electoral corruption run by the old parties created institutions as undemocratic as the Ayuntamientos set up by Primo, and yet everyone had collaborated with them.[12]

The main challenge to these tactics within the party came from Prieto, Fernando de los Rios, and Teodomiro Menéndez. At the twelfth congress of the party, in July 1928, Menéndez criticized those who had led the party to a shameful collaboration and called for an immediate retreat from Ayuntamientos and from the *Consejo de Estado* 'so that the party could enter upon a period of democratic action.' Prieto followed suit with the same argument and claimed that he also shared Fernando de los Ríos' opinion. Besteiro, Largo, and Saborit defended the tactics pursued until then, tactics which, according to Saborit, had

[12] *ES* 25 Mar. 1924, 25 Jan. 1929. For Saborit's intensive campaign explaining the issue of 'collaboration' see his speeches in Villena, Petrel, Alcoy, Palencia, Barruelo, in ibid. 13, 16 Apr., 20 July 1929; and his declaration there 20 Nov. 1929. For Androve see ibid. 11 Nov. 1924. For Besteiro 10 Feb. 1925. For Largo see *Unión General de Trabajadores, Semanario* 14 Oct. 1926.

saved the Socialist movement from collapse. As far as Largo's participation in the Consejo de Estado was concerned, the 'collaborationists' claimed that it was a matter for the UGT to discuss, and that those who brought the question to the party congress were leading a vindictive campaign against Largo Caballero.

The final vote, approving the tactics pursued by the party by 5,064 to 740, proved that those who represented 'the audacious and adventurist spirit characteristic of men who had been educated exclusively for political action', were in the minority, while the hegemony of those who represented 'the methodical, constructive spirit . . . that gives priority to concrete matters, like wages and social laws', remained unshaken.[13]

Under the leadership of the collaborationists, a spectacular increase in UGT activities took place during the Dictatorship. This made the UGT the strongest and best-organized union in the country. However, it must be stressed that the increase in membership was much smaller than might have been expected under such favourable circumstances. One obvious reason is that the main bulk of the Anarcho-Syndicalists seemed to prefer to join the *Sindicato Libre* in Catalonia rather than Socialist organizations. Despite the special efforts made by the UGT to attract the Catalan proletariat, the Catalan workers remained indifferent. Special appeals were made to members of the *Sindicato Unico* to adhere to the UGT once their centres had vanished; prominent Socialists made frequent propaganda tours in Catalonia announcing the imminence of a 'new era' for the Catalan working class; and Pablo Iglesias appealed emotionally from his sick-bed to Catalan workers to abandon their 'false radicalism . . . ominous apoliticism and stupid terrorism . . . the day that the Catalan proletariat joins the UGT will be a day of mourning for Spanish employers.' Yet this day did not come, and Socialists had to confess that Catalan workers were basically hostile to socialism. They were 'subordinated to the bourgeoisie and ignorant of both their rights and their duties'. Catalonia had its own version of socialism in a tiny new party—the *Unió Socialista de Catalunya*—with a mouthpiece of its own—*La Justicia*

---

[13] The reports on the congress in *ES* 1, 3, 5, 10 July 1928. For Teodomiro Menéndez as the representative of a minor trend in the Federacion Socialista de Asturias see David Ruiz Gonzalez, *El Movimiento Obrero en Asturias*, pp. 189, 206–8. Llaneza, a supporter of the majority line, was a more authentic representative of Asturias.

Social—which preached the united front of the proletariat, which Socialists opposed as 'a manœuvre of the paid agents of Moscow'. The Socialists were equally hostile to the Catalanist nationalistic features of the new party. Thus, with the UGT leading a precarious existence in Catalonia throughout the Dictatorship, and the PSOE claiming to have no more than 267 affiliates in the region, it would not be wrong to conclude that the impressive Socialist campaign in Catalonia bore no fruit.[14]

However, the number of affiliates was not the only indication of strength. The greatest achievement of the UGT was that it became the only syndical organization with a national apparatus and was thus enabled to strike roots in most Spanish provinces. The increase in membership in the year after the fall of the Dictatorship was a direct consequence of the systematic labour of organization and propaganda during the Dictatorship.[15]

Such was the propaganda carried on in country districts in Galicia, Aragón, Extremadura, Andalucia, Levante, and New

[14] For Anarcho-Syndicalists joining the Sindicato Libre see *Boletín de la Agrupación Socialista Madrileña* 1ᵉ semestre 1930; G. Brenan, *The Spanish Labyrinth*, p. 184. For the hegemony of the libre in Catalonia and the spectacular increase in its membership during the Dictatorship see below, p. 174. For the widespread Socialist propaganda in Catalonia see *ES* 11 Oct. 1923, 6 Sept. 1925, 13 Sept. 1925 (a week tour by Saborit there); 24 Sept., 16 Nov. 1929 (propaganda of T. Gómez among railway workers). For limited activities of the Catalan Federation of the UGT see for example *LV* 6 Mar., 21 July, 11 Aug. 1929. And a weekly supplement of *El Socialista* dedicated to Catalonia from September 1925 onwards. For the Unió Socialista see *ES* 12 Sept., 24 Oct. 1923, 14 Apr., 15 Aug., 8 Dec. 1924.

[15] The available data on the membership of the UGT provide the following picture, according to *Anuario Estadístico* 1931; *ES* 31 Dec. 1923, 1 Mar. 1924; E. Santiago *La UGT* p. 45; and J. Maurín, *Los hombres*, p. 198:

December 1923   −210,977 affiliates in 1,275 sections
July 1927   −223,349 affiliates in 1,347 sections
December 1929   −228,501 affiliates in 1,511 sections

It should be taken into account that during the same period 15,000 affiliates left the UGT, mostly rural workers, whom the Socialists were not in a position to favour because C.P.s did not exist in the rural areas, and because of the predominance of Catholic syndicates there. This makes the increase in the number of urban workers due to the C.P.s all the more impressive, see for this E. Santiago, *La UGT*, p. 45; *El Dependiente Español* Sept. 1928. For the increase during 1930 from 228,501 members to 277,011, more than during all the seven years of Dictatorship, see also *Anuario Estadístico* 1931. When dealing with all these figures one must also bear in mind that the real number of affiliates might have been bigger than the number of those who paid their membership fees and consequently figured in the statistics. See *BUGT* Feb. 1929 lamenting this fact.

Castile. It was aimed at attracting tenants, small landowners as well as landless workers. By the beginning of 1924, in spite of governmental restrictions, Socialist emissaries began to explain the basic principles of socialism to rural workers, urging them to set up their local and regional organizations with the aim of merging them in a national federation. A special weekly supplement was annexed to *El Socialista* to provide information on rural matters and to spread socialism in rural districts. To the Galician peasants UGT propagandists promised the abolition of caciquismo and the *foros*. They also urged those who had supported revolutionary 'direct action' to join a peaceful and more promising socialism. For Extremadura and Andalucía, the Socialist formula was that of expropriation of latifundios. The landless peasants in those regions were told that 'land should not be private property . . . we want to socialize land and make it collective property'. The simplistic slogan of the *reparto* was dismissed as demagogical, since only a well-organized collectivization could avoid a process by which the rich would buy the land owned by poor peasants who lacked adequate means to exploit it, thus again creating latifundios. An attempt was also made to pacify small landowners in Levante, Aragon, and Castile. Cordero assured them 'we are not enemies of small property . . . we make a clear distinction between the property exploited by the small peasant for his own living . . . and capitalist property'. The Socialists also presented themselves as defenders of tenants against their landlords. They demanded more favourable tenancy contracts which would guarantee the tenant against arbitrary eviction and give him compensation for improvements. A substantial part of Socialist propaganda was directed at agricultural workers. Their unionization was presented as the only means of improving living conditions, for increasing wages, and for extending to them the benefits of social legislation already enjoyed by industrial workers. The principle that work should be first given to local workers before cheap labour was imported from outside, a principle which Largo Caballero would convert into law as Minister of Labour of the Republic, was already defended as a means of sustaining wage levels.[16]

[16] The information of *El Socialista* on propaganda in rural districts is immense. See for example *ES* 18 July, 30 Oct. 1924, 17 July 1925, 9 Mar., 17 Nov. 1926; and

The promulgation in May 1928 of the decree extending the corporative organization to the countryside was obviously welcomed by Socialists who hoped that 'the legitimate representatives of agricultural workers', namely the Socialists, would dominate the committees. But the *Confederación Nacional Católico Agraria*, which had a strong following in some rural areas, was anxious to prevent the formation of the C.P.s which, it feared, could become the Trojan horse through which socialism would infiltrate into the countryside and thus become the 'instrument of the revolution'. Moreover, the decree explicitly favoured the Socialists by providing representation in the C.P.s for minorities, which in rural areas were the Socialists, whereas in urban C.P.s, where Socialists were in the majority, no representation was provided for minorities. The pressure of landlords and the opposition of Catholic syndicates dictated the government's dilatory tactics which resulted in the virtual abolition of the decree. In spite of the indefatigable labour of Lucio Martínez (the UGT's representative in the *Comisión Interina de Corporaciones Agrícolas*) on behalf of the implantation of the Committees, these were not set up. Nevertheless, socialist propaganda in rural districts continued as 'the task of sowing' socialist ideas and principles of organization. This was enough to alarm the right who saw 'a well organized Socialist Party infiltrating the countryside in order to capture the strong force of social conservation that is the peasant'.[17]

However, despite the effort to build a rural power base, agricultural workers did not join Socialist organizations, and

---

Vicente Risco, *El Problema Político de Galicia*, p. 189 (for Galicia). For Andalucía and Extremadura see *ES* 15 May 1924, 18 Jan., 11-21 May 1929 and *BUGT* Feb. 1929. For small landowners see *ES* 9 Apr., 5 Sept., 3 Oct. 1924, 21, 27 Mar. 1929. For small tenants see *Unión General de Trabajadores. Semanario* 7, 14 Oct. 1926; and *ES* 1 June 1928, 9 Apr. 1929. Similar demands were made on behalf of the Catalan Rabassaires, see *ES* 14 Aug. 1925. For agricultural workers see ibid. 8 Mar., 28 June 1929. See also Largo's article in *BUGT* Apr. 1929 summing up Socialist agrarian propaganda and May Day demands.

[17] *ES* 25, 26 May, 1928 welcoming the decree. For opposition from the right and Catholics see Aunós, *España en Crisis*, p. 292; *El Diario de Valencia* quoted in *ES* 1 June 1928; and *ABC* quoted in *ES* 31 May 1929; see also ibid. 12 Oct. 1928. See AHN Leg. 45: Governor of Pontevedra to the Ministry of the Interior, 28 June 1927 no. 691; the Ministry of the Interior to Governor Salamanca, 13 Mar. 1926 no. 247; Leg. 51: Liga Nacional de Campesinos to Ministry of the Interior 31 May 1926 no. 247, all reflecting the pressure from the right against Socialists infiltration to the countryside. For the

many even deserted them. The UGT remained throughout the Dictatorship an essentially urban organization. This was the factor which originated the idea of creating the *Federaciones Nacionales de Industria* in order to create industrial rather than craft unions. These big concentrations would be a more appropriate means of struggle against employers on a national scale and, as Largo Caballero pretentiously put it, 'will enable us to act like the organized workers in England who, when they assume power, do it without breaking with the existing political situation'. Rather than a syndical weapon, the new structure, which was approved by a congress of the UGT in September 1928, was the instrument which the UGT hoped would enable it to act on a national scale and 'face national problems' instead of local and narrow labour demands.[18]

But as long as the political situation remained unchanged, the syndicates of the UGT continued to concentrate on labour issues through the C.P.s, and only occasionally made use of strikes. The *Sindicato Minero de Asturias* even agreed to a wage reduction in order to save Spanish coal mines from an imminent crisis due to the competition of British coal; but when conditions deteriorated even the authority of Llaneza could not prevent a strike. However, Primo de Rivera was able to keep the Sindicato Minero in a generally docile attitude. Even when the government decided to tax workers' wages—which even employers referred to as unjust—the workers' reaction was, according to Calvo Sotelo, the Minister of Finance, 'restrained'. Although strikes against the tax did take place in Catalonia and some other places, the UGT preferred to conduct a peaceful campaign. The years 1923–9 witnessed a sharp drop in the number of strikes, a fact which should be attributed not only to the coercive authority of the Dictatorship, but also to the conciliatory

---

Socialist Campaign on behalf of C.P.s in the agriculture see *ES* 10 May, 8 Nov. 1929. The last quotation is from *La Epoca* quoted in *ES* 5 Mar. 1929. For the CONCA see below, p. 174.

[18] For the desertion of rural workers see E. Santiago, *La UGT*, p. 45. It is also interesting to compare the data brought by E. Malefakis, *Agrarian Reform and Peasant Revolution*, p. 159, indicating that in August 1922 there were 65,405 rural workers in the UGT, with the number of 27,340 incorporated in the *Federación Nacional de Trabajadores de la Tierra* in April 1930, for this see *BUGT* 1930. For the National Federations of Industry see *UGT Semanario* 2, 23 Dec. 1926; *ES* 1 Mar. 1924. Decisions of the Congress in *BUGT* Jan. 1929.

relations between the strongest union in the country, the UGT, and Primo's government, in a period in which both wages and the cost of living of a working-class family showed a downward tendency.[19]

Since the leadership of the UGT was at the same time that of the PSOE, the tactics of the party throughout the Dictatorship did not differ from those of the union. It refused to take part in any of the conspiracies organized against the regime by both republicans and monarchists. Even over an issue like the Moroccan War, on which the Socialists were very militant until 1923, no serious popular protest was organized by the party during the bloody campaigns of 1924–5.[20]

Instead, the PSOE concentrated on propaganda and organization, thus achieving a considerable increase in the number of its members. The party mouthpiece, nevertheless, went through a financial crisis due to its limited circulation, the consequence of the fact that many local groups had their own newspapers and that the majority of the members of the UGT were not affiliated to the party and did not read *El Socialista*, in spite of being constantly urged by their leaders to subscribe to that newspaper. On the other hand the *Consejo de Gráfica Socilista*, created by the party in 1926 under the presidency of Besteiro to supervise the publication of pamphlets, was a success and contributed to the promotion of a socialist consciousness among workers. Yet the public meeting was still the most widespread medium of propaganda, and the *Escuela de Militantes*, inaugurated in January 1929 to provide party propagandists with a doctrinal formation, was a reflection of the growing attention paid to this

[19] For the Asturian crisis see David Ruiz, *El Movimiento Obrero*, pp. 190–200; Saborit, *Asturias*, pp. 218–19; *HL* Nov. 1927. For the tax see Calvo Sotelo, *Seis Años*, pp. 126, 169; *BUGT* Mar. 1929; *The Times* 14 June 1927, 18, 19 Jan., 1–3 Feb. 1928 mainly reporting on protest strikes. *La Unión Ferroviaria* 19 Feb. 1929 reflected the more common protest: a petition. For employers' attitude to the tax see *Industria* Feb. 1928. For statistics of strikes showing a drop from 465 strikes in 1923 to 165, 181, 96, 107, 87 in each of the years up to 1928 see *Banco Urquijo* Sept. 1929. It should be also borne in mind that a certain degree of unemployment in the mines, building, and textile industries further contributed to keep down strikes as a common means of workers' protest, see for this *Industria* Jan. 1928; *ES* 1 May 1925; Berenguer, *De la Dictadura*, p. 52. The cordial relations with the dictator were even reflected in the fact that the censorship was lenient toward *El Socialista*: see Celedonio de la Iglesia, *La Censura por Dentro*, pp. 62–3. For wages and cost of living see above, p. 18.

[20] For conspiracies see Marco Miranda, *Las Conspiraciones*, p. 61; Cordero, *Los Socialistas*, pp. 74–6; *ES* 9 Feb. 1930.

matter. The result of these campaigns was the foundation of *Agrupaciones Socialistas* in many places where the party had no branch until then, as well as the enlargement of those already existing. The participation of prominent figures of international Socialism, like Van Roosbroeck, Wolfgang Schwartz, and others, in congresses and public gatherings of the Spanish Socialist Party, as well as the frequent participation of Spanish delegates in meetings organized by the Socialist International, contributed to strengthen the self-confidence of the PSOE. This was further accentuated when the party was joined by outstanding intellectuals, like Jiménez de Asua, Negrín, Araquistáin, and was praised by the prominent physician Marañón. They gave the PSOE prestige and a halo of respectability and responsibility, but also contributed to accentuate its reformist, liberal, and middle-class characteristics.[21]

Indeed, many considered the Socialist movement as 'the equivalent of the bourgeoisie among workers'. Besteiro's proposals for constitutional reform in the party congress were far from revolutionary, and according to a liberal ex-minister, Baldomero Argente, could have been adopted by any liberal party. The most daring political demand on May Day was that of a 'return to constitutional normality' and an investigation into the Moroccan responsibilities, though accompanied by the traditional affirmation that 'the aspiration of the working class is to socialize the means of production and exchange'. Largo Caballero even expressed himself in the *Consejo de Estado* on

---

[21] For membership of the PSOE see *ES* 9 Apr. 1925, 1 Jan. 1926, 18 Sept. 1930; *EP* 5 Jan. 1930; and J. Maurín, *Los Hombres*, p. 199, from all of which the following figures emerge: December 1924—5,400 members, 1925—8,555, 1928—8,251, June 1929—10,282, December 1929—12,757. For the circulation of *El Socialista* see Tuñón de Lara, *El Movimiento*, p. 775 claiming that in 1928 it was 9,186 copies. However see *ES* 16 Jan. 1925 pointing out that the circulation of the May Day edition increased from 56,438 copies in 1923 to 85,312 in 1924. For financial difficulties see *BUGT* Jan. 1929; and *ES* 10 Jan. 1929. The Socialists had even to ask members of the Second International for financial help to maintain its press: AHN Leg. 45: from Spain's representative in Berne to the Foreign Office with a copy to the Ministry of the Interior, 27 Mar. 1924 no. 442. For propagandists and pamphlets see Saborit, *Besteiro*, p. 259; and *ES* 11 Jan. 1924, 8 Oct. 1926. For the propaganda in the provinces see the weekly supplement of *El Socialista Informaciones de Provincias*; and for an example of a fruitful campaign in Guadalajara see SAA: Gomez Diez to Alba, 30 Mar. 1925. For international activities see Saborit, *Asturias*, p. 113. For intellectuals see *NE* 30 Jan. 1930; *EP* 1 Oct. 1929; *ES* 11, 23 May 1929, 3, 7, 9 Jan. 1930. Maranon's article 'El Unico Camino' in ibid. 6 Aug. 1929.

behalf of an outright restoration of the 1876 constitution, for which he had the wholehearted support of the Monarchist Romanones.[22]

In spite of their recognition that the implantation of socialism 'requires the existence of democratic norms in bourgeois society', the Socialists rejected invitations both from the bourgeois left to implant such norms and from the extreme left to establish socialism without a bourgeois intermediary stage.

To the Anarcho-Syndicalists and Communists Saborit declared that the Socialist Party was determined to make 'the revolution which had been achieved with violence in Russia, by lawful means'—namely through an electoral victory. Therefore no united front was possible with the partisans of revolutionary action. Largo Caballero rejected appeals from the CNT on the ground that it wanted to reconstruct its forces at the expense of the UGT, and Cordero blamed the Anarcho-Syndicalists for all the misfortunes of Spain. Their apoliticism, he said, enabled the 'oligarchy' and 'reaction' to exercise exclusive rule. As for the Communists, who were doctrinally nearer to the Socialists than to the Anarcho-Syndicalists—during the Dictatorship they claimed to support 'any bourgeois constitution which would offer sufficient opportunities for the development of proletarian action'—they were too small a party to be taken into consideration; neither had their defamatory campaign against the 'bureaucratic collaborationist triumvirate of Largo–Saborit–Cordero' encouraged the Socialists to forge an alliance with them. The efforts of the Communist leader, Bullejos, to cultivate an extreme wing within the UGT was unsuccessful. If there was a significant oppositional element within the Socialist movement it was that presented by the *Prietista* tendency, which wanted to lead socialism towards the right—an alliance with bourgeois Republicans—rather than towards the left.[23]

[22] For 'bourgeois' image see Q. Saldaña, *El Momento de España: Ensayos de Sociología Política*, p. 29. For Besteiro see his speech in 1933 in Saborit, *Asturias*, pp. 285–9. Baldomero Argente in *EI* 17 Aug. 1929. Socialist defence of the proposition in *ES* 4, 6 July 1928 at the party congress. For May Day and Largo Caballero see ibid. 21 Apr., 11 Nov. 1924, 27 June 1925.

[23] For the attitude towards the 'Frente Unico' and the bitter relations with both Communists and Anarcho-Syndicalists see the decisions of the UGT Congress in *BUGT* Jan. 1929; Cordero, *Los Socialistas*, pp. 355–8; *ES* 18 Oct. 1923, 11 Feb., 8 May 1924, 4 Aug. 1927, 2 Mar. 1927. For the Communists' arguments for a united front see *La Antorcha* 1, 15 Jan. 1926, 3, 17 June, 23 Sept. 1927; and Dolores Ibarruri, *Memoires de la*

But neither were the Republicans successful in their approach to the Socialists. Polemical debates rather than serious negotiations were the dominant feature in their relations. Lerroux's favourable attitude to the occupation of the Moroccan protectorate and his good relations in the past with the 'antidemocratic and revolutionary workers of Catalonia' were highly suspicious, while the 'collaborationism' of the Socialists irritated the Radicals. Even the most 'republican' among the Socialists, Prieto, was dismissed by them as a 'humbug, a rotter, a fool, the wretched mediocre comedian of politics, and a cynic', an attack to which he answered by relating all the real and imaginary stories about Lerroux's corruption. Socialists considered historical republicanism as an integral component of the old regime, which had to disappear in order to pave the way for the establishment of a true republican state. Marcelino Domingo reacted to the refusal of Socialists to make a pact with Republicans so long as they were not a coherent and united force, by casting doubt on their real power which, he said, was a myth, since the majority of workers were either Syndicalists or Communists. The foundation of the PRRS was obviously, among other things, an attempt to attract to the republican field those workers and middle-class militants who resented the collaborationism of the PSOE, and its refusal to forge an alliance with Republicans. However, the Socialists did not cease to point out that they were essentially republicans and federalists who were simply opposed to the *caudillismo* of historical republicanism, to the unreality of its conspiratorial tactics, and to the bourgeois state that historic republicans wanted to create. 'Monarchists and Republicans', as Araquistáin put it, 'are, as far as we are concerned, the right'. Whereas for the Republicans, the Republic was the final aim, for the Socialists, it was a step towards socialism.[24]

Prieto, Teodomiro Menéndez, and Fernando de los Ríos

Pasionaria, p. 105. Alvarez del Vayo was in 1929 among the few in the Socialist camp 'on the frontiers of communism'. See his criticism on the tactics of the party and the Socialist official reaction in *ES* 17, 23 May 1929.

[24] For republican arguments see *El Republicano* 20 Nov. 1928; *EP* 18 Aug. 1929. See the polemical debates in *ES* 15 Feb., 25 Mar., 3, 14 Apr., 7 Nov., 26 Dec. 1924, 12 Feb. 1926, 16, 17 June, 9 July, 9 Aug. 1928, 8 Dec. 1929. *El Sol* 25 Apr. 1928 expressed the republicans' hopes that the Socialists might start to act as a political organization, and not only as an economic body.

understood at an early stage that the Socialist Party was not strong enough to achieve by itself the 'interim stage' of a bourgeois Republic. Prieto had been in close contact with Republicans, a fact which seems to have worried the dictator himself, while Fernando de los Ríos claimed that the duty of the party was 'to help to implant a regime which would offer guarantees of freedom and justice . . .' His overt opposition to the regime made him the only prominent Socialist leader to be prosecuted, and the only one who personally challenged the dictator. In the twelfth congress of the party, Prieto emphasized his discrepancy with the majority when he warned the party from isolating itself from the main stream of Spanish democracy, and he urged it to collaborate with the Republicans for a change of regime. However, the congress accepted the majority line, as presented by Largo Caballero:

No one is more bitterly opposed to the present regime than I am; but since we do not possess the means to change it, we must content ourselves with the maintenance of our organization . . . [which] given the total collapse of the political parties, is the only hope of the country for the future.

However, the final resolution included a concession to the *Prietista* minority by stating that 'The PSOE, without giving up any part of its doctrine, and always with the interests of the working class in mind, declares its readiness to support any serious and efficient action aimed at establishing a regime of full freedom.' The constant argument of the majority had always been, and would continue to be until late 1930, that the Republicans did not give an impression of the 'seriousness and efficiency' required for a revolutionary movement; therefore Prieto continued his dissident campaign for which he was attacked by the majority as 'a bourgeois liberal' who made use of 'demagogic tactics . . . which sow messianic illusions among people, and which destroy any organizational and fighting spirit.'[25]

[25] For Prieto's relations with Republicans see UA: Prieto to Unamuno, 30 Mar. 1928; his correspondence with Weyler in *La Ultima hora* 8 Feb. 1932; M. Maura, *Así*, p. 58; Prieto, *Convulsiones* i, 33. For Teodomiro Menendez's relations with Republicans see AHN Leg. 45: Governor of Oviedo to the Ministry of the Interior, 12 Nov. 1927 no. 156. For de los Ríos see *ES* 11 Apr. 1929; and his letter to the dictator in *HL* Jan. 1929. For the congress see the censored debates in *ES* 1, 3, 7 July 1928; and Prieto's

Once the appeals from both the right and the left were rejected, the only way open to the PSOE as an independent political alternative for the future was, according to Largo Caballero, to increase its political control over the UGT, among whose ranks he started to notice growing anti-collaborationist feelings. The significant difference between the number of members of the UGT and the PSOE was an indication that the majority of UGT members considered it as an *exclusively* trade union body, while in *political* matters many belonged to Republican parties, to the Communist Party or to no party at all. Largo Caballero strove to establish political co-ordination between the UGT and the PSOE because, as he put it, the exclusively economic action of the proletariat was inadequate for satisfying the aspirations of the Socialist movement, which could be fulfilled only through political action. This, because of the disintegration of the Republican parties, should be the task of a firm alliance between the UGT and the PSOE. Such an alliance would enable the working class to consolidate its material gains through legislative means either through parliamentary action or 'by a Socialist government itself'. Thus the social revolution was presented as the culmination of an evolutionary process which would lead socialism 'to assume political power'. To his critics, who alleged that he wanted to fuse the UGT and the PSOE, in order to further subordinate the party to the reformist tactics of the union, he answered that his programme consisted of simply giving an 'organic character' to the co-operation that had always existed and which in 1917 had launched the UGT into a revolutionary strike. Largo Caballero obviously understood that, in the coming years, contrary to what had happened during the Dictatorship political rather than economic issues would be the most crucial preoccupation of the country. Marcelino Domingo congratulated him, hoping that this would be the beginning of a political move by the Socialists against the Dictatorship. The approaching of the end of the Dictatorship further convinced Largo Caballero of

---

uncensored speech, the resolution and additional information in *El Republicano* Nov. 1928; *HL* June 1928; and Saborit, *Asturias*, pp. 284–5. For further polemics between Prieto and the majority see *ES* 18, 19, 23 May 1929.

the need to 'politicize' the UGT, so that the Socialist movement could play a leading role in future political events.[26] However, before Largo Caballero's proposition could materialize, the acceleration of the process of the fall of the Dictatorship in 1929 and the pressure coming from local UGT and PSOE sections provided an opportunity for the Socialists to play a major role in the collective *coup de grace* that most of the political forces in the country gave to the dictator by refusing to support his scheme of legitimizing his regime through a Consultative Assembly and a constitution.

None the less, two main stages should be noticed in relation to the Socialist attitude to the Assembly: a conditional rejection at first and a definite refusal later. Already, before the promulgation of the decree creating the Assembly, the UGT had been feeling the pulse of its sections on the question of participation. Largo Caballero, as secretary of the UGT, propagated the idea, which corresponded with his 'collaborationist' line, that the union should be represented in the Assembly, 'so long as this could be done in a dignified manner'. But the majority in the National Committee, in which the regional delegates reported on the opinions that they had gathered from the sections, decided that an extraordinary congress should be summoned to discuss what was considered a vital matter. The National Committee also indicated, however, that the invitation to join the Assembly, when it came, should be rejected if the UGT was not allowed to elect its own representatives. And Saborit later claimed that had the decree allowed an autonomous designation of deputies by the UGT, the majority in both National Committees would have recommended to the congress to accept the dictator's invitation. But when the congresses took place in the first week of October 1927, the decree was already known, and no mention was made of the Socialist request. The dictator reserved to himself the

[26] For Largo Caballero's campaign see his *Presente y Futuro de la UGT*, pp. 31–2; *ES* 1, 27 Mar. 1924, 6 Aug. 1925, 19 Feb. 1926, 9 Oct., 31 Dec. 1929. For his critics see Andrade, *La Burocracia Reformista*, p. 214; Prieto in *ES* 26 Mar. 1924; Maurín, *Los Hombres*, p. 186. The 'co-operative relations' which had always existed between UGT and PSOE are reflected in the almost identical composition of the Executives of both. Out of eleven members elected in the congresses of the UGT and PSOE in 1928 for their respective executives, eight were elected for both. For M. Domingo see his *Autocracia y Democracia*, pp. 299–302.

right to designate the Socialist delegates in the Assembly. Both congresses therefore refused.[27]

The matter was again brought up for discussion two years later, when the dictator proposed to modify the composition of the Assembly and gave in to the pre-condition of the Socialists that they should elect their own representatives. But now, in July 1929, new circumstances led the Socialists to reject the whole proposition.

The Assembly had already elaborated a constitution, and the Socialists had had the opportunity to express their rejection of a draft prepared by what they considered an undemocratically designated parliament. They rejected the constitution as a *Carta Otorgada* which, according to Prieto, was so reactionary that even the Carlist pretender Carlos VII would not have accepted it. The National Committee of the UGT bitterly criticized the constitutional draft for 'closing all the legal ways' to Spanish socialism in its aim to create a republican state and a socialist society by lawful means. The alternative proposed by the Socialists was similar to that suggested by the Republicans, just as their criticism of the constitution was fundamentally identical. It consisted in a proposition to hold general elections under universal suffrage in order to elect a Constituent Cortes which would work out a democratic constitution.[28]

Additional factors in July 1929 were the increasing difficulties and unpopularity of the regime which was now shaken by growing resentment in the army, the 'Valencia Revolution' of Sánchez Guerra and the rebellion of the students. Moreover, the most attractive element of the dictatorship, i.e. its economic prosperity, suffered a serious setback in 1929 with the depreciation of the peseta, the abolition of the extraordinary budget, so important for the financing of public works, and increasing

[27] For 'feeling the pulse' of the sections see the circular of the UGT Executive *UGT. A Las Secciones* 5 Sept. 1926 in AHN Leg. 51: 'Mitines 1926'. For Largo's and Prieto's attitude see the former's *Mis Recuerdos*, pp. 90–1; *ES* 10 June 1929. For the debates in the National Committees and congresses see *ES* 11, 23 Sept. 1926; *Unión General de Trabajadores. Semanario* 4 Nov. 1926; Saborit, *Besteiro*, p. 240; and *BUGT* Aug. 1929: the speech of Largo in a meeting of the National Committee surveying previous debates.

[28] For the criticism against the constitution see Saborit, *Besteiro*, pp. 248–9; Besteiro and Prieto in *El* 11 July 1929. See also the UGT manifesto of August 1929 in *BUGT* Oct. 1930; articles in *ES* 9, 10–14, 18, 24, 28 July; 3, 7 Aug. 1929, and E. Santiago, *La UGT*, pp. 47–9.

unemployment.[29] The same opportunistic considerations that had dictated 'collaboration' required now a shift of tactics.

Under such circumstances, the National Committee of the UGT met on 11 August to discuss the invitation of the dictator. Besteiro and E. Santiago alone advocated acceptance, claiming that the only reservation that they had in 1927 (i.e. the autonomous election of representatives) had been removed by the last decree. Besteiro summed up his attitude in these words:

I think that the tactics of *retraimiento* and abstention are erroneous, and have always produced fatal results for the cause of democracy ... The adoption of an abstentionist attitude, at this moment at least, would mean inactivity, indifference and impotence in the face of a vital question for the country and for the working class ... The real problems would be then resolved according to the convenience and wishes of the reactionary elements.

The abstentionist attitude of the majority was represented by Largo Caballero who questioned the right of the National Committee to disregard a previous decision of an extraordinary congress. Largo, the personification of collaborationism, suddenly put his prestige behind the case for abstention; a dedicated trades union leader, sensitive to the feelings of local unions, he now believed the union and the party could be better preserved by leaving Primo's sinking ship. Saborit followed suit. He even argued that he would have refused to join the Assembly, even if the congress had not decided as it did, because the Socialists were now invited to give, by their presence in the pseudo-parliament, approval to a constitution elaborated in their absence and rejected by most political sectors. 'Even if we do in the Assembly whatever we like,' he concluded, 'it would mean drowning ourselves politically without glory' in a body which had been discredited in its two years of ephemeral existence, and to which the mass of Spaniards was totally indifferent.[30]

The Socialist attitude was a serious setback for the dictator who blamed them for acting as politicians rather than as

[29] For the difficulties of the regime in 1929 see above, pp. 14–21. For the economic aspects see also Berenguer, *De la Dictadura*, p. 10; and Balcells, *Crisis Económica*, p. 89.

[30] For the debates, local pressures and decision of the National Committee, see *BUGT* Aug. 1929, and Gabriel Morón, *El Partido Socialista ante la Realidad Política Española*. The Socialists' deliberations are also adequately surveyed in Villanueva, *El Momento Constitucional*, pp. 54–80.

representatives of the workers. Their abstention was their first overt collective action against a regime which had been spoiling them for years. A rightist newspaper feared that now the Socialists might abandon their evolutionary policy for one of rebellion.[31] But they did not have further opportunities. The abandonment of the constitutional draft by the dictator himself, the gradual death of the Assembly, and the subsequent fall of the regime gave the Socialists the merit of having substantially contributed to the elimination of the limited alternatives that the Dictatorship could still use for its survival.

2. TOWARDS COLLABORATION WITH THE BOURGEOIS REPUBLIC

Whereas for most of the political groups the fall of the Dictatorship was a starting signal for reorganizing their forces, for the Socialists it was the beginning of a period in which their policy during the Dictatorship would bear fruit and would make them the best-organized party in the country and the central axis of the leftist coalition.

The year 1930 witnessed a substantial increase in UGT membership though official restrictions on propaganda were frequent.[32] In April 1930, the labour of propaganda in rural districts was brought to a solemn conclusion with the formation of the *Federación Nacional de Trabajadores de la Tierra*, which absorbed 157 agrarian sections with 27,340 affiliated members as well as the agrarian programme of the UGT which, apart from the immediate aim of improving conditions of agricultural workers, aimed at 'an absolute transformation: the integral liberation of labour, by turning the land into common property'. But the designation of a moderate *Besteirista*, Lucio Martínez, as secretary of the FNTT, and the basic moderation of the whole Socialist movement at that time, were an indication that the FNTT, in spite of the depressed situation of rural workers, would not preach revolutionary methods and would concentrate on concrete demands that could be achieved by traditional

[31] *LV* 18 Aug. 1929.

[32] See above, p. 114; E. Santiago, *La UGT*, p. 46, and *BUGT* Mar. 1931 where the same E. Santiago claimed that 81,540 membership cards were issued in 1930. For an increase of almost 50 per cent in the National Union of railway workers see *La Unión Ferroviaria* 10 Apr. 1931. For official restrictions see a large number of rejections of petitions to hold meetings in AHN Leg. 45: 'Socialistas 1930'.

trade unionist methods, such as rural C.P.s, the establishment of which the Socialists constantly demanded. The FNTT, said Sánchez Rivera, should demonstrate that agrarian reform could be achieved 'without violent tumults and without shooting in the streets'. And Lucio Martínez himself made special efforts to attract 'the so-called middle class' of small landowners.[33]

The main power, however, of the UGT lay among urban workers, a fact which, for the time being, exempted it from the overwhelming revolutionary pressure later to be exerted by the great mass of landless labourers that would swell the ranks of the FNTT during the Republic.[34] The UGT continued throughout the Benerguer period to organize the national federations of industry, four of which were founded simultaneously with the FNTT. The federations contributed to the confidence of the UGT in its capacity to cope with the circumstances of economic evolution and with industrial development, 'which increases every day the complexity of social life'. The activities of the UGT reached at times spectacular intensity as when during four weeks of April 1930, the *Casa del Pueblo* of Madrid accommodated two international conferences, seven union congresses and a grand gathering in commemoration of Pablo Iglesias. Even a union like that of the teachers, which had no contacts with nor favouritism from the Ministry of Public Instruction during the Dictatorship, emerged in 1930 with a more vigorous life. Such were also the cases of the Federation of Artists, an important organization in a period of growing attention to entertainment in big cities, and the extremely popular football players' association, both of which joined the UGT by the end of the Dictatorship, to the irritation of the right. But the UGT was not able to extend its hold to traditionally anarcho-syndicalist areas, like Catalonia, Valencia,

[33] For the FNTT see *BUGT* Jan., Mar., May, June 1930, *ES* 1 Aug., 28 Nov. 1930, 4 Feb. 1931; García Menéndez, *La España Rural (Hambre de Tierra y sed de justicia)*, pp. 259–65; and E. Santiago *La UGT* pp. 45–6. A clear revolutionary shift of the FNTT seems to have taken place only in 1934, see Malefakis, *Agrarian Reform*, pp. 320–1, 334. G. Jackson, *The Spanish Republic and the Civil War 1931–39*, pp. 29–30 is inaccurate in claiming that the UGT used the C.P.s 'to begin' the organization of rural workers. The decree creating them was implemented only by the Republic, and this is precisely an explanation for the spectacular development of the FNTT then.

[34] Out of the 277,011 members the UGT had in late 1930 about 40,000 were registered in the FNTT, In mid-1932 there would be 392,953 FNTT members out of 1,041,539 Ugetistas. See Malefakis, op. cit. 290–2.

and Galicia, especially now that the CNT was awakening from the lethargy of the Dictatorship. The efforts to 'conquer' Catalonia, which were unsuccessful during the Dictatorship, were all the more so when the rise of the CNT compelled the Socialists 'to struggle in an unfavourable ambiance', as Besteiro put it. *Ugetistas* found it unbearable to sit in C.P.s in Catalonia, because of that same 'ambiance'.[35]

A major concern of the UGT throughout the Berenguer period was to preserve the social achievements of the Dictatorship. Such achievements were endangered by the crusade led by both the government and public opinion against the legacy of the Dictatorship. When the government published a decree limiting the excessive interventionism of the state in regulating economic life, the UGT blamed the government for serving the exclusive needs of capitalists who would now use their liberty 'to exploit consumers'. The Socialists would have preferred that a revision of the economic legislation of the Dictatorship should take place in a Cortes or in a National Economic Council in which they hoped to be the workers' representatives. But, in spite of the fact that these demands were not met, and that the Berenguer government was not as committed as the Dictatorship to the working class, the UGT did not modify its basic conduct. It continued to struggle by peaceful means against the income tax on wages, its members took their posts in the undemocratically designated Ayuntamientos where they led a clamorous campaign both in defence of workers' interests and of socialist propaganda. The Ayuntamientos and Diputaciones became a well exploited rostrum, and this irritated the right who accused the Socialists of practising 'politics instead of administration'. *ABC* spoke of 'the Socialist dictatorship in the Madrid Ayuntamiento'.[36]

---

[35] For the national federations see *ES* 20 Mar., 19 Apr. 1930; *BUGT* Apr., Nov. 1930. For the Artists see *Unión de Espectáculos.* Jan. 1931, football players: *ES* 31 Aug., 3 Sept. 1929. For teachers see *Trabajadores de la Enseñanza. UGT. ITE.*, Madrid, 1 Jan. 1931. For Catalonia see *BUGT* Feb., May, Sept. 1930; *ES* 26 Mar., 4 Sept. 1930; *LV* 24 Aug., 2 Sept., 10 Oct. 1930. For the C.P.s in Catalonia see: *Nuestro Programa. Organo de la Dependencia Mercantil de Barcelona* July 1930 relating the difficulties met due to Anarcho-Syndicalist boycott of C.P.s; see also *LV* 4 Oct. 1930; and *SO* 18 Jan. 1931.

[36] For opposition to revision of socio-economic policy see *ES* 1 Feb. 1930; *BUGT* Mar. 1930. For the tax see ibid. Sept. 1930. For Ayuntamientos see *Boletín de la Agrupación Socialista Madrileña* 4 trimestre 1929; Alcalá Galiano, *The Fall*, p. 79. For Saborit's pro-workers speeches and activity in the Madrid Ayuntamiento see selected examples in *ES* 27 Feb., 6, 9 Mar. 1930. For other Ayuntamientos, see ibid. 5 Mar. (Orense, Arjonilla,

The preservation of the C.P.s against a growing offensive of employers was probably one of the gravest preoccupations of the UGT during the Berenguer period. The employers' arguments were not different from those they had brought up before Aunós, except that now they hoped to exploit in their favour the revisionist policy of the government. However, the new Minister of Labour, Señor Sangro, refused to give in to employers' demands in spite of his personal distate for many of the regulations of the corporative system. In a year which witnessed both the awakening of anarcho-syndicalism and an alarming increase in strikes mainly by non-*Ugetistas*, the abolition of the C.P.s would have increased social unrest by tempting *Ugetistas* to use the strike weapon. The employers' campaign was, therefore, unsuccessful; and even when the *Unión General de Patronos Comerciantes e Industriales de Madrid* decided, on 2 January 1931, to retire from the C.P.s the 'anarchist employers', as the Socialists chose to call them, were compelled by a special order from the minister to accept the decisions made by the C.P.s although they were not represented on them. Such decisions could not but be adverse to their interests. The Socialists, on the other hand, blamed the Ministry of Labour for its utter disregard of many cases of non-compliance by employers with the decisions of the C.P.s[37]

However, in spite of the difficulties encountered by the Socialists in the C.P.s, they did not join the majority of strikes which took place in 1930. The strikes were mostly the work of the CNT and the Communists where they had sufficient power to bring them about, as in Andalucía, Valencia, Bilbao, Catalonia, and Galicia. The first big wave of strikes in June was started in Seville by the initiative of the local CNT. From there it spread to other parts of Andalucía. The Communists in Bilbao followed suit. In July and August, it was again the CNT

Villanueva de los Castillejos), 9 July (Jaén), 5 Oct. 1930 (Seville); the quotation in *ABC* 14 Mar. 1930. For Ovejero's similar labour in the Diputación see *ES* 9, 28 Mar. 1930.

[37] For the employers' campaign against the C.P.s see *El Mercantil Patronal* Feb. 1930–Feb. 1931; *El Eco Patronal* 1 Jan. 1931; *ED* 30 Dec. 1930, 4 Mar. 1931; and E. Aunós, *La Reforma Corporativa*, pp. 139–40. For the attitude of employers' bodies in Catalonia see *LV* 13 Feb., 27 Apr. 1930. For Sangro's attitude see his speech in Aunós, *La Política Social*, pp. 132–6; and *ES* 23 Jan. 1931. For the UGT's position see *BUGT* Oct. 1930; Jan., Oct. 1931; *ES* 2, 5, 8 Feb., 19 Aug. 1930.

which led the major strikes of dockers in Santander, railway workers in Gerona and Málaga, miners in Langreo, construction workers in Córdoba, and fishermen in San Sebastián. Later in the autumn the wave of strikes continued, stimulated either by real grievances, as exercises in revolutionary gymnastics, or as the accomplishment of deals with the Republicans. The Socialists denounced the summer strikes for their 'obscure origin'. *El Socialista* defined the party's attitude:

This senseless movement has the unfortunate virtue of strengthening reaction and of weakening the democratic, Republican and Socialist forces. ... Therefore, we shall not collaborate in that unfortunate labour, and we appeal to Socialists, our sympathizers, all real democrats, and to the working class, to resist the illusory suggestions that might push them to sporadic movements without any clear syndical or political ends.[38]

The Communists in Bilbao, who seemed to have struck as a protest against Socialist hegemony in the C.P.s, were dismissed as 'irresponsible elements' by the local UGT. Even when it agreed to join a strike with other elements, including the Communists, as was the case in the political strike declared in Bilbao on 5 October as a protest against a meeting of the *Unión Monárquica*, the UGT acted in a responsible manner by firmly resisting violent intimidation from the Communists, who wanted to prolong the strike indefinitely, and who tried constantly, occasionally with the support of the Nationalist workers, to challenge UGT's hegemony. In most cases, the UGT preferred to bring labour disputes to the C.P.s, which generally prevented a strike; thus in Asturias in May 1930, Llaneza achieved a wage increase of 7 per cent through the C.P., and thus removed the menace of strike; again, the painters' union in Madrid a few months later went through a similar process. Only when negotiations failed did the UGT recommend a strike, as in the case of the metal workers in November. Indeed, the *Asociación del Arte de Imprimir* was relating not only its own experiences when it claimed that most of the material achievements in 1930–1 were made possible either through C.P.s or through political pressure.[39]

[38] *ES* 28 June 1930.
[39] The marked increase in the number of strikes in 1930 is especially illuminating

The UGT strike of mid-November in Madrid was called under pressure from one of its most extreme sections, the *Federación local de Edificación*. When two workers were killed by police in a riot which developed during the funeral of four workers of that federation who had died in an accident, the federation declared a strike without consulting the *Casa del Pueblo*. On the next day the Casa del Pueblo decided to follow the lead of the building workers, by declaring a forty-eight-hour general strike. However, from that moment, the Casa del Pueblo effectively controlled the strike by issuing orders to the workers on how and when to return to work, in order to prevent extremists within the UGT or CNT elements from turning the strike into a revolutionary movement, or from extending it outside Madrid. To the Anarcho-Syndicalists, who

when compared with the data available on strikes during the Dictatorship. In the years 1924–8 636 strikes with a total of 251,355 strikers were registered, whereas in 1930 alone there were 402 strikes and 247,461 strikers. See for this *Banco Urquijo* Sept. 1929; and *Anuario Estadístico* 1931. The substantial increase in the cost of living in 1930 and unemployment undoubtedly created the appropriate ambiance for Anarcho-Syndicalist and Communist agitators. For the cost of living see *Anuario Estadístico* 1931 and *Boletín de Información Social del Ministerio de Trabajo y Previsión* July 1931. Both sources indicate that the index for a working class family went up from 165·4 points in April 1930 to 176·8 points in March 1931, while the general index went up during that same period from 181 to 187 points. Moreover, in some regions, and among some sections of the working class wages did not rise enough to keep up with this upward trend in the cost of living, see data in Tuñón de Lara, *El Movimiento*, pp. 755–67. There are no general figures of unemployment, but there are clear indications of the gravity of the problem, see for this *ES* 16 Jan. 1931; *ABC* 29 May 1930. The problem was especially depressing in Andalucía where both Anarcho-Syndicalists and Communists were active in organizing strikes, see *Democracia*, Jaén, 28 Nov. 1930; 'La Crisis Agraria Andaluza de 1930–1' in *Estudios y Documentos* (Ministerio de Trabajo y Previsión Dirección General de Acción Social Madrid 1931), pp. 14–16 speaking of 100,000 unemployed in Andalucía; see also on unemployment Tuñón de Lara, *El Movimiento*, pp. 833–4; and Balcells. *Crisis Económica* pp. 17, 124: 17,253 unemployed were registered in the province of Barcelona by the end of 1930. It was, however, only in October 1932 that the relatively high figure of 400,000 unemployed was registered in the country as a whole, see *Economic conditions in Spain*, May 1933. For strikes the best concentrated account is that of Mola, *Obras*, pp. 353–4, 373, 383, 385. *The Times* gives remarkably detailed reports on strikes as well as the British Embassy and its Consulates, for example F.O. 371/15041: Grahame to Henderson, 25 June–2 July 1930. See the CNT manifesto in *LV* 23 July 1930 claiming responsibility for the Andalucian strikes; and *Somatén* July 1930 stressing the Communist role in the summer strikes; and Maurín, op. cit. 69–70 claiming that the strikes were launched by the enemies of the C.P.s. For the strikes in the north against the U.M. and Socialist–Communist rivalry see *ABC* 5, 7 Oct. 1930; and the account of the sides in *ES* 5, 7 Oct. 1930, *La Batalla* 12 Sept., 10, 17 Oct. 1930; and *ABC* 11 Mar. 1930. For miners, painters, and metallurgical workers see *ABC* 1 May, 12 Oct., 11 Nov. 1930. See *Boletín oficial de la Asociación del Arte de Imprimir* November 1931 for a summary of achievements through peaceful means.

proceeded in Barcelona to a revolutionary strike under the pretext of 'sympathy with the Madrid proletariat', and to the extremists in Madrid, the Socialists said, 'A popular movement with concrete aims can fail either because of a lack or because of an excess of force. The first reduces it to impotence, while the latter can go beyond the concrete and limited aims and can endanger the whole movement.'[40] The impressive achievement of the UGT was in making this a manifestation of disciplined and controlled power, which could be used at any given moment. Precisely this discipline, rather than the anarcho-syndicalist revolutionary irresponsibility, frightened the right. *La Vanguardia* wrote in an alarmist vein about 'the three days of absurd dictatorship of the Casa del Pueblo', in which, 'the working class had demonstrated its power'.[41]

The November strike had demonstrated that the UGT had to fight CNT and Communist elements both within the UGT affiliated syndicates and outside them in order to maintain and defend its reformist tactics. An example of an extreme UGT syndicate, was that of the 'workers of administration and distribution'. It developed strong opposition to the 'bourgeois' tactics of the UGT and preached the slogan 'Toward Socialism? Yes! But with the Communists', while the CNT made constant efforts to set up 'minorities of opposition' within UGT syndicates. None the less, the firm control of the reformist leadership of the Socialist movement over the UGT brought the Communists in their so called 'Pamplona Conference' to decide on concentrating their efforts on the 'reconstruction of the CNT on a new basis' rather than on a futile attempt to conquer the UGT from inside. Neither was the *Cenestista* effort more successful, as was, indeed, proved when their *Grupo de Educación Sindical* in Madrid was expelled from the *Sociedad de Albañiles El Trabajo* by the

[40] *ES* 26 Nov. 1930.
[41] For the extremism of the building federation see *La Vanguardia Mercantil* Jan. 1930, on how they passed a motion forbidding members who had paid jobs in the UGT to have a casting vote in their section, because these functionaries tended to curb syndical radicalism. This included Caballero and the president of the federation, Anastasio de Gracia; see *SO* 28 Oct. 1930 how members of this federation in Madrid joined the CNT. For how they pushed the UGT to strike see F.O. 371/15042: Peterson to Henderson, 24 Nov. 1930; *La Vanguardia Mercantil* Dec. 1930. The Socialist account on the strike is in *ES* 15, 19 Nov. 1930. *BUGT* Dec. 1930. For the right's reaction see *LV* 20 Nov. 1930; *ABC* 16 Nov. 1930; and *Somatén* Dec. 1930. *LE* 17 Nov. 1930 wrote about the 'failure of the Communist attempt'.

Ugetista majority. The pretext of a *Frente Unico* as a means of dominating the UGT was equally rejected by the UGT, which pointed out that it was another weapon of the extreme left against those whom they called 'the social fascists'.[42]

The Socialists, on the other hand, had ready answers to the allegations about their reactionary stance. The *Boletín de la UGT* had a monthly column entitled 'How do the anti-reformists act?' in which precise facts were given to prove that the CNT had been using peaceful action in labour relations incompatible with their revolutionary language. The contacts of Pestaña, the CNT leader, with *Inteligencia Republicana* in Barcelona, the constant negotiations of the CNT with the authorities in order to legalize their syndicates, and its political flirtation with the bourgeois left—all together convinced the UGT that if anyone had in the past misled the working class, it was the CNT with its insistence on the incompatibility of political action with the class struggle. The CNT now recognized that only a political struggle could serve the working class, and therefore, it was the CNT who were responsible for the political backwardness of the Spanish proletariat by its consistent apoliticism.[43]

It was precisely on political action that the political wing of the Socialist movement, the PSOE, concentrated its attention until its actions culminated in a revolutionary coalition with the Republican forces. The PSOE defined itself on the political map and *vis-a-vis* the Berenguer government as a liberal Republican party. A manifesto of February 1930 put it this way:

We are facing again a government born in the shadow, having its origin in intrigues, and arbitrarily nominated by a power which no longer reflects the national will ... Berenguer ... is the symbol of a declining Spain in a painful process of disintegration ... for the sake

[42] For leftist syndicates within the UGT see *La Vanguardia Mercantil* May, Nov. 1930; *BUGT* Apr. 1930; *Boletín de la Agrupación Socialista Madrileña* 1 semestre 1930; *SO* 28, 29 Oct. 1930. For Communists see *La Batalla* 13 June 1930; *La Vanguardia Mercantil* Sept. 1930; Comín Colomer, *Historia del Partido Comunista* i, 219–22. For Frente Unico see *La Batalla* 12, 26 Sept. 1930; *La Vanguardia Mercantil* Feb.–Mar., Sept. 1930; and for a favourable attitude from a left wing in the 'juventud socialista Madrileña' see *Rebelión* 23 Aug., 6 Sept. 1930. For UGT's reaction see *BUGT* Oct. 1930.

[43] For the journalistic campaign against the CNT see *BUGT* Mar., Apr., Aug.–Nov. 1930. For Socialist allegations on the politicism of the CNT see *ES* 1, 9, 22, 27, 30 Mar., 13, 18, 19 Aug. 1930.

of order and security it is necessary to strengthen ... clear and firm republican convictions to which we adhere fervently ...[44]

It was made clear that a republican regime should be established as a vital stage towards socialism. The government was, therefore, asked to proceed, in consecutive order, to municipal, provincial, and general elections which should culminate in a revision of the 1876 constitution.[45]

What further contributed to accentuate the liberal features of the party was its moderate standing in social matters. It emphasized its willingness to preserve private property and its opposition to violent means for enforcing the collectivization of property 'because it is socially and technically impossible. The new forms of property and the new methods of work cannot be created by laws and decrees', but through social evolution.[46]

Their anti-clericalist campaign added an important element to those already held in common with bourgeois Republicans. Araquistáin, a Socialist, was the founder of the Lay League, and Socialist speakers constantly denounced the politically reactionary Church as an instrument of the monarchist state. However, secular education and the separation of Church and state to curb the excesses of clericalism, 'the major enemy of liberal and democratic progress', were proposed by Socialists in a much milder way than by leftish Republicans. That 'Republic and religion are absolutely compatible', as Socialists said, was not precisely the kind of thesis maintained by the Radical-Socialists of Alvaro de Albornoz and Marcelino Domingo. The Socialists, moreover, welcomed the advent to the party of prominent intellectuals not only because it increased their prestige, but also because it modified 'the predominantly *obrerista* physiognomy of the party', and, therefore, made Spanish Socialism 'a great hope for the implantation of a liberal policy in our state'.[47]

---

[44] Quoted in Saborit, *Besteiro*, pp. 263–4.

[45] Cordero and de los Ríos in *Boletín de la Agrupación Socialista Madrileña*, 4 trimestre 1929; and *ES* 30, 31 Jan., 2 Feb. 1930. For similar attitudes adopted at a union level see *La Unión Ferroviaria* 10 Feb. 1930.

[46] *ES* 8, 14 Mar. 1930.

[47] *ES* 4, 6 June, 15 July, 1 Aug. 1930. For intellectuals see ibid. 15 Mar. 1930 and above, p. 119.

Yet in order to become a respectable partner in the liberal-Republican camp, the Socialists had still to go through a process of rehabilitation after the charge of collaboration with the Dictatorship. As soon as the Dictatorship was over, Socialists started to 'prove' that they had never 'collaborated', that they had been persecuted like anyone else, and that their present strength was the result of their 'constant protest' against the Dictatorship rather than of any alleged collaborationism.[48]

However, the 'collaboration' issue involved nothing but a question of dignity. So long as the Socialists maintained and even increased their power, Republicans courted them. The membership of the party increased in the period between June 1929 and June 1930 from 10,282 to 17,590 and eighty-nine new sections were founded. This indicated that the increase was due not only to the development of existing sections but also to the creation of new ones through a consistent labour of propaganda. Special departments of 'organization and propaganda' were set up; emissaries from Madrid found their way to remote miners' districts in Galicia, to Melilla in the Moroccan protectorate, and to the *Ciervista* stronghold in Murcia, where a May Day speech by Saborit caused a local newspaper to write: 'Murcia is no more a city in which advanced ideas could not strike root because an all-absorbing *caciquismo* destroyed them in the bud'. Activities of 'Agrupaciones Socialistas' were reported from Las Palmas, Guadalajara, Granada, and Valladolid, when other political forces were said to be inactive. And in Sax, the Socialist section was to campaign against an attempt by Romanones to get a foothold among agrarian elements in Alicante. But the largest gatherings were held in the proletarian quarters of urban centres like Zaragoza, Santander, and Madrid, where the basic principles of socialism were presented to the workers in simplistic and sometimes demagogical terms, like those used by Regina García in two meetings in Madrid:

The workers produce everything and do not enjoy anything. See how peasants grow crops but cannot afford to buy them. See how masons build palaces, yet they live in shacks. And, on the other hand, look at those who do not produce anything but enjoy everything. They do not have any concern for the people but call them dirty and

[48] For the journalistic apologetic campaign see *ES* 12, 16, 21 Feb. 1930. For allegations about persecution of Socialists see E. Santiago, *La UGT*, pp. 54–5.

descamisados, while they can always wash themselves because they have soap at home.[49]

However, Largo Caballero, in his systematic campaign for a political alliance of UGT–PSOE, pointed out where he thought the real answer to social grievances lay: in the institutionalized politicization of the UGT rather than in demagogic agitation or syndicalist apoliticism. Until September 1930, when the National Committee of the UGT rejected his proposition, he kept on preaching. He pointed out that even the apolitical CNT was adopting a political line and, since the UGT had already embarked on indubitable political acts like the strike of August 1917, he saw no scruples of principle that could hinder the formation of a 'well-organized bloc between UGT and PSOE in the forthcoming electoral campaign'. A Socialist majority in the parliament could be achieved not by 'a simple alliance of sympathies and affinities', which already existed, but only by an alliance based on 'clear commitments' and on 'a proper programme'.[50]

The Executive of the UGT discussed on 14 August Largo Caballero's proposition and decided 'to recommend to the sections to take part in the elections in co-ordination with the Agrupaciones Socialistas'. This 'recommendation' did not satisfy Largo Caballero and his supporters who wanted to make this co-ordination obligatory. They brought the matter before the larger forum of the National Committee where they were again in the minority. Besteiro, who was becoming a consistent opponent of Largo Caballero's initiatives, in what had the

[49] The statistic in *ES* 18 Sept. 1930. For the generally not very spectacular increase in existing sections see *Boletín de la Agrupación Socialista Madrileña* 4 trimestre 1929, 4 trimestre 1930 showing an increase from 1,070 to 1,354. For propaganda in the provinces see the following examples: *ES* 27, 30 Aug. 1930; Cordero in Melilla 18 Oct. 1930. For Murcia see *Levante Agrario* (Murcia) 2 May 1930; and AHN Leg. 29: From Governor of Murcia to Minister of the Interior, 1 Dec. 1930 no. 16; see official reports from other provinces in ibid: Las Palmas 6 Dec. 1930 no. 482, Guadalajara 30 Nov. 1930 no. 1562, Granada 6 Dec. 1930 no. 481, Valladolid 30 Nov. no. 1564; For Alicante see below, p. 197–198. For the proletarization of Madrid see *El Economista* 21 Sept. 1930 quoting a memorandum of the Ministry of Labour. See also Javier Tussell Gomez: *La Segunda Republica en Madrid. Elecciones y Partidos políticos*, pp. 11–15. For Socialist meetings in proletarian quarters like Puente de Vallecas and Puente de Segovia see *ES* 27 Aug., 16, 23 Sept., 14 Oct. 1930; Regina García's speech is in ibid. 12 Sept. 1930.

[50] Largo's campaign in *ES* 6 Apr., 25 May, 11 Sept. 1930; *Boletín de la UGT* June, Aug. 1930. He was supported by E. Santiago in *La Aurora Social* (Oviedo) 6 June 1930, and Araquistáin in *BUGT* July 1930.

aspect of a struggle for power in the movement, opposed an organic alliance as a menace to 'the natural transformation' of both organizations; and the *Besteirista* Trifón Gómez, warned that the UGT, 'in which there were even monarchist members', might disintegrate if political control were imposed by the party. The *Caballeristas* were finally defeated. Their rivals passed a motion which did not differ essentially from the resolution of the Executive, and which invited the PSOE 'to consider the convenience of . . . the presentation of the largest possible number of Socialist candidates, as well as the elaboration of a common campaign for the triumph of these candidates'.[51]

The failure to create a large Socialist Party, which was what Largo Caballero and his supporters meant, in fact, by 'an organic alliance', reduced the prospects of a Republic being set up by the political action of the working class alone, and increased those of an alliance, which was established a month later, with the Republican parties for the same purpose. Moreover, as Juan Sapiña, a supporter of a pact with the Republicans put it, the fusion of the UGT with the PSOE might have accentuated the class intransigence of the Socialist movement, and would have, subsequently, made impossible an alliance with Republicans. Largo Caballero did not deny that this was precisely his intention.[52] The intensification of workers' economic grievances at a time when the 'boom' was showing clear signs of exhaustion, and the fear of losing ground to the more extremist CNT, which was making capital out of the workers' discontent, were imposing on Largo Caballero, always attentive to the voice of grass-root militants, a greater awareness of the need to give the Socialist machine a more genuine working-class base. He started, albeit slowly and gradually, a personal transformation that would turn him later in the thirties, when the bourgeois Republic had disillusioned him and the Socialist masses, into the champion of the 'Bolshevik line' in the Spanish Socialist movement, a line that would play a fateful role in the last two years of the Republic.

---

[51] The debate in the National Committee is in *BUGT* Oct. 1930, and the resolution of the Executive is mentioned there in Largo's speech. See for an opposition to Largo's proposal from leftist elements in the UGT, *La Vanguardia Mercantil* July, Oct. 1930. For Besteiro's attitude see *ES* 30 Aug. 1930.

[52] *ES* 18 June 1930 (Sapiña), 1 May 1930 (Largo Caballero).

Now, however, grass-root pressure was far from being overwhelming, and Largo Caballero was still a believer in the liberal Republic. He agreed that 'as long as capitalism has not accomplished its historical mission' socialism could not be established, and even a Socialist government would not be able to bring socialism within twenty-four hours. His conclusion was that Socialists might therefore be compelled by the circumstances to participate in bourgeois governments. Besteiro, though the strongest opponent of this conclusion—an attitude strikingly incompatible with his strong support of 'collaboration' with the Dictatorship—agreed that the most urgent objective of the Socialist Party was that of establishing a 'democratic Republic'; even novice but radical Socialists like Jiménez de Asua and Araquistáin recognized that a Republic would have to be 'an essentially bourgeois Republic', though sympathetic towards socialism. It should create the appropriate means for 'the education and the organization of the working class for the full realization of its ideal'.[53]

Thus the immediate political dilemma of the Socialists was no different from that of most of the parties. It was Republic versus Monarchy rather than socialism versus capitalism. None the less, this was not enough to smooth away difficulties between Republicans and Socialists. The latter had reservations about the kind of Republic planned, especially since ex-monarchists started to talk about a conservative Republic. A 'Republic of white gloves' headed by a Maura or a Sánchez Guerra 'would change nothing but the central figures of the state and its façade', whereas the Socialists wanted 'a profound modification of the fundamental laws and of the civil code, mainly as it affects property rights in land'. Therefore, a warning from *El Debate* that the Republic would have to move constantly towards the left, was fully supported by *El Socialista*. However, Socialists put greater emphasis on the 'lack of seriousness' of Republicans and on their differences of opinion, as the main reason for their reluctance to enter into a formal alliance with

---

[53] For Largo Caballero see *ES* 14 Jan., 8 Apr., 1930. Besteiro's speech in Saborit, *Asturias*, pp. 285–7; *ES* 8 Apr. 1930; and *EP* 12 Oct. 1930. For Jiménez de Asua see *ES* 15 Mar. 1930; and his *Política*, pp. 34, 37. For Araquistáin see his *El Ocaso* pp. 269–74. The last quotation is in *ES* 1 June 1930. See also M. Maura, *Así*, pp. 47, 59; and *LV* 6 Feb. 1930 on how Republicans considered the Socialists as the central axis of the situation.

them. Republicans were asked to discipline their ranks, to put an end to *personalismo* and *caudillismo*, and to reach an agreement between themselves which would make of their numerous groups a coherent bloc. Besteiro called on them to make up their minds about a minimum programme for a Republic 'full of concern for the working class'; then, he promised, the Socialists would be strong supporters of the alliance and subsequently of the new regime.[54]

Not until the pact of San Sebastián did the Republicans give an 'impression of seriousness' according to most of the Socialist leaders. Besteiro rejected on grounds of lack of 'seriousness' two propositions by Republican delegates in May and July. The National Committee of the party explicitly warned its sections not to make alliances with any political force unless authorized to do so by the National Committee that had been authorized at the last congress to decide what might be the 'serious and efficient action' deserving the support of the Socialist Party.[55]

This reluctance to make concrete agreements with the Republicans caused Prieto and de los Ríos to intensify their campaign on behalf of an outright agreement with the bourgeois left. Prieto's activities were now concentrated on fomenting the idea of 'a National bloc formed by the elements of opposition to the regime'. Without waiting for an affirmative decision of his party, he became deeply involved with Republicans. His participation in meetings of homage to Sánchez Guerra and E. Ortega y Gasset caused the Executive of the party to 'express its displeasure' with his activities 'which tend to commit the party to which he belongs, and break with recent resolutions'. It was also alleged that Prieto, recognizing that it was impossible to reach an agreement on a national scale, had made contacts for a regional alliance in Biscay, which would include even Nationalists and Traditionalists, for the implantation of a Basque Republic which, he hoped, might stimulate other regions to follow suit. This seems to be a false and malicious

[54] For the conservative Republic see *ES* 13, 14 Mar., 1, 23 Apr., 11 May, 1 June 1930. Agreeing with *El Debate* see *ES* 26 Mar. 1930. For the indiscipline of Republicans see ibid. 4, 9, 22 Feb., 26 Mar. 1930; Besteiro in ibid. 8 Apr. 1930. See also an article in *El* 11 Apr. 1930.

[55] *Alianza* May, June–July 1930 on Besteiro's contacts with Republican delegates. The warning to the sections in *ES* 29 June 1930.

accusation, if one considers Prieto's close links with the left Republicans of San Sebastián under the leadership of Sasiaín, together with whom Prieto exerted pressure against any concessions to the right in the Basque country. The allegation served, however, to discredit Prieto. The editorial board of *El Socialista* warned the regional sections of the party not to get involved in regional movements 'which might divide and weaken our forces'. The cantonalist movement during the first Republic was cited as an example of what could happen. The popularity of Prieto in Republican circles further created hostility in the party against him. Cordero blamed him for being the cause of violent criticism of the party for its failure to consider national matters; and *El Socialista* reminded its readers that 'this solidarity between Prieto and our enemies is not a new phenomenon'. Only Fernando de los Ríos in the party Executive and Lacort in the National Committee supported Prieto's attitudes. The former himself was active in Republican circles, and already in March he was, together with Azaña and Alvaro de Albornoz, in a delegation which started negotiations with the Catalan Revolutionary Committee.[56]

Prieto and Fernando de los Ríos, though isolated in the governing bodies of the party, were supported by elements in the *Agrupación Socialista Madrileña* and among the local youth of the party, as well as in Bilbao and Granada, their respective strongholds. The *Federación Socialista Asturiana* also bluntly expressed its readiness to make alliances with any anti-monarchist party striving to set up a Republic. Already at the beginning of the year, the Madrid section of the party urged the party to make 'any circumstantial political alliance' necessary for the implantation of a democratic regime. By the end of March, some of its members bitterly criticized the exclusive concentration of the party on administrative work in Ayuntamientos and

[56] For Prieto's personal contribution to the Republican effort see M. Maura, *Así*, pp. 58–9; and his inflammatory speeches against the Monarchy and on behalf of an anti-monarchist front in *ABC* 26 Apr. 1930 (Ateneo of Madrid); *El Sol* 20 Apr., 4 May, 2 July 1930 (Bilbao and Madrid); *EP* 2 Oct. 1930 (Logroño); *ABC* 2 Oct. 1930 (Zaragoza); and his interview with *LV* 25 Apr. 1930. *El* 14 Mar. 1930 quoted Prieto as proposing a conservative Republic. For the San Sebastián Republicans see *EP* 8 Mar. 1930; and *Alianza* June–July 1930. For the San Sebastián meeting see above, pp. 80–84. For the party's attitude towards him see *ES* 20, 29 Mar., 1, 5, 23, 25 Apr. 1930. For F. de los Ríos see ibid. 18 Sept. 1930; and Aiguader *Cataluña*, pp. 75–6.

Diputaciones, and asked for an extension of the sphere of activities of the party to 'a more radical field', and for a consideration of the possibility of 'making alliances with the anti-dynastic left . . . taking into account that the Socialist Party is not strictly a workers' party and, therefore, must strive to attract both intellectuals and the middle class'. However, in a further meeting of the Madrid section in April, the demand of these members to discuss the question was rejected by an anti-collaborationist pro-*Besteirista* majority of 135 to 72.[57]

In the youth section of the party in Madrid, however, the differences of opinion over the alliance with Republicans developed into an overt split. As in both Monarchist and Republican parties, the leadership of the PSOE had exercised a close control over the youth sections in order to avoid the emergence of radical trends. One of these young Socialists approved this institutionalization of the youth when he said: 'We, as apprentices of socialism should do nothing but occupy the battle position which the party assigns to us'.[58] The National Committee of the National Federation of Socialist youth reaffirmed in April 1930 its adherence to the tactic of the party, by supporting its reserved attitude towards any political pact with Republicans.[59] Yet a radical wing under the leadership of Graco Marsá, Ramon Pinillos, and Navarro Ballesteros encouraged by Gabriel Morón's critical attitude towards the party's reformism, accentuated its opposition to the official view of the party. However, whereas Prieto and de los Ríos represented, as the Communist leader Bullejos put it, an exclusively political left mainly interested in closer relations with the liberal bourgeoisie, the radical wing of the youth section combined in its credo both political and social leftism. When the PSOE and the UGT were condemning the summer wave of strikes and the 'irresponsible' revolutionarism, their newspaper, *Rebelión*, praised them as a positive awakening of the proletariat from the years of repression, an awakening which might culminate in a 'real social transformation'. This, they argued, could not be achieved

---

[57] *Boletín de la Agrupación Socialista Madrileña* 4 trimestre 1929; *ES* 30 Mar., 12 Apr. 1930. For Granada see ibid. 18 Sept. 1930. For Asturias see David Ruiz, *El Movimiento Obrero*, p. 216.

[58] *ES* 16 Apr. 1929.

[59] *ES* 9 Apr. 1930.

by parliamentary means or by any other form of bourgeois legality, but through an armed insurrection of the working class and an outright nationalization of all means of production. Such ideas were utterly opposed to the official line of the party; and in September 1930, the group of Graco Marsá retired from the party with loud accusations against the 'oppressive bureaucratic rule' of the reformists over the party.

Among other allegations, the dissident group, which promised to fight the bourgeoisie from outside the party better than from within, claimed that a campaign of defamation against Prieto was being elaborated in the National Committee. This allegation meant a change of emphasis. Instead of emphasizing the demand of *fighting* the bourgeoisie, the group started to attack the party for not making an *alliance* with that same bourgeoisie. The dissidents clearly supported a bourgeois Republic as a necessary stage towards socialism. What they doubted was whether the triumvirate Largo–Saborit–Cordero would ever be likely to proceed from a bourgeois Republic to socialism. The fact that Besteiro, no less responsible than Largo Caballero and the others for the collaboration with the Dictatorship and for the reluctance to pact with Republicans, was never denounced, was an indication of his authoritative prestige in the Socialist movement.[60]

The minor dissidence of Graco Marsá's group and nonconformist tendencies in Granada, Asturias, and Bilbao, though indicative of a dissatisfaction with the party's refusal to forge a revolutionary alliance with Republicans, and of the fact that Prieto and Fernando de los Ríos were not completely isolated, fell short of forcing a change of policy. Even the 'serious' alliance

[60] For G. Morón see his bitter criticism against both the social reformism of the party and its isolation from democratic movements in the country in his books, *El Partido Socialista ante la Realidad Política Española*, and *La Ruta del Socialismo en España. Ensayo de Crítica y táctica Revolucionaria.* In the first book the emphasis was on a critical survey of the collaborationism, the indifference of the Socialist movement towards the *political* preoccupations of the bourgeois left, and the reluctance of the party to get in touch with Republicans; whereas the second is an attack on the excessive reformism of the party during the first year of Republic. For Morón's thesis see also *NE* 18 Mar., 8 Apr. 1931; *ES* 21 Feb. 1930; *Rebelión* 20 Sept. 1930. For Bullejos see *La Batalla* 18 July 1930. For the split see *Rebelión* 28 June, 26 July, 13, 20, 27 Sept. 1930. Ramos Oliveira remained, however, in a minority within the group of 'the 35 *indeseables*', as the majority called them, by opposing an alliance with Republicans and preaching an exclusively proletarian revolution; see for this *Rebelión* 19 July, 2 Aug. 1930.

of Republicans forged in San Sebastián, though it exerted a positive influence in that direction, was not a decisive factor. The Socialists continued to reject Republican appeals, as Besteiro did in late August in a meeting with 'San Sebastián' delegates, on the ground that a programme consistent with the minimal Socialist demands should be previously agreed upon. In a further meeting that same month in the Ateneo, Besteiro urged the Republicans to strengthen their own union, to which the Socialists should not adhere, but, he added, 'we should discuss the common points which we would all commit ourselves to defend, and in this intimate contact, without violating the autonomy and the independence of our party ... we should realize a common action, whatever the consequences may be'. Besteiro did not want to commit the party to an unconditional collaboration which might lead the Socialist movement to subscribe a policy 'which is not genuinely its own'.[61]

He emphasized that, as far as matters of programme were concerned, the elements of San Sebastián had not offered anything which might satisfy the Socialists. The greatest preoccupation of the Republicans in San Sebastián was that of appeasing the Catalans, and the Socialists were far from satisfied with the way they did it. Anibal Sánchez denounced the extreme nationalist language of the Catalan delegates and referred to the concessions given to them as to 'a highly dangerous error were it not impossible to put it into practice'. He claimed that the commitment of the Republicans to the Catalans, and their eagerness to attract both the Socialists and the Anarcho-Syndicalists were an indication of their awareness of the weakness of their forces compared with the objects that they aspired to achieve. This, and the total disregard of economic and social questions in the San Sebastián meeting, in spite of Prieto's participation—another act of insubordination—did not encourage the Socialists to conclude a concrete agreement with Republicans.[62]

[61] For Besteiro's meetings with Republicans see Saborit, *Besteiro*, p. 265; and his speech in the UGT congress of 1932 in ibid. 278–81.

[62] Besteiro in *ES* 22 Aug. 1930; Anibal Sánchez in ibid. 11, 14 Sept. 1930. The speeches delivered at the huge Republican gathering in the Madrid bullring were criticized for their utter disregard of questions of interest to the Socialists: ibid. 30 Sept., 2 Oct. 1930. The Republicans hoped that at least the 'discipline' of the meeting would satisfy the Socialists: *Alianza* Sept.–Oct. 1930.

Therefore, when in mid-September the *Agrupación Socialista de Granada*, which adopted Fernando de los Ríos' attitude, suggested the Republican alliance to the National Committee, Saborit's proposition that 'there is not sufficient ground for any pact with Republicans', was voted by the majority. None the less, the erosion of the party's attitude was reflected in the fact that the representatives of Levante, Andalucía, Aragón, and Extremadura adopted Fernando de los Ríos' attitude, asking for an outright alliance even if that would mean that a socialist Republic would not be installed in the near future. And those who, like the representatives of New Castile, opposed the alliance, did not suggest breaking off relations with the Republicans.[63]

But, finally, the consistent contacts of the Republicans with the CNT, the Communists and the military, and the fact that the National Committee of the UGT failed to agree, in its meeting on 15 September, on a political union with the PSOE, convinced some of the party leaders that the revolution might start without the Socialists, who might then 'lose any control of the revolutionary movement' that might finally overwhelm them. This was the mood that prevailed in a meeting of Besteiro with the members of the Executive on 4 October, and which finally brought them to decide 'to intervene in the movement, and to authorize the president of the Executive [Besteiro] to continue his conversations with the other elements who are committed to the revolution'. Besteiro's declarations to *El Imparcial*, a couple of days later, still referred to the 'old fashioned' doctrines of the Republicans. This strengthened the assumption that the agreement made with them was the result of the circumstances rather than of a narrowing of the doctrinal gap. On the seventeenth both the UGT and PSOE Executives met again to approve a motion promising total support for the revolutionary movement 'to fight the Monarchy'. No mention was made of whether any agreement on a programme was reached with the Republicans, and this, anyway, did not seem to be a central issue any more. On 20 October the Executive of the party met to discuss precise details of the revolutionary *coup* which, according to what Alcalá Zamora and Azaña reported

---

[63] *ES* 18 Sept. 1930.

to a commission composed by Besteiro, Largo Caballero, Fernando de los Ríos, and Saborit, would start on 28 October. The Socialists were given the role of following the military once they were in the streets, so that the revolution should not be another *cuartelada*. Instructions were consequently issued to the sections for a revolutionary strike.

In that same meeting Largo Caballero brought up the question of whether the Socialists should accept ministerial posts in the Provisional Government. Besteiro, who since negotiations had started had maintained that Socialists should preserve their autonomy in order to carry out a socialist policy, was now the greatest opponent of 'ministerial collaboration', fearing that it might compel the party to support any decision of the Provisional Government in which the Socialists were in the minority. The supporters of 'ministerial collaboration' (the *Caballerista* faction), though recognizing the solid doctrinal grounds on which Besteiro based his arguments, claimed that this was a revolutionary period, and that the ministerial posts provided the Socialists with a historic opportunity to lead a revolution. Besteiro, though by no means a radical figure, refused to let his opponents claim a monopoly of the revolutionary spirit. His attitude was presented as tactically shrewd and doctrinally radical. He wanted to have the best of both worlds: to collaborate with the Republicans and to keep socialism as a movement free if necessary to fight the bourgeois government in the street. He was, however, in the minority, together with Saborit, Lucio Martínez, Trifón Gómez, Anastasio de Gracia, and Anibal Sánchez. Subsequently three Socialists were designated to the Provisional Government. These were Fernando de los Ríos and Prieto—who could see it as their personal victory, and Largo Caballero who had already exercised 'ministerial collaboration' during the Dictatorship as member of the *Consejo de Estado*.[64]

---

[64] For details of the debates which culminated in the decision to collaborate in the provisional government see T. Gómez's speech in the October 1932 UGT congress, quoted in Saborit, *Besteiro*, pp. 304–12; Besteiro's speech in the PSOE congress that same year in pp. 277–81, see also pp. 265–6, 269. Besteiro in *El* 7 Oct. 1930. M. Cordero, *Los Socialistas*, pp. 76–9. Largo's account in *Mis Recuerdos*, pp. 107–9 is rather confused. Prieto's argument, in *Convulsiones* ii, 351, that the participation in the revolutionary committee was an 'intimate collaboration' rather than a ministerial participation is an unsuccessful exercise in logic which tended to erase the negative

Thus compelled by the circumstances, rather than by their free choice, the Socialists joined a movement which had no very promising prospects. They were asked to play no more than a secondary role, that of following the army—in itself a sufficient reason for Trifón Gómez to consider resigning from the Executive—to collaborate with their traditional enemies from the CNT, and to agree precipitatedly in favour of ministerial collaboration, a sensitive issue for Socialists everywhere. Mutual accusations between the CNT and the UGT went on as usual. The Anarcho-Syndicalists pointed out that the revolutionary prospects of the movement were sparse if it relied on UGT masses 'good only for voting', while Socialists denounced the chain of strikes launched by the CNT throughout October, and warned the Republicans against thinking that a revolution might be achieved through violence and barricades. The revolutionary movement, it was suggested, must separate itself from the CNT, because 'without them there is still a possibility of triumph, but with them there is none'. The Socialists even accused the CNT of betraying the October revolution by revealing in the editorials of *Solidaridad Obrera* details of the revolution, which they wanted to fail because of Socialist predominance in the Revolutionary Committee, and as a protest against the refusal to reach an official agreement with them. Cordero predicted that, even in the case of success, the Anarcho-Syndicalists would become the fiercest enemies of the Republic. Neither was the prospect of a military *coup* very attractive to the Socialists.[65]

The mixed feelings with which the Socialists entered a movement which was not properly socialist, as well as failures of organization, explain why they were subsequently reluctant to fulfil their role adequately in December 1930. The failure of the October revolution because of Mola's efficiency and the insubordination of the CNT, brought Besteiro and Saborit to suggest a total withdrawal from the movement. This was

connotation that 'ministerial collaboration' had for Socialists, see for example *ES* 13 Dec. 1930. See Mola, *Obras*, p. 421; and E. Santiago, *La UGT*, pp. 64–5 on Socialist emissaries in the provinces, spreading instructions of strike.

[65] For the 'October revolution' see above, pp. 93–4. For Trifón Gómez see Saborit, *Besteiro*, p. 307. For the Anarcho-Syndicalists see *SO* 5, 21 Oct. 1930; *ES* 7, 17, 26, 30 Oct. 1930; and E. Santiago, *La UGT*, pp. 65–71.

rejected on the ground that the Socialists were now too involved, and their withdrawal might discredit them as traitors. So, towards December *El Socialista* started to speak in a blunt revolutionary language about an imminent change of regime. Instead of 'peaceful means', a 'violent struggle' against the 'defenders of the old regime' was predicted.[66]

Yet on 15 December the Socialists, though fully loyal to their commitments in the provinces, did not strike in Madrid, the most sensitive and crucial point. In fact, already on the twelfth the UGT affiliated railway workers could have saved the Jaca insurrection from failure by declaring a strike in Zaragoza, thus preventing the sending of military reinforcements to Huesca. Their failure to do so might be the result of the fact the Jaca *coup* came as a surprise, and that they had instructions to strike on the fifteenth. This they did, together with Communists and Anarcho-Syndicalists all over the country. And, in Barcelona, José Jove, the UGT president and its representative in the Revolutionary Committee, took the lead by starting the general strike, while Pestaña still hesitated because of the UGT's failure to strike in Madrid. Jove had a written order from Largo Caballero and he acted accordingly.[67]

In Madrid, however, lack of clarity over the role that the Socialists were expected to play, imprecise instructions, and insubordination torpedoed the strike. On 14 December, Largo Caballero gave instructions to Muiño, the secretary of the *Casa del Pueblo*, to declare a general strike on the following day as soon as the army in the Montaña Barracks had struck. Muiño, on the spot, transmitted the order to Trifón Gómez, the president of the Casa del Pueblo. On that same evening, when the Executives of the UGT and the PSOE met to discuss the matter, the failure of the revolutionary movement was imminent, since the arrest of the Provisional Government indicated that the authorities were on the alert. Largo Caballero demanded

[66] Largo Caballero, *Mis Recuerdos*, pp. 109–11; *ES* 7 Nov., 9 Dec. 1930. See in Saborit, *Besteiro*, p. 307 how T. Gómez presented the attitude of Besteiristas following the failure of the October movement.

[67] For Jaca and the 'December revolution' see above, pp. 94–99. *BUGT* Feb. 1931 gave a full map of the revolutionary and Socialist strikes of December. These resulted in the arrest of 952 Socialist militants all over the country, in the closure of 223 Socialist centres, and in several killed and injured. For Barcelona see Rafael Sánchez Guerra, *Proceso*, pp. 73–6.

that the general strike should be declared even if the military should fail to act. Given the unpromising circumstances the executives rejected his proposition and supported a rather ambiguous resolution that 'the Madrid working class would declare a strike only in the case of the military rebelling or if the movement of strikes in the provinces should require it'. The state of mind in the Casa del Pueblo depressed the army's spirit. Many of the conspirators deserted the movement on the same evening. Consequently, the units in the Montaña barracks remained there on the next morning. The first aeroplanes from Cuatro Vientos took off at about 8.00 a.m. when most of the workers were already at work, as Queipo de Llano realized earlier in the morning. When Largo Caballero understood that no strike had been declared he rushed to Besteiro's house, where they both decided to summon the Executives to consider the possibility of declaring a strike on the following day. But the Executives rejected again Largo Caballero's demand, and he went to give himself up to the authorities, together with Fernando de los Ríos.

The main controversy over the question of who had deliberately betrayed the movement was, according to Largo Caballero, connected with the question of whether the strike was to be dependent on the previous action of the military or whether it was to take place independently of this action. He himself had undoubtedly given firm orders to strike. But it was irrelevant for him to insist that he had stressed that the strike should be declared even if the military remained inactive, because the decision of the Executive on the evening of the fourteenth was a legal procedure to abolish his order. However, on the morning of the fifteenth Besteiro himself gave Muiño a personal order to declare the strike when he saw the aeroplanes from Cuatro Vientos. Muiño bluntly refused, alleging that the strength of the military insurrection was insignificant. The most that could be now done was to warn the government that, in case of further executions, the general strike would be finally declared.

It seems, therefore, clear that neither Largo Caballero, as Mola had wrongly alleged, nor Besteiro had torpedoed the strike. The damage was done by the failure of the military to make a sufficient manifestation of power and Muiño's insubordination. Largo Caballero's accusations of sabotage on the part of Besteiro, Saborit, and Trifón Gómez are supported by the fact that they were opposed to the 'ministerial collaboration'. Yet there is no clear-cut indication of a causal relation between their attitude towards 'ministerial collaboration' and the failure to declare the strike. It should be, however, pointed out that Trifón Gómez, as president of both the Casa del Pueblo and the *Sindicato Nacional Ferroviario* (the railway union) and an 'anticollaborationist' *Besteirista*, was not very anxious to declare the strike. His syndicate, according to his own testimony, was committed to declare the strike in those places in which there was *no* military movement, and not to declare it where the army acted. The logic of all this was to provide transport for the insurrectionist army and to deny it to loyal units. Since the army in Madrid did not act, he should have declared a strike there; yet, like Muiño, he did not.

An additional factor, however, must be taken into consideration: The decision of the Executive that stipulated that the strike should be the consequence of and combined with military insurrection might have proved to be impractical, since many workers were at work before the military could act. Therefore, Muiño's refusal to obey Besteiro's order might have been the result of the technical impossibility of contacting the workers once they were at work. The clearest consequence of this episode, as far as the Socialist movement was concerned, was growing mutual suspicion between its leaders. This would poison relations between them and accentuate a tendency towards factionalism of which the debate of the ministerial collaboration was a starting point and which would continue well into the Republic.[68]

The Socialists were now in a difficult and embarrassing position. They recognized that the movement had failed, but

[68] The accounts of the events of 15 December are many and contradictory. See: Largo Caballero, *Mis Recuerdos*, pp. 111–13; E. Santiago, *La UGT*, p. 80; M. Cordero, *Los Socialistas*, pp. 80–7; Trifón Gómez's speech in the UGT Congress of 1932 in Saborit, *Besteiro*, pp. 308–12, and his speech in the Congress of the National Union of Railwaymen: *ES* 8 May 1931; Besteiro's speech in the PSOE Congress that same year in Saborit, op. cit. 271–2; Queipo de Llano *El Movimiento*, pp. 94, 98–9, 123–8; Rafael Sánchez Guerra, *Proceso*, pp. 116, 125–6; Mola, *Obras*, pp. 513, 518, 543–4, 564, 577; M. Maura, *Así*, p. 73. Juan Andrade, *La Burocracia Reformista*, pp. 157–9; and C. Falcón, *Crítica de la Revolución*, pp. 62–4—both represent an extreme left blaming the Besteiristas for boycotting deliberately the revolution.

they claimed that the Madrid working class 'had completely fulfilled its duties', and that the elected bodies of their organizations would discuss in due time the omissions, if there were any. To criticism from the right they answered that the movement to which they were committed was by no means communist, but rather a movement in which 'limited concessions of a social character, mainly in agrarian questions' were promised to the working class.[69]

However, the lessons of December and the fact that Lerroux, a *persona non grata* for many Socialists, became the leader of an alternative Revolutionary Committee once the original Committee had been arrested made Socialist membership in it little more than a formality. The national committees of both the UGT and the PSOE decided in the beginning of February that the circumstances that had determined the previous resolution to collaborate with the Republicans still prevailed. But, from now on, every proposition for common action would have to be discussed by the Executives, taking into consideration 'the possibilities of action which might exist at that moment'. Yet neither was Lerroux active, nor were the Socialists too anxious to get involved in revolutionary action.[70]

The Socialists, like the Republicans, now realized that the only effective action that could be taken against a government in a constant mood of alert was that of closing its legal way out from an embarrassing anti-constitutional position. The answer was electoral *retraimiento*.

Yet, it should be stressed that the Socialists had been, throughout the last year, the foremost opponents of electoral retraimiento. Though they had been demanding that municipal and provincial elections should precede the general elections and that full constitutional guarantees should be granted, they made it clear that the Socialist Party 'is not, and by no means should be, abstentionist'. They wanted to enter the Cortes to insist on the investigation of responsibilities, and to exploit the electoral campaign for spreading their propaganda. To Marcelino Domingo's abstentionist preachings *El Socialista* answered that a revolution could be better brought about from within

[69] *ES* 19, 21, 28 Dec. 1930; 10 Feb. 1931; *BUGT* Feb. 1931.

[70] *ES* 12 Feb. 1931; *Boletín de la UGT*, Feb. 1931; Mola, *Obras*, pp. 604, 607. See also above, pp. 99–100.

parliament than from outside it. If the Republicans abstained, it was because they lacked any substantial force and aimed to isolate the 'interventionist' Socialists from the political forces of the left. Even on the eve of the December revolution, when the government was still determined not to give in to demands from both right and left to reverse the order of elections, and when the Socialists were convinced that the control of the Ministry of the Interior over the elections would make them 'the dirtiest and most violent ever held', they refused to join the abstentionist choir. Consequently, the Socialist Party was very active in carrying on its electoral preparations. UGT workers were urged to realize the importance of getting into parliament the largest possible number of Socialists, and they were promised that their representatives would struggle there for better education, public works, economy in public expenditure, the abolition of *latifundios* etc. Syndicates were encouraged to give donations for the electoral fund, which they did; and candidates were designated both by the Executive and by the local sections.[71]

However, a change of attitude became apparent by the beginning of January 1931, following the failure of the revolutionary movement, and with their prestigious leaders either under arrest or in exile. Neither an Ordinary nor a Constituent Cortes were now presented as an adequate solution. Electoral corruption and the government's insistence on holding the general elections first were now a cause for a growing fatalism over the results of the elections. Under these circumstances, the official abstention of the totality of the Republican groups by the end of January created a situation in which the Socialists might have been again isolated from the advanced forces in the country, had they not decided to abstain. This

[71] For the initial campaign against retraimiento see *ES* 14 May, 18, 23, 25 July, 13, 21, 22 Aug., 12 Dec. 1930; *NE* 11 Oct. 1930. For demands of a reverse order of elections see AHN Leg. 29: 'Elecciones generales Diputados a Cortes 1930', reporting on petitions from the Socialist sections of Jaén (2 Sept. 1930 no. 57). Badajoz (24 Aug. 1930 no. 301), Morón (23 Aug. 1930 no. 41), Mieres (26 Aug. 1930 no. 23), Barruelo (26 Aug. 1930 no. 75), Utrera (17 Sept. 1930 no. 634), Cueta (18 Aug. 1930 no. 60), and Valladolid (30 Dec. 1930 no. 1589). For electoral propaganda and donations see *Boletín de la Agrupación Socialista Madrileña* 4ᵉ trimestre 1930; and *ES* 22, 26 Aug., 20 Sept., 28 Oct. 1930. For designation of candidates see *AHN* Leg. 29: reports from 30 December coming from Jaen (no. 1580), Córdoba (no. 1594), Granada (no. 1568), Huelva (no. 1552), Cáceres (no. 1550), Almería (no. 1555), Badajoz (no. 1582), Oviedo (no. 1606); and *ES* 24 Oct., 21 Dec. 1930.

they did in a meeting of their Executives on 3 February with a majority of 50 to 4, putting the Berenguer government in an equally embarrassing situation as Primo de Rivera's when they abstained from taking part in his Assembly. Now, as then, the right considered the Socialists' abstention as a fatal blow to the regime.[72]

With the fall of the Berenguer government, though not 'organically united', both the UGT and the PSOE were committed to the bourgeois republican revolution. The division in the leadership between *Caballeristas* and *Besteiristas* had more to do with the struggle for power within the Socialist movement, than with the *ad hoc* necessity of establishing such a Republic. Both factions, and indeed the anti-collaborationists not less than their opponents, were committed to the bourgeois Republic, and were to 'collaborate' during the next months in its creation.

[72] For the change of attitude in January see *ES* 4, 6 Jan. 1931; *El Sol* 31 Jan. 1931; the final decision to abstain in *ES* 4 Feb. 1931. See *SO* 25 Jan. 1931 stressing the isolated anti-abstentionist position of the Socialists. For the impact of the Socialist *retraimiento* see *LE* 4 Feb. 1931; and *El Sol* 10 Feb. 1931.

IV

THE INCOHERENT DEFENCE OF THE MONARCHY

The Monarchist parties, which entered the Dictatorship in a state of fragmentation, were further disbanded by Primo de Rivera's policy of ostracism and persecution. On the other hand, the refusal of their main figures to collaborate with the anti-constitutional rule of both the king and the dictator increased their political isolation, though it helped to preserve their dignity. Dignity and a sincere attachment to constitutional forms were what lay behind the active rebellion of some of them, and the passive *retraimiento* of most of them in the last crucial months of 1929. In both cases they contributed substantially to diminish the alternatives left to the dictator for perpetuating his rule. Furthermore, the attempt to liquidate their parties proved to be of fatal consequence for the Monarchy, which was left, immediately after the fall of the dictator, without the traditional foundations of its existence, i.e. the dynastic parties. However, it should be stressed that the symptoms of the post-dictatorial period affected the Monarchist parties as well. The alarming menace of an increasingly massive mobilization of leftist opinion stimulated the old dynastic parties to attempt at last what they had never felt the need to do in the past: to 'modernize' their organizations and doctrines. They were becoming aware that an open struggle to attract the masses, rather than their manipulation through the Ministry of the Interior, was the key for the survival of the Monarchy. But the failure of the Berenguer government was, among other things, the consequence of the Monarchists' unwillingness to create a coherent bloc, and of the revival of old strifes between their factions.

I. OSTRACISM AND *RETRAIMIENTO* 1923–1929

Primo de Rivera represented and interpreted a public weariness, shared by the *políticos* themselves, with the 'inertia of civil governments'.[1] García Prieto, who had previously declared that only over his dead body could the military assume power, added Primo de Rivera to his list of saints a few hours after his dismissal for having removed from him 'the burden of the government'. Nor did the monarchist *ABC* see any reason for mourning when contemplating this funeral of 'old politics'.[2]

Primo de Rivera had to create the 'phantom of the old regime', to use Unamuno's expression, in order to justify his rule. Old politics were from now on denounced constantly, and by contemporary standards a festival of ruthless maltreatment of politicians was initiated. 'Politician', according to *El Socialista*, became a more contemptuous word than 'thief'. The names of politicians were removed from streets, they were denigrated in the official notes of the dictator, published in a press which was closed to his adversaries, and they were deprived of their local political strongholds. A circular to the governors explicitly ordered them to dismiss any state functionary suspected of being 'in contact with politicians of the old regime'. A special decree in October 1923 prevented ex-ministers from holding posts in public companies. Thirty-four prominent figures of the old regime, among them Romanones, Sánchez Guerra, Sánchez de Toca, and the Marqués de Cortina were affected by this measure.[3]

Deprived of political rights and personally humiliated, politicians led a boisterous and ineffectual opposition of epistolary criticism, intimate *tertulias*, and club murmurings. When they were allowed to speak in public, as they did in a commemoration of Cánovas, their tone was one of 'exquisite courtesy'. The writing of books, which were not subject to censorship, was also a dignified way to defend the old regime, while others like Santiago Alba and García Prieto hoped for a 'fair trial' in order to refute the dictator's accusations. A way of retaliating

---

[1] The ex-ministers Rafael Gasset and Romanones in *El* 28 Sept. 1930, and *El Diario Universal* 8 Oct. 1923.

[2] García Prieto quoted in Ramos Oliveira, *Historia de España* ii, 459. *ABC* 14 Sept. 1923.

[3] UA: Pérez de Ayala to Unamuno, 17 Dec. 1925; *ES* 4 Oct. 1923, 12 Jan., 26 Mar. 1924. For lack of freedom to answer the dictator's attacks see RA Leg. 63 no. 38: Correspondence between Primo and Romanones 23, 29 July 1925, n.d., and the director of 'El Pueblo Vasco' to Romanones, 30 July 1925. The circular is in AHN Leg. 45: 2 Nov. 1923 no. 33. For public companies see *The Times* 15 Oct. 1923; and F. O. 371/9490: Howard to Curzon, 9 Nov. 1923.

against the king was to avoid public receptions in the palace, though some, like the Conservatives Bugallal and the Marqués de Lema, could not resist the temptation of 'paying their respects to the king'. Their attachment to parliamentarism brought them to reject appeals like that of Primo de Rivera and the king for the collaboration of 'all good Spaniards to the exclusion of none'. Neither had an encouraging record in defending parliamentarism; and some politicians tried unsuccessfully to increase their influence with the queen, by trying to play on the constitutional tradition which they assumed that she had inherited as an English princess. But this, as well as direct pressure on the king, were rejected by Alfonso not only in November 1923, in the euphoric phase of the new regime, but also in September 1924, when the directory was passing through its most difficult hours in Morocco.[4]

This lack of official favour put the dynastic parties in a process of rapid disbandment. 'This is a period of desertions' wrote one of Antonio Maura's followers.[5]

In the Liberal Party, with García Prieto devoted to reading and to playing with his grandchildren, and with Alba in exile, Romanones was to witness how the party was disappearing. Eleven *Romanonista* ex-ministers considered themselves his personal clientele, yet he had no party to lead. He could see his 'friends' only at funerals, where they looked to him 'as if they have just emerged from some attic, where they had been put by the landlord as useless items'. His colleague Villanueva, who was now followed 'by nothing but his shadow', had to cancel a meeting commemorating Sagasta because of lack of participants.

[4] For meetings see *The Times* 1 Nov. 1924, 19 Jan. 1926, 7 Mar. 1928. For epistolary gossips see Burgos y Mazo, *Los Constitucionalistas* i, 122–38, ii, 59–108, 130–48, his correspondence with Sánchez Guerra, Villanueva, and others. For books see Romanones, *Las Responsabilidades Políticas del Antiguo Régimen*; and Ossorio, *Mis Memorias*, pp. 143–4 on the publications of the *Sociedad de Estudios Políticos Sociales y Económicos*. For receptions see F.O. 371/11096: Rumbold to A. Chamberlain, 30 Jan. 1925, reporting a conversation with the queen; and RA Leg. 68 no. 19: Romanones to Duque de Miranda, 16 Jan. 1927. For an appeal for collaboration see *The Times* 26 Jan., 24 Mar. 1925. For the queen see UA: Marañón to Unamuno, n.d. and her conversation with the British Ambassador mentioned above. For the appeals to the King see Romanones, *Notas* pp. 217–19, *LE* 15 Nov. 1923; RA Leg. 63 no. 66: ex-premiers and ex-ministers to the king 12 Sept. 1924; and another letter mentioned in F.O. 371/11936: Rumbold to A. Chamberlain.

[5] MA Leg. 322: Blas Aguilar to Antonio Maura, 10 Apr. 1924.

Many had deserted to join either the Republicans or the UP. Romanones' consolation was his private fief of Guadalajara, where his clients were 'in a silent and expectant attitude without losing their faith in their leader and in his future', despite efforts by the new authorities to ruin his influence there. But on a national scale this was an insignificant factor. He therefore tried to launch an energetic campaign, calling upon liberalism to rouse itself and take up the cudgels for the restoration of the constitution. He initiated an assembly of all the Monarchist leaders committed to the principle of Constitutional Monarchy. At the beginning of 1925 he also appealed, in a dramatic way, to 'all liberals who were ready to forget the old procedures' of parties based on personal relations, to collaborate in the formation of a 'broad' and 'modern' Liberal Party. The response, even among Liberals, was not very enthusiastic. The *Albistas* suspected that Romanones was again looking for power; and they, anyway, refused 'to play the game in order to consolidate the Monarchy, against whom we have a dispute pending'. The failure of such initiatives as well as earlier refusals of the dictator to authorize Romanones to address his followers left the party without organization; and in an international congress of Liberals, in July 1928, Lloyd George lamented in public the lack of organization among Spanish Liberals, 'because of the circumstances'.[6]

Neither were Romanones' conspiratorial activities successful in restoring the Constitutional Monarchy. His involvement in the attempts against the Dictatorship was halfhearted, his private business ventures being no less dear to him than public liberties. Nevertheless, he became a receiving centre for all those who wanted to denigrate the regime. Romanones' constant

[6] For the ex-ministers and Romanones as the main Liberal figure see RA Leg. 89 no. 8: a censored article of *La Voz Valenciana*, and Leg. 33 no. 1: 'Ex-ministros Romanonistas'. For funerals see Hurtado, *Quaranta anys* ii, p. 220 (relating a conversation with Romanones). For Villanueva see RA Leg. 28 no. 35: Belmonte to Romanones 13 June 1925; and MA Leg. 322: Blas Aguilar to Antonio Maura, 10 Apr. 1924. For UP and republicans see F.O. 371/9490: Howard to Curzon, 22 Nov. 1923; *EP* i, 28 May 1929; and Belmonte to Romanones in RA Leg. 28 no. 35. For Guadalajara see SAA: Emilio Gómez Diez to Alba, 30 Mar. 1925; and RA Leg. 63 no. 63: Victor Felipe Serrano to Primo de Rivera 5 Dec. 1923. For the assembly see the mentioned letter of E. Gómez Diaz and RA Leg. 78 no. 5: a censored article in a Catalan newspaper. See also Romanones' articles in *El Sol* 28 Feb., 4 Mar. 1925. For earlier attempts to address his followers see *The Times* 8, 9 May, 14 July 1924. Lloyd George in *ES* 12 July 1928.

appeals to the king to return to constitutional rule, promising that this would gather the politicians around him and 'forget the past', provoked only angry official notes from the dictator. This eroded his belief in the old system; and as time went on, he doubted if there were still many politicians who were ready to serve the king. By the end of the Dictatorship, he was suggesting the designation of a 'neutral government' to summon a Constituent Cortes that would have to bring into question some of the prerogatives of the king.[7]

On the left of the Liberal Party, the Albista *Izquierda Liberal* was also in disarray. Its leader Santiago Alba spent his time in business and in seeking personal rehabilitation, after having been picked out by the dictator as the personification of all the corruptions of the fallen regime. From his exile in Paris he abstained from taking any part in any of the conspiracies against the dictatorship, thus setting an example to his followers in Spain who, consequently, avoided conspiratorial activities. This, however, did not prevent the dictator from persecuting the *Albistas* who had their main stronghold in Valladolid and sixty-three ex-deputies and ex-senators scattered in the country with their personal clientele. After they submitted a petition both to Primo de Rivera and to the king in October 1923 asking for a fair trial for their leader, they began to be harassed. Their correspondence was frequently intercepted, their centres were closed, *El Norte de Castilla*, their mouthpiece, was frequently suspended, and their militants were banished. In Valencia a fine of 1,000 pesetas was levied on a man for having mentioned Alba in a public speech, and a bullfighter's career was threatened by the authorities for daring to dedicate a bull to Alba. Nevertheless, Albistas continued to protest, and when Alba was finally acquitted, they ratified in a clandestine manifesto, signed, among others, by Chapaprieta, Roig i Bergadá and Natalio Rivas, both their loyalty to their leader

<hr />

[7] For Romanones in the conspiracies see F.O. 371/10593: Gurney to MacDonald 2 Aug. 1924; RA Leg. 53 no. 6, Leg. 7 no. 29, Leg. 28 no. 10, Leg. 63 no. 80: Letters on the Sanjuanada from Carlos Ascain 11 July 1926, General Aguilera 17 Aug. 1927 and n.d., Rafael Suarez n.d. For his business ventures as an impediment to confrontation with the regime see his own testimony in *HL* Oct. 1927. For denigration see RA Leg. 23 no. 6, 28 no. 5: 'Noticias Sobre la Toma de Alhucemas'; anonymous to Romanones July 1925. For appeals to the king see Maura, *Bosquejo*, pp. 234–5; and *El* 27 May 1926. For a 'neutral government' see RA Leg. 63 no. 31: Romanones to the king, n.d.

and their opposition to the regime. Royo Villanova, an Albista Professor, even attacked the dictator *ex cathedra*, rejected the king's invitation to the palace, and renounced his title of senator.[8] Less committed to the monarchist principle, members of the 'accidentalist' Reformist Party became increasingly alienated from the regime. Their leader, Melquiades Alvarez, who was at odds with the 'rotten' pre-dictatorial regime, was initially ready to accept the Dictatorship as 'a heroic measure for preventing a social danger'. But when it refused to give way to a constitutional regime, the Dictatorship turned into odious Caesarism; and he joined the opposition to overthrow it. The Liberal Union, whose formation was his idea, was intended to bring an end to the Dictatorship by a *coup*. However, despite his conspiratorial contacts, Melquiades Alvarez was not persecuted like other politicians. Never a minister, he was not identified with the vices of the old regime. But like all the others, he was not allowed to address meetings of his followers, even in the semi-privacy of the banqueting hall. His party, therefore, enjoyed no better fate than the others. Its members were loyal to the Monarchy so long as it respected a democracy open to social and political improvements. With a king violating the constitution and a dictator governing arbitrarily, many moved towards republicanism.[9]

It is evident that as one moves to the right of the political map, the attitude towards the Dictatorship was more lenient.

[8] For Alba's persecution and exile see Julio Zarraluqui, and Angel Marsá, *Figuras de España, Santiago Alba, el Hombre, el Símbolo*, pp. 169–226. See also Alba's appeals for rehabilitation in SAA: Alba to the king, and Alba to Magaz, 1 Oct., 1 Dec. 1923. For refusal to join conspiracies see ibid: Rodrigo Soriano to Alba, 7 Feb. 1925, 2 Mar. 1930. For the Albistas see Chapaprieta, *La Paz* p. 146; García Venero, *Alba* pp. 219–22, 248. The manifesto is in *HL* 1 May 1927. For Royo see ibid. 1 July 1927, and his *Un Grito Contra el Estatuto*, pp. 28–9. See also an Albista meeting in which acts of protest were related: *La Voz Valenciana*, 17 Feb. 1930. For Valladolid see José Altabella, '*El Norte de Castilla*' *en su Marco Periodístico (1864–1965)*, pp. 120–1, 154–5, 157.

[9] The main stronghold of the party in Asturias seems to have remained unshaken, but the bridgehead of Madrid was deprived of important elements who felt more strongly the new political ambience, see David Ruiz, *El Movimiento Obrero* pp. 201, 204. For Melquiades' criticism of the old regime see César González Ruano, *El General Primo de Rivera* pp. 63–4. For his attitude to the Dictatorship see his prologue to Carlos Blanco, *La Dictadura y los Procesos Militares*, pp. xiv–xvi. For his role in the Sanjuanada see RA Leg. 5 no. 29: 'Información Sobre los Sucesos de la Noche de San Juan'. See his conversation with Republican leaders on the 'Union Liberal' in Azaña, *Obras* iii, 886–7. For meetings see *The Times* 8, 9 May, 14 July 1924. See also García Venero, *Melquiades Alvarez*, pp. 344–5, 347, 353.

Nevertheless a crisis of confidence took place there also; and the tension between collaboration and opposition brought about open breaches in those parties and public alienation from the 'new regime'. Such was the case of the Conservative Party. Its leaders paid oral tribute to the Constitutional Monarchy, but neither Bugallal nor the Marqués de Lema were ready to criticize the king for his unconstitutional actions. Members of the party acclaimed the coming of the new regime as well as many of its subsequent steps to preserve 'order'; and some received *enchufes* (cushy jobs) in reward. In Huelva, this trend caused the virtual dissolution of the local branch; while La Cierva called openly upon his followers to support the new regime actively. He moved so far towards a collaborationist position, that Primo de Rivera suggested that he should succeed him. Ministerial posts were also offered to Sánchez de Toca and Bugallal, but they refused. The latter maintained that the Conservative Party could not disassociate itself from the constitutional legacy of its founder, Cánovas: a system that respected both the sovereignties of the people and of the king.[10]

However, the way in which the Conservatives disassociated themselves from Sánchez Guerra indicated that they were more devoted to the sovereignty of the king than that of the people. It was on behalf of the latter that Sánchez Guerra went into exile and later led an open rebellion, without finding any substantial support in the party of which he was the leader. In fact, a split in the party was evident from early 1925 when Sánchez Guerra was said to be 'violating the conservative character of the party by a policy of *rapprochement* with the left'. This *rapprochement*, as Ossorio y Gallardo pointed out in March the same year, was the reflection of 'a crisis of the conservative feeling', a growing alienation from the Alfonsist Monarchy, and a quest for democratic procedures. Sánchez Guerra, however, did not try to impose his opinion on the orthodox Conservatives who were more identified with Bugallal, who

[10] For acclamation of the new regime see Hipolito Finat Rojas, Marqués de Carvajal, *Cual Es el Horizonte Político de España? Reflexiones del Hombre de la Calle*, pp. 206–9. For 'enchufes' and Huelva see *ES* 3 Apr. 1924; and RA Leg. 28 no. 27: a speech of Burgos y Mazo in mid-1930. For Bugallal and Lema see *The Times*, 7 Mar. 1925, and RA Leg. 75 no. 6: 'Declaraciones de Bugallal 13 June 1925'. For La Cierva see his *Notas*, pp. 298–300, 305; and F.O. 371/11936: Rumbold to A. Chamberlain, 16 Sept. 1926.

unofficially took over the leadership of the party. When Sánchez Guerra went into exile, the magnates of the party were not ready to support him even financially. And in November 1929, when he was still under arrest for his abortive coup, Bugallal wrote to him that he opposed the attempts to bring the Dictatorship to an end by 'tragic means', an attitude which was adopted earlier in the year by the party organ, *La Epoca*. Sánchez Guerra ceased to be a party leader when he became a public hero; and in December 1929 Conservative ex-ministers were preparing the enthronement of Bugallal as the leader of the dispersed party.[11]

Also sympathetic to the new regime were the *Mauristas*. Benito Andrade, a member of the group, claimed that 95 per cent of them welcomed the Dictatorship. Their representatives in the Madrid *Diputación* rushed to acclaim any measure on behalf of 'the revival of Spain'. Antonio Maura also believed that the Dictatorship had an important task to fulfil: to uproot the vices of the old regime, and to carry through the longed-for 'revolution from above'. He therefore gave his blessing to those of his followers, like Calvo Sotelo, who collaborated with the new regime.[12]

Nevertheless, the dictator did not follow the advice of the old man, who soon became disillusioned. Maura upbraided the Directory for its failure to make any reform worth mentioning. He dismissed the UP as a new version of *caciquismo* rather than a national movement. He exhorted his followers not to join it; while his attack on Primo de Rivera as 'the creation and tool of the notorious Juntas de Defensa' (of 1917) brought some to resign from posts in the new administration. This led to a lofty exchange of letters between Maura and the dictator, who publicly attacked *Maurismo* as an abortive movement.[13]

[11] For the breach see Sanchez Guerra's letter to *El Sol* 28 Feb. 1925; Ossorio, *Una Crisis del Sentido Conservador*. For refusal to support him financially see Burgos y Mazo, *Los Constitucionalistas* ii, 16. Bugallal's letter is in Rafael Sánchez Guerra, *El Movimiento* pp. 214–16. *LE*, 30 Jan. 1929. For the ex-ministers see *EP*, 14 Dec. 1929.

[12] For 95 per cent see Benito Andrade in *LE*, 30 Oct. 1930. The declaration of the members of the Diputación is in Lerroux, *Al Servicio*, pp. 259–60. For Maura see G. Maura, *Bosquejo*, pp. 54–5. See F. Acedo Colunga, *Jose Calvo Sotelo. La Verdad de Una Muerte*, p. 46.

[13] MA Leg. 322: Antonio Maura to Adolfo Rodriguez, 4 Oct. 1924; Luis de los Terreros to Antonio Maura, 2 Oct. 1924; Maura, *Bosquejo*, pp. 82–5, 106–7; Dionisio Pérez, *La Dictadura a Través de sus Notas Oficiosas*, pp. 58, 60.

A similar progression from support to alienation from the Dictatorship took place in the Carlist movement as well. Carlists acclaimed the *coup* because it destroyed the liberal system to which they had always been hostile, and because they hoped it would set up a new regime more consistent with their doctrines of a 'Christian representative regime'. The pretender, Don Jaime, even claimed enthusiastically that the *coup d'état* was 'a convergence towards our doctrines, the fruit of our own action, the expression of a purely traditionalist spirit'. Victor Pradera, the most loyal collaborator of Primo de Rivera, had a detailed programme of 'regeneration' which he proposed to the dictator; and in a series of articles in *El Debate*, he welcomed the military uprising as 'illegal but necessary'.[14] But it was soon realized by Carlist leaders that the only point they had in common with Primo de Rivera was negative: his crusade against the liberal parties. He had no intention of creating a 'Traditionalist' Spain, nor of breaking his allegiance to the 'usurper' Alfonso. Thus, both *Jaimistas* and Traditionalists became an ineffective opposition to the regime. While Pradera remained faithful to the dictator, Vázquez de Mella and Don Jaime came to inspire an attitude of *retraimiento* from the institutions of the new regime—so much so that the ex-Deputy Esteban Bilbao was expelled from the party for joining the UP and assuming the presidency of the *Diputación* of Biscay.[15]

The *Lliga Regionalista* of Catalonia was the conservative party that moved more drastically than any other from 'support' to 'alienation' from the Dictatorship. The Lliga, a genuine representative of the Catalan bourgeoisie, not only welcomed the *coup d'état*, but also bore a collective responsibility for it, by creating an ambiance of hysteria around the terror in Catalonia, and by manifesting its readiness to acclaim any champion of 'peace' and 'order'. Some of its prominent leaders seemed to have a previous knowledge of the *coup*, and when it finally took place, Cambó, the party leader, exclaimed that this was 'the only sweet that we have been able to taste in a bitter year'. The

---

[14] See the manifesto of the Catalan Traditionalists in *LV* 16 Sept. 1923; the Duque de Madrid in Martínez, *Las Jornadas*, pp. 193–5; Don Jaime in *ES* 4 Oct. 1923; for Victor Pradera see his *Al Servicio de la Patria. Las Ocasiones Perdidas por la Dictadura, passim*.

[15] *The Times* 22 Sept. 1927 (Vázquez de Mella), 17 Jan. 1928 (Pradera); Román Oyarzun, *La Historia del Carlismo*, p. 501. Don Jaime in *Estampa* 29 April 1930. For Esteban Bilbao see *El Cruzado Español* 6 Mar. 1931.

Lliguista president of the *Mancomunidad,* Puig i Cadalfach, claimed that between an 'illegal' *coup* and 'corrupt politics', the Lliga chose the first. Moreover, the party organ did not conceal its 'satisfaction' at the fall of the old regime. The official history of the party denied allegations of collaboration in the *coup,* yet it is evident that the first measures of the dictator were in absolute coincidence with the Lliga's wishes. Such were the measures against the Anarcho-Syndicalists, the creation of the *Somatén,* the guardian of the 'bourgeois peace', and the designation of 'strong' men like Martínez Anido and Arlegui to deal with public order. Primo de Rivera also promised, at a very early stage, protectionist tariffs to the Catalan industrialists, politically represented by the Lliga. One of the reasons for their alienation from the last monarchist government was precisely the latter's threat to reduce tariffs on products imported from Belgium, Germany, and the U.S.A. When they needed lower tariffs—as for imported American fuel oil and raw cotton for their factories—the dictator did not hesitate to satisfy their demands. The euphoria with which the Chambers of Commerce and Industry of Catalonia greeted the dictator was fully rewarded with 'social peace' and the highest tariffs in Europe.[16]

However, the political bait did not materialize. Primo de Rivera promised to give the regions 'all the power and freedom compatible with the existence of a single state'. He even suggested that the Mancomunidad should draw up an autonomy scheme. But, as soon as he was firmly in the saddle he promulgated a series of anti-Catalanist decrees. 'Regionalist feelings are incompatible with a great fatherland', declared the dictator, to the Catalans' dismay. Primo's shift of policy caused a political breach between him and the Lliga, and its leaders became bitterly critical towards him. Attempts by the authorities

---

[16] For the Lliga and the origins of the *coup* see Maurín, *Los Hombres,* pp. 122, 124–6; García Venero, *El Nacionalismo Catalan,* pp. 306–9. Cambó in Lerroux, *Al Servicio,* p. 264. Puig in *LV* 19 Sept. 1923. The official organ is *La Veu de Catalunya* 18 Sept. 1923. The official history is Lliga Catalana, *Historia d'Una Política Actuacions i Documents de la Lliga Regionalista 1901–1933,* p. 362. See also Puig in *El Sol* 15 May 1930. For the tariffs see F.O. 371/9490, 9493: Howard to Curzon (quoting reports from the British consul in Barcelona), 21, 29 Sept., 31 Oct. 1923; *The Economist* 26 Nov. 1927, 23 Nov. 1929. For the Chambers of Industry see *LV* 15, 18 Sept. 1923. They were the first to congratulate the dictator. For social peace see the testimony of the captain general in J. Milego, *El General Barrera,* pp. 73–89. See also a study on the Lliga: Isidre Molas, *Lliga Catalana* i, 144–5.

to bridge the gap between the government and the Lliga failed, once it was made clear that the Local Government Act of 1924 provided for the dissolution of all the *Diputaciones*, except those of the Basque country. The Lliga now moved to a position of illegality and opposition. Its centres were dissolved and its leaders persecuted. It could still carry on some activities in the cultural and the international fields. Joan Estelrich made the issue of Catalan aspirations a legitimate item in the agenda of the League of Nations; while his colleagues in Spain promoted a Catalanist cultural renaissance.[17]

This confrontation with the Dictatorship did not push the Lliga towards an exclusive Catalanism ('Catalunya endins'), as it did to some sectors of the Catalan left. Cambó recognized that the 'Catalan differential fact', as it was called, had been accentuated by the persecutions of the dictator. But he also held that the constitutional and legal recognition of this 'differential fact' could not be achieved through a separatist policy. Centuries of historical and geographic union with Spain should not be denied as Rovira i Virgili had denied them; Cambó suggested neither separatism nor assimilation, but a solution of concord. This would be 'a mutual sentimental disarmament', by which Spain would recognize the 'Catalan differential fact', and Catalonia the historical unity of Spain. This solution could be brought about by a 'Catalunya enfora' policy once the Dictatorship was over. This appeal by Cambó for solidarity with Spain could not but be enhanced when, because of his open opposition to the regime, he was treated by the dictator like all the other discredited politicians. He openly criticized the persecution of the Catalan clergy; he urged the government to abandon the Moroccan Protectorate, and he denounced the inflationist policy of Calvo Sotelo as well as the floating of the peseta, as intolerable for business. Cambó was now, according

---

[17] For Primo's promise see *LV* 16 Sept. 1923; *The Times* 15 Sept. 1923 spoke of 'Home Rule'. For the breach see Puig's letter to Primo following the decrees in *ABC* 2 Mar. 1930; his conversation with him in December that year in *La Veu de Catalunya* 4 Mar. 1930. For the attempt to bridge the gap see Perucho, *Catalunya Sota*, pp. 68–81. For persecution see Hurtado, *Quaranta Anys* ii, 225; *The Times* 12 Nov. 1925; and Lliga, *Historia d'Una Política*, pp. 363–4, 367–9. For international campaign see Perucho, op. cit. 215–49; and J. Estelrich, *La Qüestió de les Minories*, pp. 85–94. For culture see Cambó, *Per la Concordia* , pp. 36–44.

to the dictator, a man 'whose patriotism has been proved of doubtful quality'.[18]

Thus, by the time the dictator tried to transform his 'parenthetic' rule into a regime with a constitutional framework, the bulk of the political forces of the old regime were alienated from him. Moreover, they were determined to abstain from supporting his constitutional schemes, thus obstructing his effort both to legitimize the new regime by their adherence to it, and to legalize it by means of a constitution. While presenting their views on the dictator's plans, the old politicians also seized the opportunity to define their political positions for the future.

The idea of convoking the so-called Consultative Assembly was interpreted by alarmed politicians as an attempt to perpetuate the Dictatorship, and as an unconstitutional step by the Monarchy in its disregard for national co-sovereignty. Politicians like La Cierva and Gabriel Maura, who accepted the invitation to the Assembly with the excuse that they were thus contributing to restore 'normality', did not alter the general trend of abstention on the part of others like Romanones, Bergamín, Cambó, Sánchez Guerra, Melquiades Alvarez, and even the orthodox Conservative Bugallal. The monarchist press gave moral support to this trend. This opposition, however, remained diffuse and incoherent when the ex-presidents of Chambers failed to meet in June 1927 in order to elaborate a common plan of action; thus Sánchez Guerra's appeals to the king warning him that, by becoming an absolute monarch, he was separating from himself all the constitutional monarchists, represented the strength and views of one isolated man.[19]

However, if in 1927 Primo de Rivera was strong enough to disregard the criticism of the politicians, their *retraimiento* in

[18] For Cambó's ideas see his *Per la Concordia, passim*; and his *España, Cataluña y la Nueva Constitución*, pp. 32–43, 53–89, 91–106. For their endorsement see Isidre Molas, *Lliga*, p. 151. For Cambó's criticism see Pabón, *Cambó* ii, part i, 548, 553–5; Diaz-Retg, *España Bajo el Nuevo Régimen*, pp. 182–98; and Cambó, *La Valoración de la Peseta*, especially pp. 99–111, 113–27, 129–31. The last quotation is from *The Times* 21 Nov. 1927.

[19] See Bergamín and Romanones in *LE* 2 Oct. 1926; *HL* 1 Oct. 1927; *The Times* 16 Nov. 1927; Cambó in *Per la Concordia*, p. 169; for Melquiades see García Venero, *Melquiades*, p. 355. For the press see *ABC* 20 May 1927, 1 Jan., 24 Aug. 1928; and a survey in F.O. 371/12717: Rumbold to A. Chamberlain, 6 Sept. 1927. For the failure to meet see RA Leg. 2 no. 42: Bugallal to Romanones 26 June 1927. For Sánchez Guerra see RA Leg. 53 no. 48: Sánchez Guerra to the queen mother, n.d.; and *HL* July 1927, May 1928. See also above, p. 29–30.

1929 was certainly a severe blow to his attempts to save his uncertain rule. Whereas in 1927 he said that the 'for ever extinguished' voices of the 'políticos' would not be heard in the Assembly, he now proposed seats for ex-ministers to help decide on the new constitution. After a series of contacts between ex-premiers and ex-presidents of Chambers, a negative attitude was elaborated, with Cambó and Reformist leaders joining the *retraimiento*, and a hesitant Romanones in the minority. *El Imparcial*, that saw the possibility of a genuine constitutional revival, denounced this 'torpid obfuscation, reprehensible pride and sectarian doctrinairism of the politicians'; and *El Debate* cast on them the responsibility for the failure of the Dictatorship to become 'a national movement'. But the official decision of the politicians as well as the demonstrative designation by cultural associations of outcast politicians like Alba and Sánchez Guerra as their representatives in the Assembly seemed to represent the general tendency among constitutional monarchists.[20]

This was further proved by an overwhelming rejection of the constitutional draft of the Assembly by the mouthpieces of constitutional monarchism. Any parliament or draft which were not based upon the 1876 constitution were rejected out of hand. Both Liberals and Conservatives agreed that the Assembly's draft disregarded the basic principles of parliamentarism and national sovereignty. If there were any advanced clauses in the new constitution, they said, they could be added to that of 1876 without an entirely new constitution having to be drawn up. Even if the new draft was perfect, they added, it was still unacceptable, because it had not been elaborated by a demo-cratically elected body. Only a group of nominees by the dictator could, according to *El Imparcial*, have drawn up this 'utopian and fantastic conception of reactionary politics'. Nor did the voice of La Cierva, a member of the committee which

---

[20] For the decree see Maura, *Bosquejo*, p. 347. For contacts and common decision see *LE* 30 July, 7 Aug. 1929; *EI* 30 Aug. 1929; *LV* 14, 21 Aug. 1929, 1 Sept. 1929. See a detailed survey of the 'políticos' attitude in F. Villanueva, *El Momento Constitucional*, pp. 27–53. For Romanones see Burgos y Mazo, *Los Constitucionalistas* ii, 155–6. Romanones had, however, an 'authorization' from his 'friends' to join the Assembly, see RA Leg. 14 no. 5: *Relación de los Amigos que Contestaron a la Consulta por su Asistencia o no a la Asamblea* (348 were on behalf, 121 against and 268 abstained). See *EI* 29 Aug. 1929; *ED* 13 Sept. 1929. For the 'outcast' see *EI* 2, 25 Oct. 1929.

elaborated the new constitution, represent that of the Conservatives, whose organ *La Epoca* attacked the undemocratic draft, and whose leader Bugallal was opposed to the idea 'of giving a constitution to a people which had already got one'.[21] The Lliga, unlike the Conservatives and the Liberals, had no sentimental attachment to the 1876 'Castilian' constitution. It recognized the need of substantial modifications to limit the absolute power of the king. However, the new draft's disregard of Catalan aspirations, rather than its 'undemocratic origin' which they took pains to stress, brought them to reject it.[22]

Unfortunately for the dictator, not even on the extreme right did he find substantial support. The Carlists did not find in the draft their principle of 'Dios, Patria y Rey' and provisions for a 'Christian society', though Pradera would have preferred it to the 'liberal' constitution of 1876. Not even the Catholic syndical movement, alienated from the regime because of its favouritism towards the Socialists, was prepared to support either the Assembly or its constitution. *El Debate*, which ran a consistent panegyric of the Dictatorship, though strongly in favour of the new constitution's provisions for 'strengthening the executive', expressed some democratic scruples when it exhorted the dictator not to promulgate his constitution by decree, but through elections or plebiscite. When analysing this coolness of both right and left, *La Vanguardia*, another supporter of the dictator, had to suggest that the whole idea be dropped.[23]

The imminence of the fall of the Dictatorship brought the men of the old regime to take up positions looking to the future. The Conservatives agreed on the need to set up a conservative 'government of transition' which would summon an Ordinary

[21] Since mid-July 1929 an immense number of articles and editorials in both *El Imparcial* and *La Epoca* had been putting forward these reservations. See selected references in *EI* 9, 16, 18, 21 July, 16 Aug. 1929 (Romanones, García Prieto, Marqués de Lema, Baldomero Argente, Pérez Caballero), 7, 19 July, 14 Nov. 1929 (editorials); *LE* 18 July, 13 Dec. 1929 (Bugallal, Marqués de Santa Cruz, La Cierva, Sánchez de Toca), 8, 10, 26, 27 July, 7 Aug. 1929 (editorials). For a concentrated analysis of the Conservative view see Marqués de Carvajal, *Cual Es el Horizonte* pp. 21–2, 209–13, 219–21.

[22] Cambó, *España, Cataluña* pp. 107–12; *LE* 26 July 1929 (Ventosa), 7 Aug. 1929 (quoting *La Veu*).

[23] For the Carlists see *El Cruzado Español* 2 Aug., 13 Sept. 1929; Luis Navarro Canales, *La Cuestión Religiosa en el Anteproyecto Constitucional* pp. 9–13; Pradera, *Al Servicio de la Patria*, pp. 365–83. For the syndicates see *LV* 8 Aug. 1929. *ED* 7, 16 July, 23 Oct. 1929. *LV* 11, 12 July 1929.

Cortes and restore the 1876 constitution. The Liberals, on the other hand, feared that such a government might be a prolongation of the Dictatorship under the auspices of the UP, or of some other ultra-conservative group. They therefore asked for a period of free political mobilization to culminate in a general election under a Primo government, rather than under any conservative group anxious to perpetuate its rule. However, both Conservatives and Liberals had a common objection to the opening of a constituent process, which might involve the country in a long period of unrest and instability. Cambó had clearer vision of what a period of transition implied. He was convinced that whether a Constituent Cortes were summoned or not, a constituent process would in any case be opened with the fall of the Dictatorship. And consistent with his plans for 'political intervention', he renewed in September 1929 his political contacts, in order to be able to play an important role in the new situation.[24]

When the 'new situation' finally emerged with the dictator's resignation, the old parties could claim credit for it. Their consistent contumacy, and their refusal to provide the dictator with a political backbone for his schemes to perpetuate his rule contributed to the exhaustion of his alternatives. Now they were determined to disassociate both themselves and the king from a dangerous identification with the fallen regime.

2. A MONARCHIST COUNTER-OFFENSIVE 1930–1931

The republican revival in the 'new situation' was not met by indifference on the monarchist side. Despite years of inactivity it is evident that, once the left accelerated its anti-monarchist campaign throughout the Berenguer period, monarchist opinion was also mobilized. Just as the left was aware of the golden opportunity to undermine the Monarchy, so the monarchists understood that a campaign on behalf of the king and the basic principles of a 'Christian society' was a question of self-preservation. Just as on the republican side, in the monarchist

[24] For the Conservatives see *LE* 13 (Bugallal), 17, 23 Dec. 1929, 4 Jan. 1930 (editorials); *EI* 4 Jan. 1930 (Bugallal). For Liberals see ibid. 15, 28 Sept., 10, 17, 20–22, 24, 29 Dec. 1929, 5 Jan. 1930. For objection to Constituent Cortes see *LE* 12, 17 July 1929; *EI* 10 Dec. 1929. For Cambó see *LV* 30 July, 2 Aug., 21 Sept. 1929; Cambó, *Per la Concordia*, pp. 183–93; Pabón, *Cambó* ii, part i, 581–4.

camp there was also a great number of local and provincial groups, as well as diffuse manifestations of monarchism. However, whereas *Alianza Republicana* and the 'San Sebastián coalition' became a melting-pot for the dispersed expressions of republicanism, the monarchists were not able to co-ordinate the numerous and isolated monarchist initiatives into a great national movement. Old rivalries and the pettiness of leaders, whether local or national, condemned them to sterility in the face of a Republican movement whose greatest force lay in its unity.

The monarchist counter-offensive started as soon as Sánchez Guerra launched his attack on the king, in his speech of 26 February. The next day numerous broadsheets were scattered over Madrid and Barcelona with 'Vivas' to the king from aeroplanes and motor cars. All over the provinces official establishments became crowded with people who came to declare their loyalty to the Monarchy, and hundreds of telegrams arrived at the royal palace with huge files of signatures. These came from Spaniards in the Moroccan Protectorate, citizens in provincial towns, ladies' organizations like the *Real Patronato del Soldado*, Catholic bodies like the *Asociación Católica de Represión de la Blasfemia*, and non-Marxist syndicates. Many came to sign personally at the palace, taking a good opportunity to visit the inside. These and other monarchist demonstrations were in many places initiated either by members of the nobility or by the local authorities. Such was the case of the enthusiastic welcomes for the king staged in San Sebastián, Seville, Barcelona, and Zaragoza, and of the conspicuous file of 75,000 signatures which arrived from Santander, a city of 89,000 inhabitants.[25]

The climax of this monarchist gathering around the king, a gathering which reflected both lack of organization and disunion among Monarchists, was the meeting in the Madrid bullring at

[25] For 'Vivas' see *The Times* 28 Feb. 1930; *LV* 2 Mar. 1930. For files of signatures see *ABC* 5, 6, 8, 9, 14 Mar., 4, 22 Apr. 1930 (from San Sebastián, Barcelona, Córdoba, Avila, Salamanca, the ladies, Morocco, Catholics); *EI* 30 Mar. 1930 (Santander); *LV* 7, 28 Mar. 1920 (Barcelona). For crowds in the palace see *ABC* 8, 11 Mar. 1930. For 'organized' demonstrations see *The Times* 7 Mar. 1930 (La Granja); *ABC* 14, 16, 20, 28 Mar., 5, 13, 15, 16 Apr., 7, 9, 20 May 1930 (Valencia, Bilbao, La Coruña, San Sebastián, Seville, Barcelona, Zaragoza, Almería, Murcia); *LV* 6 Mar. 1930 (Cádiz).

the end of April. Mutual misgivings prevented the representation of the Monarchist left in the meeting, which thus became a Conservative gathering of Bugallal's friends, aristocratic clients, 'patriotic' women, and probably also curious republicans. The manifestations of loyalty that arrived from the provinces were 'official' and lacked a genuine popular character. The speeches in the meeting were characterized by stereotyped monarchist phrases about the nation that loved its king and the 'consubstantiality' between both. Only Goicoechea's speech had precise references to the political situation; but when Bugallal embarked upon a boring speech about the origins of the Monarchy, the discovery of America, and 'the glory of the race', he found himself talking to a half empty bullring.[26]

Nevertheless the monarchist campaign, however diffuse, continued. Sections of Monarchist Youth were founded to be 'enthusiastic propagators of the monarchist ideal'. The Madrid section was personally encouraged by the king. In Valencia, it campaigned with meetings and pamphlets on behalf of 'Religion and Monarchy'; in Barcelona it elaborated a platform of compromise between *españolismo* and regionalism, while in Seville, Valladolid, Bilbao, Córdoba, Zaragoza, León, and Burgos youth section were engaged in pro-Alfonso initiatives. In the case of Madrid, however, there was a failure to maintain a persistent devotion to the cause. Long summer holidays paralysed the activities of these sons of good families, as their leader Vegas Latapié later confessed. During the winter he managed to stage some manifestations, but regular activities were boycotted because of lack of enthusiasm and a central organizer.[27]

The union of Monarchists which could not be achieved on a

---

[26] For the mutual misgivings see Romanones in *ABC* 22 Apr. 1930; *El* 20 Apr. 1930. For 'official' support see an example in AHN Leg. 51: The Mayor of Plasencia to the Minister of the Interior 19 Apr. 1930 no. 567. For the meeting see *ABC, Estampa* 22 Apr. 1930; F.O. 371/15040: Grahame to A. Henderson, 23 Apr. 1930.

[27] For Madrid see *El* 7 Mar., 4 Apr. 1930; *ABC* 9 May, 28 Nov. 1930, 21 Jan. 1931 and S. Galindo Herrero, *Los Partidos Monárquicos Bajo la Segunda República*, p. 62. For other places see *ABC* 25 Apr., 16 July, 26 Sept., 2, 10 Oct. 1930 (Valencia); 9 Dec. 1930 (Bilbao); 20 Mar. 1930 (Valladolid); 9, 27 Apr. 1930 (Córdoba); 22 Apr. 1930 (Burgos); 2 Dec. 1930 (León); 1 May 1930 (Zaragoza); *El* 9 Mar. 1930 (Seville); *LV* 25 Apr., 20 May, 31 July, 24 Oct. 1930 (Barcelona).

national level was nevertheless successfully organized in some towns. In Córdoba, the ex-Deputy Manuel Enriquez Barrios set up a common committee for all the Monarchist forces in the area, from the rightist *Casa Social Católica* to the Liberals. In Jaén, local Conservatives and Liberals organized a coalition not only for daily propaganda, but also in order to negotiate a common candidature for the forthcoming elections; while in León it was the mayor who managed to gather local monarchists in a common group. The strongest coalition was that of Seville under the presidency of the Marqués de Torrenueva. It was an alliance of disparate groups like *Albistas, Liga Católica,* Liberals, and Conservatives, in which each group preserved its own significance, but agreed to a minimum political programme of 'Monarchy, Constitution, and Parliament', and to a common economic platform which emphasized a desire for agricultural protectionism. Monarchist national figures like La Cierva, Goichoechea, and Royo Villanova, who attended a huge meeting staged in November by the Seville coalition manifested their appreciation of the work done by the local Monarchists, but were unable to extend this unity on a national scale.[28]

Attempts to stimulate monarchist feelings through non-political associations and the spreading of 'Christian morality' were also made, to curb the republican offensive. Such was, in Madrid, the *raison d'être* of the *Casa de la Democracia Monárquica,* which endeavoured to find jobs for unemployed workers as well as to propagate among them the principles of 'authority' and 'Monarchy'. Equally dedicated to overcoming the 'corrupt' influence of the leftist offensive was 'Spanish Action on Behalf of Cultivated Conversation and Good Manners'. In Barcelona, such clubs as the *Institución Alfonso Victoria, Centro Cultural Monárquico, Liga Ciudadana Cultural, Peña Ibérica, Acción Española, Acción Nacional,* and *La Raza* combined with their monarchist propaganda an extreme 'españolismo', to such an extent that even a centralist journalist was alarmed by their total disregard of Catalan sentiments.[29]

---

[28] Córdoba: *EI* 13, 16 Mar. 1930. Jaén: *ABC* 13 Feb., 6 Mar. 1930. León: ibid. 9 Mar. 1930. Seville: *ED* 25 Feb. 1930 (editorial), *EI* 26 Feb. 1930, *ABC* 14 May, 28 Sept., 4 Nov. 1930, *LE* 18 Nov. 1930. See also Burgos y Mazo, *Los Constitucionalistas* iii, 123.

[29] For organizations see *ABC* 7 May, 3, 10 June, 6 Sept., 29 Oct. 1930; *LV* 15 Feb., 5, 6, 8, 12 Mar., 22 July, 20 Aug., 11, 20, 29 Nov. 1930; *LE* 11 Feb. 1931 (the journalist).

The best organized and most active campaign was that run, in huge gatherings throughout the country, by the *Campaña de Orientación Social.* It was founded to propagate the 'four basic principles of society', as men like Severino Aznar, Ramiro de Maeztu, Pio Zabala, and Angel Herrera—all prominent Catholics—perceived them. These were religion, family, order, and Monarchy. The 'consubstantiality' of the latter with Spain, and the monarchist feeling as a consequence of 'conviction, aesthetic considerations, tradition, and instinct' were put forward as the ideological and historical answer to the leftist challenge to one concrete act of the king: the violation of the constitution. The assumption of the organizers was that Spain was going through a period of confusion in which even those foundations of society were in question. The alarming symptoms of sexual freedom, an upsurge of pornographic literature, permissive manners, and corrupting films were attacked as 'dissolvent' factors. Stability could be restored only by making religion once more the major unifying factor, by strengthening the sanctity of the family against dissolvent tendencies, and by defending order through complete submission to the Monarchy.[30]

Attempts to coin slogans to attract the proletariat were also made by tiny Monarchist pseudo-Socialist groups, like the *Partido Socialista Monárquico Obrero Alfonso XIII,* the *Asociación Monárquica Obrera,* and the *Unión Obrera Monárquica.* The last two groups, the first in Barcelona and the latter in Madrid, were led by non-workers who were mainly interested in 'harmony' between workers and employers, and in the support of Monarchist candidates in the elections. Neither was the first group more 'Obrerista'. It existed before the Dictatorship as an 'element of order' in syndicalist Barcelona. Later its members joined the UP, and now they were propagating in a great number of meetings blind allegiance to the king, 'social order' and 'national unity'. With the class struggle an anathema, the

---

[30] For 'Orientación' see reports on meetings in *ED* 15, 29 Apr., 6 May, 11 Nov., 9 Dec. 1930; *LE* 1 Dec. 1930; *ABC* 11 Apr., 21, 28 Oct., 25, 27 Nov., 11 Dec. 1930. For an insight into the motivation of the campaign see also Juan de Hinojosa, 'La Lucha Contra la Inmoralidad Publica' in *Problemas Sociales Candentes* (Publicaciones del 'Grupo de la Democracia Cristiana'), pp. 57–110. For Angel Herrera's propagandists in the campaign see J. M. Pemán, *Mis Almuerzos,* p. 78.

'socialist' content was represented by vague economic formulae. But not even the active support of the king and the local authorities in Barcelona were sufficient to increase the impact of the group, which was nothing more than the reflection of a desire to dissuade urban workers from joining the swelling trend to the left.[31]

The menace to the Monarchy and to the basic foundations of society had also stimulated monarchist women to fight against the leftist trend. The Association of Spanish women, an organization sponsored by aristocratic ladies, denounced the 'immoral and unpractical' ideology of their feminist counterparts. When it called for 'a greater participation of women in politics', what it had in mind was 'a crusade on behalf of religion, the fatherland and the king'. Even without suffrage, the ladies of the Association claimed, women could exercise their influence through propaganda in meetings and in the press, and by exerting pressure on their husbands in order to make them use their vote 'properly'. In May 1930 they set up a 'Feminine Committee For Peace, Progress and The Honour of Spain', which not only published leaflets and organized pro-monarchist subscriptions, but also tried to persuade housewives to boycott those merchants who advertised their products in the leftist press. Equally active in the clamorous monarchist counter-offensive were orthodox women's organizations like *Acción Católica de la Mujer* and the *Unión de Damas Españolas del Sagrado Corazón*, both sponsored by the church. Together with their campaign aimed at canalizing women's activities towards 'their natural functions', keeping them away from 'emancipatory and revolutionary' ideas—for which both organized special courses— they had instructions from the *Juntas Diocesanas de Acción Católica* to join any manifestation of loyalty to the king. The Bishop of Madrid–Alcalá called upon them to set up 'a league of defence of our Catholic monarch, to which all good Spaniards should belong', an idea strongly supported by the Primate of the Spanish Church, Cardinal Segura. If not formally, at least

---

[31] See information on the group *Alfonso XIII* in *LV* 11, 15 Mar., 24 Apr., 29 July, 5 Sept., 4 Nov., 2 Dec. 1930, 20 Jan. 1931; *ABC* 22 Apr., 28 Dec. 1930, 24 Jan. 1931; *EP* 31 Oct. 1930. For the two other groups see *LV* 16 Apr., 27 Nov. 1930; *ABC* 28 Nov. 1930, 23 Jan. 1931.

practically, such a league existed through the energetic propaganda of these women whether in the streets, the press, or meetings.[32]

Indeed, it is fairly obvious that the powerful ecclesiastical establishment was essentially monarchist and that throughout the Berenguer period it took sides with the monarchists in their effort to curb the left. It did so through its pastorals and educational institutions scattered all over the country, through its large network of lay organizations like *Acción Católica*, *Confederación Nacional Católico-Agraria* with its 5,000 syndicates and 600,000 affiliates, committed to anti-Marxism; and through the *Sindicatos Católicos*, and *Sindicatos Libres*, whose membership had increased substantially during the dictatorship, and the Association of Catholic Students.[33]

Both the 'Libres' and the 'Católicos' received special attention from Cardinal Segura. In a speech at the congress of the National Confederation of Catholic Syndicates in 1928, he explicitly called upon the members to serve faithfully 'our august king who cares especially for the Catholic worker'. During the Berenguer government, and encouraged by the influence of *Acción Católica*, they were there to raise their voice against the waves of political and revolutionary strikes. As part of this consistent campaign, in December 1930 Segura was able to unify the 'Católicos' and the 'Libres' into a powerful Catholic

[32] For the first Association see information on its activities and ideas in its organ *Mujeres Españolas* 5, 19 Jan., 23 Feb., 2, 9, 16, 23 Mar., 9 Nov. 1930, 11 Jan., 1, 13 Feb. 1931; *ABC* 17, 25 Apr. 1930. For the boycott see ibid. 23 May 1930 denouncing it as an 'unfair' measure; and *EI* 12 June 1930. For the Catholic women see their campaign and courses against revolutionary ideas in *Acción Católica de la Mujer* Jan.–May, Nov. 1930; *La Unión* Jan.–Apr., Nov. 1930. Acción Católica had for this purpose 8 provincial newspapers, and 81 cultural centres with 18,488 pupils: See *ACM* Jan. 1930. For official pro-Monarchy instructions see ibid. Apr.; and *La Unión* May 1930. For information on meetings, leaflets etc. see ibid. May, July 1930; and *ABC* 6, 8, 11, 20 Mar., 4, 22 Apr. 1930.

[33] *Anuario Estadístico de España* 1931; in 1930 the Church had 1,536 educational institutions and a regular clergy of 81,400. For a non-biased and unemotional account of the enormous material power of the church in 1925 see Torrubiano Ripoll, *Rebeldías*, especially pp. 29–61, 73–84. For the CONCA see statistics in *EI* 8 Nov. 1930. See for how the Church supervised its activities on a local level *El Labrador*, Teruel, 15 June 1930. Agustin Revuelta Martin, *Ventajas que la Sindicación Católica Reporta a la Clase Agraria*, pp. 20–1. For the flourishing of the Sindicatos Libres during the Dictatorship see Aunós, *La Política Corporativa*, p. 128. He points to an increase from 50,000 to 150,000. See also *LV*, 24 Sept. 1929: 143,027 affiliates were represented in the national congress, and the optimistic accounts in 1929 and 1930 in *Boletín del Sindicato Católico de Tipógrafos y Similares de Madrid 1930 (Memoria de 1929), 1931 (Memoria de 1930)*.

syndical force committed, under Church auspices, to keeping Catholic workers away from revolutionary ideas.[34] Church encouragement was also given to the Catholic Association of Students in an effort to curb the overwhelming predominance of the FUE. But, apart from protesting against the politicization of the campuses, they did not seem to be able to attract the student youth, and in Seville, for example, they had to move outside the campus for their demonstrations.[35] The Church believed that only a strong united front of Catholics and the cultivation of political awareness could curb 'the enemies of the Church and social order', as Segura put it.[36] To the creation of such a front were directed the main activities of *Acción Católica*. It preached the intervention of Catholics in politics, whether directly or through 'propaganda in defence of Catholicism and its civilization . . . the family . . . the authority of parents, and moral life', all of which would create 'harmony between social and political life'. When, in mid-1929, the political forces of the country were rising out of a long lethargy and 'anti-religious as well as anti-Monarchist parties' were making their appearance, *Acción Católica* referred to its national congress as to 'the first general mobilization of the Catholic forces of Spain'. The rise of anti-Monarchist parties was made possible by the separation of Catholics from politics, therefore *Acción Católica* campaigned for the 'circumstantial union of all the Catholics affiliated to political parties'. In March 1930 Segura, alarmed by the leftist offensive, urged the flock under his care to join those political parties whose doctrines did not contradict those of the Church, and to vote in the next elections on behalf of those candidates 'who offer the most solid guarantees for the good of religion and the fatherland'. In the spring of that year

---

[34] Segura's speech is in *Boletín del Sindicato Católico de Tipógrafos y Similares*, Madrid, Dec. 1928. For his and Church influence on the syndicates see *ES* 28 Nov. 1926, 11 Feb. 1927, 19 Sept. 1929; and Padre Sisinio Nevares, *El Porqué de la Sindicación Obrera Católica* (Biblioteca de Fomento Social. Madrid, n.d.) *passim.* For campaign against revolutionary strikes see *ABC*, 16, 20 Nov., 17 Dec. 1930; and *Manifiesto que la confederación Regional de Sindicatos Libres del Centro de España dirige a Sus Afiliados y a la Opinión en General, con Motivo del 1 de Mayo 1930* in HMM, A/1696. For the unification see *La Ciencia Tomista* Mar.–Apr. 1931.

[35] Federico Tedeschini, *Discursos y Cartas Sobre Acción Católica Española*, pp. 32–4, 60–1, 109–10; *Boletín de Acción Católica* 25 Mar. 1929. for their campaign against politicization see *ABC* 6 May, 4 Nov. 1930. For Seville see ibid. 9 Mar. 1930.

[36] *Boletín de Acción Católica* 10 Feb. 1929.

prominent members of both the secular and the regular clergy adhered to the monarchist campaign. The Bishop of Avila, in a letter to the king, the Archbishop of Santiago, that of Seville as well as a representative of the Dominican order, in declarations either to the press or to their flock, made strong monarchist affirmations, stressing the 'consubstantiality' of the Monarchy with religion, and calling on everybody to gather around the king.[37]

It seems therefore incorrect to claim, as did *La Ciencia Tomista*, that 'the Church had kept a prudent silence' throughout the year that preceded the Republic.[38] The ecclesiastical establishment was a bastion of monarchism. Its spokesmen justified any strong measure that the Berenguer government might take against revolutionary attempts and the excesses of republican propaganda. Segura was alleged to have a proposal for a 'strong' Monarchist government that could fulfil this task better. This included hard-liners such as La Cierva, Goicoechea, and Pradera. Alfonso was 'the unshaken axis of national life' according to the Jesuit *Razón y Fe*; and Canon Hilario Yaben took great pains to provide doctrinal grounds for his belief in the superiority of the Monarchy over a Republic, the symbol of 'chaos' and 'national disintegration'. While the anti-monarchists were preaching political and social change, the Church was defending the political status-quo, and was both attacking the 'new wave' of morality and taking positions against the leftist press and intellectuals. No wonder that a liberal Canon, Garcia Gallego, was deeply alarmed by the identification of the Church with an 'absolute monarchy'. For the sake of both he suggested constitutional reform.[39]

---

[37] For the ideas of Acc. Cat. on political involvement see *Boletín de Acción Católica* 10, 25 Jan., 10 Feb., 25 Aug., 10 Sept. 1929. For Segura in March 1930 see *ABC* 9 Mar. 1930. For the figures of the clergy see *ABC* 14 Mar., 10, 22, 27, 30 Apr. 1930. For Segura and the increase in Acc. Cat.'s activities under his leadership, see J. Requejo San Román, *El Cardenal Segura*, pp. 101–12, 128–9.

[38] *La Ciencia Tomista* Mar.–Apr. 1931.

[39] For justifying measures see *La Ciencia Tomista* Jan.–Feb., Mar.–Apr. 1931; *Razón y Fe* 10 Jan. 1931. Segura in *EP* 5 Nov. 1930. The 'unshaken axis' in *Razón y Fe* 10 Mar. 1931. Hilario Yaben, *Monarquía o Republica?*, *passim*. For the defense of the status quo against the new morality etc., see the activities of the *Asociación de Padres de Familia* in *ABC* 25 Apr., 6 May, 24 Oct. 1930; *Patria Española* 22 Nov. 1930; see how these ideas were spread at a local level in *Semana Parroquial Organo de la Juntas Parroquiales* 14 Dec. 1930; and *La Cruz de la Parroquia*, Alcalá de Henares, 28 Dec. 1930. For a 'campaign of

However, the great monarchist potential that undoubtedly existed remained, throughout the Berenguer period, divided among its various components. Attempts to unify all the various and varied initiatives in a common front resulted in failure. The awakening of monarchist feelings was essentially a series of passionate reactions to the constant attacks from the left. The Sánchez Guerra speech, the 'anti-patriotic' campaigns of the Ateneo, the revolutionary strikes and the abortive republican *coups*, were the main stimulants of Spanish monarchism. Otherwise, as *ABC* pointed out, it was 'a prolix movement without any organic coherence'.[40]

It seemed that the nobility, motivated by an instinct of self-preservation, were the main force interested in creating a Monarchist front. 'The Russian Tsar was overthrown', recalled the Duque de Almenara Alta, 'because his aristocracy did not rally behind him.' *Acción Nobiliaria* was founded to bring about such a rally, and also in order to create a bloc which would be the 'strongest supporter of Monarchy, fatherland, and religion'. It strove to create a common committee for all the Monarchist groups, an idea also welcomed by the monarchist press. It succeeded for as long as it did not reach the operational stage. *Acción Monárquica*, which was founded by elements of Acción Nobiliaria to reach a united electoral candidature for Madrid, managed to include in its executive committee representatives from all the Monarchist groups in the country, from the Scouts up to the Conservatives and Liberals. But apart from organizing common protests against the 'Soviet hurricane' and from doing a useful job in getting monarchists on to the electoral register from which they had been omitted, neither Acción Monárquica nor *Reacción Ciudadana*, founded in November 1930, were ever able to elaborate a common political programme and strategy.[41]

---

defence' against the leftist press see *Boletín de Precios de la Cooperativa del Clero*, Dec. 1930. J. García Gallego, *Por Donde se Sale? El Momento Actual de España*, pp. 703, 708–11, 501–4.
[40] *ABC* 9 Dec. 1930.
[41] Almenara Alta in *ES* 26 June 1929; for attempts to create a bloc see Marqués de Lema, Vicente Piniés, and César Sanz respectively in *ABC* 3 Apr. 1930, 3 Feb. 1931, 25 Jan. 1931, Almenara Alta in 26 Feb., 12 Mar. 1930. For the press see *ED* 25 Jan. 1930; *LE* 18 Jan. 1930; *EI* 12, 13 Mar., 26 Apr. 1930. For Acción Monárquica see *ABC* 23 Mar., 2 Apr., 1 May, 22, 25 June, 11, 20 July, 5 Sept., 12 Oct. 1930; *LV* 27 Dec. 1930. For Reacción Ciudadana see *ABC* 6, 15 Nov. 1930.

3. THE 'OLD PARTIES' BETWEEN 'MODERNISM' AND THE REVIVAL OF 'OLD POLITICS'

The awakening of 'apolitical' monarchism was supported by an attempt of the old parties to reorganize. Furthermore, the strength of the republican offensive had also compelled these parties to coin slogans of modernization. However, the Berenguer government was to witness not only the history of this experiment's failure, but also a return to old rivalries and old divisions.

a. An incoherent conservatism

In 1929 Conservatives were aware of the fact that their party, as it existed before the Dictatorship, had never tried to attract the masses. The example of England and 'the predominance of an agrarian and conservative spirit in Spain', stimulated some to believe in the possibility of creating a 'Conservative Party of opinion on the English style'. For this purpose, without descending to 'populacherismo', it had to be stressed that 'conservative' was not a synonym of 'plutocrat', but the very essence of Spain's quest for order, religion, and social peace. This modern notion of conservatism was supposed to embrace and guarantee the interests of the working class, small business and small property owners. The Marqués de Carvajal pointed out how it was becoming impossible in politics to disregard the increasing power of the working class and the radicalization of public opinion. He therefore suggested that parties should strive to increase their contact with the 'street' and to establish an 'open democracy'. Once such a large Conservative Party was established, La Epoca argued, the Liberal Party would no longer have a raison d'être, thus establishing a two-party system in the English style with a Conservative and a Socialist Party alternating in power.[42]

But the formation of the Berenguer government with a majority of Conservatives helped to remove from the agenda, for the time being, the issue of a 'modern' party. With the feeling of being in power and a belief that the Ministry of the

---

[42] Marqués de Carvajal, *Cual es el Horizonte. . .?*, pp. 26–9, 113–16, 129–30. See how these ideas were endorsed by *La Epoca* 20, 23 Feb., 25 Mar., 1 July, 8, 13 Aug., 4 Dec. 1929; and supported by *ED* 20 Feb. 1929 (here also Bugallal).

Interior would anyway 'arrange' electoral results, 'renovation' became unnecessary. Conservatives suddenly started to refer to the government as if it was a definitive government and not a transitory one. As far as they were concerned, this government was 'normality itself', and they hoped to see it not only running the next elections, but also ruling the country afterwards. According to Bugallal nothing had really happened, and there was no need even to restore the constitution, which was still 'unshaken'. His main concern was to clear the Ayuntamientos of *Upetistas*, so that 'fair' general elections could be held. In a dull doctrinal speech to celebrate his election to the leadership of the party, he set out the principles that the Conservatives stood for: Constitutional Monarchy under the 1876 constitution, 'moderate protectionism', a budgetary policy concerned with increasing income and reducing expenditure, a reform of the Comités Paritarios to curb the workers' predominance, and strong opposition to any degree of expropriation. Conservatives who followed the offical line even refused to wave the banner of 'political responsibilities', because of the constitutional irresponsibility of the king and his 'sacred' person.[43]

Without any 'new definition', in a period in which everyone was expected to say something 'new', the Conservative Party met with no popular response. Even merely reviving old Conservative circles ran into difficulties. The election of Bugallal as leader of the party was questioned as premature by supporters of Sánchez Guerra like Bergamín, Hernández Lazaro and Abilio Calderón who threatened to lead their traditional clientele out of the party. In Alicante, the retirement of Salvador Canals left the local branch in a state of confusion, in spite of being favoured by the government in the matter of official posts. In Córdoba and Seville, when local Conservatives started to reorganize their forces, it was not in order to be subordinated to a central discipline, but in order to create local concentrations; while in Valladolid Conde de Gamazo was interested in strictly regional matters and in the defence of the

---

[43] For the Conservative features of the government see Berenguer, *De la Dictadura*, p. 63; *ED* 31 Jan. 1930. *ABC* 9 Mar. 1930: the commemoration of a Conservative ex-Premier was almost a cabinet meeting. For the government as 'normality' see *LE* 30 Jan., 3, 4, 17, 27 Feb., 7 July, 27 Oct., 3, 11 Nov. 1930 (editorials). For Ayuntamientos see Bugallal in *ABC* 4 Feb. 1930. For his speech see *LE* 11 Feb. 1930. For responsibility see *EI* 23 Apr. 1930 (Bugallal); *ABC* 9 May 1930 (Sánchez de Toca); and *LE* 7 Mar. 1930.

traditional protectionist aspirations of Castilian wheat growers.[44] 'Reorganization' in other places was a simple caciquista revival. *Bugallalista* strongholds were giving signs of life throughout the year in Valencia, Huesca, Zaragoza, and Galicia, Bugallal's private fief. The ex-minister Vicente Piniés went to revive 'old friendships' in Teruel; while in Murcia, La Cierva led, as an 'independent' Conservative, his 'friends', to whom he made his apologia for his collaboration with the Dictatorship. He reminded them that the main task of Conservatives was 'to defend the king against his defamers'. In Soria the Vizconde de Eza who claimed to have retired from politics, but confessed that he followed Bugallal, was confident that his 'men' would gain the elections in the province.[45]

Yet the current fashion of 'modernization' was not abandoned altogether, at least not as a tactical necessity. Youth sections were being set up in the provinces, and Rodríguez de Viguri, a senior member of the party, was appointed to supervise and to control their activities. Frequent meetings were held to discuss questions of the constitution, economics and 'international peace', but all roughly within the lines traced by Bugallal. Propaganda efforts were made through manifestos and meetings. The demand to make contact with the British Conservative Party, and 'to imitate' its organization was again put forward, and an ultra-modern political secretariat was organized with the help of the Minister Weiss. The secretariat was supposed to draw up a detailed register, not only of members of the party, but also of other conservative forces, and was to include sections for propaganda, legislation, reforms, and press. But the whole matter seemed to be more of a governmental measure than a great 'modern' achievement of the Conservative Party.[46]

Furthermore, if by 'modernization' any geniune openness

[44] For the dissidents see *ABC* 12, 14, 15 Feb., 5 Mar. 1930. For Canals and the case of Alicante see *El Agrario*, Alicante, 25 Oct. 1930; RA Leg. 25 no. 6: 'Política Agraria en Alicante'; Leg. 49 no. 21: Unión Agraria to Berenguer 10 Nov. 1930. For the other cases see *LV* 19 Feb.; *ABC* 13 Mar. 1930; and *Unión Monárquica* 15 Jan. 1931.

[45] *El* 20 Feb. 1930 (Valencia); *ABC* 29 Apr. 1930 (Huesca, Teruel, Zaragoza). For Galicia see ibid. 12 Sept., 24 Oct. 1930; and Vicente Risco, *El Problema Político de Galicia*, pp. 111, 182–3, 185, 230–1. For La Cierva see his *Notas*, p. 336; *LE* 6 Oct. 1930; and *ABC* 28, 30 Sept. 1930. For Eza see an interview in ibid. 18 Sept. 1930.

[46] For the youth and propaganda see *ABC* 21 May, 5, 11, 15, 22, 27 June, 6 Sept., 1 Oct., 6, 19 Nov. 1930; *LE* 15, 16 Oct. 1930. For the British Conservatives see *ABC* 5 July 1930; *LE* 20 Sept. 1930. For the secretariat see *ABC* 12, 13 Nov. 1930.

towards the left was ever meant, it was soon overshadowed by a move to the right. Compelled by the anti-dynastic left and the advances of the Liberal Party, the Conservatives were pushed to adopt orthodox views, or rather to direct their energies towards attracting the extreme right. Once the possibility of a great Liberal Party assuming power under Santiago Alba was raised during the summer,[47] Bugallal suggested that the best way of avoiding it was by setting up a coalition of conservative forces, under the doctrinal lead of his party.[48] This meant an openness towards ultra-rightist elements like *El Debate*, *Acción Nobiliaria*, Catholic syndicates and agrarian conservatives. A special appeal was made to the latter 'because the country is where the petty bourgeoisie is the strongest bastion of social conservatism, the most impregnable wall against revolutionary tumults'. Faced with the leftist offensive, the Conservative *La Epoca* claimed, there was no alternative but to act as 'defenders and saviours of western civilization'.[49]

None the less, the appeal to agrarian elements was utterly rejected. Throughout the Berenguer period agrarian organizations were spreading among small landowners. The main features of this movement were social and political conservatism, a particular interest in agrarian matters, and a refusal to be patronized by professional politicians. The credibility of 'old politics' was at its lowest point among conscious agrarians, who had been campaigning for years on behalf of demands such as credit facilities and 'protection'. The *Partido Nacional Agrario*, the *Liga Agraria*, the *Liga Nacional de Campesinos*, and *Acción Castellana*, all of which represented the small and middle peasants in Spain, though all defending monarchism and Catholicism, campaigned against the empty agrarian oratory of politicians, and made consistent efforts to prevent the infiltration of representatives of the Monarchist parties into their ranks.[50] Conservative 'agrarianism', socially and politically

---

[47] See below, pp. 199–201.

[48] *LE* 18 July 1930.

[49] *LE* 15, 21, 29 Oct. 1930, 1, 7 Jan. 1931. See also *EI* 2, 4 Jan. 1931.

[50] For the various groups see *ED* 28 Oct. 1930 (on Acción Castellana), 12, 26 Oct., 8 Nov. 1930 (articles on the spectacular increase of the movement); AHN Leg. 51: Governor Cáceres to Ministry of the Interior 28 Oct. 1930 on the local Liga Agraria; *El Campesino* Oct., Nov. 1930 (the organ of the Liga Nacional); and articles in *LV* 30 Oct. 1930; *ABC* 7 Nov., 3 Dec. 1930; as well as a report in F.O. 371/15042: Grahame to A. Henderson, 29 Oct. 1930, surveying with special interest this agrarian movement.

threatened by the 'urban values' such as democracy and liberalism, was on its way to becoming a coherent proponent of Catholic corporatism rather than of liberal monarchism.[51]

The appeal to the right was also part of the efforts of the Conservatives to save the Berenguer government from the electoral boycott of both the dynastic and anti-dynastic left. The Conservatives maintained that general elections should precede the municipal elections as against the Liberals' campaign on behalf of an inverted order. *El Debate*, which initially supported the Liberals, later endorsed the Conservatives' view, when it realized that this was a good banner under which to cement the union of the conservatives.[52] The Conservatives even rejected the demands of Liberals that the designation of mayors by royal order should be abolished, in order that the general elections should be made on a democratic basis. The government's policy was devotedly supported by the Conservatives as the best way of bringing a Conservative majority to the next Cortes. In what was considered by the liberal *El Sol* an anachronistic speech, and by *El Debate* a genuine Canovist concept, Bugallal also rejected out of hand the idea of a Constituent Cortes. It was 'unconstitutional' to summon such a Cortes, he said, and added that 'a nation should not be submitted to daily plebiscites', and to 'explosions of passion'.[53]

The failure to create a strong conservative alternative to support the Monarchy was also due to the isolation of other conservative parties and groups. Together they might have become a political backbone of the regime, but separated they were a manifestation of the division and incoherence of Spanish conservatism.

With no original methods or content, the *Mauristas*, who represented a so-called rejuvenated conservatism, ran independent and sterile activities in their dispersed centres in Mallorca, Madrid, and Catalonia. Though they continued to pay tribute to Maurista slogans of 'citizenship' and 'electoral sincerity', they differed, under Goicoechea's leadership, from *Bugallalistas*

---

[51] See *El Campesino* and *España Agraria*, 1929–30. These organs were the precursors of the CEDA rather than the defenders of Alfonso XIII's uncertain crown.

[52] *ED* 18 June 1930.

[53] For the party's ideas on the order of the elections and on mayors see *LE* 22, 29 Sept., 3 Nov. 1930, 14 Jan., 2, 4, 11, 12 Feb. 1931. For Bugallal see *El Sol* 1 Jan. 1931; *ED* 2 Jan. 1931; and *LE* 1, 7 Jan. 1931.

and *Ciervistas* only in name. They campaigned against the revolutionary strikes and on behalf of the defence of 'Monarchy, social order and a *prudent* and gradual restoration of constitutional liberties'. This led an ex-Maurista, Benito Andrade, to point out, by the end of 1929, their identification with the Conservatives, and therefore, to suggest that they should join them, instead of leading an ineffective separate campaign.[54]

Equally sterile was the attempt of Gabriel Maura to patronize another pseudo-Maurista group entitled *Derecha Nacional*. It resulted in the precarious existence of a tiny group confined to the geographical boundaries of Barcelona and to the doctrinal limits of both political and social conservatism. In spite of its declared aim and consistent efforts to unify the 'healthy elements of the right, in order to avoid the formation of dispersed groups, which might justify the return to shameful situations', the Derecha Nacional was no more than one of these 'dispersed groups'.[55]

Such groups were also created by the liquidation of the *Unión Patriótica*, following the fall of the dictator. Many of its members, however, poured into any established party, whether republican or monarchist, in an attempt to save their skins. But others joined ephemeral groups founded by the collaborators of the dictator. Such were the *Partido Social Conservador* of Yanguas in Linares, the *Derecha Social Democrática* in Seville under the inspiration of José Pemartín, the *Unión de Antiguos Combatientes de la Dictadura* in Logroño, and the *Casco de Hierro Ciudadano* in Cuenca.[56]

A more significant trend, however, was started in April 1930, when the ex-ministers of the Dictatorship officially founded the *Unión Monárquica*, a conservative party that aimed at defending the heritage of the Dictatorship. Primo de Rivera had given his blessing in February to the then embryonic

[54] For information on centres, activities and ideas see *ABC* 7, 28 Feb., 15, 25 Apr., 25 June, 10, 12, 15, 18 July, 19 Nov., 9 Dec. 1930; *LV* 23 Feb., 4 Jan., 15 Oct. 1930, 4, 20, 30 Jan. 1931. See also Goicoechea in 'Orientación Social': *ABC* 28 Oct. 1930. Andrade in *LE* 30 Oct. 1929.

[55] See information and their relations with Gabriel Maura in *ABC* 23 Feb. 1930; *LV* 15 Feb., 1 Mar., 4, 17, 23 Apr., 4 June, 5 Sept., 8, 12 Nov. 1930.

[56] For a movement of escape to the right and to the left see Calvo Sotelo, *Seis Años*, pp. 24–7; Berenguer, *De la Dictadura*, pp. 76–7, 80–1; and references in *ABC* 11 Feb., 6, 14, 27 Mar. 1930; *EP* 16 Feb. 1930; *ES* 15 Feb. 1930. For the groups see *EI* 16 Mar. 1930; *ABC* 2, 6 Mar., 29 Apr. 1930.

initiative, and urged *Upetistas* to join the new party. In its manifesto of foundation the UM combined an emphasis on the concrete achievements of the fallen regime with an attempt to acquire respectability in public opinion by advocating 'strictly legal and constitutional means'. Although it was joined by many centres of the UP, Guadalhorce took great pains to deny that the UM was nothing but the UP in disguise. Unlike the latter, the UM, he argued, was 'strictly political, constitutional monarchist, ready to join any monarchist bloc'.[57]

It is evident, however, that the UM was a party of the extreme right. It rejected the leftist campaign for the investigation of the *political* responsibilities of the Dictatorship, though its leaders were ready to be judged for their *administrative* responsibilities. They became uncompromising defenders of the king, manifesting a marked lack of vindictiveness towards him for having 'bourbonized' Primo. Their 'parliamentarian' and 'constitutional' slogans were weakened by the demand for a 'strong executive' and by an endorsement of the social, economic, and Catalan policy of the Dictatorship. Ramiro de Maeztu, a fanatic ideologist of the UM, even claimed that the fact that Guadalhorce had engineered the 'Confederaciones Hidrográficas' was a sufficient reason for electing him leader of the party. The fact that the UM leaders were the only group of people who had recently been responsible for 'achievements' in the social and economic fields, made the party confident of being the only 'modern conservative party' with a clear programme of 'national reconstruction'. *El Debate*, a protagonist of extreme right monarchism, was delighted with the new party. It was acclaimed as a 'mature' organization and as the 'only conservative force still dynamic and alive'. It should be the central nucleus of a mass movement, that would absorb the traditional Conservatives (Bugallalistas, Ciervistas, Mauristas), and would form a 'stable, conservative and traditional government' to stop the socialist–communist avalanche.[58]

---

[57] *Unión Patriótica* 18 Feb. 1930 (Primo), 15 Apr. 1930 (Manifesto). For UP centres joining in see *ABC* 5, 10, 13 July 1930 (Cadiz and Lugo); *Unión Patriótica* 2 July 1930 (Madrid); *LV* 11 May, 23 July, 6, 12 Dec. 1930 (Barcelona). See Guadalhorce in *Unión Patriótica* 15 May, 1, 16 June 1930.

[58] For responsibilities see *Unión Patriótica* 15 Apr. 1930. For the king see Calvo Sotelo, *Seis Años*, pp. 491–2; *ABC* 2, 5 Mar. 1930 (Yanguas and Guadalahorce). For the programme see *Unión Patriótica* 1, 15 May, 15 July 1930 (a speech by Guadalahorce),

This coalition could not be brought about, however, because the UM was anathema to other Monarchist parties, and was treated by the government, which was taking great pains to disassociate itself from the Dictatorship, as a political underdog. Its constant appeals to other parties to form a united front were either dismissed as likely to stain their reputation or remained unanswered.[59]

The UM, therefore, made its own electoral preparations, and ran such an impressive campaign of propaganda, unequalled by any other Monarchist group, that even its enemies had to confess that it was virtually the only Monarchist party in the field.[60] Branches and youth sections were set up and meetings were held in many provincial capitals like Valencia, Vitoria, Bilbao, Zaragoza, Badajoz, and Barcelona. The most spectacular campaign of the summer was that run in Asturias, with the acclamation of business circles who felt themselves threatened by working-class agitation, and in Galicia, where the UM hoped to capitalize on Calvo Sotelo's Galician connections. On 27 August the ex-ministers were in Oviedo whence they went to Gijón, where a banquet was organized in their honour by industrialists and mineowners in the area who were most grateful to them for their defence of their interests. In Mieres, Guadalahorce unveiled a monument to himself. In Pavia a banquet was given to the propagandists and Guadalahorce's speech on that occasion inspired a local commentator to refer to him as 'a positive value, a hope for Spain'. They then moved on to Cudillero, Ribadeo, Luarca, and Ortigueira, where they promised that when they assumed power they would solve the problem of the *foros*, a burdensome land tenure of minute holdings on which most Gallegos depended for their poor living. In El Ferrol the Chamber of Commerce organized a special reception, from which they rushed to La Coruña, and

---

and *Unión Monárquica* 4 Aug. 1930 (Guadalahorce on Catalonia); Ramiro de Maeztu in *Unión Patriótica* 15 July 1930. See also a defence of the 'achievements' in Lorenzo Pardo, *La Confederación del Ebro. Nueva Política Hidráulica.* For confidence in being 'modern' see *Unión Monárquica* 4 Aug. 1930. *ED* 26 June, 10 July, 12 Sept., 3, 10 Oct. 1930 (editorial).

[59] For appeals see Guadalahorce in *ABC* 25 June 1930; Pemán in *Unión Monárquica* 18 Sept. 1930; and in *ABC* 9 Dec. 1930. For reactions see *Unión Monárquica* 1, 15 Oct., 15 Nov. 1930, and *El* 7 Aug., 5 Oct. 1930.

[60] Berenguer in *ED* 12 Sept. 1930; Mola, *Obras*, p. 403; and *ABC* 8 Oct. 1930.

then to Mellid, Noya, Villagarcía, Melou, Ribadavia, Carballino, Orense, and Lugo.[61]

In its propaganda, the UM also made clear that it differed substantially from the Constitutional Monarchist Conservatives. It introduced an aggressive new style and terminology into the lexicon of the Spanish right, which was mostly attached to the traditional formulae of liberalism. Now José Antonio, the son of the dictator, attacked the 'superstition of national sovereignty' on behalf of the 'public good'; while Pemán said that the UM, rather than the Liberal-Conservatives, was the genuine right, with the Socialists rather than the Liberals, as the genuine left. The UM, he added, was the real defender of 'Monarchy', and 'tradition', and if the Socialists wanted power, they would have to win it not only in the polls, 'but also in the streets'. The dilemma was 'between Moscow and us'. 'Us' meant family, fatherland, honour, army and sexual morality. If the right choice was not made, then 'Spain will sink'.[62]

Less noisy, but also less influential, was the *Partido Laborista Nacional* founded by Aunós, another ex-minister. His corporative plank as well as his campaign on behalf of 'less politics' and more 'economics and administration', might well have been compatible with the UM's platform. The same could be said of his dismissal of universal suffrage as leading to 'social slavery'. Like the UM *Laborista*, the party's organ, was always sympathetic to the king, though Aunós claimed to have an 'accidentalist' approach to the forms of government. His group, however, did not gather any substantial strength, though it had a few scattered centres. In December it was ready to support in the forthcoming elections any conservative party which showed a certain respect towards its programme.[63]

As in the case of the *Laboristas* and the UM, so with regard to

[61] For branches and meetings in the provinces see *Unión Monárquica* 4, 15 Aug. 1930; *ABC* 18 July, 6, 27 Aug., 7 Sept., 8 Oct., 1, 2, 4 Nov. 1930; *LV* 30 Aug. 1930. For Asturias and Galicia see *Unión Monárquica* 3, 18 Sept. 1930; *ABC* 28 Aug., 7, 9 Sept. 1930. The commentator is in *La Región*, Oviedo 28 Aug. 1930.

[62] For José Antonio see *ABC* 25 July 1930, 17 Jan. 1931. Pemán in *Unión Monárquica* 1 Oct. 1930. See also meetings in ibid. 15 Oct. 1930, 1 Jan. 1931.

[63] See manifestos in *EI* 30 Mar. 1930; *ABC* 11 Apr., 2 July 1930; assembly of the party in ibid. 11 July 1930; and centres in *LV* 29 Apr., 1, 15 May 1930. For 'accidentalism' and monarchism see survey of articles of 'Laborista' in F.O. 371/15041: Peterson to A. Henderson, 14 July 1930. For elections see *ABC* 27 Dec. 1930.

the noisy group of *Legionarios de España*, one must not look in it for an effort to save the Monarchy, but for the roots of the *Falange* and Franco's Spain. Founded in April 1930 by a physician from Valencia, Albiñana, who became officially its *Jefe Nacional* in July, it appealed to all 'honest people who feel proud to have been born Spanish'. His men swore to challenge any one who uttered a subversive cry, and, indeed, on several occasions brawls ensued in cafés and in the streets in consequence. Their propaganda had a highly alarmist tone. It denounced leftist groups like the FUE as 'communists' and 'antireligious', and it stimulated the creation of the phantom of 'the international offensive' led against Spain by communists, Freemasons, and Jews, especially the latter, who were directly responsible for all disasters from the loss of the Netherlands up to the defeat of Annual. To meet this offensive, Albiñana suggested the formation of a 'strong' government under La Cierva or Martínez Anido. Albiñana made use also of social slogans to attract members of the Catholic syndicates, whom he considered as an 'españolista' and 'anti-internationalist force'.[64]

But Albiñana's appeal for a united front was disregarded, as was that of the UM. When he paid tribute to 'constitutional monarchism' it was seen as a tactical device, or as a respectable pretext under which he introduced into Spain pseudo-fascist methods and conceptions. Albiñana expressed no appreciation for the old Monarchist parties either. They were the 'bad monarchists', as against the UM for which he showed his sympathies.[65]

Neither did the Carlist movement contribute to the formation of a coherent conservatism for the defence of the Monarchy. Their accelerated reorganization after the fall of the Dictatorship was aimed at accentuating their struggle against the liberal system, which Berenguer endeavoured to restore. At the zenith of the monarchist campaign, in the spring of 1930, the *Jaimistas* refused to join the monarchist front, not sparing in their attacks even *El Debate* and Bugallal. Instead, they campaigned separately

---

[64] For foundation, organization, street quarrels, and propaganda see *ABC* 12 Apr., 6, 7, 10, 16, 18 July; 4, 5, 8 Oct., 25 Nov. 1930. *La Legión* 1 Jan., 13 Feb. 1931 (articles by Albiñana). See also José María Albiñana, *Prisionero de la Republica*, pp. 50–61, 67–74.

[65] *El* 5 Apr. 1930; *ABC* 30 July, 8 Oct. 1930; and Alcalá Galiano, *The Fall*, p. 97.

for their traditional principles as the only alternative to 'anarchy' and the 'communist offensive'.[66]

Neither did the *Lliga Regionalista*, a socially conservative element, give any help towards the creation of a politically conservative front. Its attitude towards the Berenguer government started by being one of abstention and coldness. According to Ventosa i Calvell, this was the consequence of their resentment against the king whom they blamed as the architect of Primo de Rivera's anti-Catalanist decrees. Their inhibitions towards both the Monarchy and the government only increased when Berenguer showed a reluctance to rescind the decrees. Only after he finally repealed them, at the end of May, did the Lliga adopt a position of recognizing the compatibility between the Monarchy and Catalan aspirations. But even this change of attitude did not turn the Lliga into a propagator of monarchism. In the first general assembly of the party after the Dictatorship, Ventosa i Calvell reaffirmed Cambó's thesis of 'neither assimilation nor separatism'. He exposed a quasi-'accidentalist' theory by claiming that, although the Lliga did not believe that the Republic was indispensable, the Monarchy was not either, and democracy could flourish in both systems. Yet, he added, rather than go through a tumultuous change of regime, the Lliga preferred to adopt the existing system to its needs, by 'transforming' it through active intervention in Spanish politics. This was an opportunistic attitude, of which the Lliga was fully aware. The Lliga was a 'conservative, accidentalist and Catalanist' party, said Valls i Taberner. When a Lliga sponsored plan of autonomy elaborated by the *Diputación Provincial* of Barcelona was rejected by the left on the ground that that body was designated undemocratically by the government, Joaquín Pellicena reacted in a clear-cut 'accidentalist' way. He said that the democratic nature of a measure was not the only criterion which could make it acceptable to the Lliga, and an anti-Catalan decision reached democratically would be utterly rejected. 'For us', he said, 'a dictatorship that restores our

---

[66] On reorganization there is a great deal of information in *El Cruzado Español* of 1929–30; *ABC* 4, 7 Feb., 29 Apr., 1, 8 May, 21 Oct. 1930; *LV* 9 Mar., 13 May, 22 Aug. 1930; 6, 7 Jan. 1931. For resentment against 'liberal monarchists' see *El Cruzado Español* 28 Feb., 4 Apr., 6 June 1930, 9, 23, 30 Jan. 1931. for Carlism as the 'sole' answer to communism see ibid. 17 Oct., 17 Nov., 26 Dec. 1930.

liberties to us is a more legal regime than a liberal regime that denies them.'[67]

This new trend did not at all please orthodox monarchists who dismissed the Lliga as 'antiespañolista'. Its desertion by some of its members and the growing power of the Catalan left was interpreted as a consequence of its opportunism.[68]

However, the Lliga was by no means disappearing. Although it was virtually non-existent as a party by the end of the Dictatorship,[69] it profited from the way by which Berenguer designated the new *Ayuntamientos*, and achieved predominance in a considerable number of them. So much so that allegations were made about an agreement between the government and the Lliga for the 'orientation of local politics' in Catalonia. At the same time, a revival of *Lliguista* centres was taking place in that region, propaganda meetings were held and new juntas were elected. In addition the *Unió Catalana* was founded to carry on cultural activities within the political tradition of the Lliga.[70]

Though it would be true to a great extent to conclude, with the centralist Gaziel, that the Lliga was not 'a firm buttress of Madrid governmentalism',[71] the imminent threat to the social and political system from the leftist offensive brought the Lliga as an essentially conservative group closer both to the Monarchy and to the government. The fear of an electoral defeat and the revolutionary movements stimulated this move.[72]

In fact, Cambó had been trying since the fall of the

[67] For the impact of the decrees see SAA: Ventosa i Calvell to Alba, 27 May 1930. See declarations about republicanization of Lliga members: Vallés i Pujals in *EI* 27 Mar. 1930; Teixidor Comes in *LV* 3 May 1930. For the general assembly see *El Sol* 21 June 1930; and *Historia d'Una Politica*, pp. 382–4. See a similar thesis presented by Joaquín Pellicena in *LV* 28 Sept. 1930; Valls i Taberner quoted in Isidre Molas, *Lliga*, pp. 161–2; J. Estelrich, *El Moment Politic*, pp. 17–20, 31, 44–6; *Catalunya Endins*, pp. 81, 87–91; *De la Dictadura a la Republica*, pp. 85–99, 111–37. In all the cases he criticized the Catalan left for making the Republic a 'conditio sine qua non'. He emphasized the circumstantial compatibility between Monarchy and Catalanism.

[68] *EI* 15 June, 12 Nov. 1930; *ABC* 11 June, 11 July, 12 Oct. 1930; *NE* 1 June 1930.

[69] Isidre Molas, *Lliga*, p. 157.

[70] For Ayuntamientos see *EI* 28 Feb., 2, 5, 27 Mar. 1930; *EP* 2 Mar. 1930; for reorganization see *ABC* 22 Feb., 6 Mar., 26 June 1930; *LV* 13 July, 9 Sept., 8, 9, 15, 22 Oct. 1930; Isidre Molas, *Lliga*, pp. 156–60. For 'Unió Catalana' see Estelrich, *De la Dictadura*, pp. 67–84; *El Sol* 26 Oct. 1930; *LV* 6 June, 9 Nov. 1930, 10, 27 Jan. 1931.

[71] *LV* 27 June 1930.

[72] *EI* 12 Nov. 1930; *ABC* 14 Dec. 1930.

Dictatorship to create a Spanish–Catalan political alliance that would strengthen the links with Madrid, preserving the vital interests of Catalonia and the Catalan bourgeoisie, now threatened by the collapse of the Dictatorship's 'law and order'. The menace to the political and social system had brought him to suggest a series of constitutional and social reforms that would appease the left, yet would not harm the right. It was supposed to represent a 'dynamic conservatism' different from that of Bugallal, and also more likely to preserve the fundamental features of the system. The Canovist system was outdated, and the Lliga should become the Catalan branch of a national party instead of pursuing the anachronistic tactics of playing off Conservatives and Liberals. Cambó hoped that his 'national party' would meet· with 'considerable co-operation all over Spain, which would assure' him 'the support of the most select elements of both the Spanish inteligentsia and the economic forces of the country'.[73]

But Cambó's enterprise failed to materialize during the Berenguer period. With the assistance of Gabriel Maura, he tried during the spring and the summer to establish a political axis Alba–Maura–Cambó. This was an attempt to bring about a 'leftist' Alba government, that would disarm the republican movement, and would guarantee a statute of autonomy to Catalonia. However, Alba's closer attachment to manœuvres with the Liberals,[74] and Gabriel Maura's hesitance to get rid of Berenguer before he held the general elections reduced the triumvirate to a duumvirate of Maura–Cambó. By the end of the Berenguer government they were still talking about a 'big' party manipulating *Maurista* terms of 'citizenship' and 'anti-caciquismo'. They made contacts with the Catholic Angel Herrera, who was sympathetic, as well as with the *Upetista* Pemán. They also managed to find a positive response among traditional Maurista and conservative circles in Mallorca, Galicia, Valencia, and Biscay. A high functionary in the Ministry of the Interior, Montes Jovellar, a friend of theirs, was

[73] For his appeal and early contacts to create the 'national party' see *ABC* 5, 6, 8, 9 Feb. 1930; *LV* 7, 8 Feb. 1930. His politico-social programme was published under the strains of the revolutionary ambiance, see *ABC* 10, 13 Dec. 1930. His remark on Bugallal is in *El Sol* 6 Jan. 1931.

[74] See below, pp. 199–201.

alleged to be preparing electoral favours for the new party, which was finally founded only after the fall of Berenguer.[75]

The latter, though leading a strictly Conservative government, was finally brought down without having behind him a strong coalition of conservatives either to support him or to succeed him. There were many political manifestations of conservatism as we have seen. As *El Debate* lamented, though, they manifested a disunity and a mutual rivalry when the Monarchy needed more than ever a solid backing from its natural supporters. They failed to reach even tactical unity, and as 'anaemic remnants ... exhausted by the years', to use Berenguer's expression, they were useless.[76]

b. 'Republican-Monarchists'—The Constitutionalists

The Conservatives' position was further undermined and some of its main power bases were demolished when prominent members of the party became the leaders of the Constitutionalist movement. This movement brought under attack the 'irresponsibility' of the king and the concept of an Ordinary Cortes, both cornerstones of the Conservative doctrine. It was indeed, in Sánchez Guerra's protest of 1927, a protest that was rejected by orthodox Conservatives, that the Constitutionalist bloc originated. This started under the leadership of the Conservative Burgos y Mazo and the Liberal Villanueva. They proposed a Constituent Cortes to reform the constitution and to pass verdict on the responsibilities of the Dictatorship. Under this programme they were active in the frustrated *coup* of January 1929; and a year later they constituted the main political nucleus that activated the military under General Goded to conspire, thus creating the final pressure on the king to get rid of Primo de Rivera. They were reluctant to disperse even when

[75] For the contacts with Alba–Maura see Pabón, *Cambó* ii, part ii, 36–8, 45, 52–4, 59; La Cierva, *Notas*, p. 311; *EI* 13 May 1930; and Rovira i Virgili's article in *El Sol* 13 June 1930. For Gabriel Maura see MA: 'Cartas a Prudencio Rovira': Gabriel Maura to Prudencio Rovira, 14 Aug. 1930. For Maura–Cambó and the response see *LV* 28 Nov. 1930, 13 Jan., 4, 14 Feb. 1931; *ABC* 21 Jan. 1931; Vicente Risco, *El Problema Político de Galicia*, p. 231; Cierva, *Notas*, p. 321 (on Montes Jovellar); Pemán, *Mis Almuerzos*, pp. 97–100 (on Herrera and himself).

[76] *ED* 28 Jan. 1931; Berenguer, *De la Dictadura*, p. 112.

Berenguer formed his government, hoping that he might thus be pushed to adopt a Constitutionalist 'solution'.[77]

With the fall of the Dictatorship the Constitutionalists came out to join the anti-Alfonso campaign. The first bloc was established in Seville with Conservatives under Burgos y Mazo, *Alcalá Zamoristas* under José Centeno, *Albistas* under Blasco Garzón, and Republicans under Martínez Barrios. It called for a Constituent Cortes that would uncover the 'political intrigues' of the king. In his first public speech in Seville, on 25 February 1930, Burgos y Mazo said that the group was ready to accept 'any form of government' decided by the Constituent Cortes, though he personally thought that the Republic 'was a more perfect form of government than the Monarchy'. He rejected the unquestioned acceptance of the monarchist principle, and he substituted it for that of the *Fuero Juzgo*: 'You should be King if you do good, but if you do not, you should not be King'. Several weeks later, Burgos y Mazo transformed the Conservative party of Huelva into a *Partido del Centro Constitucional.*[78]

Sánchez Guerra's speech at the end of February 1930 stimulated the bloc further. Though he himself opposed a Constituent Cortes, he demanded a reform of the constitution, which the king had made a 'kitchen rag' of, thus rebuffing those Conservatives who still used that 'rag' as a flag. Villanueva estimated that the speech paved the way 'for continuing the campaign of the bloc', an opinion 'shared by all the members'. Melquiades Alvarez now contributed to the bloc the prestige of his name, if not the insignificant material strength of his party, many of whose members were joining republicanism, leaving their party as a 'walking corpse'. Bergamín, another prominent Conservative who in 1929 spoke about a 'conservative Republic' was now encouraged to adopt a Constitutionalist position and

[77] See Villanueva's declarations in *HL* Oct. 1927; the manifesto *Partido Constitucionalista. Manifesto al País*, without date, but certainly written under the Dictatorship, in RA Leg. 28 no. 43. See also Burgos y Mazo, *Los Constitucionalistas* ii, 18–21, 168–94, iii, 10–12.

[78] For the Seville bloc see SAA: Blasco Garzón to Alba 2 Feb. 1930; Burgos y Mazo, *Los Constitucionalistas* iii, 12–33. Their manifesto is in Burgos y Mazo, *De la Republica a...?*, pp. 66–8. The speech in Seville is in Burgos y Mazo, *Al Servicio de la Doctrina Constitucional*, pp. 129–97. For Huelva see RA Leg. 23 no. 27: an extract from *Diario de Huelva*. See also his speech in *ABC* 6 May 1930; and his open letter to Berenguer in *EI* 23 Mar. 1930.

to take his Andalucian clientele away from the Conservative Party. Though still committed to the monarchist principle, he was not committed to the king, a similar position to that adopted by Sánchez Guerra.[79]

It was, indeed, evident that the Constitutionalist 'solution' was not suggested in order to destroy the Monarchy. It was aimed at damming the republican stream and canalizing it into less extreme and clear-cut leftist definitions. Bergamín, who in April suggested a 'strong rightist party' against revolution, by the end of the year believed that monarchism was so shattered that only a Constituent Cortes could consolidate it, and that the king should go in order to save the Monarchy, dissociating it from his personal blunders. Even Burgos y Mazo had earlier referred to Constitutionalism as a 'conservative solution', because if the left did not get a Constituent Cortes, it would use revolutionary means leading to 'sovietism'. The Fabian tactics of Berenguer and the upsurge of republicanism were pointed to by Burgos y Mazo as the main reason why, in the autumn and winter of 1930, many monarchists joined the bloc who had previously advocated an Ordinary Cortes. And, after the 'December revolution', Sánchez Guerra, who was consistently reluctant to join the call for a Constituent Cortes, subscribed to a common manifesto of the bloc leaders on behalf of a Constituent Cortes as the only solution that might still save the country from revolution.[80]

However, the political ambiance in the country did not seem to favour a middle-course solution between Monarchy and Republic. The Constitutionalist campaign was seen as a ramification of the republican movement. Its leaders did not make a secret of their denunciation of the king, thus collaborating, willingly or unwillingly, with the anti-monarchist campaign. When they asked for a constitutional reform, they meant precisely a reform of the prerogatives of the Monarchy,

[79] Villanueva in *ABC* 28 Feb., 8 Aug. 1930. For Melquiades' constitutionalism see *ABC* 29 Apr. 1930; *El* 15 June 1930. For his party see *El* 26 Feb. 1930. Bergamín in *LE* 19 June 1929, 28 Feb. 1930; and *El* 10, 13 Apr. 1930. For Sánchez Guerra and the Constitutionalists see Burgos y Mazo, *Los Constitucionalistas* iii, 75.

[80] Bergamín in Berenguer, *De la Dictadura*, pp. 114–15; and later in *ABC* 13 Feb. 1931. Burgos y Mazo in ibid. 26 Feb. 1930. For the upsurge of 'Constitutionalism' see Burgos y Mazo, *Los Constitucionalistas* iv, 9–15. The manifesto of December in *El* 19 Dec. 1930.

recognizing the legitimacy even of its abolition. Their real significance is probably best illustrated by Bugallal's attack on them as 'revolutionary agitators', and by Lerroux's appeal to the left to support them as 'a step towards the Republic'.[81]

c. The failure of the Liberal alternative

The prospects of more 'open' politics and the growing 'socialist menace' had stimulated Liberals to coin 'modern' slogans, as did the Conservatives. In fact, in August 1928 it was alleged that Baldomero Argente had suggested the creation of a Liberal–Conservative bloc to curb the 'socialist threat'. Earlier in the year, young Liberals proposed, for the same reason, the creation of a 'Liberal Socialist Party'. In 1929 Baldomero Argente as well as the Liberal organ *El Imparcial*, took up the cudgels for the creation of a Liberal Party wide enough to attract proletarian elements as well as members of the middle classes eager to join a 'modern Liberal Party'. This could bring about the creation of a new two-party system of Socialists and Liberals with the latter advocating a welfare state against the 'excesses of sovietism'. The possibility of Conservatives and Socialists alternating in power was rejected. Such a *turno* could only condemn the country to frequent and sudden changes, whereas a large Liberal party could be a 'bridle' for both conservatism and socialism.[82]

With the fall of the Dictatorship the elaboration of a new Liberal image started to take place. Romanones suggested in February the creation of a 'democratic Monarchy' in which the king would be the 'hereditary president' of a Republic governed by two great parties, one Liberal and the other Conservative. *El Imparcial* supported this view enthusiastically; and García Prieto as well as other elements of the 'Democratic' fraction of the party, echoed it when they talked about a 'crowned Republic' and 'progressive programmes'. This new 'openness' was intended to prove, as *El Imparcial* put it, that all the radical innovations were possible within a Monarchy governed by a 'big' Liberal Party, which would 'radically transform Spanish

---

[81] See evaluations of the movement in *EI* 11 Feb. 1930; *LV* 4 Mar. 1930, and 13 Feb. 1931; *ED* 23 July 1930. Bugallal in ibid. 2 Jan. 1931; and Lerroux in *ES* 14 May 1930.

[82] Baldomero in *El Sol* 9, 19 Aug. 1928; the young Liberals in *ES* 19 Jan., 15 Feb., 3 Mar. 1928. Baldomero in *LV* 21 Apr. 1929; and *EI* 20 Nov., 3, 4, 6 Dec. 1929.

society' by collaborating, if necessary, even with the Socialists. This would make unnecessary the whole republican movement, and would satisfy those who 'suffered from the obsession of incompatibility' between Monarchy and progress.[83]

Romanones' speech of 'definition' in mid-July was not, however, exactly an indication that he was pursuing 'radical transformations'. Apart from a vague appeal on behalf of a 'reform of the land system', he remained bound to old formulae. He dismissed the quest for a Constituent Cortes as 'illegal', but he rejected the demands for an inquiry into the responsibility of the king in bringing about a no less 'illegal' Dictatorship. His declaration that the Liberals would remain friends of the king so long as he remained a friend of the constitution was another contradiction, considering the widespread belief that the king had long ceased to be a 'friend of the constitution'. Only later would Romanones understand his tactical blunder in letting 'responsibilities' become the exclusive banner of the left. The imprecise tax reform which he mentioned was later interpreted as a scheme for financing an insurance against unemployment and the abolition of the Dictatorship's income tax, a demand put forward earlier by the Socialists. *El Imparcial*, however, could now claim that the Liberals had 'one indivisible doctrine and one indisputable leader'. Romanones' programme was explained in detail emphasizing the *laissez-faire* economic policy, the quest for a 'social basis', and the difference from the Conservatives who were ready to sacrifice 'democracy' for the sake of 'order'.[84]

The Liberals however were during the first months of 1930 in disarray, and the public arena seemed to be exclusively occupied by Conservatives. This, and the disquieting desertion of Liberals to republicanism and socialism, created the impression that the Liberal Party was a series of dispersed 'molecules'. Moreover, the exclusively Conservative colour of the Berenguer government caused dismay to the Liberals, who feared that

---

[83] Romanones in *ABC* 6, 12, 13 Feb. 1930; for the Democrats see *LV* 18 Feb. 1930, *Estampa* 27 May 1930 (García Prieto); *ABC* 6 Mar. (Juan Alvarado), 9 Mar. 1930 (the Democrats of Córdoba). See how *El Imparcial* developed the issue in many editorials: 5, 8, 11, 12 Feb., 30 Mar., 4, 5, 10–12, 25 Apr. 1930.

[84] The speech in *ABC* 17 July 1930. Commentaries in *EI* 18, 25, 26 July, 2, 9, 14, 16, 20 Aug. 1930. For responsibilities see RA Leg. 49 no. 4: undelivered speech prepared for the congress of 'Union Agraria'.

they would be discriminated against and that their organization might be obstructed from the Ministry of the Interior. Romanones, so familiar with the rotative system, believed initially that his party's 'turn' was next. But bitter criticism of the Fabian tactics of the government, because of the frequent suspension of personal liberties and the excessive favour shown to Conservatives, soon became commonplace among Liberals. The automatic designation of city councillors and provincial deputies was rejected as 'undemocratic'. Instead, it was suggested that the functionaries of the last Liberal government dismissed in 1923 should be restored. It was clearly feared that under the present government and administration, the general elections would be 'made' on behalf of the Conservatives.[85]

However, the Liberal party, which was virtually non-existent by the end of the Dictatorship,[86] gradually started to reorganize in many provinces. In Catalonia centres were already opened or inaugurated in February, electoral offices were opened in April, and lectures on 'doctrinal orientation' were given. Since Romanones' 'definition' this 'orientation' adopted a strictly *Romanonista* character. It was emphasized that he was the man who conceded to Catalonia its statute of autonomy in 1919; and now he was the only one who possessed a 'political genius' and a 'disciplined party' with which he would soon become the 'saviour of Spain'. The regional leader, Gassol, appealed in late August to Catalan opinion assuring it that the Liberal Party had absorbed in its programme Catalan aspirations: an 'absolute decentralization' as long as it was compatible with national unity. This propaganda line did not coincide with centralist declarations of *El Imparcial*, whose editor Luis Massó made it clear that he represented Romanones' views. None the less, if not for doctrinal at least for tactical reasons Romanones defended the decentralizing thesis, at a meeting in Barcelona. In Madrid, it was Romanones' deputy, Ruiz Jiménez, who led the local reorganization of the party, setting up youth branches and committees at a district level. In Alicante, though some of

[85] For the impression of disarray see *EI* 2 Mar., 4, 8, 10 Apr. 1930. Romanones in *ABC* 29 Jan., 5 Feb. 1930. For criticism against the government see *EI* 23 Feb., 4 Mar., 26 Apr., 5, 28 June, 12, 23 July 1930; Berenguer, *De la Dictadura*, pp. 186–91; see Tomas Valverde, *Memorias de un Alcalde*, pp. 88–91.

[86] *EI* 5 Sept. 1929 (editorial).

the Liberals who awoke from years of silence chose an anti-monarchist newspaper as their mouthpiece, the ex-councillors of the party followed Alfonso Rojas in his reorganizational initiative. In the province of Seville sixty-nine local committees and leaders were elected in *pueblos*, which were Romanonista strongholds. Similar efforts were going on in Murcia under the direction of the Romanonista ex-Deputy José Maria Guillamón and with the personal encouragement of Romanones. In Jaén the Liberals woke from seven years of lethargy to declare that they were 'in the same position as in September 1923'. In his fief of Guadalajara, Romanones personally supervised the reorganization of the party, while his son, the Marqués de Villabragima, paid special attention to Jaén. Romanones was considered the patron of Liberal centres in other places, such as Cadiz, Almería, San Fernando, and Ibiza.[87]

Considerable efforts were also made by the Liberals of the province of Alicante to patronize the local agrarian movement of small landlords who gathered in the *Unión Agraria* in order to defend their interests. Once their leaders, Pascual Carrión and Emeterio Abad, approached the Liberals to adopt their demands, Romanones hurried to snatch the opportunity of playing the champion of agrarism. Consequently, the Unión Agraria became the branch of the party in Alicante, and spread its agrarian doctrine. This consisted of a commitment to fulfil the UA's demands for state assistance in promoting irrigation schemes and in protecting wine and fruit production 'without utopian revolutionarism or improper reactionary attitudes'. Romanones now stressed that *Agrarismo* was not just one of the components of his party's plank, but the most fundamental one.[88]

---

[87] For Catalonia see *LV* 9 Feb., 2 Mar., 19, 20, 29 Apr., 1 May, 20 July, 3, 22, 24, 27 Aug., 10, 17 Oct., 2, 11, 30 Nov. 1930; *El* 29 Mar. 1930; RA Leg. 72 no. 45: Luis Massó y Simó to Romanones, 13 May 1930. For Madrid see *ABC* 8 July, 26 Aug., 7, 12, 28 Oct. 1930. For Alicante see ibid. and *LV* 8 Feb. 1930. For Seville see RA Leg. 9 no. 5: 'Presidentes y Secretarios de los Comités de la Provincia de Sevilla'. For Guadalajara see ibid. Leg. 52 no. 19: 'Creación del Circulo Liberal de Guadalajara' 1 Sept. 1930. For other places see *La Voz de Cadiz* 18 Nov. 1930; *La Voz Liberal*, Jaén, 7 Nov. 1930; *Heraldo de San Fernando* 2 Nov. 1930; RA Leg. 75 no. 6: Leopoldo Colombo (San Fernando) to Juan de Aramburu 28 July 1930. See also *ABC* 29 Mar., 30 Apr., 17 June, 18 Oct., 13 Nov. 1930.
[88] RA Leg. 75 no. 6: *A los Agricultores de Nuestra Provincia, Alicante*, 5 Apr. 1930; Leg. 49 no. 21: *Agricultores Alicantinos*; *La Voz de Levante* 3 Oct. 1930; *El Agrario, Organo de la Unión Agraria Provincial*, Alicante, 25 Oct., 1 Nov. 1930.

This attempt to infiltrate *Romanonismo* into the province of Alicante alarmed the rival political forces, which made every effort to curb the Liberals. Socialists and Republicans started a campaign of defamation against both Romanones and the UA. Even the government was now inclined to stop the *Romanonista* offensive. While at the beginning of the year the Ministry of the Interior favoured the UA with the concession of posts of mayors and deputy mayors, assuming that it was a good barrier against republicanism in the province, now that Romanones was there, the mayors were dismissed, and a strict control was imposed on the functionaries of the UA. This left the Liberals with no political basis in the region. Romanones could think of no better solution than that of 'installing' Liberals in key posts. But that was precisely what he could not do so long as he himself was not in a position of power. The anti-Romanonista ambiance was such that Romanones had to cancel his visit and speech to the UA congress, under the pretext that he was ill.[89]

Though the whole 'Alicante enterprise' stimulated an agrarian programme by the Liberal Party on behalf of landless peasants, and small and middle landowners, there is no evidence that *Romanonismo*'s dream of becoming a mass party with a considerable social backing ever materialized. There are no indications of substantial increase in the size of the party. The reorganization which we have earlier summarized was no more than an attempt to return to the strongholds of the past and to revive old connections.[90]

This could not be different as far as the *Izquierda Liberal* was concerned. Alba no longer considered himself as party leader. He did not even authorize the reopening of centres carrying his name. Groups like the *Partído Monárquico de la Izquierda Liberal* set up in Seville by Rodriguez de la Borbolla as well as the Izquierda Liberal in San Fernando, were private initiatives rather than the expression of the existence of a 'national' party.

[89] For the Socialists' and Republicans' campaign see RA Leg. 49 no. 24: *Problemas Agrarios, Ante Una Cruzada*, Sax. Nov. 1930, and ibid: Francisco Guillen Herrero to Emilio Tato. For lack of official favour see ibid. Leg. 49 no. 21: Unión Agraria to Berenguer 10 Nov. 1930; and Leg. 75 no. 6: 'Política Agraria de Alicante', and 'La Política en la Provincia de Alicante'. For cancelling the visit see *ABC* 9 Nov. 1930.

[90] For the sudden and enormous interest in agrarian issues see *El* 22, 26, 28, 31 Oct., 8, 12, 19, 21 Nov., 11 Dec. 1930, 29, 30 Jan., 4 Feb. 1931; and RA Leg. 49 no. 24: 'Apuntes Notas y Datos para el Discurso Agrario', a series of detailed programmes.

Alba did not even give any special encouragement to his friends in Valladolid, his former political stronghold. When the *Albista* Federico Santander accepted the mayoralty of the city, he was representing himself according to Alba, who said that 'an Albista Party does not exist any more'. He could not avoid, however, the impressive awakening of the Albistas in Valencia, nor that of his friend Natalio Rivas who returned to his private fief of the Alpujarras to renew the network of relations he had built up over the years as cacique. Only Royo Villanova was able to act as a national figure in order to spread Alba's political views on the need to unify all 'Spanish democrats' in a frankly liberal party with a defined plank on economic matters, for which there was no need either of a Republic or of a Constituent Cortes.[91]

Yet Alba's political standing and the role that he was to play during the Berenguer period were an example of how a politician without a party, but with clear political convictions and a dignified past, could become the axis of Spanish politics at a given time. He personified the alternative of a leftist yet not extreme government that might save the Monarchy by adapting it to democratic institutions. This would avoid both the republican solution and a sterile return to 'old politics'. It is true, however, that Romanones and García Prieto had played on similar slogans, but their return to old procedures and their lust for power reduced their credibility; whereas Alba's *otium cum dignitate* aroused the admiration of the public.[92]

Alba was by no means ready to preside over a Liberal government of groups of *Romanonistas* and *Garcíaprietistas*, but seriously considered a proposition to head a 'broad liberal coalition', which was proposed to him by Romanones and other Liberals, and to which the king seemed to be inclined to give power. But Romanones' insistence on doing politics in the old

[91] For the first initiatives and Alba's inhibition see *ABC* 16 Mar. 1930; SAA: Alba to Alejandro Manzanares 24 Nov. 1930; *Heraldo de San Fernando* 25 Oct. 1930. For Federico Santander see García Venero, *Alba*, p. 277. Natalio Rivas in *ABC* 10 Apr. 1930. For Valencia see the meeting in *La Voz Valenciana* 17 Feb. 1930. For Royo see *ABC* 28 Feb., 2, 29 July, 16 Oct. 1930; *LV* 15 Feb. 1930. For another echo of Alba's ideas see Teofilo Ortega, *La Política y un Político*, *passim*.

[92] For Romanones' 'manœuvres' see the correspondence cited in García Venero, *Alba*, pp. 279–81, 284–5. For Alba's popularity see his short visit in Barcelona in *ABC* 23 Apr. 1930; and Hurtado, *Quaranta Anys* ii, 280.

style constantly irritated Alba. Such was his proposition to
restore the dissolved Cortes in 1923, in which there was a
Liberal majority, as the 'shortest way of returning to normality'.
Neither Alba nor the Conservatives took the proposition too
seriously. It emerged and died as an ugly manifestation of an
absolute disregard of public opinion and the new social and
political forces that had emerged in the country since 1923.[93]

Yet Alba's political prestige as well as the 'Liberal alternative'
received clear encouragement when the king made a personal
visit to the expatriated politician in Paris, at the end of June.
On the eve of the meeting, both Romanones and García Prieto
promised their support for any solution that Alba might suggest
to the king. What Alba proposed to the monarch was a plan of
'sincere' elections, a constitutional revision in an Ordinary
Cortes which would democratize the Monarchy on the model
of Belgium and England, together with an investigation of
'responsibilities'. The king, in what was a reflection of the
strains under which the Monarchy was living, accepted Alba's
plan. The latter began to believe that his plan for a 'leftist
government' was about to be realized with the setting up of a
coalition of Liberals, Republicans, and Socialists.[94]

But Alba's plan was jeopardized by the indifference of both
right and left. The Conservatives realized with dismay how the
power was slipping away from their hands. Gabriel Maura was
ready to support Alba so long as he belonged to a predominantly
conservative 'axis' with himself and Cambó, and not as a
'prisoner' of the left. Villanueva did not see how the Constitutionalists could support a government not committed to summon
a Constituent Cortes, while the anti-dynastic left rejected the
plan out of hand. Furthermore, Romanones, in a manifestation
of pettiness combined with a lust of power, simply disregarded

[93] For the 'liberal coalition' see Alba in *Estampa* 18 Mar. 1930; SAA: letters from
Almodovar del Valle and Tomas Angulo to Alba, 18 May, 18 June 1930, and García
Venero, *Alba*, pp. 283–4. For the 1923 Cortes see ibid. pp. 286–9; and a clear support
from the Liberals in *El* 24, 27 May, 10, 12 June, 3 July 1930.

[94] Extracts of the plan were published already by the end of May, see *ES* 25 May
1930. See the full plan in *ABC* 24 June 1930; and the king's preparedness to accept the
'Liberal alternative' in SAA: Alba to Duque de Almodovar del Valle, 25 June 1930.
See also Chapaprieta relating his conversation with Alba in *ABC* 20 June 1930. For
Romanones–García Prieto 'blank cheque' see their correspondence with Alba in
García Venero, *Alba*, pp. 291–2.

the 'blank cheque', which he had given to Alba on the eve of his meeting with the king, a 'blank cheque' which Alba considered as a precondition for his engagement in the 'Liberal coalition' enterprise. He refused to be the 'prisoner' of an extreme left government. In his speech of 'definition' in mid-July Romanones was more eager to organize his own following, to cultivate his image as the leader of a 'disciplined' party, and to suggest a centre-left government rather than to reiterate his support of Alba's 'leftist solution'.[95]

A last attempt to reach a definite agreement between the Liberal leaders was made at the so-called 'Hendaye meeting' late in September. But the only agreement that they seemed to have reached was that of sticking to the idea that the next Cortes should be 'Ordinary' rather than 'Constituent', and that the municipal and provincial elections should precede the general elections. It was also decided to approach Melquiades Alvarez to join the 'Liberal bloc', which he refused to do so long as the 'bloc' did not accept the idea of a Constituent Cortes. No 'Liberal concentration' determined to assume power had emerged from the meeting. This obviously placated those conservatives who, like the editor of *El Debate*, believed that only a strong conservative coalition was likely to defend the crown, while any Liberal combination would only precipitate the move towards a Republic.[96]

By the end of the year, it had become obvious that the whole 'Alba solution' was impractical. The revolutionary strikes of October and November convinced Alba that the Republicans and the Socialists were leading the country to what might end in 'communist chaos'; and he dismissed any possibility of a collaboration with these 'operetta revolutionaries'.[97] A collaboration with the Constitutionalists was equally improbable so long as Alba continued to reject the Constituent Cortes as a

[95] For the rejection of the plan see *El Sol* 25 June 1930 (editorial and information); *LE* 27 June 1930; Romanones, *Notas*, pp. 231–2; for the anti-dynastic left see Romanones in *ABC* 24, 25 June 1930; and Jiménez de Asua in García Venero, *Alba*, p. 298. For Romanones see his speech in *ABC* 7 July 1930; and Alba's letter to García Prieto quoted in García Venero, op. cit. 307–8. For the Liberals' collaboration as a precondition see his letter to both Romanones and García Prieto in ibid. 300.

[96] See *ABC* 25, 27 Sept. 1930; *EI* 28 Sept. 1930; *LE* 25 Sept. 1930; *ED* 28 Sept. 1930; Mola, *Obras*, p. 399; Berenguer, *De la Dictadura*, p. 188.

[97] SAA: Alba to Tomas Angulo, 24 Nov. 1930; *LE* 1 Dec. 1930; and *ABC* 23 Nov. 1930.

revolutionary slogan, and to stick to his belief that the reforms suggested by the leftist press could be well achieved in Ordinary Cortes. That is why the press which was supposed to pave the way for his 'leftist government' was alienated from him.[98] On the right, Romanones refused a request from Alba to postpone his personal propaganda until a common programme of action should be elaborated by all Liberals. This seemed hardly indicative of any substantial degree of close agreement between them. The fact that Alba remained in Paris, that Romanones continued his partisan campaigns, and that Berenguer continued the slow march towards general elections were enough to indicate that the whole idea of a left-Liberal alternative to the Berenguer government had entered a blind alley.[99]

d. The fall of the Berenguer government

The Liberals did not make a secret of their desire to get rid of Berenguer's Conservative government. Their insistence on a consecutive order of municipal, provincial, and general election was not motivated only by a 'scruple of legality', as they themselves confessed. It was mainly the result of their fear that the government was 'making' the elections for the Conservatives. Allegations on the government's partiality, at a local level, for Conservative candidates were launched almost daily. The Liberals had more reason to worry when, in November, Marzo, an apolitical figure, was replaced as the Minister of the Interior by Matos, who seemed to be more aware of the political struggle lying ahead. This, and the publication by the government of a proper political programme for the next Cortes, indicated that this Conservative government had no intention of giving way in the near future. The Liberals hoped that local elections might provide them with a solid power base in the Ayuntamientos and Diputaciones to 'support' them in the general elections. Simultaneously, the government was discredited by the Liberals for its inability to control the political situation, shattered by revolutionary strikes and students'

[98] SAA: correspondence with the editor of *El Sol*: Urgoiti to Alba, 16 July 1930; Alba to Urgoiti, 21 July 1930.

[99] *ABC* 9 Nov. 1930; F.O. 371/15042: Grahame to A. Henderson, 11 Nov., 23 Dec. 1930.

agitation—both of which could be appeased only by a Liberal government open to 'radical transformations'.[1]

When it became clear that the 'Liberal bloc' would not materialize, and, therefore, would be unable to force the king to form a Liberal Ministry, the Liberals, mainly through the intrigues of Romanones, started to put pressure on the government in a final and successful attempt to get rid of it altogether. At the beginning of January 1931, Romanones made a tactical advance towards the Constitutionalist position, when he declared that he would accept a Constituent Cortes if previously decided on by an ordinary parliament. His suggestion was based on the assumption that if a 'national government', in which the Liberals would be represented, would preside over the elections, a majority of anti-Constitutionalists would anyway be elected.[2] But a week later he realized that a 'national government' was impractical. Nor was his demand from the government of special guarantees of its electoral sincerity sufficient to bring down the government. These guarantees included election of mayors in 800 villages and the abstention of the government from sending 'governmental delegates' to the polls.[3] If he, together with Cambó and García Prieto, who collaborated in this move, had hoped for a moment that the government would reject this formula of 'partial municipal elections', and thus provide them with a pretext for boycotting the elections, and bringing down the government, they were soon disappointed, because the government rushed to give these and further guarantees which the Liberals had not asked for.[4]

[1] For insistence on the order of the elections see the reflection of an intensive Liberal campaign in *ABC* 10 June, 17 July, 20 Sept. 1930 (Romanones); *LV* 24 Aug. 1930 (the Catalan Liberals); *ABC* 12 Aug., 14 Sept., 6 Dec. 1930; and *La Voz Liberal*, Jaén, 7 Nov. 1930 (Ruiz Jiménez); *ABC* 25 Oct. 1930 (Marqués de la Hermida); *EI* 24 Sept. 1930 (Luis Massó y Simó); RA Leg. 68 no. 16: 'El Ferrol, Elecciones Gobierno de Berenguer'. SAA: Alba to Amós Salvador, 30 Oct. 1930. Even La Cierva, *Notas*, pp. 320, 322. had allegations of his own. Berenguer, *De la Dictadura*, p. 192, had 'estimates' on a Conservative victory. For the political intentions of the government see *ABC* 26 Nov. 1930; *ED* 14 Nov. 1930; Berenguer, op. cit. 208–11. See also editorials in *EI* 27, 30 Nov. 1930, 2, 4, Jan., 12–14 Feb. 1931. For attacks on the government as unable to 'appease' the left see ibid. 25, 30 Sept., 15, 16, 24 Oct., 14, 21 Nov. 1930.

[2] *LE* 7 Jan. 1931; *EI* and *ABC* 8 Jan. 1931.

[3] *ABC* 16 Jan. 1931.

[4] RA Leg. 63 no. 60: minute of a telephone conversation between Cambó and García Prieto, 29 Jan. 1931; and between Romanones and Cambó, 30 Jan. 1931. See also *ABC* 29 Jan. 1931; *El Sol* 31 Jan. 1931. For the guarantees conceded by the government see *LE* 2 Feb. 1931.

The Liberals had now no reason to use the electoral *retraimiento*, but the question of the kind of Cortes to be summoned remained as a weapon in their hands. The Constitutionalists and Reformists decided to abstain, thus refusing to be the extreme left in a parliament from which Republicans and Socialists had already made it clear that they would be absent. The reaction of Romanones and García Prieto was to suggest a formula to appease the Constitutionalists and to undermine the government's commitment to fight the 'Constituent' thesis. According to the new formula, the Liberals would 'go to the elections', but would ask in the first session of the Ordinary Cortes, that it should be dissolved and that constituent elections should be declared immediately. At the same time, Alba was elaborating his personal abstention, after he had reached the conclusion that both Republicans and Socialists had abandoned their revolutionary tactics, and were looking for a legal formula. He hoped that by his abstention he might cause the fall of the government, and then a wide leftist coalition could be created to run the municipal elections. On 10 February, he made public his retraimiento, alleging that elections 'made' by the Berenguer government would produce 'a Conservative ministry in the old style'. He made a final appeal to the left to rally around him for a legal struggle on behalf of common interests. This, in fact, was a basic change of attitude. His previous support of an Ordinary Cortes was replaced by a call for a Constituent Cortes, since no other formula could satisfy the left. This 'desertion', as *El Imparcial* put it, depressed the Ministry of the Interior, who saw now no other way out but the resignation of the government.[5]

The final *coup de grace* to the government was given on 13 February 1931 in a common note to the press by Romanones and García Prieto, after a previous consultation with Cambó. They reaffirmed their position already made public on 31 January. This amounted to a virtual abstention, which, they said, they were forced to adopt in view of the long series of

---

[5] For the Constitutionalists' abstention see *ABC* 30 Jan., 6 Feb. 1931; Burgos y Mazo, *De la Republica...?*, pp. 85–9. The Liberal formula is in a common note of García Prieto and Romanones in *El Sol* 31 Jan. 1931. For Alba see his note in *ABC* 10 Feb. 1931, and his motives as related to Cambó in Pabón, *Cambó* ii, part ii, 74; *EI* 11 Feb. 1931. For the Minister of the Interior see La Cierva, *Notas*, p. 337.

abstentions by other political sectors. By adhering to the retraimiento of the left they had undermined the old, and now anachronistic, 'fair play' between Liberals and Conservatives, just as they had done to Maura in 1909. Romanones was, indeed, fully aware that he was contributing to the overthrow of the government, and on the same evening of the thirteenth he mentioned to Berenguer the name of Admiral Aznar, as his possible successor, and he telephoned to General Cavalcanti in what seemed to be an attempt to neutralize the army in the approaching crisis.[6]

If there was still any doubt that the government had no alternative but that of resignation, the General Union of Employers came out on the same day with an abstention of its own, as a means of exerting pressure on the government on behalf of a reform in the Comités Paritarios. Romanones could easily claim that his attitude was influenced by the employers' position and by the declining monetary situation, which could be solved only by a political change. Political uncertainty was, indeed, blamed by financial circles as the reason for the depreciation of the peseta, and hence of the instability of business.[7]

Thus, under pressure similar to that which had been brought upon Primo de Rivera—political isolation and economic failure—Berenguer decided to give way to the proposed political change. He pointed out, however, that the Liberals' attitude was the main reason for his resignation. The Liberals, on the other hand, congratulated their leader for bringing an end to a government that was 'a protector of reactionaries and supporters of dictatorships', in order to pave the way for a 'national government' that would save the Monarchy from the Republican bid for power.[8]

[6] The note in *El* 14 Feb. 1931; a special note of Cambó in *ABC* 14 Feb. 1931. For Romanones' awareness see his *Las Ultimas Horas de Una Monarquía*, p. 8; Berenguer *De la Dictadura*, p. 316. For Cavalacanti see *ABC* 14 Feb. 1931. *The Times* 16 Feb. 1931 called the whole affair 'Count Romanones' *coup*'.

[7] *El Mercantil Patronal* Feb.–Mar. 1931; *Boletín de la Cámara de Comercio de Madrid* Apr. 1931; *The Economist* 24 Jan. 1931; *Banco Urquijo* Dec. 1930, Jan., Feb., Mar. 1931; Berenguer, *De la Dictadura*, p. 273.

[8] *El* 15 Feb. 1931.

V

THE FALL OF THE MONARCHY AND THE PROCLAMATION OF THE REPUBLIC

I. A MONARCHIST SAN SEBASTIÁN PACT

The issue of Monarchy versus Republic which was in the background of political activities throughout the last year, reached its culminating point during the Anzar government. Both the Monarchists and the Republicans made last-minute efforts to close their ranks for the forthcoming electoral struggle, thus sharpening their differences and accentuating the plebiscitary character of the municipal elections of April 1931, which both admitted should decide between Monarchy and Republic. But the history of the Berenguer period had also shown what the next two months would further emphasize: the left was much more determined and capable of transforming its revolutionary alliance into an electoral pact than the Monarchists were able to collaborate between themselves for the defence of the regime. However, it is by no means true that the Monarchists were either indifferent or absent from the political arena. They realized the precarious position of the regime, and made considerable efforts to defend it. It was the vigour of their enemies and the discredit of the Monarchy in an increasingly politically-minded society, rather than lack of unity among Monarchists, which finally brought down the Monarchy. Unity between personalistic factions of Monarchists was irrelevant in a period of massive political mobilization.

In fact, the constitution of the Aznar government was an example of the capacity of Monarchist leaders to close their ranks when the regime was threatened. The fall of the Berenguer government was the result of a breach between Conservatives and Liberals—the two main Monarchist factions. This, and the growing demand for a 'leftist' solution, brought the king to cast upon Sánchez Guerra, now a Constitutionalist leader, the task of forming a new government. The king even agreed to a minimum programme which included the abolition of Primo's legislation and the freezing of his own prerogatives until after the Constituent Cortes had given its verdict. By agreeing to introduce an alteration in the oath of allegiance of the government, the king went so far as to recognize, for the first time, that the 1876 constitution no longer existed. Although he did not object to the presence of anti-monarchist figures in the new government, he still insisted on the inclusion of Romanones and García Prieto who, he believed, would be his defenders in a government that would not consider the preservation of the Monarchy its main task. The king's insistence, and the refusal of leftist figures like Marañón, J. Ortega, and the Republicans in the Model Prison to take part in the government, could only result in the formation of an unrepresentative cabinet threatened by both the Monarchist and anti-Constitutional right, and by the ambiguous attitude of the Republican-Socialist coalition. Sánchez Guerra therefore retired. An abortive attempt by Melquiades Alvarez to succeed where he failed finally put the lid on the so-called 'Constitutionalist solution'.[1]

The failure of the Constitutionalists brought relief to the Monarchists, who were now delivered from the nightmare of a Constitutionalist 'solution' which would effectively exclude the 'pure' Monarchists from power. The possibility of a leftist government supported by the enemies of the king was, according to *El Debate*, an invitation to the left to realize, with the blessing of the king, the revolution which it had failed to carry out in the streets. It was, therefore, with satisfaction that *ABC* announced the collapse of 'the house of cards' of constituent politics.[2] Moreover, the Monarchists could now claim that the king was not an obstacle in the way of the left's achieving power by legal means.[3] This was precisely the impression that the king was interested in creating.

A Monarchist coalition government was suggested to him by Romanones, García Prieto, La Cierva, and Bugallal already on 14 February—one day before Sánchez Guerra was called to the palace—and on that same evening Romanones urged Aznar to come from Cartagena, at the special request of the king

---

[1] For Sánchez Guerra see *ABC* 17, 18 Feb. 1931, Chapaprieta, *La Paz*, pp. 147–8; Burgos y Mazo, *Los Constitucionalistas* iv, 84–6. For Melquiades see *ABC* 18 Feb. 1931.
[2] *ED* 17 Feb. 1931, *ABC* 18 Feb. 1931.
[3] *El* 17, 18 Feb. 1931, *ED* 18 Feb. 1931.

himself.[4] Romanones and the king shrewdly prepared the Aznar alternative while reluctantly giving a chance to the Constitutionalists which both hoped would fail. Hence their insistence on the inclusion of Romanones and García Prieto in any proposed government, an unacceptable condition to both Sánchez Guerra and Melquiades Alvarez. Now the king and his advisers could appear as liberals who had been ready to invite the left to power. It was the left which had rejected the invitation. The Aznar solution could now be presented not as an anachronistic insistence of the Monarchists to hold power against public opinion, but as the *only* way to govern the country.[5]

As soon as La Cierva knew that Sánchez Guerra had asked the anti-dynastic left to participate in his government, he started a series of meetings with Monarchist leaders in order 'to save the country'. His efforts resulted in a kind of 'Monarchist San Sebastian pact', which embraced most of the Monarchist factions, and which like the Republican San Sebastian pact, recognized Catalonia's right for autonomy. As soon as the failure of the Constitutionalists had become obvious, Romanones 'accepted' La Cierva's initiative for setting up a coalition, and rushed to 'convince' his Liberal colleague, García Prieto. The negotiations between the Monarchist leaders, which started on the evening of the 17 February, culminated on the night of the eighteenth at Berenguer's office with the king's blessing, in what people in the street called a cannibals' feast[6] to share the spoils of the government between the various factions. Apart from the disreputable UM and *Albiñanistas*, all parties were represented. The key posts of Premier and Minister of the Interior were given to apolitical figures in order not to alienate any of the factions. Aznar, an admiral with no authority over his ministers, was a very 'convenient' Premier who allowed each ministry, in Romanones' words, to become 'an independent canton'. The Ministry of the Interior in the hands of Hoyos, another apolitical figure, was a guarantee that none of the factions represented in the government would be favoured

[4] *ABC, ED* 15 Feb. 1931.

[5] For the constutionalists' refusal to serve with liberals see *ABC* 17 Feb. 1931; Burgos y Mazo, op. cit. 80–2. For their consideration of the whole affair as a 'manœuvre' see Burgoz y Mazo, *De la Republica a . . .?*, pp. 89–95. Romanones in his *Las Ultimas horas*, pp. 72–3 stressed the king's 'liberalism'.

[6] *The Times* 20 Feb. 1931.

either in political appointments or in electoral matters. And—
what is more significant—it reflected the government's determination not to 'make' the elections according to the old
procedures. The *Lliga's* support for the new government, for
which Ventosa Calvell received the Ministry of Finance, was
given in return for the recognition by the government of
Catalonia's claim for administrative autonomy and the adoption
of Cambo's quest for a stabilization of the peseta, the floating of
which had introduced confusion and instability into the Catalan
business world. The concession to the Liberals and, indeed to
the anti-dynastic left as well, was the government's decision to
hold first municipal and then general elections as 'the only
means of attracting popular sympathies', according to Romanones. The opponents of a Constituent Cortes, mainly the
Conservatives, were appeased by the ambiguous definition
given to that Cortes in the governmental message to the people:
it would not deal exclusively with constitutional questions and
would be entitled to act simultaneously as an Ordinary Cortes.
Being a bicameral parliament it would also preserve, through
the Upper House vested interests in the new constitution, while
the form of regime would not be open to revision.[7]

However, mutual suspicions and pessimism predominated in
the government, despite the Monarchist euphoria which
acclaimed the new cabinet as the incarnation of 'the monarchist
spirit' and which praised the victory of 'peace, order and
concord'. Gabriel Maura noted sadly that the ministers did not
represent 'the voice of the masses, but that of parties and
groups'. A minister for the first time in his life, Maura had the
feeling of 'escorting the crown to the cemetery', while García
Prieto anxiously looked forward to the elections to relieve him
of his ministerial burden. With the Minister of the Interior
politically unaffiliated, every group in the government—and

[7] For the negotiations see: *ABC* 18 Feb. 1931; Joaquín Nadal, *Seis Años con Don F.
Cambó*, pp. 77–9; Berenguer, *De la Dictadura*, p. 332; Hoyos, *Mi Testimonio*, pp. 47–9,
50–1; Romanones, *Notas*, pp. 232–3; La Cierva, *Notas*, pp. 339–40, 342–5. For the
programme see *ED* 20 Feb. 1931; La Cierva, op. cit. 341–2, 345–6. For the Catalan issue
see *Historia d'una Política* pp. 388–90; Cambó in *LV* 27 Feb. 1931; J. Estelrich, *De la
Dictadura*, pp. 214, 217–19; and *Revista de Catalunya* March 1931 (an article by Ferran
Soldevila). Romanones is quoted from his *Las Ultimas Horas*, p. 42. For electoral sincerity
see AHN Leg. 47: Circular to the Governors No. 28, 7 Mar. 1931. Cambó was deeply
concerned with the depreciation of the peseta. See his *La Valoración de la Peseta*.

there were as many as there were ministers—managed to have a number of provincial governors under its control. This emphasized the atomization rather than the union of Spanish Monarchists. There is no evidence that the alliance went beyond the superficial governmental level or that any programme of collaboration in the provinces was ever evolved.[8]

The only promising and exceptional case was that of the foundation of the *Partido del Centro Constitucional* by a fusion of *Mauristas, Derecha Nacional*, Regionalists, and other conservative groups. Cambó brought conservative elements to believe that he might have the formula for conciliating anti-separatist regionalism with the basic interests of the socially and politically conservatives of Spain. After that the *Bugallalistas* in Lugo,[9] and the regionalist *Union Valenciana* transferred their loyalty to him, he pretentiously appealed, at the end of February, to his 'friends in Aragón, Levante, Castile, León, Galicia, Andalucía, La Mancha and Extremadura' to support him in his decision 'to extend my activity into Spain'. Gabriel Maura, who had been in close contact with Cambó throughout the last year, pointed out to him the identification of Mauristas with his ideas as to the need to set up a 'modern' party based on Catholicism, monarchism and constitutionalism, a party which, though rejecting the Republic, would oppose a simple return to old politics, and, therefore, could absorb all the monarchists who wanted to bring about an end to the unrepresentative parties of the old regime which, anachronistically, were still the major political incarnation of monarchism. The *Centro*, however, was conceived by Maura also in negative terms, a characteristic position of monarchists on the eve of the fall of the Monarchy. It was an organization aimed at fighting the 'anti-religious', the 'anti-monarchists', the 'separatists', the 'Communists' as well as the 'collaborators with the Dictatorship'. The party was officially founded on 3 March at a closed meeting of Maurista and *Lliguista* leaders. Subsequently the political committee of the *Lliga* ratified its adherence to the new party, and, while stating

[8] For the euphoria see *ABC, LE* 18 Feb. 1931, *LE, El, LV* and *ED* 19 Feb. 1931. Even the financial sector reacted favourably with an improvement in the rate of the peseta, see *The Times* 20 Feb. 1931, *Financial News*, London, 23 Feb. 1931; see Gabriel Maura, *Recuerdos*, pp. 198–9. For García Prieto see his letter to Romanones in RA Leg. 63 no. 18. For the governors see Mola, *Obras*, p. 748; and La Cierva, *Notas*, p. 347.

[9] *NE* 25 Mar. 1931.

that it would continue to act in Catalan politics 'with an independent personality', it also made it clear that it had become the Catalan branch of a new national party, thus jeopardizing its chances in forthcoming struggles with the Catalanist left. Apart from the immediate adherence of Maurista centres throughout the country, the new party (encouraged by civil governors loyal to Maura and Cambó) was joined by a great number of conservative groups scattered in the provinces, like the followers of General Saro in Ubeda, Montes Jovellar in Granada, and Conde de Güell in Barcelona. Cambó noticed a few years later, that his party consisted of the basic elements which would form the skeleton of the CEDA.[10]

The immediate reaction of monarchists to the creation of the new party was positive. Baldomero Argente referred to it as to the first serious attempt to organize a mass monarchist party. He saw the mission of the *Centro* as 'gathering the dispersed energies of socially conservative Spain—whose frontiers correspond with those of monarchist Spain—and converting them into a powerful instrument for the transformation of the country'. *El Debate* and *ABC* hopefully believed that the Centro, a coalition likely to absorb the collective energies of the wealthy and panic-stricken classes, was that long-awaited conservative party which would be soon called to assume power because of its emphasis on the 'real problems' of the economy and agriculture, and because of the abandonment of regional exclusivism by the Catalan bourgeoisie. The Liberals who used to dismiss the *Bugallalistas* and *Ciervistas* as insignificant factions, foresaw now the emergence of a conservative party, with a clear social basis, worth taking into consideration as a political rival. Even *El Sol* welcomed the new party as a 'modern and European right of which Spain would not have to be ashamed'. Only the Conservatives, who feared for their monopoly of conservatism, and therefore saw the Centro as evidence of further disintegration among the monarchists, were critical towards the new party. But they could not overshadow the initial euphoria which surrounded its foundation. Even the

---

[10] *La Veu de Catalunya* 4 Mar. 1931, *ABC* 10, 18, 19, 25 Mar. 1931; *LV* 18 Mar., 5 Apr. 1931; Nadal, *Seis Años*, pp. 85–7. See also ibid. 325–9: Maura–Cambó's exchange of letters; and also MA: Gabriel Maura to Indalecio Abril, n.d. (uncatalogued letter). For the CEDA see Cambó quoted in Pabón, *Cambó* ii, part ii, 98.

king, in his anxious quest for a solid support for his uncertain crown, seemed to be interested in encouraging the new party. Unfortunately for him, the Centro came too late, and in the April elections it was no more than one additional small party.[11]

However, the recent government crisis had considerably roused monarchist opinion, and every opportunity was taken to show loyalty to the king. Such was the huge demonstration on the return of the queen from England, and a pilgrimage of thousands of people to the queen mother's tomb in the Escorial. Donations to the Civil Guard were also a way of showing loyalty to the Monarchy. The king's political ability in overcoming the recent crisis strengthened the conviction of many that, as a women's newspaper put it, 'we probably lack statesmen, but we have a king'. Although the current activities of the governmental parties were limited, the *Juventud Monárquica Independiente*, under the energetic leadership of Vegas Latapié, was there to make constant efforts in spreading monarchist propaganda, and, when necessary, even to defend the king's prestige in physical clashes with his enemies.[12]

But it was the extreme Monarchist right, rather than the old traditional parties, which carried on the most vociferous campaign on behalf of the Monarchy. The UM, though disappointed at not having been invited to the government, manifested its satisfaction with the failure of the 'pre-revolutionary' experiment of the Constitutionalists, and promised to support the Aznar government 'as far as it personifies the principles of authority, Monarchy and order'. The UM was the only Monarchist party which still had the capacity to hold huge gatherings on a national scale, such as the commemoration of Primo's death, meetings of monarchist affirmation, and even to start the publication of new monarchist reviews, like *Ideal Patrio* in Salamanca and *La Idea* in Valencia. The other monarchist outcasts—the *Albiñanistas*—continued in their efforts

[11] Argente in *LV* 3, 10 Mar. 1931; *ED* and *ABC* 4 Mar. 1931. The Liberals in *El* 5 Mar. 1931; *El Sol* 5 Mar. 1931; The Conservatives in *LE* 4 Mar. 1931. For the king see La Cierva, *Notas*, p. 348.

[12] For the demonstrations and donations to the Civil Guard see *ED* 18 Feb., 4 Mar. 1931; *La Unión*, March 1931; *Mujeres Españolas* 1 Mar. 1931. ibid. 22 Feb. 1931 is the women's newspaper. For the Juventud Monárquica see Galindo Herrero, *Los Partidos Monárquicos* pp. 68–9; *Unión Monárquica* 19 Mar. 1931; and *ABC* 21 Feb., 8, 27 Mar., 1 Apr. 1931.

to save the Monarchy from its 'international' enemies. They organized anti-amnesty campaigns pressing the government not to yield to the demands of the left and the FUE. Nonetheless, Albiñana had a fatalistic feeling that he was leading a lost war. Militant monarchism was in the minority, while the institutionalized parties were unable to curb the left. His hysterical invitation to 'republicans who have the guts to stand up for their Republic' to meet his men in the streets was a ridiculous attempt to turn away from the course towards peaceful elections. Not even a young new group of nationalists—*La Conquista del Estado*—bothered to support him. Their message—as was indeed that of Albiñana—was the defence of 'Hispanic values' rather than the Monarchy. History has come to regard both groups as forerunners of the later anti-monarchist Falange rather than as the militant defenders of a decadent Monarchy.[13]

2. THE LEFT: NON-COMPROMISE AND AGITATION

The Provisional Government, though confined in its majority in prison, managed to influence the course of events and to be a political factor no less decisive than the official government. It was they who moulded the political ambiance in the country and the overwhelming leftist pressure which led to 14 April.

Their key position in the political map was reflected in Sánchez Guerra's attempt to enlist them in his government, while they were awaiting trial for rebellion. This bizarre and unprecedented step was the result of the radical transformation of Spanish politics in the last year. The Monarchy depended now either on the collaboration of the Republican-Socialist movement, or on the Provisional Government's willingness to grant the regime a truce. The political prisoners rejected both demands; but, in a moderate public note, they welcomed the formation of a Constituent government as the first stage towards their victory, and as the capitulation of the Monarchy to republican pressure, which they were determined to continue to exert until the final victory. Their concession to Sánchez Guerra was reflected in the emphasis in the memorandum on

---

[13] For the UM see *Unión Monárquica*, 1, 19 Mar. 1931; *ABC* 17 Mar. 1931. For Albiñanistas see *La Legión* 19, 26 Mar., 2, 9 Apr. 1931; *ABC* 11 Apr. 1931; and R. Sánchez Guerra, *un Año Histórico*, pp. 100–6. *La Conquista del Estado* 14, 28 Mar., 4, 11 Apr. 1931.

their belief in victory through elections rather than by violence.[14] But when the Aznar government came to power, the Republicans obviously changed their attitude. What started as an extraordinary crisis ended with 'a new government of old men', as had many others before 1923. The campaign of agitation was, therefore, to be continued and intensified. However, purely revolutionary actions were not considered seriously, though Mola's department was on constant alert. The Provisional Government had no confidence in Lerroux, who presided over an alternative Revolutionary Committee. Neither were the Socialists to be trusted after their obvious shortcomings on 15 December, nor were they eager to be pushed into a revolutionary movement. They were now divided, more than at any time in the last year, over the issue of 'ministerial collaboration'. In a meeting of the National Committees of both the UGT and the PSOE, Besteiro's proposition not to designate a representative to the Revolutionary Committee was rejected in favour of a contrary motion by a majority of 35 to 12 with 5 abstentions. As a demonstration of disagreement with the decision, four major leaders—Lucio Martínez, Ovejero, Saborit, and Besteiro—resigned from the Executive. Though, as Saborit claimed, rather than a definite split it was 'a small discrepancy over a question of tactics', the party was not united either; and as such it was a dubious partner for a revolution. However, the *Caballerista* majority, by putting revolutionary republicanism before its class politics, was still able to impress both a defender of the present order like Cambó, as 'a contribution of undeniable value' to the republican movement, and a leftist intellectual like Ortega, as leading to an 'exemplary unanimity' between Republicans and Socialists for the establishment of the new state.[15]

Even without new *coups* the Republican coalition was able to harass the government and to incite public opinion. From its

[14] For the visit of Sánchez Guerra to the prison see *ABC* 17 Feb. 1931; M. Maura, *Así*, pp. 123, 125; R. Sánchez Guerra, *Proceso*, pp. 141–4. The note in *ABC* 17 Feb. 1931. See also *ES* (editorial) 17 Feb. 1931; Azaña in *La Tierra* 2 Apr. 1931; and Prieto in *La Gaceta de la Revolución* 25 Feb. 1931, all expressing the great self confidence of the Provisional Government.

[15] For the attitude to the government see *Vanguardia*, Badajoz, 23 Feb. 1931; *ES* 19,

confinement in the Model Prison, the Provisional Government was in contact with immense crowds of citizens who came to pay it daily tribute. A verdict against the prisoners in their trial, which opened on 20 March, would have made them the martyrs of a widespread national movement. This was the reason why Romanones, Ventosa, and Gabriel Maura exerted pressure for their acquittal. But unfortunately for the regime, even their acquittal in what was a republican meeting rather than a trial, did not gain the government public sympathy. Their advocates made every effort to defend their clients by undermining the Monarchy's prestige. They deliberately chose a long crowded route from the prison to the law court which, they insisted, should be big enough to contain a large public. Amid frequent applause, and supported by the lenience of the judges, both the accused and their defenders managed to put the Monarchy in the dock. Ossorio, Jiménez de Asua, and Bergamín pointed out the illegitimacy of the regime which ruled unconstitutionally and, therefore, had no right to judge and punish a rebellion, while Sánchez Román claimed that in December the Revolutionary Committee was the incarnation of the will of the majority of the citizens, 'who wanted neither disorders nor tyranny'. The vague allegations of the prosecutor about the communist character of the movement were easily refuted by the authoritative claim of Alcalá Zamora that he personally was the guarantee that 'we were not going to jump into chaos'. The verdict adopted the basic arguments of the defence by stating that the accused were motivated 'by the painful impression' created on them by the situation into which the country had been thrown, and had, therefore, acted in a 'pardonable obfuscation'. The result was a virtual acquittal, the effect of which was strengthened by General Burguete, one of the judges, when he publicly denounced the dictatorial tendencies of the regime and emphasized the army's solidarity with the people. For the left it was a moment of great confidence; those

22 Feb. 1931; *NE* 25 Feb. 1931. For Mola see *Obras*, pp. 721, 724–5, 730–3, 811–12. For Socialist reluctance to consider revolutions see *ES* 18 Feb. 1931. The meeting of the National Committees in Saborit, *Besteiro*, pp. 276–7; *BUGT*, March 1931; and E. Santiago, *La UGT*, pp. 86–9. Saborit in *ES* 24 Feb. 1931. Cambó in *LV* 11 Mar. 1931; and Ortega in *El Sol* 13 Mar. 1931. See also *NE* 4 Mar. 1931 on the republican euphoria at the Socialists' decision.

just released were 'the first government of the second Spanish Republic'.[16]

The agitation, however, was kept alive by a pro-amnesty campaign following the death sentence on Captain Sediles, one of the leaders of the Jaca rebellion. But the Aznar government, the 'weakest government in the world' as a French newspaper put it,[17] rushed to concede amnesty having in mind both the unfortunate execution of Galán and a violent threat from the Socialist Party warning that the people might 'rise *en masse* against the tyranny'. Yet the campaign went on on behalf of other political prisoners, as an instrument of political mobilization.[18]

This was also the significance of the continued agitation of leftist students which, with the support of Republicans and Socialists, contributed to discredit the regime further in its last days of precarious existence. Thrown into the streets by Berenguer's order to close universities for thirty days, they organized in Republican and Socialist centres the so-called 'unofficial university' by enlisting mainly leftist professors like Ortega, Besteiro, and Ovejero. The 'free university' was rightly seen by both right and left as a political republican movement. The reopening of the universities by the beginning of March only brought an increase of tension—the Revolutionary Committee, despite denials from the FUE, was stirring up the students. The death sentence on Sediles was another excuse for demonstrations which continued after his amnesty, now on behalf of all political prisoners. The climax was a two-day battle, on the 24–25 of March, between students and the police in front of the faculty of medicine, during which both made use of guns. The result of the battle in 'the Kasba of rebellion', as Mola called the faculty, was one Civil Guard killed and eighteen wounded

[16] For ministerial pressure for acquittal see La Cierva, *Notas*, pp. 358–9. For the 'meeting' see Maura, *Así*, p. 136, Castrovido's 'El mitin republicano de las Salesas' in *El Pueblo* 26 Mar. 1931; *ES* 21, 22, 24 Mar. 1931. See also Jiménez de Asua's highly political defence speech in his *Defensa de una rebelión*, especially pp. 5–6, 50–9, 67–83. The verdict in J. Gutierrez-Ravé, *España en 1931*, pp. 67–71, Burguete in *ABC* 1 Apr. 1931, and in *NE* 1 Apr. 1931. Last quotation in *ES* 25 Mar. 1931.

[17] *Le Journal*, Paris, 28 Mar. 1931.

[18] The campaign on behalf of Sediles in *ABC*, 19 Mar. 1931; *La Gaceta de la Revolución* 6 Mar. 1931. The Socialists in *ES* 19 Mar. 1931; *La Gaceta* 19 Mar. 1931; and E. Santiago, *La UGT*, pp. 92–4. For the last statement see meetings pro-amnesty in *ABC* 24 Mar. 1931, *ES* 25 Mar. 1931; and Mola, *Obras*, pp. 772–3.

from both sides. This bloodshed aroused a widespread protest from leftist sectors; professors asked for the resignation of Mola, and the FUE followed suit with a declaration of 'incompatibility between the universities and a regime that had no answers to our demands but the guns of the Civil Guard.'[19] The events of Madrid had their repercussion in provincial universities like Salamanca, Valencia, Valladolid, Seville, Zaragoza, Santiago, and Barcelona. In Barcelona, the students even declared the Republic and asked the people to support them, while in most universities violent clashes with the police took place, and republican slogans were used. The leftist press exploited the events. It told how Ramón Sampere, before dying from injuries received in front of the faculty, cried 'Viva la Republica'.[20] Mola was denounced as a rough soldier who confused the streets of Madrid with the mountains of the rebellious Rif. The students made it clear in a public manifesto that not even Mola's resignation would satisfy them. Their goal was a republican Spain: to bring an end to the regime. And, indeed, not until the declaration of the Republic did the FUE's agitation stop.[21] By then it had played a decisive role in discrediting the political machine in public opinion, thus paving the way to a peaceful Republican takeover.[22]

[19] *Heraldo de Madrid* 24 Mar. 1931.
[20] *El Sol* 31 Mar. 1931.
[21] For the 'free university' see *El Sol* 27 Feb. 1931 mainly on Madrid; and for the provinces see *El Heraldo de Aragón* 21 Feb. 1931; *El Pueblo Gallego* 24 Feb. 1931; *Noticiero Sevillano* 24 Feb. 1931; *Noticiero Granadino* 24 Feb. 1931; *Día Gráfico*, Barcelona, 24 Feb. 1931; *El Norte de Castilla*, Valladolid, 24 Feb. 1931. The rebellious students and their supporters among the professors in the May 1968 days in Paris ran a similar experiment—'the université critique'—which they hoped to establish on the ruins of the old university, see Belden Fields, 'The Revolution Betrayed' in Seymour Lipset and Philip Altbach, *Students in Revolt* p. 155. For the free university as a republican movement see *ABC* 25 Jan. 1931, *NE* 25 feb. 1931; and for allegations on the Revolutionary Committee's involvement in the agitations see Mola, *Obras*, p. 763; *Ejercito y Armada* 8 Apr. 1931; *Heraldo de Madrid* 24 Mar. 1931. For the 'battle of the faculty of medicine' see Mola, *Obras*, pp. 763–98; Hoyos, *Mi Testimonio*, pp. 71–98. For the students using guns see *The Times* 26 Mar. 1931; and *Heraldo de Madrid* 25 Mar. 1931. Wanting publicity, and for anti-monarchist propaganda, they invited journalists to cover the battle, see Luis de Armiñan, *La Republica . . . Es Esto?* pp. 105–12. For the provincial universities see *El Sol* 27, 31 Mar. 1931; *La Tierra* 26 Mar. 1931, *Heraldo* 26, 27, 28 Mar. 1931. The above mentioned newspapers and *ES* 26 Mar. 1931 also led the campaign against Mola. The public manifesto in *El Sol* 27 Mar. 1931 was wholeheartedly welcomed by republicans, see *NE* 1, 8 Apr. 1931.
[22] Cf. 'Los estudiantes—una deuda de gratitud' in *El Crisol* 21 Apr. 1931.

3. A MONARCHIST EXPERIMENT IN A MODERN ELECTORAL CAMPAIGN

The superficiality of the Monarchist alliance in the government was reflected in the flimsy and uneasy collaboration, and sometimes overt rivalry, between Monarchist groups all over Spain, on the eve of the municipal elections decreed by the government for 12 April. Although they suffered from a certain degree of fragmentation, the efforts made by monarchists and other supporters of the regime to defend the king, and the basic principles they stood for, were nevertheless by no means negligible, and Monarchist coalitions, either partial or total, emerged in almost every provincial capital and large town.

Madrid was the nerve centre of the electoral campaign, and it was there that the Monarchists started by displaying a lamentable spectacle of rivalries before they managed to forge an electoral alliance. Hoyos was not authoritative enough to impose a common electoral strategy on Liberals and Conservatives, and Aznar was indifferent. The UM, though suspect to public opinion when the Dictatorship was denounced by both right and left, still insisted on a considerable representation in the alliance. *Albiñanistas, Laboristas,* and *Mauristas* were there to increase the confusion.[23] Although Romanones indicated in the first week of March that the Monarchist coalition was a fact, negotiations went on until the last week of the month in order to conciliate demands of the various groups. *ABC* noticed with sadness that whereas the leftist coalition was successfully overcoming doctrinal differences of opinion between its members, the Monarchists were engaged in the traditional spoil-sharing. In a fierce personal attack it summed up its opinion on the national leaders of monarchism.

Not only have they betrayed monarchist opinion, but also the majority of their followers. As for the government . . ., a heterogeneous mixture of egoism and colourless neutrality, it manifests indifference towards the interests that it should have embodied and unified . . . The truth is that those responsible for the failure to form a united slate in Madrid are Romanones, Bugallal, Guadalhorce, Cambó–Maura.[24]

[23] Alcalá Galiano, *The Fall*, pp. 163–4.
[24] Romanones in *ABC* 7 Mar. 1931. The quotation in ibid. 24 Mar. 1931.

An additional problem was the reluctance of the traditional Monarchists to pact with the UM. This was a reason why apolitical organizations like Chambers of Commerce, Catholic syndicates, and *Orientación Social* threatened not to support the Monarchist slate because it did not represent all the Monarchist forces. The Chamber of Commerce even warned that its members would vote for the UM, and *El Debate* even encouraged this party to fight alone in order to achieve 'a moral victory'. It was finally the pressure of the 'apolitical' forces which brought the coalition to terms with the UM, thus allowing the Monarchists to present a common slate to the public on 24 March, after having overcome the question of each group's share in the coalition. A last moment insistence by the *Albiñanistas* that they be included was simply disregarded. But the insistence of the *Unión General de Patronos Comerciantes e Industriales de Madrid* to present its own separate candidature, as an act of protest against the government attitude to their demands to reform the Comités Paritarios' regulations, and against the politicization of municipal life, was a serious setback.[25]

Among Monarchists in the provinces there was a general quest for union which, in most cases, was brought about, either through the intervention of the governors, who were themselves stimulated by the Minister of the Interior[26] or by local initiatives. These coalitions were sometimes wider than that of Madrid. In Alicante it included all the Monarchists from the Integrists on the right up to the *Izquierda Liberal* on the left. In Valencia it consisted of all the traditional parties, the *Centro*, local regionalists and *Jaimistas*, with the *Albistas* refusing to join such a rightist alliance, though in other places, like Palencia, where they had a substantial force and were able to dominate the majority of the places on the coalition list, they did join it. The same happened in Gijón with the Reformists, and in Huelva where the Constitutionalists had a stronghold under Burgos Mazo. Especially wide coalitions were also made in

---

[25] For the 'apolitical' forces see *Unión Monárquica* 1 Apr. 1931; *El Debate* 17 Mar. 1931, there also the quotation. More on the negotiations in Hoyos, *Mi Testimonio*, pp. 109–10; and an emphasis on the rivalries in J. Cortés-Cavanillas, *La Caída de Alfonso XIII*, pp. 191–7. For the presentation of the slate see *ABC* 25, 26 Mar. 1931. The Albiñanistas in *La Legion* 26 Mar. 1931. For the employers see *El Mercantil Patronal* April 1931; and *La Nación* 19 Mar. 1931.

[26] Hoyos, *Mi Testimonio*, pp. 53–4.

Murcia, Cuenca, Cadiz, Málaga, and León, where even *Upetistas* had six places in the coalition.[27] The general pattern, however, was that of coalitions in the majority of the provincial capitals between Liberals, Conservatives, with the occasional adherence of *Centristas* and Catholic groups, leaving aside the UM and the Carlists to the right and Constitutionalists to the left. Such was the case in Badajoz where the Centristas were separated from the coalition, Toledo where only Conservative, Liberals and 'apoliticals' made up the slate, Córdoba where the Centristas did not join the alliance and the UM had to fight alone, and Peñafiel where the *Albistas* went on a separate slate.[28] An exceptional case was that of Seville where the Liberals, headed by Conde de Halcón, the city mayor, refused to join the coalition, presided by the Conservative Marqués de Torrenueva, when their demand to get half the places in the coalition, leaving the other half for the other five groups, were rejected. Therefore, the Liberals of Romanones and the Albistas went on a separate slate, thus seriously fragmenting the Monarchist forces.[29]

Nor were the Liberals ready to collaborate with the *Lliga Regionalista* in a city like Barcelona. They had not the slightest chance of success by acting separately, as they did. Also the emergence of ephemeral Monarchist slates like the *Derecha Social, El Grupo Católico de Barcelona, Candidatura Católico-Monárquica, Unión Nacional,* and *Candidatura Independiente Administrativa,* was not exactly a contribution to the efforts of the only big Monarchist party, the *Lliga,* to fight the overwhelming offensive of the Catalan left. Sala's *Unión Monárquica Nacional,* which in

[27] *ABC* 15, 24, 27 Mar. 1931 (Alicante, Valencia, Palencia, Gijón); *El Liberal Sevilla* 12 Apr. 1931 (Huelva); *El Centro,* Cuenca, 3 Mar. 1931; and *ABC* 3, 5 Apr. 1931 (Cuenca. Cádiz, Murcia); *Unión Mercantil,* Málaga 11 Apr. 1931; *El Norte de Castilla,* 5 Apr. 1931 (León). For the coherence of the Constitutionalist bloc on the eve of the elections, in alliance mainly with Albistas, see Burgos y Mazo, *Los Constitutionalistas* iv, 107–16. They were, however, by no means unconditional friends of the Monarchy.

[28] *ABC,* 24, 27 Mar. 1931 (Toledo, Badajoz); *ABC, Sevilla* 2 Apr. 1931 (Córdoba); *El Norte de Castilla* 5 Apr. 1931 (Peñafiel). See for more alliances: *La Voz de Galicia* 4 Apr. 1931 (Ferrol); *ED* 7 Apr. 1931 (Santander); *El Norte de Castilla* 5 Apr. 1931 (Valladolid). *ABC* of the second half of March is very informative on such coalitions see 17, 18, 21, 24, 27 Mar., 4, 5 Apr. 1931 (Aranjuez, La Carolina, Pontevedra, Ciudad Real, Salamanca, Jaén, Santiago, Soria).

[29] *El Liberal, Sevilla* 2, 4 Apr. 1931; *ABC, Sevilla* 1, 2, 5 Apr. 1931.

Tarrasa failed to persuade the Lliga to join a Monarchist candidature, decided in Barcelona to abstain from the elections altogether. Nor were the Traditionalists successful in their attempt to reach an agreement with the *Lliga* and they also decided to abstain.[30] The Monarchist forces were obviously less coherent in the Basque provinces where the struggle was complicated by the existence of the *Partido Nacionalista Vasco*, strong Carlist branches, and Republicans. The only chance for Monarchists, given their different concepts of Monarchy, was in joining the Carlists in 'anti-revolutionary' candidatures. Such alliances were made possible in Pamplona, San Sebastián and in many other places in Navarra, Alava, and Guipúzcoa, because the Carlists, who were allowed to make alliances according to the 'local circumstances', seemed to be more concerned with the preservation of the religious and social values that they had in common with Alfonso's defenders, than with an improbable restoration of the 'legitimate' Monarchy.[31]

The Monarchist coalition, however, was deprived in many places of the support of both an increasingly important agrarian movement and of the Constitutionalist group, which consisted of the followers of prestigious national leaders like Alba, Sánchez Guerra, and Melquiades Alvarez. Apart from exceptional cases in which they collaborated with the Monarchists, the Constitutionalists, though they were basically monarchists, prepared their separate candidatures with an electoral platform which challenged both the authority of the king, by asking him to suspend his prerogatives until the Constituent Cortes had given its verdict on responsibilities and constitution, and the government's concept of the constituent parliament. Their standing on the border between Monarchy and Republic obviously shattered the solidarity of the monarchist front, just as the apolitical agrarian movement managed to win votes which otherwise would have gone to the traditional parties.

[30] *LV* 6, 26, 29, 31 Mar. 1931 (Liberals and the ephemeral groups), 5 Apr. 1931 (UMN); *El Cruzado Español* 10 Apr. 1931 (Traditionalists). See for the UMN also A. Joaniquet, *Alfonso Sala*, p. 332.
[31] For Pamplona and San Sebastián see *Diario de Navarra* 1 Apr. 1931, *ABC* 3 Apr. 1931. For Carlist's instructions see *El Cruzado* 27 Mar. 1931; *El Siglo Futuro* 1 Apr. 1931.

The suspiciousness of small and middle peasants towards professional politicians, whom they blamed for the neglect of agricultural interests, led them to prepare their own separate candidatures where they were able to do so. Such was the attitude adopted by the *Bloque Agrario*, an organization of small landowners in Castile, and the *Secretariado Nacional Agrario*, a conservative organization which was cultivated by Primo during his Dictatorship, and had many branches all over the country. The attitude of the newly founded *Partido Nacional Agrario*, with its attention focused on the Castilian wheat growers' interests, was more sympathetic towards agrarian planks in the platforms of Monarchist parties, like the *Centro* for instance. Yet it also tended to present its own candidatures.[32]

The power of the leftist effort had not only stimulated Monarchists to be more united; it also had compelled them to run, for the first time, an intensive and modern electoral campaign, which they had never felt the need to do so long as their rule did not depend on public opinion. The Liberals in Madrid were in contact with an advertising company that proposed to direct their electoral campaign in the city with a budget of 67,350 pesetas. Aeroplanes were used to drop monarchist manifestos, public meetings were held in large halls, and the monarchist press, whether daily organs, periodical publications or bulletins sponsored by the Church, was filled with editorials, manifestos, and reports on meetings. Even the aristocracy made considerable efforts out of an instinct for self-preservation. Balls were cancelled to allow the nobility to take part in electoral activities, and some even rushed home from abroad especially for the elections. *Acción Nobiliaria* and *Acción Monárquica*, both aristocratic bodies which were the main sponsors of the Monarchist coalition, called upon their members to exert their influence on their middle-class friends, while an aristocratic women's organization, which proudly claimed that 'never before have women been so motivated by sentiments of political awareness', asked its members to dictate to their

[32] For the Constitutionalists see *El Sol* 25 Mar. 1931; *ABC* 20, 24, 27, 28 Mar. 1931. For the 'Bloque Agrario' see *El Campesino* Jan., Feb., Mar., and Apr. 1931. The 'Bloque' managed to win over some 200 mayoralties in rural villages, to have the majority in some 400 Ayuntamientos, and the minority in 1,500 villages; For the 'Secretariado Nacional Agrario' see their organ *España Agraria* 1, 15, Mar., 1, 15 Apr. 1931. For the 'Partido Nacional Agrario' see *ABC* 25 Feb., 7, 10, 28 Mar. 1931.

husbands how to vote. The manifestations of the monarchist reaction were so intense in Madrid, and their electoral centres were so crowded, that their opening hours had to be extended, thousands of volunteers had to be enlisted to help the general effort, and a special committee of co-ordination of propaganda had to be set up.[33]

The defeat of the Monarchy was not the result of the indifference of its supporters, as the frustrated defenders of the fallen regime later claimed.[34] It was rather their campaign for the preservation of the existing order. It was precisely this old order that the overwhelming offensive of the left had been able to undermine throughout the last year.[35] The monarchists were compelled to accept, rather unwillingly, the leftist emphasis on the political and plebiscitary character of the municipal elections. They admitted that they would have 'an obvious and inevitable aspect of political contest'. *El Debate* pointed out that not only the election of new municipal administrators was on the agenda, but also 'the battle for the sake of order and social peace, both of which are, at the moment, inextricably tied up with the Monarchy'; Dato's grandson, the Conde de Guevara, put it bluntly when he wrote in a public manifesto that 'the question to which these elections will give a definite answer is which regime should govern us, Monarchy or Republic.'[36]

Thus under consistent pressure from the left, the monarchists virtually abandoned the 1876 constitution, according to which the Monarchy was an undisputable institution which under no circumstances should become an electoral issue. Efforts were now made to denigrate the future Republic. It was presented as

---

[33] For the Liberals see RA Leg. 9 no. 12; *Estudio de Publicidad directa* 14 Mar. 1931. For aeroplanes *ED* 12 Apr. 1931. For aristocracy, Marqués de Valdeiglesias, *La Sociedad Española 1875–1949*, pp. 239–40; *ABC* 27 Mar. 1931; *ED* 7 Apr. 1931; *Mujeres Españolas* 5 Apr. 1931; and *La Unión* April, 1931. See also the meeting organized by Acción Nobiliaria in *ABC* 12 Apr. 1931. For enthusiasm and increased efforts see *ABC* 26 Mar. 1931; *ED* 8, 9, 12 Apr. 1931.

[34] See for example Albert Despujols, *La Gran Tragedia de España 1931–1939*, pp. 27–33; Alcalá Galiano, *The Fall*, pp. 89–92.

[35] M. Maura, *Así*, p. 142.

[36] See *LE* 23 Mar. 1931; Romanones in *ABC* 31 Mar. 1931; *ED Debate* 9, 11 Apr. 1931; and the manifestos; *Propaganda Electoral Monárquica ante las Elecciones Municipales en Madrid*; and *Propaganda Electoral de la Candidatura Monárquica* in HMM, A/1700, 1691. See also Romanones, *Las Ultimas Horas*, pp. 129–31 on how the monarchists unwillingly compelled by the left to accept the challenge of a plebiscite.

a period of anarchy that would overthrow the values of religion, property and family for 'Russian barbarism', because even the conservative Republic was nothing but an avenue leading towards the inevitable social revolution. Alcalá Zamora and Maura, both bitterly attacked as traitors, to their past and to their class, would play the inglorious role of Kerensky, and a programme allegedly written by Galán was presented as a 'proof' that communism was indeed the ultimate goal. These black prophecies warned against a regime in which 'bolshevik Jews will dominate our beloved Spain, spreading terror and misery, corrupting and ultimately destroying our traditional home life'. This would cause, they said in what sounded like an imminent threat, an immediate flight of capital which would throw the country into economic chaos, and then 'your wives and children will have to queue, as in Russia, in order to get a miserable mess'. Marín Lázaro even alleged, in a public meeting, that the revolutionaries had planned the sharing out of women. Moreover, the fact that not only the economic well-being, but also religion, social order and the unity of Spain would be seriously threatened, would probably result in 'an immediate civil war'.[37]

The monarchists excluded none from their appeals for support. The victory of the Monarchy was in the interest of aristocrats who, otherwise, might lose their titles; of the clergy opposed to the victory of 'crude materialism and sensuality'; of the military who deplored the lack of discipline of the Jaca mutineers; of the businessmen who might become bankrupt in a chaotic Republic, even of 'the good workers'.[38] The population of Madrid was warned of the threats to their status as dwellers of the capital, because in a federal Republic, Madrid would be like any other provincial city. The city would be ruined, 'neither the

---

[37] The communist threat was probably the most common allegation in monarchist propaganda. See for example: *ED* 8, 10 Apr. 1931; *LE* 6 Apr. 1931; *EI* 8, 12 Apr. 1931, Goicoechea, García Cortés, and Marín Lázaro in public meetings: *LE* 9 Apr. 1931; *ABC* 10, 12 Apr. 1931. See the manifestos *Hoja de Propaganda anti-Republicana; Propaganda Electoral en Contra de las Candidaturas Republicanas;* and *Por qué Hay que Votar Contra los Revolucionarios?* in HMM A/1860, 1681, 1685. For attacks on Maura and Alcalá Zamora see the public meetings in *ABC* 8 Apr. 1931; *ED* 9 Apr. 1931; *LE* 11 Apr. 1931. For civil war see *ABC* 7 Apr. 1931.

[38] *LE* 6 Apr. 1931. For the workers see also *ED* 11 Apr. 1931 on a meeting in a proletarian quarter.

commerce, the industry, the public shows, the hotels, nor the public cafés' would be maintained at their present standard.[39]

Attempts were also made to defend the king against those who defamed him. His personal courage, as well as his 'democratic spirit' shown during the recent crisis, were praised. Some went back to the origins of Primo's *coup*, like Conde de Limpias, who claimed in a public meeting that the acceptance of the Dictatorship by the king was a purely democratic act. A more mystical concept of the Monarchy was also spread in the meetings of *Reacción Ciudadana*, an 'apolitical' organization which was founded to stimulate the monarchist electoral campaign. When it held a meeting in Avila, the streets were occupied by monarchist demonstrators, some of whom arrived from Salamanca. A Catholic propagandist, Martínez Agullo praised the hereditary Monarchy and its strong attachment to religion, while Gil Robles, the future Caudillo of the CEDA, spoke about his 'deep and old conviction' that 'the best rule is that which finds its incarnation in one person'.[40]

Madrid provided the prototype of the monarchist electoral campaign in the provinces. Everywhere the topics of the communist threat, the quest for the preservation of the social order, the warnings of imminent republican economic chaos, a clear attempt to play on the fears of the well-to-do classes, and the defence of the king, were frequently used. As in Madrid, municipal programmes were issued to praise the labour of Monarchist city councillors and to present plans for the future. Public meetings were held, youngsters distributed leaflets in the streets, and in Seville, Valencia, and Zaragoza hundreds of thousands of manifestos were thrown from aeroplanes. Reacción Ciudadana intensified its activities as 12 April approached. Gil Robles took part in four of their meetings in less than a week in Segovia, Torrelavega, Avila, and Béjar, meetings which emphasized the 'eternal' social and religious values. The general

[39] *LE* 25 Mar. 1931; *ED* 9 Apr. 1931; Conde de Vallellano's platform in *Unión Monárquica* 1 Apr. 1931. See also the manifesto *Al pueblo de Madrid* in HMM A/1680.

[40] For the defense on the king see *The Times* 13 Apr. 1931; *ABC* 12, 24 Apr. 1931 (Gil Robles), 31 Mar. 1931 (Martínez Agullo). For Avila see AHN Leg. 16: from Governor Avila to Minister no. 429, 10 Apr. 1931. See also the manifesto *Don Quijote Votando* in HMM A/1716. For Gil Robles in Reacción Ciudadana's meetings see also Gutierrez-Ravé, *Gil Robles, Caudillo Frustrado*, pp. 17–19.

tendency, however, was that of reluctantly accepting the leftist challenge that the elections were political in character, and, therefore, praise for the Monarchy and defamation of the Republic were commonplace. The choice was, according to Hernando Larramendi in Santander, between 'a despotic and cruel Republic and a Monarchy which guarantees internal peace'; and a manifesto of the Monarchist coalition in Valladolid warned that only a 'violent and bloody convulsion' could bring about a change of regime. Pathetic speeches, like that of the Duque de Canalejas in Salamanca, emphasized the difference between a peaceful and flourishing city under the Monarchy, and a republican regime in which 'your beautiful cathedral will be converted into a garage and your tombs and altars will be profaned'.[41]

Even the Lliga in Barcelona was compelled, by the leftist emphasis on the need to change the regime, to stress its monarchist significance rather than its Catalanist personality. The presence of Ventosa in the government and the foundation of the *Centro* had undermined the Lliga's position as a Catalan party allowing the left to gain ground on its expense. Cambó appeared as the defender of social order against 'the fashion for revolutions'. He stressed the government's recognition of Catalonia's right to administrative autonomy, according to the *Mancomunidad* of 1919, as a proof that Catalan aspirations were perfectly compatible with the Monarchy. Pedro Rahola emphasized this point when he denounced the Catalan left for its insistence on solving the Catalan problem by violence when 'the Spanish state' was doing it 'by legal means'. *Acció Catalana* was, according to the Lliga's leaders, who seemed to have completely underestimated the *Esquerra*, the incarnation of a republicanism which refused to recognize the Spanish state and the Lliga's material achievements for Catalonia. However, an appeal to leftist opinion was also made by an insistence on the need to investigate the 'administrative responsibilities' of the

---

[41] Speeches and editorials from the provinces illustrate this variety of topics. See examples: *ED* 11 Apr. 1931 (Salamanca); *El Norte de Castilla* 5, 8 Apr. 1931 (Valladolid); *La Voz de Galicia* 10, 11, 12 Apr. 1931 (La Coruña); *Diario de Navarra* 12 Apr. 1931 (Pamplona); *ABC Sevilla* 8, 9, 10 Apr. 1931 (Seville); *ABC* 9, 12 Apr. 1931 (Valencia, Santander, Cuenca, Bilbao, Murcia). For Reacción Ciudadana see Gil Robles, *No Fue Posible la Paz*, pp. 30–1; *ED* 7 Apr. 1931; *ABC* 24 Mar. 1931. For aeroplanes see *ABC* 12 Apr. 1931; *ABC Sevilla* 12 Apr. 1931.

Dictatorship. The political responsibilities were not mentioned, both because the Lliga had early contacts with the dictator, and because no monarchist had demanded an investigation which could involve the king. The Lliga's alleged indifference to the form of regime, provided it respected democratic values, though it was mentioned occasionally, as it was by Puig be Bellacasa, could not be taken seriously when its enemies were Republicans, nor could it contribute to an electoral victory, when the choice was obviously between Monarchy and Republic. The Lliga, however, was optimistic on the eve of the elections, and Cambó rejected Maciá's proposition for an electoral alliance. Despujols, the captain general, was confident that, unless the CNT decided to vote, the Lliga would triumph.[42]

The decisive character of the elections led the ecclesiastical establishment all over Spain to the realization that it must take a definite side. It took the side of the Monarchy against the Republic, and called upon Catholics to vote for it. Mugica, the bishop of Vitoria, warned against supporting any party 'like the Republican-Socialist coalitions' which might attack 'the sacred rights of the Church'. Any violation of this instruction 'would be judged by Jesus Christ on the Day of Judgement'. The counsels given by the Pope against electoral abstention were spread with the warning that to abstain is 'to collaborate in the ruin of social order'. Bishops exhorted their flocks to ensure that city councils be 'in good hands', or in the words of the Bishop of Vich, in the hands of 'those who will know how to guarantee the well-being of religion'. At the level of the parish, the style was sometimes ruder. A priest in Alcalá de Henares threatened his flock with whips and scorpions if they abstained, while his colleagues in the proletarian quarter of Puente de Vallecas and in a remote village in the province of Oviedo turned their sermons into vulgar monarchist speeches. *Acción Católica*, always a defender of religion and order, explained 'how to vote' in posters, and organized 'apolitical' meetings in which the 'duties of the Catholics in

---

[42] See Cambó's manifesto in *La Vea de Catalunya* 11 Apr. 1931. For the Lliga's achievements and attacks on Acció Catalana see *LV* 20, 27, 31 Mar., 4, 8, Apr. 1931. For responsibilities see ibid. 24, 31 Mar. 1931 (here also Puig). For optimism see Mola, *Obras*, p. 759; and Hoyos, *Mi Testimonio*, pp. 110–11. He gives the evidence on the pact suggested by Maciá to Cambó.

electoral matters' were explained according to ecclesiastical instructions.[43]

4. THE REPUBLICANS LEAD THE NATION TO A PLEBISCITE

It was the tragedy of Spanish monarchism that, at the moment of its greatest political mobilization, it was faced by an uncompromising coalition of Republicans and Socialists, who were determined to use the municipal elections as an unprecedented manifestation of anti-monarchist power, if not as an immediate means for bringing in the Republic. After having abstained from the proposed general elections because of the government's refusal both to hold municipal elections before the general election, and to summon a Constituent Cortes, the left had now its preconditions officially fulfilled, and it decided to participate in the forthcoming struggle. The national committee of *Alianza Republicana* pointed out the significance of the elections. The Republican Socialist coalition, it claimed, was not interested in the number of city councillors that each party would have, but in 'measuring the forces of Spanish democracy' and in making an 'instructive plebiscite', of, as a Radical Socialist manifesto put it, 'a general mobilization of the left', as a stage towards the longed-for Republic. According to Azaña the demonstration of the suffrage should be so impressive as 'to strengthen the authority of the revolutionary movement, by proving that it represents the state of the public spirit'.[44]

The Socialists, who decided to participate in the elections 'because of the predominantly administrative character' of the *Ayuntamientos*, conceived them as part of their united action with the Republicans 'for the establishment of a new regime in Spain'. Their National Committees, therefore, recommended that their branches should forge electoral alliances with the Republicans 'wherever possible'. They justified this by arguing that, since they had agreed with the Republicans on the fundamental

---

[43] For Mugica see *BOO de Vitoria* 15 Apr. 1931. See also Bishop Tuy in *La Voz de Galicia* 7 Apr. 1931; Bishop Orense in *BOEO de Orense* 10 Apr. 1931. For the parish level see *La Cruz de la Parroquia, Alcalá de Henares* 22 Mar. 1931; *ES* 4 Apr. 1931. For Acción Católica see *Acción Católica de la Mujer* April, 1931; *ED* 25 Mar., 10, 11 Apr. 1931; *LV* 2, 9 Apr. 1931. See also J. Sánchez, *Reform and Reaction*, pp. 75–7.

[44] *ABC* 3 Mar. 1931; *El Sol* 10, 24 Mar. 1931. Azaña in *SO* 10 Apr. 1931. For a similar revolutionary view see *NE* 8 Apr. 1931.

question of the change of regime, why should not they agree on 'a strategic step', i.e. joint action in the municipal elections. Furthermore, the old parties were united in a governmental coalition which was 'the General Staff of the monarchist defence', and the Socialists should not insist, at such a time of emergency, on doctrinal differences with the Republicans. The major consideration was that of fighting 'the reserve troops of the Monarchy'. However, already at this initial stage of the electoral campaign, the Socialists made it clear that they would preserve both their organizational and doctrinal autonomy. Their coalition with the Republicans was circumstantial, and, as soon as the Republic was established, they would strive alone to bring about the social revolution by fighting against their present allies, who would then rule over a bourgeois Republic.[45]

But now they were both running what García Venero, himself a Republican activist, called 'one of the most skilful' electoral campaigns in 'world history'.[46] The monarchist effort, which was large in comparison to its efforts during the old regime, was overshadowed by an impressive demonstration of coherent power. On Sunday 29 March, 500 electoral meetings were recorded all over the country, and the left credited itself with most of them. When the biggest halls in Madrid were filled with immense crowds, hundreds of people still gathered outside. There were speakers who in twenty-four hours appeared in five meetings: no wonder that some lost their voices and could hardly be heard by the public. When on 5 April, eight Republican meetings were held in Madrid (with only one Monarchist meeting) more than twenty-five speakers, among them most of the members of the Provisional Government, took part in them, and some rushed to speak in more than one meeting.[47]

The general tactics of the campaign consisted of presenting to the public no particular programme which might alienate a section of the voters. The main emphasis was put on the common

[45] *BUGT* Mar., Apr. 1931; *ES* 4, 8, 18 Mar. 1931.
[46] García Venero, *Alba*, p. 328.
[47] For the 500 see *The Times* 31 Mar. 1931; *ES* 1 Apr. 1931. The reports of both *El Sol* and *El Socialista* on Republican electoral meetings are full of information, see for example: *ES* 4, 5, 7–11 Apr. 1931; *El Sol* 8–10 Apr. 1931. For crowds outside see the meetings in the four big halls of Madrid in *ES* 31 Mar. 1931, and the meeting in Vallecas in ibid. 10 Apr. 1931. For the eight meetings see *The Times* 13 Apr. 1931; and *ES* 7 Apr. 1931. Pedro Rico lost his voice: ibid. 11 Apr. 1931.

denominator of anti-monarchism and Republic. Though each had in mind a different Republic, no one insisted on his own. Nor was the municipal issue more than a marginal one. The major question, of which the left had been able to make political capital during the last year, was stressed now: was King Alfonso an accomplice in the *coup d'état*? Had he violated the constitution?[48] The Republican candidature, declared Pedro Rico, 'represents the protest against those who trampled the constitution underfoot'. Miguel Maura presented the issue more vividly when he declared in Madrid, 'There is a definite struggle, with no mercy shown, a struggle to death, between the people and the regime. This war was unleashed on three dates: June 1921, September 1923, December 1930'. Some posters added 1909 to this list of the Monarchy's crimes. Annual and Galán's execution were exploited to the full for their emotional capacity. Speakers blamed the Monarchy for the backwardness of the country. Fernando de los Ríos pointed out that Spain had an extremely high death rate and that a great proportion of its children did not receive any kind of education because of the king's insistence on diverting 30 per cent of the budget to the Ministry of War. Alcalá Zamora made the dynasty's historic record a target of his eloquence. He asked:

Was it not from the palace that emerged the street riots organized by Ferdinand VII, military pronunciamientos and dictatorships?... The altar of the motherland cannot be in the palace that issued the message inviting the French invasion ... Even family virtues were violated by this degenerate family of Bourbons. You should ask Isabel II.

Confronted with such a Monarchy, a public manifesto argued, the Republic was the embodiment of order and well-being. The threat that Spain might disintegrate into anarchy lay in the Monarchy 'which had debased the spiritual values of the nation', and was on its way to bring a disaster to the economy, a disaster of which the alarming depreciation of the peseta was a symptom.[49]

---

[48] Maura, *Así*, pp. 141–2.

[49] *ES* 3 Apr. 1931 (P. Rico). The Socialist manifesto in *Manifiesto del PSOE y UGT*, in HMM A/1695; *ES* 7 Apr. 1931 (Maura). See the posters in *Propaganda Electoral de la Candidatura Republicana–Socialista* in HMM A/1637; and Galán and Annual in E. Ortega's speech in *El Sol* 7 Apr. 1931, and Arrazola's in *Heraldo de Chamartin* 10 Apr. 1931, *ES* 3, 10 Apr. 1931 (de los Ríos, A. Zamora). The public manifesto is *Al Pueblo de Madrid* in HMM A/1679.

The government was also frequently attacked for being the representative of 'the old tradition of caciquismo', which allowed it to rule regardless of the nation's will. A loan contracted by the government with an American bank was presented as a proof of arbitrary dealings, without the supervision of an elected parliament, and of 'lack of patriotism', because it subordinated the country to 'foreign capitalism'. Largo Caballero even warned, introducing an international aspect to the electoral campaign, that Spanish capitalism might initiate a fascist take-over in order to preserve its interests against the leftist offensive. Therefore, he concluded, 'our struggle is international as well as national . . . if we overthrow the Monarchy, fascism will also die in Europe'.[50] Largo Caballero, just as did his rivals on the right, was anticipating the 'civil war language' of the mid-thirties.

While blaming the right for planning fascism, the left was compelled to set the public mind at rest that it did not have a communist regime in mind, as the monarchists alleged. A conservative and moderate Republic was, therfore, presented to the electorate, by both right and left Republicans. The men of the *Derecha Republicana* went ostentatiously to mass to prove that religion would suffer no harm. The coalition assured Catholics that it would only fight clericalism, but would not persecute any religion.[51] What the Republicans did not promise, was that they would not tolerate other cults. Freedom of religion was most unwelcome to the Church. But the left did not stand for the persecution of the Catholic Church. An extremely anti-Catholic programme of the *Agrupación de Librepensadores de Madrid*, produced by *El Debate* as a proof of Republican intentions, did not represent the official attitude of the Republican coalition on the eve of the elections. The public was obviously impressed by Alcalá Zamora's confessions as 'a believer in the good God', and by Rafael Sánchez Guerra's claim that precisely because he was a Catholic and a man of order he became Republican.[52]

Order was promised also to capitalists and investors. Alcalá

[50] Against the government see *Manifiesto al PSOE y la UGT* in HMM A/1695. For Morgan's loan *ES* 31 Mar., 2 Apr. 1931. For fascism see *El Liberal* 8 Apr. 1931; *ES* 5 Apr. 1931 (Caballero).
[51] Alcalá Galiano, *The Fall*, pp. 167–72. Sánchez, *Reform*, p. 74.
[52] *ED* 12 Apr. 1931; *Heraldo de Chamartin* 10 Apr. 1931; *The Times* 13 Apr. 1931. See the coalition's manifesto in *El Liberal* 8 Apr. 1931.

Zamora called upon the bankers not to be afraid because 'the banks would not be assaulted' in the case of a Republican victory. On the contrary, the Republic would stabilize the peseta 'for the benefit of bankers'.[53] Even Socialists and left Republicans were ready to give assurances of order and moderation. Largo Caballero warned businessmen that only under the Monarchy's arbitrariness were their interests in danger. As for the Republic, he said, 'do not be afraid. It is not going to be communism nor anarchy . . . the organized working class . . . knows that it cannot go now to a socialist Republic, or to complete economic equality; it only wants a real political equality'. This working class, Alcalá Zamora explained, would be the 'honest guardian' of this moderate Republic.[54]

However, this did not mean that the Socialists ruled out their socialist Republic. They had only postponed it to give way to the bourgeois Republic, as was claimed by electoral manifestos to the postal workers and to the National federation of Waiters. An immediate achievement, which was promised to the workers, apart from 'political equality', was that of a general amnesty for social and political prisoners. Indeed, a great many of the electoral meetings both in Madrid and in the provinces were pro-amnesty gatherings.[55]

The Republicans, though obviously emphasizing the political significance of the elections, rejected Monarchists' allegations that they lacked any municipal programme. Alcalá Zamora said that the mere fact that the left insisted on an investigation of responsibilities was in itself a municipal programme, which only the Republicans could fulfil, because the responsibilities lay with the right. Saborit, who was an industrious city councillor, spoke frequently on administrative questions; and Republican candidates in the overcrowded poor suburbs presented detailed municipal platforms, promising an improvement in every aspect of daily life, or dismissing their rivals' plans as an attempt to

---

[53] ES 10 Apr. 1931.

[54] ES 7, 11 Apr. 1931; El Sol 7, 11 Apr. 1931. See Francisco Escola speaking for Acción Republicana in ES 3 Apr. 1931. A respectable Republic was also preached by the prestigious team of the Agrupación al Servicio de la República, see their manifesto A los Electores de Madrid in HMM A/1637.

[55] ES 8, 10 Apr. 1931 (the manifestos). For reports on pro-amnesty meetings in all the country see ibid. 24 Mar., 11, 12 Apr. 1931.

preserve the vested interests of old caciques and ex-collaborators with the Dictatorship.[56]

The Republican propaganda in Madrid, as in the provincial capitals, was supported by the anti-monarchist agitation of the students, as well as by the leftist youth. Simultaneously with official Republican–Socialist coalitions, an anti-dynastic alliance of their youth sections was set up, including leftist groups like the *Izquierda Universitaria* and the *Groupo La Tierra*. They exploited the ambiance created by the university troubles, and emphasized in their propaganda their incompatibility with the Monarchy, contributing to convert the elections to the Madrid Ayuntamiento into a battle for 'the central bastion of monarchism'.[57]

Republican–Socialist coalitions elsewhere managed to convert local elections in cities, towns, and even small villages into a major political struggle against the Monarchy. Republican–Socialist coalitions were set up 'in places in which an electoral campaign has never taken place'.[58] It was an enthusiasm unknown before in Spain. A newspaper in Seville remarked: 'We do not remember in Seville ... a similar effervescence ... The present system, so different from that of previous elections, reminds us of the methods used in the presidential elections in America.'[59] The civil governor of Badajoz recorded in the first week of April eighteen Republican in contrast to two monarchist meetings in the main towns of the province; and in the municipal district of Murcia forty such meetings were planned for the period. The absolute predominance of the left in Valencia caused *ABC* to claim that the monarchists 'must be hiding'. Some were perhaps, but many simply joined the republican wave. Thousands of people gathered in electoral meetings not only in cities like Granada where 15,000 people gathered in the bullring to hear Fernando de los Ríos, but also in small towns like Torrevieja and Villa de Don Fadrique; and in rural villages like Paderne,

---

[56] *ES* 10, 11 Apr. 1931 (Saborit, Alcalá Zamora). For municipal programmes see: *Propaganda Electoral contra Aurelio Regulez Candidato a Concejal* in HMM A/1683; *Propaganda Republicana Dirigida a los Electores de Canillas, Pueblo Nueva (Vicálvaro)* in HMM A/1712; *Heraldo de Chamartin* 1, 10 Apr. 1931; *ES* 5 Apr. 1931.

[57] *A los Jovenes Obreros y Estudiantes. El Bloque Antidinastico* in HMM A/1679; *El Sol* 8 Apr. 1931. The last quotation: *Al Pueblo de Madrid* in HMM A/1679.

[58] *ES* 8 Apr. 1931. See for the particular case of Serón ibid. in 3 Apr. 1931.

[59] *El Liberal sevilla* 12 Apr. 1931. For a similar situation in La Coruña see *La Voz de Galicia* 8 Apr. 1931.

Coiros, and Zalamea de la Serena peasants gathered to listen to overt attacks on their caciques. Everywhere Republicans and Socialists forged their own alliances, though there were places like Lorca, Úbeda, and Murcia in which local considerations caused a party to retire from the coalition. The country was no longer witnessing the 'inertia of the provinces', which, according to Ortega had enabled the Monarchy to perpetuate its rule, but the longed-for 'civil uprising of the provinces' from which he hoped that a new Spain might emerge.[60]

The Republican–Socialist coalitions in the provinces had the same pattern of propaganda as in Madrid, stressing the plebiscitary character of the elections, though also emphasizing local problems. In Badajoz, the demand for a Republic came together with that of 'a maximum autonomy for the region and Ayuntamientos', and of 'the sweeping away, once and for all, of rural caciquismo'. As for those who were afraid of the disorder of the Republic, the *Derecha Republicana* was in the coalition to reassure 'landlords and property owners', and to promise that the Republic would avoid anarchy and would not persecute the Church. In the province of Seville, the existence of vociferous communist candidates and a great deal of unemployment, compelled the Republican–Socialist coalition to make use of a more extreme brand of oratory. In a meeting at Gerena the workers were urged to prepare for the revolution, and a local lawyer promised them free advice in the case that they were arrested while 'fighting for the ideal'. The unemployment and hunger in Utrera caused a Republican speaker to say that 'rather than going to the Ayuntamiento, we should go to the revolution'. And in Cazalla de la Sierra, Hilario Brito, though recognizing the constituent character of the elections, declared that 'a regime cannot be overthrown in the polls, but in the street'. The 'shameful' state of negligence in the proletarian quarters of

---

[60] For Badajoz see AHN Leg. 30: Governor Badajoz to the Minister of the Interior 11 Apr. 1931. *ABC* 1, 12 Apr. 1931 (Murcia and Valencia). *Vanguardia*, Badajoz, 9 Mar. 1931 claimed 6,000 liberals joined republicanism in Valencia. For a similar process in Seville and Palma del Río see *El Liberal, Sevilla* 8, 11, 12 Apr. 1931. For Granada see *ED* 7 Apr. 1931. For the towns and villages see a few examples in *ES* 3, 4, 5 Apr. 1931. For coalitions see few cases in *ABC* 15, 17, 18, 20, 21, 24–26 Mar. 1931 (Huelva, Santander, Murcia, Las Palmas, Valladolid, Lorca, Jaén, Salamanca, Úbeda); *Vanguardia*, Badajoz 9, 16 Mar. 1931 (Badajoz); *La Voz de Galicia* 3–5 Apr. 1931 (Coruña, Vigo, Pontevedra). For Valencia see also Alfons Cuco, *El Valencianisme*, p. 199. For Ortega see *El Sol* 15 Feb. 1931.

Seville was, according to the Socialist Egocheaga, a proof that time had arrived to change both the regime and the municipal administration. In Guadalajara and Sagunto, *Romanonista* strongholds, the 'incompatibility of the nation with the Monarchy' and the demand for the immediate establishment of a Republic were stressed by local Republicans and Socialists together with the political elimination of 'the clients of *Romanonismo*', and for improvement in municipal services for the lower classes. In Puertollano, in the province of Ciudad Real, the target was the chamber of Commerce and the Association of Landlords, whose 'manœuvres', it was hoped, would be brought to an end by the Republic.[61]

In Barcelona both the propaganda and the frame of electoral coalitions were obviously different from elsewhere. The major Republican Parties—the *Esquerra* and *Acció Catalana Republicana*—which hoped to profit from the excessive *españolismo* of the Lliga, refused to consider an electoral alliance with 'Spanish' parties like the tiny Socialist and the divided Radical Party, both of which managed to forge a pact between themselves and with various autonomous groups, but were unsuccessful in their approach to ACR, despite all being members of the San Sebastián coalition. The issue was a purely Catalan one, and the Catalan left preferred to accentuate its 'personality'. Apart from the Catalanist emphasis which caused it to reject the alliance, ACR seemed to have been confident in its own power, and claimed that a leftist coalition against the Lliga would only increase its popularity.[62]

The Esquerra, on the other hand, was a totally new power and very much lacking in self-confidence. So much so that it proposed to the ACR an alliance which was utterly rejected, both because of the 'soviet' character of Esquerra and because of its alleged weakness. Nevertheless, the Esquerra started to run a highly

---

[61] For Badajoz see *Vanguardia*, Badajoz 16 Mar., 6 Apr. 1931, and the meeting in Mérida in *ES* 1 Apr. 1931. For Seville see *El Liberal, Sevilla* 1, 8, 10, 11 Apr. 1930. For Guadalajara and Sagunto see RA Leg. 49 no. 16: *Al Pueblo de Guadalajara*; Leg. 75 no. 6: *Al Pueblo Saguntino. ES* 1 Apr. 1931 (Puertollano).

[62] For ACR see *LV* 24 Mar., 7 Apr. 1931; and J. Bofill i Mates, *Una Politica*, pp. 63–5. For the Republican–Socialist coalition see *LV* 25 Mar. 1931. It included Radicals, Derecha Republicana, Federals, Socialists, Radical–Socialists and a Partido Republicano Social. For dissidences in the Radical Party and personal ambitions on the eve of the elections see Lerroux, *Mis Memorias*, p. 597.

effective electoral campaign. Its meetings were much more crowded than those of any other party. It profited from the revolutionary image of 'grandfather' Maciá and from the demagogic style of many of its speakers. Ventura i Gassol, Maciá's deputy, related to the public the bitter experiences of his exile and that of Maciá. The party's propagandists emphasized their 'intransigence' over the issue of 'Monarchy or Republic', 'against Catalonia or on its behalf'. Both Aiguader and Maciá maintained, in a public meeting, that once the elections are over, the republican Ayuntamientos would have to meet to declare the Republic. This should be, according to Amadeo Aragay, a Republic that would embody the three tenets of the Esquerra: Catalanism, republicanism, and socialism. In fact, the Esquerra was the only political party in Catalonia which could absorb the social demands of the working class, both because of the weakness of Catalan socialism and the fact that the ACR and the Radical Party were predominantly middle-class parties. Lluhí Vallescá was aware of this, and he stressed the quest for 'the emancipation of the working class'. The Esquerra was, therefore, able to appeal to a wide public both of workers attracted by its populist style and of the lower strata of the bourgeoisie who admired the figure of Maciá.[63]

ACR appealed to the public in a milder style, though obviously anti-monarchist and pro-Catalanist. Its propagandists did not seem to have noticed the Esquerra's existence, and they aimed their attacks at the Lliga, denouncing it for having collaborated with the Dictatorship, and for now supporting a Monarchy which was 'incompatible with Catalanism'. The ACR's speakers insisted also on undermining the Lliga's claim that its men were the greatest contributors to the improvement of material life in Catalonia, by pointing at the achievements of their own men in the same field. On the eve of the elections Rovira i Virgili was confident that his party's policy within Catalonia and its negotiations with the Provisional Government would result in the rapid recognition of 'Catalan liberties' by

---

[63] For the pact proposed to ACR see *LV* 21 Mar. 1931; Bofill i Mates, *Una Política*, pp. 65–7. For the initial lack of confidence of the Esquerra, see Solá Cañizares, *El Moviment*, p. 116. For propaganda meetings see Pabón, *Cambó* II, part ii, 107–8; Hurtado, *Quaranta anys* iii, p. 22; *LV* 31 Mar., 7 Apr. 1931. See also Macia's manifesto in Aymani i Baudina, *Maciá*, pp. 168–9.

the Spanish state. The Provisional Government promised to both Rovira and Bofill that though the Republic should not necessarily be federal, it should be *federable*.[64] It was, however, as the Captain General Despujols remarked, the CNT in Catalonial which possessed the key to success in the elections. Its 'apolitical' mass of potential voters could give the victory to any party. It is obvious that it favoured the Esquerra whose foundation was generally welcomed by it and whose electoral meetings were crowded with Syndicalists. Despite claims that the bourgeois Republic would perpetuate 'the calvary' of the working class, as the extremist Mauro Bajatierra put it, and despite denials that the CNT had any interest whatsoever in the elections, or any contacts with bourgeois Republicans who had 'betrayed' the December revolution, the National Committee of the CNT decided on 19 March that, without committing itself officially, the *Cenetistas* should vote for leftist candidatures. Peiró, 'probably the leader who, at this moment, incarnates more than anyone else the spirit of the CNT', had recently admitted the necessity of a political as well as an economic struggle against capitalism. The CNT obviously hoped that two of its most elementary demands, amnesty for social and political prisoners and the legalization of its syndicates, would be more easily achieved under the Republic than under the Monarchy. Hence, its massive support for the Republican left in regions where it was strong as in Catalonia, Valencia, and Andalucía. *Solidaridad Obrera* could, therefore, claim on the eve of the elections: 'We take for granted the victory of republican ideas all over Spain'.[65]

Nor was the tiny and divided Communist Party with its separate candidatures in Madrid, Catalonia, and Andalucía, able to endanger the chances of the Republican–Socialist coalitions seriously, in spite of directing its electoral propaganda

[64] See a report of five electoral meetings in one day in *LV* 7 Apr. 1931. See also ibid. 31 Mar. 1931. See Rovira's article in *El Sol* 25 Mar. 1931; and Bofill i Mates, *Una Politica*, pp. 72–3.
[65] The last quotation is *SO* 12 Apr. 1931. For 'Cenetista' participation in Esquerra meetings and support see *La Batalla* 2 Apr. 1931; and Maurín, *La Revolución*, p. 80. For attitude towards the bourgeois Republic see *SO* 13, 19, 25, 31 Mar., 3, 8, 11 Apr. 1931. For a decision to support the left see Mola, *Obras*, p. 760. For Peiró see *SO* 4 Mar. 1931. For the quest for legalization and amnesty see ibid. 3, 5, 24, 26–28 Mar., 1, 2, 5, 7 Apr. 1931.

mainly against them. The class emphasis, which the realistic PSOE had abandoned in the campaign, the denigration of leaders like Maura, Alcalá Zamora, and Caballero, who were at the height of their national prestige, and the weakness of both the official Communist Party and the dissident *Bloque Obrero y Campesino*, combined to explain both the insignificance of the 'communist threat' and the fact that its candidatures were nothing but a minor embarrassment for the Republicans.[66]

These were confident of their victory on the eve of the elections. Some had limited hopes of 'dismantling the municipal organization' so that the general elections could be held in still more favourable circumstances,[67] others pointed out that the persistent efforts of the right to forge an alliance was a clear recognition of the power of the left. This was further emphasized by the support given by the government to monarchist financiers to buy the leftist newspapers *La Voz* and *El Sol*. The monarchists were 'frightened' and support for the Republic was 'unanimous'. Therefore, the victory would be 'crushing', and the Republic 'might be declared tomorrow' said *El Liberal* of Seville.[68]

5. MONARCHIST ABANDONISM AND A REPUBLICAN TAKE-OVER

The municipal elections held in 9,259 Ayuntamientos all over the country resulted in a numerical victory of the Monarchists, thanks to their traditional dominance in rural districts. But the elections in 45 out of 52 provincial capitals and in many other large towns and cities resulted in a landslide victory for the Republicans, a victory which they could claim, as the monarchists had previously feared, was a plebiscitary verdict against the Monarchy.[69]

[66] For the weakness and division see Dolores Ibarruri, *Mémoires*, p. 119; Mola, *Obras*. pp. 734–5; and *La Batalla* 5, 12 Mar. 1931. For electoral propaganda see: *Trabajadores; El Partido Comunista de España ante las Eleciones Municipales; Obreros Madrilenos* in HMM A/1677; *La Batalla* 5 Mar., 9 Apr. 1931.

[67] *EC* 11 Apr. 1931.

[68] *ES* 24 Mar., 9, 10 Apr. 1931; Maura, *Así*, p. 143. For *El Sol* see *NE* 25 Mar. 1931. *El Liberal Sevilla* 12 Apr. 1931. For a similar confidence in the imminent proclamation of the Republic see a speech of Basilio Alvarez on 11 April at Porrino (Galicia) in his *Dos Años de Agitación Política* i pp. vi–vii.

[69] *ABC* 7 Apr. 1931. The Monarchist press, however, though deeply depressed by the results, was far from an abandonist conclusion. It preferred to look forward to the general elections, see *ED, LE, ABC, EI* 14 Apr. 1931. For the results of the elections see Appendix I.

In fact, the behaviour of most of the ministers in the Aznar government during the two last days of the Monarchy was motivated by their recognition that the Monarchist victory in rural districts did not represent authentic public opinion. 'This rural monarchism', whose reflection in the polls was frequently the result of the manipulations of local caciques, was according to Gabriel Maura an expression of 'sheep-like obedience and routine', while the vote of the cities was 'a clear verdict of the national will'.[70] However, the government did not resign immediately on the evening of 12 April, nor had it a coherent attitude towards the crisis. The heterogeneity of its composition and the lack of an authoritative premier led its members to make a series of individual initiatives the analysis of which, combined with that of the reactions of the revolutionary Provisional Government and the growing tensions in the big cities, can provide us with the key to the chain of events which led the Monarchy to give way to the second Spanish Republic. To simplify the labyrinth of contradictory and polemical accounts, written by some of the ministers, on the two last days of the Monarchy, a schematic exposition has been adopted.[71]

The twelfth of April

4.00 p.m. In the Ministry of the Interior, the following ministers were gathered to hear the results of the elections: Hoyos, Romanones, La Cierva, and Maura. The commander of the Civil Guard, Sanjurjo, was also there for the same reason.

[70] Gabriel Maura, *Porqué cayó Alfonso XIII?*, pp. 387, 389; Romanones, *Las Ultimas Horas*, pp. 131–2. See C. Lisón–Tolosana, *Belmonte de los Caballeros*, p. 41 on the political indifference of such a village up to the proclamation of the Republic.

[71] The memoirs are: Berenguer, *De la Dictadura*; La Cierva, *Notas*; Hoyos, *Mi Testimonio*; Romanones, 'Recuerdos de las Ultimas Horas de un Reinado' in *El Sol* 3, 4, 5 June 1931; *Las Ultimas Horas; Reflexiones y Recuerdos, Historia de Cuatro Días; Notas; . . . Y Sucedió Así*; Gabriel Maura, *Recuerdos*; Gabriel Maura and Melchor Fernández Almagro, *Porqué Cayó*; Juan Ventosa i Calvell, an interview in *Revista*, Barcelona, June–July 1955; Admiral Rivera has also written an unpublished account whose content is summed up in J. Pabón, 'Siete Relatos de Tres Días. Estudio preliminar para un libro sobre la crísis de la monarquía', published in his *Días de Ayer, Historias e Historiadores Contemporáneos*, pp. 368–431. This article is a systematic and instructive evaluation of the various accounts. In addition declarations and articles in the press should be also taken into consideration. For example see: Marañón, 'Las dos y cinco de la tarde, el 14 de Abril', in *El Sol* 23 May 1931; an exchange of letters between Sanjurjo and Romanones in *El Sol* 7, 9 June 1931; Alcalá Zamora's article 'Los primeros pasos del régimen republicano', in *El Sol* 17 May 1931. See also a short account of the king's secretary in J. L. Castillo–Puche, *Diario Intimo de Alfonso XIII*.

The results in the capitals caused 'real anguish' to all; especially shocked were La Cierva and Romanones because of Republican victories in their respective fiefs of Murcia and Guadalajara. When asked by Romanones and La Cierva what the Civil Guards' reaction would be, General Sanjurjo replied that the results 'would have profound effect on the Civil Guards', upon which, he added, '*until yesterday* the government could rely absolutely'. It was decided not to bring forward the cabinet meeting, due to be held on the fourteenth. This was aimed at creating an impression of 'tranquillity and security'. Gabriel Maura was not surprised by the results. He saw them as the logical culmination of the crisis of the Monarchy which started in 1909 with the dismissal of his father, Antonio Maura, by the king. And Romanones was convinced, even before Sanjurjo's reply, that 'the battle was lost'.

Later in the evening—Romanones made a declaration to the press about 'the deplorable results of the elections' and 'the absolute' Monarchist defeat.[72]

The thirteenth of April

1.15 a.m.   Berenguer, who was very much impressed by the results of the elections, and fearing that the passivity of the government 'might cause confusion' in the army, sent without consulting anybody a telegram to the captains-general pointing out the Monarchist defeat in the big cities, and exhorting them to maintain the discipline of the army as a guarantee that the country could get peacefully through 'the logical course imposed by the supreme national will'.

2.00 a.m.   Hoyos visited Berenguer at his office at the Ministry of War to brief him on the last events. Berenguer made it clear that he objected to the decision not to advance the cabinet meeting, thus emphasizing how serious he considered the situation. He also showed his telegram to Hoyos, who approved its content.

Later in the morning   At his office in the Ministry of Labour, Maura held a meeting of *Maurista* leaders. Though all agreed that the best solution to the crisis would have been the

[72] *ABC* 14 Apr. 1931.

expatriation of the king while a Constitutionalist government summoned a Constituent Cortes, it was decided to suggest a milder course both to the king and to the Provisional Government: the Aznar government, which had just proved its electoral sincerity, would summon the constituent elections for 10 May. If the results of the elections should require it, the king would abdicate. Honorio Maura was sent to get the king's approval, and the Marqués de Cañada Honda went on a similar mission to Miguel Maura's house, where the Provisional Government was gathered.

That same morning Romanones and García Prieto went to their weekly interview with the king, who was 'serene' and who believed that there were still some options open. Romanones, however, left the palace with a bitter feeling that he might not have many more opportunities to visit it.

Early in the afternoon Honorio returned with the king's approval of the 'Maurista' proposition.

1.30 p.m. An *ad hoc* meeting of ministers took place at Aznar's office, at which, apart from himself there were Gabriel Maura, Berenguer, and Rivera, the Minister of Marine. Berenguer presented his telegram to the generals. It was approved by all of them. Contrary to Aznar's attitude that the cabinet should meet as scheduled on the fourteenth, in order not to create alarm, both Maura and Berenguer insisted on a meeting that same day. The latter was especially eager to get his telegram approved officially by all ministers.

5.30 p.m. On his way to the cabinet meeting, Aznar answered a journalist's question about the crisis by declaring: 'Is there a bigger crisis than that of a nation which goes to sleep monarchist and wakes up republican?' At the meeting, Berenguer read his telegram, which was approved by all, except La Cierva, who objected to its emphasis on the national sovereignty rather than on 'the legitimate power of H.M.'s government'. While all the ministers maintained that the results of the elections amounted to a virtual defeat of the Monarchy, and, therefore, the government should resign, both La Cierva and Bugallal insisted that the numerical victory of the Monarchy was sufficient to justify the continuity of the government in office as if nothing had happened. La Cierva made it also clear that he was prepared to preside over a government which, unlike the existing cabinet, would defend the Monarchy under all circumstances. Romanones, as the meeting became a gathering of pessimists, proposed a resolution, which he had previously written at home and which he kept in his pocket while his colleagues exhausted themselves in a futile discussion. It consisted of a recognition that the Monarchy had been defeated in the cities, of a suggestion that the king should consult 'other people' and should be advised to provide 'the national will' with the opportunity to express itself in general elections. Romanones rejected the use of force. 'The Mauser', he said 'is an inadequate answer to the manifestation of suffrage.' Aznar was designated to hand the resolution, which was a virtual resignation of the government, to the king. La Cierva was isolated. He sadly realized that 'these are not appropriate people to defend the king'.

Midnight   Cañada Honda returned with a negative reply from Miguel Maura to the 'Maurista' proposition.

The Fourteenth of April

Early in the morning   Aznar reported the government's resolution to the king. The Conde de Gimeno came to visit Romanones and told him that the previous night Casa Aguilar left the palace with the impression that the king was still determined not to give up, and was thinking of additional ways of solving the crisis. Romanones immediately sent a written note to the king, through Casa Aguilar, urging him to leave the country as soon as possible, and stressing that, in his opinion, this was 'the only solution'. He also exhorted the king to summon the government 'in order to arrange the peaceful transmission of power'. The note also expressed Romanones' fear that the failure of the king to act rapidly might precipitate bloodshed if military elements should join the Republicans, thus making the maintenance of public order impossible.

In the morning   La Cierva wrote a note to the king telling him that he personally had not 'resigned' on the previous day with the other ministers, and he was still 'at the disposition of the king'.

By 10.00 a.m. The king met his ministers for consultations in the following order:

1. Ventosa and Hoyos. The first said that the government was incapable of using force, and, therefore, the Monarchy should accept the verdict of the nation. The king agreed, and added, with Hoyos' support, that he would set up a council of regency, because of the Prince of Asturias' illness. This council would summon a Constituent Cortes. The king added that for this purpose he would consult both Melquiades Alvarez and Sánchez Guerra.

2. Romanones, García Prieto, and Aznar. Romanones insisted that the king should act according to his written advice, but the king still wanted to consult the Constitutionalists. Romanones considered this a waste of time. The king seemed finally to have given up: he urged Romanones to make the arrangements with Alcalá Zamora 'for the transition from one regime to another', and for the peaceful expatriation of the royal family.

3. Berenguer, Rivera, and Maura. The king told them that he was determined to transfer his power to a government which would summon a Constituent Cortes, and meanwhile, he would leave the country. He also charged Maura to write, on his behalf, a public declaration consisting of 'the terms and the extent of his renunciation' (*not* abdication).

4. Bugallal, Gascón y Marín, and La Cierva. The king reaffirmed his decision to leave the country, after having formed a constituent government, for which he had already summoned the Constitutionalist leaders for that evening. He dismissed La Cierva's objections as narrow-minded, and neglected his proposal of presiding over a 'strong government'. Gascón y Marín supported the king's view, while Bugallal backed his Conservative colleague.

1.00 p.m. Berenguer told Generals Sanjurjo and Cavalcanti of the king's intention to leave the country and to form a Constitutionalist government.

2.05 p.m. Romanones and Alcalá Zamora met at Marañón's house. The first asked the Republicans for 'an armistice of a few weeks' so that a Constitutionalist government, 'presided over perhaps by Villanueva could prepare the future with serenity'. Alcalá Zamora replied with an ultimatum that the king should leave the country 'before sunset'. The initially weak position of Romanones, who said bluntly that he came 'with a white flag', enabled Alcalá Zamora to impose his terms: the king would abandon his crown, though he would not abdicate, and his last government would hand the reins of power to the Provisional Government.

3.00 p.m. Romanones reported the failure of his mission to the king. The latter revealed the general content of his declaration to the nation; and he still had in mind the idea of a regency.

4.00 p.m. Romanones summoned Aznar, Hoyos, and Berenguer, and briefed them on his negotiations. In the middle of the meeting, a report came in about demonstrations in the streets and about the hoisting of the Republican flag over the central post office. They decided to declare martial law in order to protect the expatriation of the royal family. But the crowds and the excited demonstrations compelled them to drop the idea, which would lead to a bloody confrontation between army and people. An emissary was sent to ask the Provisional Government for a postponement of the transmission of power.

5.00 p.m. A cabinet meeting presided over by the king at the palace. La Cierva's insistence on defending the Monarchy even by military force was rejected by Berenguer as 'dangerous and useless'. The king reaffirmed that he would object to any bloodshed for his sake, and would immediately leave the country. Not even Bugallal now supported La Cierva. An emissary from the Provisional Government interrupted the meeting with an ultimatum that unless power was transmitted by 7.00 p.m. they could not be responsible for what might happen. Under the pressure from outside and the almost unanimous agreement of his ministers that the king should go, final arrangements were made for his journey. The king also modified the 'message of departure' written by Maura, by erasing the sentence 'I charge a government to consult the nation by summoning a Constituent Cortes'. This was the change of attitude imposed on the king by the result of Romanones' negotiations with Alcalá Zamora. The king finally admitted that not only he had lost 'the affection' of his people, but that he had to give way to a revolutionary government. Romanones urged his colleagues to come next morning to

Aznar's office in order to transmit the government officially to the Republican government.

Several obvious conclusions may be drawn from this account. Firstly, the government, except for La Cierva and Bugallal, admitted the defeat of the Monarchy at the polls, and subsequently lost its equilibrium and revealed its inability to elaborate a clear attitude towards the crisis. This basic weakness invited the ministers to make individual and un-coordinated initiatives.

Secondly, La Cierva was the only minister who still clung to the Canovist conception of the king as the source of power, a conception which considered elections and public opinion irrelevant.

Nor did his colleagues comprehend the full significance of mass politics. The possibility that a lasting Republic might be established, and might abolish the Monarchy for ever, did not cross their minds. Their sanguine attitude to the Republic is otherwise hardly explicable. They strove to solve the present 'crisis' in a gentlemanlike manner, as they had done with so many others in the past. They acted as if they were sure that the Monarchy was to be restored during the next 'crisis' within a few months or even weeks.

It was also obvious that Romanones, motivated by a conviction that 'everything was lost' even before he came to the Ministry of the Interior on the evening of the twelfth, and, therefore, before he knew about Sanjurjo's attitude,[73] started to act as the effective premier. He was the architect of the steps which led to the final capitulation of the Monarchy. Romanones was aware of the possibility that he might go down to history as the prime mover in the fall of the Monarchy. Therefore in his account written in 1940[74] he omitted his *abandonista* initiative through Casa Aguilar, an initiative which he had related in his first account.[75] In his *Reflexiones* he also made special efforts to emphasize that the king was very depressed on the morning of the fourteenth and eager to give up,[76] whereas the emphasis in

---

[73] See his article in *El Sol* 4 June 1931; and his *Las Ultimas Horas*, p. 13.
[74] *Reflexiones y Recuerdos*, pp. 102–5.
[75] *El Sol* 4 June 1931; and *Las Ultimas Horas*, pp. 17–18.
[76] *Reflexiones*, pp. 115–16. At that time the king still believed that general elections should be the solution, see J. Cortés-Cavanillas, *La Caída de Alfonso XIII*, p. 216.

the first account, written amid republican euphoria, Romanones emphasized his own initiatives, or rather his 'contributions' to the coming of the Republic. In his later account he also presented himself as the tough defender of the Constitutionalist solution in his conversation with Alcalá Zamora, up to the moment that the latter 'revealed' that Sanjurjo had already passed over to the Republic.[77] But Marañón who wrote earlier about this episode[78] does not mention Sanjurjo at all, and Sanjurjo himself, in an exchange of letters with Romanones, made it clear that it was only after the meeting in Marañón's house that he went over to the Republicans.[79] Even if Alcalá Zamora had really used this argument, it nonetheless should not have been a surprise for Romanones who already on the twelfth, had known Sanjurjo's basic attitude. It is clear that he did not become 'abandonista' following his meeting with Alcalá Zamora; he started the meeting as such, using at the very beginning, according to Marañón, the term 'white flag'.[80]

Furthermore, the king urged the Constitutionalist solution until Romanones came from his meeting with Alcalá Zamora. Then, for the first time, he admitted the necessity of transferring power to the Republicans. It should however be stressed that on that busy day of the fourteenth, the king managed also to consult both Villanueva and Melquiades Alvarez who dismissed the Constitutionalist solution as out of date. The latter exhorted the king 'to give free access to the republican ideas of the nation', and Alba called him to 'give way to the new generation'.[81] Nor was Cambó any help. After advising Gabriel Maura on how to formulate the 'departure message' of the king, he left for Paris.[82] The king was left with no alternative but that of capitulation.

This was further brought home to him when he realized that not only had his reservoir of politicians deserted him; the army, by its neutral 'abstentionist' attitude, had shaken an essential foundation of the regime—the personal bond between

---

[77] *Reflexiones*, pp. 118–22.
[78] *El Sol* 23 May 1931.
[79] Ibid. 7, 9 June 1931.
[80] Ibid. 23 May 1931.
[81] *ABC* 14 Apr. 1931. For the attitude of the Constitutionalists see Burgos y Mazo, *Los Constitucionalistas*, iv, 123–4.
[82] Nadal, *Seis Años*, pp. 98–9.

the king and his army. The experiences of the Dictatorship, the revolutionary movements and republican propaganda had acted as a disintegrating factor in the army. An atmosphere of 'pessimism and disorientation', as Berenguer put it, dominated military circles throughout the last year. And when General Burguete came out with an open attack on the regime and on the tradition of military pronunciamientos, Berenguer had to appeal to the army to maintain its discipline as 'a guarantee for the regime and its institutions'.[83] But, now, when the crown was collapsing, no general was ready to provide such a guarantee by following in Primo de Rivera's footsteps. Romanones, in his message to the king through Cañada Honda clearly pointed out the disloyalty of the army as a reason why he should go.[84] The attitude of Sanjurjo was for the king an indication that a 'strong' La Cierva government would not have the support of the army, nor was general Mola's recognition of the elections as the 'indisputable expression of the national will' likely to encourage his policemen to fight the people.[85] Berenguer's telegram did not 'paralyse' the army as La Cierva alleged. It is unlikely that it would have deterred any general from staging a last-ditch defence of the Monarchy. Not even a personal telephone call from the Minister of War prevented Primo de Rivera from carrying out his *coup*. The army of 1931, as Gabriel Maura noticed, lacked the monarchist 'coherence' of the past, and, though General Cavalcanti assured the king of the loyalty of the cavalry, none came to speak on behalf of the infantry, the artillery, or the air force.[86] Not even on the level of local garrisons was the army eager to come out against the jubilant people, and it preferred either to stay confined to its barracks or to join the people in the streets. In Murcia the garrison refused an explicit order from the governor to prevent the declaration of the Republic. In Seville it 'abstained' according to a local observer, and in Barcelona General Despujols while making efforts to cool down the monarchist agitation of a few officers, was unable to maintain order

[83] Berenguer, *De la Dictadura*, pp. 350–3; Romanones, . . .*Y Sucedió* p. 76. For Burguete see Mola, *Obras*, pp. 804–8.

[84] Romanones in *El Sol* 4 June 1931; and *Las Ultimas Horas*, pp. 79–80.

[85] For Mola and for the police reluctance see *Obras*, pp. 849, 858–9; and Hoyos, *Mi Testimonio*, pp. 145, 231.

[86] La Cierva, *Notas*, pp. 375, 378; Gabriel Maura, *Porqué*, p. 395.

without the assistance of the local Revolutionary Committee.[87] Azaña could, therefore, congratulate the army, when he took over the Ministry of War, for its 'patriotism and discipline'.[88]

The behaviour of both government and king should also be considered against the background of republican pressure, both in the streets and through negotiations, a pressure which limited further the monarchists' power of manœuvre. However, at the beginning the Republican leaders were as disoriented as the government. Most of them looked forward to the general elections rather than to an immediate solution,[89] though their press spoke of the elections as 'one of the greatest events in Spanish political history', which should culminate in a Republic, and the PSOE warned the government from trying 'to retard the inevitable consequences of the plebiscite'.[90] It was the passivity of the government and its willingness to capitulate which stimulated the Provisional Government, on the thirteenth, to publish a manifesto exhorting the Monarchy 'to submit itself to the national will', and warning that, if it failed to do so by arguing a numerical victory in the 'rural fiefs', the Provisional Government would not be responsible 'for what might happen'. Alcalá Zamora, however, was still worried of a possible military reaction sponsored by the government.[91]

In order to put additional pressure on the regime, the Republicans exhorted their men in the provinces to demonstrate in the streets.[92] Crowds, mostly non-violent, poured into the streets after the afternoon of 13 April. Republican flags appeared everywhere, and the liberal Hymn of Riego with the Marseillaise were the hits of the day. The ministers in Madrid had to look for alternative streets on their way to the cabinet meeting at the palace, in order to avoid the immense crowd which filled the Calle Mayor from the Ministry of Interior to

[87] For Murcia see *ABC* 15 Apr. 1931. For Barcelona see Mola, *Obras* p. 1042; José García Benitez, *Tres Meses de Dictadura*, pp. 54–6; Solá Cañizares, *El Moviment*, pp. 119–121. For Seville see Enrique Vila, *Un Año de Republica en Sevilla*, pp. 26–30. See *ABC*; and *LV* 15 Apr. 1931; and Buckley, *Life and Death of the Spanish Republic*, p. 39 on soldiers fraternizing with the people in the streets.

[88] *ABC* 15 Apr. 1931.

[89] Maura, *Así*, pp. 152–3; Romanones, *...Y Sucedió* p. 38; Josép Plá, *Madrid, L' adveniment de la Republica*, p. 19.

[90] *ES, EC, El Sol* 14 Apr. 1931.

[91] *El Sol* 14 Apr. 1931. For Alcalá Zamora see Solá Cañizares, op. cit. 117.

[92] Mola, *Obras*, p. 854.

the Plaza de Oriente. The meeting itself was held with the noise of the crowd echoing in the ministers' ears.[93] The demonstrations ceased to be a simple problem of public order and became a reflection of the collapse of the regime when many of them culminated in the spontaneous proclamation of the Republic from the balconies of Ayuntamientos many hours before such a scene took place in Madrid. Eibar, a town in Guipúzcoa, set the pattern. The Republic was proclaimed at 6.00 a.m. on 14 April by the new Republican councillors. This practice was followed elsewhere. The president of the *Diputacion* or the mayor received a commission of newly elected Republican councillors stimulated by an excited crowd in the streets, and handed over the government of the city. Then the Republic was declared and a manifesto was issued exhorting the people to preserve peace and order 'in order not to discredit the newly-born Republic'. In some places royal emblems were destroyed and the crowds chanted republican songs.[94]

The proclamation of the Republic in Barcelona with its separatist connotations was obviously a severe blow to the authority of the Monarchy. It started as a 'conventional' proclamation, when Companys with several newly elected councillors, having received at 1.30 p.m. the government of the city at the hands of the outgoing mayor, declared the Republic from the balcony, waving the Catalan as well as the Spanish flags. But at 2.30 p.m., Maciá rushed to seize the opportunity and proclaimed from the same building both 'the Catalan state and

[93] Gabriel Maura, *Recuerdos*, pp. 212–13; Romanones, *Reflexiones*, pp. 125–6; Maura, *Así*, pp. 154, 161. For an eyewitness see Buckley, *Life and Death*, pp. 47–8. *La Ciencia Tomista* May–June 1931 wrote with contempt of the *populacho* which filled the streets. For students' demonstrations see Antonio Gascón, *Los Estudiantes*, pp. 117–18. For the provinces see Mola, *Obras*, p. 875; and Berenguer, *De la Dictadura*, pp. 402–5. Descriptions can be also found in abundance in every newspaper of 14 and 15 April. Only in Huelva was one man reported killed, see *ABC, Sevilla* 14 Apr. 1931.

[94] For timing and description of declarations see Prieto, *Convulsiones*, i, 74–7 (Eibar); *ABC* 15 Apr. 1931 (Castellón. 3.00 p.m.; Alicante, 4.00; Almería, 5.00; Coruña, 5.00; Tarragona, 5.00; Valencia, 5.00; Gerona, 6.00; Murcia, 6.00; Santander, 6.00; Zamora, 6.30; Badajoz, 7.00; San Sebastián, 7.00; Bilbao, 7.00); *LV* 15 Apr. 1931 (Zaragoza by 1.00 p.m.). For Huelva see J. Ordoñez Marquéz, *La Apostasia de las Masas y la Persecución Religiosa en la Provincia de Huelva 1931–1936*, pp. 2–3. For Seville see E. Vila, *Un año*, pp. 11–26. For Orense see Basilio Alvarez, *Dos Años*, i, viii–ix. For students' role see *El Liberal de Sevilla, ABC*, and *El Norte de Castilla*, 14, 15 Apr. 1931. See for attempts to declare the Republic in rural districts in Extremadura, Pedro Vallina, *Mis Memorias*, pp. 303–11. The Republic was declared even in Cádiz where the Monarchists had won the elections, see *El Liberal, Sevilla* and *ABC, Sevilla* 15 Apr. 1931 on Cádiz and other places in Andalucía.

Republic' which, he promised, would seek 'a confederation with the other Spanish Republics'. Minutes later he conducted a similar scene at the *Diputación Provincial*, where he was also elected by his colleagues as 'president of the Catalan Republic'. At 3.00 p.m., the local radio transmitted the news to the whole country, in spite of Mola's objections. 'No one is obeying us anymore', he said. An attempt by the *Lerrouxista* Emiliano Iglesias to take over the Civil Government in the name of the local Revolutionary Committee, was aimed at giving 'españolista' character to the Republic. Although he claimed to have the support of a large crowd, the captain general and the police, Emiliano Iglesias' short rule was wiped out by the intervention of López Ochoa, the captain general just nominated by Maciá, and by the violent pressure of Maciá's supporters from the CNT.[95]

The events both in Madrid and in the provinces proved manifestly that the Ministry of the Interior was no longer in control of the situation. The Minister himself was not available during most of the day, and an eyewitness observed telephones ringing with no one to answer, 'watching the regime dropping like a juicy, over-ripe plum from the tree'.[96] The Provisional Government was pushed by the circumstances to pick up the fruit. Since the early hours of the day the staff of the central post office was constantly briefing the Republican leaders on the government's abandonist position.[97] Early that morning, Azaña who had been in hiding since the abortive *coup* of December, started to move about freely;[98] and when at 2.05 p.m. Romanones asked Alcalá Zamora for an armistice, the latter could appear in a position of strength, supported by the very fact that an official government came to ask for a truce, and by the republican excitement in urban Spain. He therefore

---

[95] For the proclamation of the Republic see José Gaya Picón, *La Jornada Histórica de Barcelona*, pp. 5–58; *LV* and *SO* 15 Apr. 1931. The best documented account is in *Revista de Catalunya* 1931 pp. 387–550. For Emiliano Iglesias see his testimony in *ABC* 22 Apr. 1931; J. Peirats, *Los Anarquistas*, p. 85; Ossorio, *Companys*, pp. 86–9 and Maura's interview in *Estampa* 6 June 1931.

[96] Buckley, *Life and Death*, p. 44. The governor of Palma de Mallorca was disoriented because of lack of instructions from the Ministry, see AHN Leg. 16 no. 644: Palma de Mallorca, 14 Apr. 1931.

[97] Mola, *Obras*, p. 868

[98] F. Sedwick, *The Tragedy of M. Azaña and the Fate of the Spanish Republic*, p. 76.

drew up his famous ultimatum urging that the king should leave and power be transmitted 'before sunset'.[99] About a couple of hours later, Sanjurjo came to express his loyalty officially to the Provisional Government, after getting clear knowledge about the king's intentions to leave, and after having been in close contact with the Republican leaders through his personal friend Ubaldo de Aspiazu.[1] Now the symbolic and most efficient defender of the Monarchy, the Civil Guard, was with the Republic. If anyone could guarantee order in the streets, it was not the official government, but its opponents. However, sunset approached and the government was still undecided. Rafael Sánchez Guerra and Ossorio y Florit were, therefore, sent to the Ministry of the Interior, at 5.00 p.m., to demand an immediate transmission of power; but the Minister was not available.[2] Simultaneously, the new Republican and Socialist councillors went to proclaim the Republic in the Ayuntamiento, from which Trifón Gómez appealed to an excited crowd to 'give to the world an example of the political maturity of the Spanish people'. Only after the *fait accompli* did the outgoing mayor hand over his office to Saborit.[3] Meanwhile, the crowd surrounded the Ministry of the Interior demanding the proclamation of the Republic there. To appease it, R. Sánchez Guerra and E. Ortega waved a republican flag at about 6.00 p.m., and when by 7.00 p.m. the Monarchist government had not appeared, they telephoned the Provisional Government to come and assume a power which was 'lying in the streets'. By 8.00 p.m., the Republican leaders, stimulated also by a confident and impatient Maura, reached the Ministry of the Interior amid the enthusiasm of an immense crowd. From the balcony Alcalá Zamora proclaimed the

---

[99] Alcalá Zamora, 'Los primeros pasos del régimen republicano', *El Sol* 17 May 1931; Maura, *Así*, pp. 168–9.

[1] Sanjurjo was told at 1.00 p.m. by Berenguer about the king's intentions. At 2.00 p.m. he was back at home waiting for the results of the Alcalá Zamora–Romanones meeting which ratified the capitulation of the regime; then he went to Maura's house, see Berenguer, *De la Dictadura*, pp. 379–80; Sanjurjo–Romanones exchange of letters in *El Sol* 7, 9 June 1931; and Hoyos, *Mi Testimonio*, pp. 170–1. Maura, *Así*, 165–6 is probably mistaken when claiming that it was at 11.00 a.m. that Sanjurjo came to his house; see also General Estaban Infantes, *General Sanjurjo*, pp. 129–33; and a journalistic account in González Ruano and Emilio Tarduchy, *Sanjurjo*, p. 158.

[2] R. Sánchez Guerra, *Proceso*, pp. 165–6.

[3] *ES* 15 Apr. 1931; *ABC* 15 Apr. 1931.

Republic, in a message transmitted by the radio—an instrument of power which did not obey the Monarchist government—'with the manifest assent of the triumphant political forces and of the national will'.[4]

The smoothness of the transition was completed when Maura telegraphed the governors of the provinces with instructions to give way to the local Republican forces. Apart from minor riots, the Republic was declared smoothly in most of the Ayuntamientos in the country during that night and the next day. And, in some of those in which 'caciquismo had prevented the people from expressing its will', Monarchists were prevented from taking over.[5] Army officers like Generals Riquelme, Cabanellas, and Sanjurjo then rushed to the ministry to express loyalty to the de facto government. With the communication network under its control, the Provisional Government started that same night to publish its first decrees which consisted mainly of nomination of new functionaries at the top level, and of 'the juridical statute of the government'. Azaña took over the Ministry of War by 10.30 p.m. without the presence of the outgoing minister, and his other colleagues followed suit during the next morning.[6] Thus the new regime was smoothly established simply because, as El Crisol put it, 'public authority did not exist any more'.[7]

---

[4] R. Sánchez Guerra, Proceso, pp. 167–9; Maura, Así, pp. 169–72; ABC 15 Apr. 1931.
[5] Maura, Así, p. 172; and ABC 16 Apr. 1931.
[6] R. Sánchez Guerra, Proceso pp. 170–1; ABC 15, 16 Apr. 1931. For first decrees see Estanislao de Aranzadi, Repertorio Cronológico de Legislación 1–4. For the full subordination of the communication services, see El Cartero Español 30 Apr. 1931.
[7] EC 16 Apr. 1931.

VI

THE SAN SEBASTIÁN COALITION IN POWER

I. THE UNEASY PATH OF MODERATION AND COMPROMISE

The period between the proclamation of the Republic and the convocation of the Constituent Cortes witnessed an uneasy attempt by the San Sebastián coalition, as the Provisional Government of the second Republic, to lead the country along a middle way, far from extremisms of right and left, without alienating any of its components. But the unity which was made possible by the necessity of closing the ranks against the common Monarchist enemy in power, became impossible when contradictory views within the coalition on matters of doctrine and government and when an authentic revolutionary opposition in the streets confronted the Republican alignment with a new situation: no longer a vague Republic versus Monarchy, but a rightist versus a leftist Republic. Their dilemma was explicitly put on the agenda for the first time in the crisis of May, and it was to accompany the Republican forces throughout the subsequent months until it culminated in the official breach of the coalition in October.

However, the fact that the Republic was initially 'accepted' by a wide sector of public opinion,[1] making its imposition by

---

[1] For the army see S. Payne, *Politics and the Military in Modern Spain*, p. 266; and *Ejército y Armada* 16, 17 Apr. 1931. For the Church appeal to 'respect the established authorities' see pastorals of most of the bishops in *BEO de León* 20 Apr. 1931; *BOEA de Burgos* 15 Apr. 1931; *BOO de Madrid–Alcalá* 1 May 1931; *BOEA de Sevilla* 2 May 1931; *BOEO de Orense*, *BOEO de Vitoria* 1 May 1931; *ABC* 3, 8 May 1931 (the Bishops of Salamanca and Oviedo). See also R. Muntanyola, *Vidal y Barraquer*, pp.186–8. Submission to the Republic was preached even by local priests; *La Cruz de la Parroquia*, 19, 26 Apr. 1931. The left appreciated this attitude, See *EC*, 21 Apr. 1931. For reaction of business world see *Banco Urquijo* May, 1931. For an expression of loyalty by the superior council of Chambers of Commerce and Industry see *Boletín de la Camara ... de Málaga* April, 1931. Vested interests in the Moroccan protectorate followed suit, see *España en Africa* 30 Apr. 1931. Employers were delighted with 'the admirable discipline' shown by the working class in the first days of the regime, see *El Eco Patronal* 1 May 1931; and *El Mercantil Patronal* May 1931; and *El Economista* 25 Apr. 1931 denounced the unpatriotic flight of capital. Monarchists accepted the *fait accompli* as well, see *ABC* 15, 17 Apr. 1931; *EI* and *LE* 15

extreme measures simply unnecessary, and the basic moderation of most of the parties in the coalition produced non-radical legislation which did not create serious discrepancies between the ministers. Furthermore, this legislation was, according to Miguel Maura,[2] the execution of a plan agreed upon by the government when it was still a Revolutionary Committee, and, therefore, was unlikely to produce disagreements, though differences of opinion and attitude which would later sharpen into conflict were already manifest at this honeymoon stage.

The Juridical Statute, a kind of statement of provisional constitutional principles embodied this compromise between heterogeneous elements. It recognized the principle of 'freedom of belief and of religion' longed for by left Republicans and Socialists, but it equally amounted to a compromise with the only two Catholics in the government (Maura and Alcalá Zamora) 'by protecting Catholics from any abuses by lay government'.[3] The bourgeois liberal principle of 'individual freedom' was counterbalanced by the juridical recognition of 'syndical and corporative' entities, in order to appease both the Socialists and the extreme left. A similar tendency was reflected in the clause which guaranteed private property, but recognized that it could be expropriated 'on grounds of public utility', though with 'proper compensation'. The Socialists' insistence on agrarian reform would, therefore, be met not by an indiscriminate policy of expropriation, but by the application of milder norms according to which 'agrarian legislation should correspond to the social function of the land'.[4]

It has already been established that this compromising and moderate line was followed by the government in its early legislation. The agrarian decrees were aimed at mitigating the gravity of the problem by giving Largo Caballero a free hand to issue decrees on labour questions, while postponing for the Cortes the controversial issues of *latifundismo*, expropriation, as

May 1931. For the Constitutionalists see Burgos y Mazo, *Los Constitucionalistas* 125-6, 144-5. For the Carlists see Blinkhorn, *Carlism and Crisis in Spain*, pp. 2, 40. Even the extreme left was ready to grant limited credit to the new regime, see *Mundo Obrero* 15 Apr. 1931; *La Batalla* 18 Apr. 1931; *SO* 15-19 Apr. 1931.

[2] *El Sol* 30 May 1931. For a criticism of unity as a counter-revolutionary element see Falcón, *Crítica de la Revolución*, pp. 176-86.

[3] Maura, *Así*, p. 194.

[4] See Aranzadi, *Repertorio*, 2.

well as the question of *reparto* versus collectivization, over which Republicans and Socialists differed. Equally prudent and unprovocative was the financial policy of Prieto, 'the most conservative minister in the government', according to Maura. With the 'arch-reactionary economist Flores de Lemus'—these are Prieto's words—as his adviser, he ran a conventional policy which enabled Calvo Sotelo to claim that he did not introduce any fundamental change in the financial policy of the Dictatorship. Nor were any radical measures adopted against the flight of capital, because 'the moderate elements in the government had the upper hand' when the matter was discussed. Even Azaña's military reforms, which were acclaimed by both left and right, were consistent with the general line of moderation. He was not a Spanish Carnot, and the army that he created was neither revolutionary nor republican. Even Primo de Rivera had had in mind a reform to cut the army drastically. It was the style of Azaña, rather than the content of his reforms, which was new and revolutionary.[5]

The religious policy of the government was undoubtedly the most serious test of the unity of the San Sebastián coalition. Anti-clericalism was a traditional legacy of historical republicanism. This led people to believe that drastic measures against the Church were inevitable.[6] But with the *Derecha Republicana* and an increasingly moderate Lerroux in the coalition, the pre-parliamentary religious legislation of the government had to be an acceptable compromise. After the proclamation of the Republic Lerroux and Alcalá Zamora promised Tedeschini, the Papal Nuncio, that no anti-religious steps would be taken, while he assured them of the Church support, which was indeed manifested in April, though as a cautious attitude

---

[5] For a contemporary account on the gravity of the agrarian problem see Cristobal de Castro, *Al Servicio de los Campesinos. Hombres sin Tierra, Tierra sin Hombres*, and Pascual Carrión, *La Reforma Agraria de la Segunda Republica*, pp. 37–44. For the agrarian decrees see E. Malefakis, *Agrarian Reform*, pp. 166–71. For Prieto's financial policy see A. Balcells, *Crísis Económica*, pp. 73–6, 90–1, 95–7. Maura in his *Así*, pp. 201–2, 219; and Prieto in *Convulsiones* iii, 137. Calvo Sotelo, *En Defensa Propia*, p. 119. For the military reforms see S. Payne, *Politics*, pp. 268–9, 275–8. For the offending style see Nazario Cebreiros, *Las Reformas Militares*, pp. 3–19, 284–8; and the clandestine manifestos in HMM A/1742–1745: *A Todos los Compañeros, Al Cuerpo de ex-Oficiales del Ejército*. For the acclaim of the reforms by left and right see G. Maura, *Dolores de España*, pp. 79–81; Maura, *Así*, pp. 224, 226, 228; *EI*, 6 May 1931; *El Sol*, 5 May 1931.

[6] OA: Raymond Mussey (New York) to Ortega, 23 Apr. 1931.

motivated by fear, rather than as a positive acclamation.[7] But in early May a series of anti-religious decrees enacted by the government indicated that, though they were based on the accepted principle of 'freedom of religion and conscience', which was part of the Juridical Statute, the extremists in the government were getting the upper hand. However, it seems that the moderates were able to calm down the anti-clerical demands of left Republicans and Socialists so long as the Church maintained its discreet tone. It was on 2 May, the same day that Cardinal Segura published his pastoral praising the king and warning of the dangers of the Republic,[8] that the first decree, forbidding the transfer or sale of Church property, appeared. On 6 May a more sensitive decree was issued. It ended obligatory religious education.[9]

The episode of 'the burning of convents', a sudden outbreak of mob anti-clericalism in Madrid and other cities between 11 and 13 May, following a 'monarchist provocation' on the tenth,[10] exacerbated the differences in the government over both the religious issue and the approach to the problem of public order. Maura had on the evening of the tenth previous knowledge of the plan of young *Ateneistas* to set fire to churches and convents as a protest against the government's lenience towards the Church. But he failed to convince Azaña and Alcalá Zamora of the need to take preventive measures.[11] During the next day large crowds witnessed with indifference groups of youngsters setting fire to nine religious buildings in Madrid and making unsuccessful attempts against others. The agitation among Communists and CNT in Madrid, following the clash with Monarchists on 10 May, indicates that they were no strangers to the 'burning of convents'. They also protested against the general conservatism of the government, which

---

[7] For early contacts with Tedeschini see J. Sánchez, *Reform and Reaction*, p. 84; and Cierva, *Notas*, p. 331. The picture that emerges from Vidal i Barraquer's private correspondence during the first weeks of the Republic is one of a panic-stricken hierarchy. See Batllori and Arbeloa, eds., *Archivo Vidal i Barraquer* i, 19–29.

[8] *BOEA Toledo* 2 May 1931.

[9] Sánchez, op. cit. 86–8. Segura's behaviour was used by the republican press as a reason why the government should take tougher measures, see *ES* 2 May 1931.

[10] See below, p. 277.

[11] Maura, *Así*, pp. 246–7. See also his speech in *El Liberal* 12 Jan. 1932. Alcalá Zamora in his *Los Defectos* pp. 87–8 claimed that Maura was 'blameless'.

refused to radicalize the Republic, and therefore compelled them to make in the streets the revolution that the government failed to make 'from above'.[12]

In the government the first serious crisis developed on the same day. Maura advocated strong action against the mob, and he suggested sending the Civil Guard on to the streets. The Socialists adhered to the principle that an uncontrolled rabble should not rule the streets, but they feared a blow to their popular prestige if they backed a strong policy. The left Republicans were indifferent to the fate of religious buildings, and the most they would do was to try to dissuade their friends of the Ateneo, who came to the Ministry of the Interior to ask for Maura's resignation, for the dissolution of the Civil Guard, and for the expulsion of the religious orders, from further exciting the crowd. The Radical Socialists even declared that they 'adhered to the movement of protest carried out by the republican people' against the lenience of the government towards 'the most abominable feature of the old regime'. Facing complete isolation, Maura resigned. But the possibility that the coalition might disintegrate before fulfilling its original aim— to summon a Constituent Cortes—caused his colleagues to suggest a compromise. Martial law was declared, giving to the army, rather than to the hated Civil Guard, the task of restoring peace. In addition, Maura was given full power to deal with further disturbances in his own way. A public declaration by Alcalá Zamora did not mention the crisis in the government. He limited himself to putting the blame for the incidents on both the monarchist provocations of the previous day and the 'extremist elements', who wished to radicalize the Republic. He also refused a popular demand to dissolve the Civil Guard as unjustified, because 'it is an instrument which knows and will know how to defend the Republic'. However, an attempt to meet the demands of the extremists was made by arresting prominent monarchists and by promising that judicial

[12] For the figures of between 7 and 9 buildings see ecclesiastical sources: *La Ciencia Tomista*, July–Aug. 1931; and *ACM* May–June 1931. See also *The Times* and *El Sol* 12 May 1931. For communists see *Control*, Madrid 16 May 1931; *La Vanguardia Mercantil* June 1931. For anarchists see *El Libertario, FAI, Semanario Anarquista* (Madrid) 12 May 1931, which referred to the incident as the *acción directa* of the proletariat against the Church; see also *SO* 12 May 1931.

action would be taken over matters of 'responsibilities' during the dictatorship.[13]

The lenience of the government towards the incendiaries in Madrid obviously could not act as a deterrent against the possible repercussions in the provinces, although Maura put the governors on full alert. During the three following days, outbreaks of incendiarism took place in several cities, with the greatest effect in Andalucía. In Málaga twenty-seven religious buildings were attacked, seventeen of which were set on fire. As in Madrid, property and life were respected. The fury of the mob was directed against the Church as such. The indifference of the governor and of the garrison only encouraged incendiaries, and threw Catholics, aristocrats, and functionaries of the old regime into a mood of panic. Gibraltar hotels were again crowded with new emigrés, and business circles were in dismay. This time, however, Maura was able to take immediate steps 'to save the Republic', in line with the authority which had been delegated to him by the government: martial law was proclaimed, four governors and the Police Chief were replaced, and many other functionaries on a lower level were dismissed for negligence.[14]

The 'burning of convents' crisis had manifestedly proved that the threat from an uncontrolled revolution in the streets was, for the time being, graver than the danger of provoking the Church by anti-religious decrees. A radicalization of the Republic aimed at appeasing the extreme left, and already

---

[13] For the Socialists see their manifesto in *ES* 12 May 1931. For the left Republicans see: *Poesía de Luis de Tapia con el Motivo de la Quema de Conventos* in RA Leg. 75 no. 6; the Radical–Socialist declaration is quoted in Tuñón de Lara, *La España* pp. 247–8. The Ateneo: *El Sol* 12 May 1931. For the crisis in the government see Maura, *Así*, pp. 250–259; his interview in Pierre Dominique, *Marche, Espagne*, pp. 87–8. Alcalá Zamora's declaration and the government's measures are in *El Sol* 12 May 1931.

[14] For the Governors see AHN Leg. 16: circular No. 81, 12 May 1931. For detailed reports on Málaga and other parts of Andalucía and Levante see F.O. 371/15773, 15774: Grahame to Henderson, 15, 19, 30 May, 6 June 1931 providing reports from the consuls in Málaga, Alicante, and Valencia; and Maura, *Así*, p. 261; see also *El Sol* 12, 13 May 1931. It should be noticed that no authoritative indication as to the identity of the incendiaries has been given, except vague allegations about Communists. It is, however, evident that the outbreaks took place in regions where Anarcho-Syndicalists had substantial forces. See the case of Murcia, in AHN Leg. 16: Governor of Murcia to Maura, 12 May 1931 No. 697. For business circles see ibid: MacAndrews and Co. Ltd. to Maura, 18 May 1931; and *Boletín Oficial de la Cámara de Propiedad Urbana de Madrid*, May, June 1931. For the measures of Maura see *El Sol* 14 May 1931.

reflected in tough measures against Monarchists, would be now expressed in a less compromising approach to the Church.[15] *El Socialista* warned the government that 'social peace' would be constantly disturbed unless the religious orders were expelled from the country, and the influence of thousands of priests and 'more than 5,000' Catholic agrarian syndicates was curbed.[16] Under these circumstances the government reached an agreement in principle that the Jesuits should be expelled as soon as a pretext proving their involvement in politics was found. But in subsequent meetings, when the storm of 11 May was calmed, Maura and Alcalá Zamora managed to resist the pressure by Azaña, Albornoz, and Marcelino Domingo. Prieto's insistence that this should have been done not as a punishment, but simply because the 1851 Concordat did not allow the existence of more than three orders, which did not include the Jesuits, was also shelved for the moment.[17]

However, other no less dramatic steps were taken in the aftermath of the 'burning of convents'. The Bishop of Vitoria, Mugica, was expelled by Maura for 'subversive' activities, an act for which he had the support of the government and leftist opinion. On 22 May a decree was issued declaring 'freedom of religion' in the country. This enraged Segura. He left immediately for Rome, where the Pope could only suggest the diplomatic tactics pursued by Tedeschini as the only means to safeguard religious interests. Before returning to Spain, he sent a letter to the government in which he bitterly attacked its religious policy, and when he set foot again in Spain by mid-June, he was expelled, an expulsion acclaimed by *El Socialista* as 'a step towards purging Spain of the national enemy'. The religious establishment was shocked by these latest steps. Bishops spoke with anxiety of the 'Republic of the Godless' which had unleashed 'the furious anti-religious gale' and 'storm waves of sectarian hatred' against the Church and against everything sacred. The precarious co-existence of Church and Republic was definitely shattered long before October 1931, when the

---

[15] *EC* 21 May 1931; Rafael Sánchez Guerra, *Un Año Histórico*, p. 142. For Monarchists see below, pp. 278.

[16] *ES* 17 May 1931. See similar demands in *EC* 16 May 1931; and demands from Ayuntamientos on the same style in Dominique, *Marche, Espagne*, p. 80.

[17] See Azaña, *Obras*, iv, p. 51; Alcalá Zamora, *Los Defectos*, pp. 12–13, 88; and Prieto, *Palabras al Viento*, p. 219.

anti-religious clauses were introduced into the constitution. The only achievement which the moderates in the government could claim was that they succeeded in avoiding the total separation of state and Church, a separation demanded by their radical colleagues.[18]

The San Sebastián pact was seriously threatened also by Maciá's rule in Catalonia. The pact stated that only the Cortes should decide on Catalan autonomy, after all the political forces in the region had collaborated in the elaboration of a statute. Maciá was therefore persuaded by the government and by a manifestation of 'fraternity' reflected in a personal visit of Alcalá Zamora to a euphoric Barcelona, to stick to the San Sebastián pact, and to give up 'for the sake of republican solidarity' and 'for a short period, part of that sovereignty which we have the right to exercise'. However, he later explained that the proclamation of the Catalan state was not a separatist act, but a means of exerting pressure on the Monarchist government which was still in office. A federal Republic was all that he wanted.[19] The *Generalidad*, a *de facto* semi-autonomous regime which he was allowed to establish, enabled him, however, to become the undisputed arbitrator of Catalan politics, a position which he could obviously claim because of his total victory in April.

Maciá remained a constant menace to the government. He organized the Generalidad as the 'embryo of the Catalan state', to use Rovira i Virgili's expression. It was an executive

---

[18] For anti-Church legislation after the May events see Sánchez, *Reform* pp. 98–9. For Mugica see Maura, *Así*, pp. 294–7; *BOEO de Vitoria* 1 June 1931; and the left's support in AHN Leg. 16: Republican–Socialist bloc of Vitoria to Maura, 27 May 1931, No. 1918. For 'freedom of cults' see Aranzadi, *Repertorio*, no. 282; and how it was acclaimed by leftist opinion in *ES* 26 May 1931. For Segura see Maura, op. cit. 301–4; *BOEA de Toledo* 2 May 1931, 16 June 1931; *El Sol* 19 June 1931, *ES* 17 June 1931. For negotiations with the Holy See see Sánchez, op. cit. 81–4, 99–106. For the unanimous protest of the ecclesiastical establishment and the right see *BOEO de Leon* 15 June 1931; *BOEA Toledo* 8 June 1931; *BOEA de Burgos* 30 June 1931; *BOEO de Orense* 27 June 1931; *ACM* May–June 1931; *Boletín del Sindicato Católico de Tipógrafos y Similares de Madrid*, April–Aug. 1931. See how even at a local level, in sermons and homilies, the decrees were attacked: *La Cruz de la Parroquia* 7 June 1931; and *Revista Eclesiástica, Homilías Breves* May–June 1931. For Alcalá Zamora see his *Los Defectos*, p. 87.

[19] *LV* 19 Apr. 1931. For the government's attitude, see Maura, *Así*, pp. 236–9; Bofill, *Una Política* p. 113. For Alcalá Zamora's visit see *LV* 28 Apr. 1931. For the last statement see his interview in *EC* 23 Apr. 1931.

government with authority to deal with matters of education—Marcelino Domingo, to the alarm of 'Spanish' teachers, rushed to concede to Catalonia the right of bilingualism in schools, and the university of Barcelona started to elaborate the statute of a 'Catalan university'—and administration of public works, finance, and health services. This he did by abolishing the *Diputaciones Provinciales* and by concentrating their functions in Barcelona. He did not cease to warn the government that Catalonia, rather than accept any anti-Catalanist resolution of the Cortes, even if it was reached democratically, would 'return to extremism'. He made it clear that if the Cortes did not approve the statute, 'Catalan separatism would flame up stronger than ever and a spiritual war would follow between Catalonia and Spain'.[20]

But as far as some sectors of Spanish opinion were concerned, Maciá had already declared war. Many Chambers of Commerce in the country started to boycott Catalan products. Royo Villanova, representing the wheat growers of Castile, accused Maciá of plotting with the frontier police in Catalonia to smuggle in cheap wheat from abroad, thus severely damaging Castilian interests. Economic interests in Catalonia, as well as Maciá, were alarmed by the possibility of a Spanish boycott. The Chamber of Commerce and Industry of Barcelona explained to its Spanish colleagues that whatever had happened in Catalonia, it was not separatism, but 'steps taken in complete and cordial harmony with the central government'. Maciá made special efforts to deny Royo Villanova's allegations. His colleague Rafael Campalans coined in a lecture in Madrid the slogan of 'Catalonia in the service of the Republic'; and Vidal y Guardiola lectured in the Madrid Ateneo emphasizing the great interest of Catalan industry in the prosperity of the market for its products: agricultural Spain. But he also gave warning of a counter-boycott by Catalonia which consumed

---

[20] For the Generalidad see *LV* 29 Apr. 1931; Rovira i Virgili, *Catalunya i la Republica*, p. 31. For bilingualism see *El Magisterio Español* 7 May 1931; and Marcelino Domingo, *La Escuela en la República, La Obra de Ocho Meses* pp. 61–3. For the university see RA Leg. 63 no. 20: *Notas de Interes para la Discusión del Estatuto de Cataluña*. For the Diputaciones see *LV* 5 May 1931. Maciá's declarations are in ibid. 29 Apr. 1931. Hurtado, *Quaranta Anys*, iii pp. 31–2 noticed that for the majority of the Catalans the 'concessions' of Maciá to the central government did not matter. For them, he was the 'president'.

500 million pesetas' worth of Spanish agricultural products per year.[21]

The dominance of Catalan politics by the *Esquerra* was also emphasized by the way the statute was elaborated. For that purpose, a Diputación Provisional was elected by the representatives of the Ayuntamientos. But, the fact that many of the Ayuntamientos were run by *Esquerristas* or *Comisiones Gestoras* assured that the DP, as well as the whole statute it elaborated, would be 'sectarian'. The Lliga decided, therefore, to boycott it. Similar attitudes were taken by the Federals and the DR, both attacking the undemocratic procedures of Maciá. The whole idea of the statute was opposed also by agrarian elements in the non-industrial provinces of the region. They feared that a *Barcelonista* centralism might develop, in which the competing interests of agriculturists and industrialists in tariff policy would be settled in favour of the latter. The result was a DP composed of twenty-six Esquerristas and an opposition of thirteen deputies from ACR, independent Republicans and one Radical. In his inaugural speech, Maciá exhorted the deputies to represent the will of the Catalan people 'to reclaim the sovereignty of which it had been dispossessed', thus contributing 'to establish an Iberian confederation'. However, in spite of allegations that the statute was exclusively Esquerrista, it can be argued that Maciá and his party were careful not to provoke Spanish opinion and the government. The moderation of the statute published on 20 June was recognized by neutral and Spanish observers. Even the sensitive question of tariffs was left under the central government's authority. Only *ultra-españolista* elements in Catalonia and anti-Esquerristas continued to oppose it.[22]

[21] For the boycott see *LV* 9 May 1931; *ABC* 9, 10 May, 14 June 1931. For Castilian wheat see *El Norte de Castilla* 17, 19 May 1931; and Royo Villanova, *Un Grito Contra el Estatuto*, pp. 32–4. For the Barcelona businessmen see *Cámara de Comercio y Navegación de Barcelona, Memoria* 1931 pp. 72–5. For Vidal see *El Sol* 17 May 1931. For Campalans see his speech on 14 May in his *Hacía La España de Todos* pp. 19–70.

[22] For the DP see *LV* 22, 23, 26 May 1931. Maciá in ibid. 11 June 1931. For the Lliga, ACR and the DP see ibid. 21 May 1931; Lliga, *Historia d'Una Política* pp. 391–393; Rovira, *Catalunya*, p. 61; and Solá Cañizares, *El Moviment* pp. 129–30. For agrarian elements see *Comunicación de la Asociación General Agropecuaria de la Cuenca Hidrográfica del Ebro. En Defensa del Fomento del Trabajo e Intercambio Comercial entre las Distintas Regiones de España* 16 May 1931, in OA. The statute is in A. Sevilla, *Constituciones*, pp. 259–68. For observers see *EC* 14 July 1931; *The Economist* 18 July 1931; Lliga, op. cit. 402–3. For the opposition see *Catalunya*, 15 May, 15 June 1931; *Ley y Justicia* 1 Aug. 1931.

Maciá, however, kept elements in the San Sebastián coalition—especially the right and the Socialists—in a state of tension with his policy of favouring the CNT, to whom he was indebted since they backed him in the April elections. The appointment of Companys, a lawyer who had defended Syndicalists in the past, was in itself a concession to *Cenetistas*. They responded by open support to the Generalidad. They acclaimed Maciá as 'a honest man' with whom they had 'a mutual alliance'.[23] Maciá rewarded them with a policy of persecution of their rivals, the *Sindicatos Libres* and the UGT, to the right, and the extremist group of the FAI to the left. When a May Day demonstration ended in bloodshed, Maciá came personally to apologize to a huge gathering of workers: 'If freedom for Catalonia demanded the perpetuation of the present social situation, I would have given it up . . . no order has been given by us to shoot on you. I am your friend. I am your brother . . . I am always with you . . .'[24]

These cordial relations proved their efficiency when, during the 'burning of convents', no religious building was attacked in Barcelona. But Maciá was unable, and probably unwilling, to force the CNT into accepting the arbitration of the *jurados mixtos* (the arbitration boards established by Largo Caballero). Consequently, the first months of the Republic witnessed a sharp increase in strikes in Catalonia, and general chaos in labour relations which caused a panic among employers and, by undermining Largo Caballero's policy, enraged the Socialists. The latter attacked Maciá for persecuting the UGT and for creating in Catalonia 'a dictatorship of terror' in collaboration with the CNT, 'his mine of votes'. It is, however, noteworthy that the CNT contributed to smooth away differences between Maciá and the government by exerting a moderating influence on the Esquerra's nationalist aspirations. They warned Maciá that they would support him only as long as he strove for a federal Spain. 'The workers who had given you their votes', he was reminded, 'did not do so in order that you should separate them from their Spanish brothers.'[25]

[23] *SO* 25 Apr., 11 June 1931.
[24] *LV* 3 May 1931.
[25] For persecution of the Sindicatos Libres and UGT see F.O. 371/15771, 15774: Grahame to Henderson, 17 Apr., 12 June 1931, providing accounts from the consul in Barcelona. The FAI was expelled from the national congress in June, thus allowing the

2. THE UNFULFILLED QUEST FOR THE REPUBLICANIZATION OF THE REPUBLIC

The new regime's unrevolutionary face was obviously reflected in its failure to run a radical campaign of 'republicanizing the Republic' either by making a political purge at all the levels of administration or by stopping the influx of 'new Republicans' thirsty for jobs and for a secure position. This prevented the Republic from becoming 'authentic' for those who looked for a radical change.[26]

Old functionaries continued to hold their jobs as if a change of regime had not taken place. When Prieto tried to replace the staff of the monopolistic *Compañía Arrendataria de Tabacos*, by 'safe' Republicans, he was met by the objections of other ministers. Lerroux made it clear upon assuming the Ministry of Foreign Affairs, that he would not dismiss any functionary of account of his monarchism. And he confirmed the appointment of the Spanish consuls in Buenos Aires and Montevideo despite the fact that they had always been very keen on collecting signatures of adherence to the king. He even appointed the ex-*Upetista* Agramonte y Cortijo as an assistant to the sub-secretary of the ministry.[27] Although the top functionaries were frequently replaced, much of the staff remained in office. Such was the case in the Moroccan protectorate where the High Commissioner, General Jordana, was dismissed, but the old staff continued to carry out his policy in economic as well as in political matters.[28] A similar case was that of an important Ayuntamiento like that of Madrid where it was impossible to run the city without the close collaboration of the minority of twenty Monarchist councillors, who ensured that many of the functionaries who

---

CNT to reach a resolution which advocated a minimum of collaboration with republican legality, see for this: *SO* 12–14, 16–18 June 1931; and J Brademas, *Anarcosindicalismo y Revolución en España 1930–1937* pp. 59–69. For the 'burning of convents' see F.O. 371/15773: Grahame to Henderson, 19 May 1930, an account from the consul in Barcelona. For Socialists' resentment see *ES* 6, 9, 11, 16 June 1931. For CNT's anti separatism see *SO* 19, 24, 26, 28 Apr. 1931.

[26] Maura, *Así*, p. 206, 272; Azaña, *Obras* ii 38.

[27] Prieto, *Convulsiones*, i 101. For Lerroux see *ABC* 16 Apr. 1931; and *Izquierda* 9 Aug. 1931.

[28] *España en Africa* 15 May, 15 June, 30 July 1931.

had received their jobs through the favouritism of the Monarchy were not dismissed.[29] Many others became Republicans simply in order to keep their jobs. Such was the case in the Ayuntamientos of Carabanchel, Vicálvaro, and Chamartin where ex-*somatenistas* and old caciques, now 'new Republicans', continued to head the same departments as in the past. A similar process was noticed in the city council of Seville, where the Monarchist councillors converted immediately to republicanism. Local citizens simply could not understand what was the point in establishing a Republic if they had to depend on the same men in their daily life.[30] The Ministry of Education faced a similar problem when it had to staff its new schools with hundreds of teachers who swore that they were 'more constitutionalist than Riego, more republican than Salmerón and more socialist than Pablo Iglesias'.[31] In the Ministry of Communications many came to claim that they were 'citizens with a clean republican history', for which they expected a recompense now that the 'ideal had won'.[32] Even the Radical-Socialist Galarza, the Attorney General of the Republic, confessed that only two of his functionaries were 'pre-April-the-fourteenth Republicans'.[33] It was not very astonishing, therefore, that a republican newspaper should suggest that Sánchez Guerra should be the prime minister and that figures like La Cierva, Bugallal, and Goicoechea should not be absent from the Republican parliament.[34]

This situation greatly offended those who considered themselves old Republicans, and who wanted to make the Republic an exclusive club, in which the spoils should be shared.[35] The newcomers were bitterly attacked as *conversos* 'who had changed their opinion in one day'. These included many councillors and mayors who had been originally elected as Monarchists. These

---

[29] Saborit, *Besteiro*, pp. 289–90; *España Republicana* 1 June 1931.

[30] *Heraldo de Chamartin* 4 May 1931; *El Defensor del Extrarradio* 19 June 1931; E. Vila, *Un Año*, pp. 60–1.

[31] *Trabajadores de la Enseñanza* 5 July 1931. This phenomenon night have been encouraged by the fact that the 'monarchist' system of examination for teachers was replaced by a system of 'selection'; see Domingo, *La Escuela*, pp. 75–6.

[32] *El Cartero Español* 30 Apr. 1931.

[33] OA; M. Granados to Ortega, 2 May 1931.

[34] *Catalunya* 1, 15 May 1931.

[35] Alcalá Zamora, *Los Defectos*, pp. 48–9.

a posteriori Republicans or *adherentes,* as some called them, were considered as a serious threat which might 'falsify the orientation of the new democracy'.[36] So long as *Upetistas* and *Albiñanistas,* supported by the leniency of a 'reactionary disguised as democrat' in the person of the Minister of the Interior, were holding posts in the new regime, 'loyal Republicans would be pushed to join the ranks of syndicalism and communism', as the only way to bring about 'a real revolution'.[37] Because of the government's reluctance to 'purify' the Republic, an association of office-holders started to make its own 'tests' of republicanism for new adherents, by asking them to produce evidence that they had been members of Republican organizations before the Republic was established. The infiltration of 'the quarter-past zero hour Republicans', as some nicknamed them, would not only jeopardize the material interests of authentic Republicans but would prevent any real radicalization of the Republic. The gates of the Republic must, therefore, be closed to *arrivistas* as a measure of public safety against the possibility that 'the right and secure course of the regime' might be 'strewn with obstacles and stumbling blocks'.[38]

Though some ministers set up *juntas de defensa de la republica* in order to curb the influx of new Republicans into the administration there is no indication that any serious attempt was made to radicalize the ministries as a counter-measure. The struggle for a more radical Republic against the accentuated conservatism of the Radical Party and the *Derecha Republicana,* was led within the San Sebastián coalition rather than at the administrative level. When ministers appointed or recommended their protégés for a job, it was not necessarily because of their republican purism, but as part of the traditional practice of *enchufismo.* Maura, who himself recommended his men for administrative posts, was compelled by such 'recommendations' to appoint many provincial governors who claimed to be 'republicans

---

[36] *ES* 18 Apr. 1931; *España Libre* 5 June 1931.

[37] *El Defensor del Extrarradio* 4 June, 8, 20 July 1931; *España Libre* 26 June 1931.

[38] *Avanti, Revista Decenal Defensora de los Intereses Morales y Materiales de los Empleados,* Madrid, 18 Apr., 19 May 1931; *El 14 de Abril* 30 May 1931; *España Republicana* 1 June 1931; *C.T.T. Semanario de los Trabajadores de Comunicaciones* 20 June 1931. Even *ABC* 9 June 1931 was disgusted with these *camaleones* (chameleons). 'New Republicans' appeared also in Spanish communities abroad, see *España Republicana. Organo de la Alianza Republicana en Nueva-York* April–June 1931.

since birth', but were unfit to fulfil their role as the only genuine representatives of the Republic in the provinces.[39] Maura was not a unique case. The spectacle of thousands of 'eternal republicans', with letters of recommendation, crowding the corridors of the ministries, was shocking to those who expected new standards in the administration.[40] Nepotism in the old style was the origin of the appointment of a relative of E. Ortega to several jobs in the Madrid Ayuntamiento, and of Aurelio Lerroux as a high functionary in the 'Compañía Telefónica'.[41] The phenomenon was so common that Azaña was to notice, after three months of the Republic, that only two of his assistants in the ministry had never appealed to him for a recommendation. Among his party colleagues there was at least one who promised him that the whole province of Almería would go over to the *Acción Republicana* if a party member was appointed as governor.[42]

In the rural districts, the superficiality of the change of regime was even more accentuated. The governor of Toledo lamented that the Republic had not struck roots and that 'the new spirit has not penetrated into the masses'.[43]

Many Monarchists, encouraged by local governors, started to go over *en masse* to Republican organizations, or to establish their own 'Republican centres', in order to be in with the victors. In the province of Palma de Mallorca where *Cambóistas* and *Marchistas* had the upper hand in many Ayuntamientos, their caciques rushed to express their loyalty to the new governor and to assure him that they had always been 'republicans in hiding', so that they could continue to rule the province as they always did. At Colunga, in Asturias, the traditional caciques, headed by an ex-*Upetista*, even created a new party called cynically the 'Republican–Monarchist Party',

[39] Maura, *Así*, 265–72. See Lerroux, *Mis Memorias*, p. 598 on his 'recommendations'. For Maura's recommendations see an immense quantity in SA Leg. 1304. For the epidemic of *enchufismo* during the first years of the regime see a tendentious account in Joaquín del Moral, *Oligarquía y Enchufismo*, pp. 88–111, 300–6.

[40] OA: Cortina Giner de los Ríos to Ortega, 27 May 1931.

[41] *España Republicana* 16 July 1931; C.T.T. 20 June 1931.

[42] Azaña, *Obras*, iv, 10, 36. See for further evidences of *enchufismo*, Julio Camba, *Haciendo de Republica*, pp. 91–9. Ortega's prestige was also exploited for recommendations, see OA: M. Granados to Ortega, 9, 20 May 1931.

[43] OA: José Maria Semprun to Ortega, 4 May 1931.

which, they claimed, would avoid a take-over of the administration by 'old Republicans'. This was a typical case, many similar being reported elsewhere.[44] Francisco de Cossio noticed ironically that 'the Republic had in the *pueblos* the same large number of adherents as the UP had during the Dictatorship'. After having 'voted' for the Monarchy, they rushed to find a shelter under the Republican umbrella.[45]

Galicia, a region of two million inhabitants, 1,800,000 of whom lived in poverty-stricken rural districts, yielded an illuminating demonstration of this phenomenon. The agents of monarchism who 'made' the Monarchist victory in rural Ayuntamientos were now among the first to celebrate the proclamation of the Republic. In Puerto del Son eleven liberals and seven UM were elected, but, when they took over the Ayuntamiento, they did so as fifteen Republicans and three Independents. In Orense, one week after the declaration of the Republic, the whole Liberal Party was converted to republicanism. And in Mondariz (Pontevedra) the *Bugallalistas* followed suit. New Republican centres headed by old caciques were founded in many pueblos and the governors were kept busy with applications to approve their constitutions. The office of the governor of Orense was so crowded with such new Republicans asking for political favours that he had to publish a note denouncing those 'who expect the Republic to shield their personal ambitions and to help them in hatching their political caciquismo'.[46]

Many, however, did not bother to change their affiliation, because the Republic did not rule out the possibility of non-Republicans remaining in office. A circular letter from Maura

---

[44] See for Palma de Mallorca *EC* 12 May 1931; and OA: Jose Rivero Marraro (Palma) to Ortega, 11 June 1931. For Colunga, *EC* 23 May 1931. For other cases see ibid. 28 May 1931 on Puebla de Lillo (León), Torreblanca (Castellón), Creciente (Pontevedra), Puebla de Caraminal (La Coruña), Selas (Guadalajara). *ES* 6 May 1931 reported from Serón (Almería) that even 'Albiñanistas' created a Republican centre, and claimed to be 'more republican than Robespierre'; ibid. 9 May 1931 on Fitero in Navarra.

[45] *El Sol* 28 Apr. 1931.

[46] *La Voz de Galicia* 19, 21, 24, 25 Apr., 5, 6 May 1931. For Mondariz see AHN Leg. 16: The Republican centre of Mondariz to Maura 18 May 1931, No. 1099. For illuminating accounts on the lack of political maturity of Galicia as a whole and of its rural population in particular see Domingo Quiroga, *Ensayo Sobre una Nueva Política Gallega*; and Vicente Risco, *El Problema Politico de Galicia*, pp. 83, 103–213.

explicitly prohibited the dismissal of functionaries for political reasons,[47] thus tranquillizing secretaries of Ayuntamientos who acclaimed the Republic in a mood of panic fearing that they might be replaced.[48] The governor of Valladolid followed the instructions of the minister when he exhorted both Monarchists and Republicans to collaborate for the development of the city 'without political squabbles'; while in Hornachuelos (Seville), the *delegado gubernativo* appealed to the Ayuntamiento to avoid any sectarian discrimination, because 'the Republic does not belong only to the Republicans, but to all Spaniards'. A similar approach was expressed by the Republican mayor of Seville when he promised functionaries that 'even if they are not Republicans', they would not be dismissed arbitrarily so long as they fulfilled their professional duties.[49] Monarchist councillors took their seats in Republican Ayuntamientos, sometimes with the support of Republicans who believed that 'any organism might disintegrate and become demoralized if it lacked a strong and uncompromising opposition'. But in rural districts, the hegemony of Monarchist caciques, was becoming not simply an 'opposition', but a clear obstacle even to the proclamation of the Republic.[50]

However, the fact that the Republic did not carry out a radical transformation of the administration, gave rise to growing pressure from those who considered themselves authentic Republicans. They saw with anger how 'the old caciques have established themselves in many Ayuntamientos' under the flag of the Republic. *The Federación Local Obrera* in Coruña appealed to the government to dismiss all the state, provincial and municipal employees who, by their doubtful republicanism, constituted a danger to 'progress and liberty'. The existence of many noisy *Calvosotelista* groups in the local administration of Galicia brought some to the conclusion that, though the

[47] *El Norte de Castilla* 25 Apr. 1931; AHN Leg. 16: Circular No. 188, 14 Apr. 1931.

[48] *Boletín del Colegio Oficial del Secretariado Local de la Provincia de Palencia* March–April, May 1931. For a Monarchist secretary in the Ayuntamiento of Pontevedra who could not be dismissed see *La Voz de Galicia* 25 Apr. 1931.

[49] For Vallodolid see *El Norte de Castilla* 24 Apr. 1931. For Hornachuelos and Seville see *El Liberal, Sevilla* 19, 22 Apr. 1931.

[50] *El Liberal, Sevilla* 19 Apr. 1931. For the docile behaviour of a Monarchist opposition in Santiago, see *La Voz de Galicia* 21 Apr. 1931. For rural districts see the cases of Sanlúcar de Barrameda (Cádiz), and Araya (Alava) in *EC* 28 Apr., 12 May 1931.

Republic had been proclaimed, 'the revolution so badly needed by Spain had not yet taken place'.[51] A regional agrarian congress held in Pontevedra by representatives of the area's small farmers echoed the urgency of the problem when it urged the government, if it wished to give any meaning to the change of regime, to replace all the Monarchist authorities with 'people with a republican lineage', and to dismiss all those judges who were known to be 'agents of caciquismo'. Furthermore, the investigation into the 'responsibilities' of the Dictatorship should not only include the shortcomings of ministers, but also of their local agents in rural districts, the caciques.[52] The 'overproduction of circumstantial republicanism in rural Ayuntamientos' demanded, according to the purists, 'a republican *cordon sanitaire*' to avoid a conservative take-over of local administration. Otherwise, some socialists argued, it would have been better if the Republic had carried out 'three days of revolutionary violence, in which the caciques of the pueblos could have been hanged from the telegraph poles'.[53] A more institutionalized solution, however, was suggested by the new *Federación de Republicanos Rurales* which appealed to the electorate not to vote for any candidate whose republicanism did not go back before 15 December 1930 and which exhorted the government to dissolve all the Monarchist Ayuntamientos and not to authorize 'this bazaar of new Republican centres' unless they were created by old Republicans.[54]

The May events had, however, stimulated Maura to consider a radical step towards 'republicanizing' rural Ayuntamientos. Under pressure from rural districts, and with the conviction that circumstances had changed because of 'the evident monarchist provocations',[55] Maura decided by mid-May to hold new elections in at least 882 Ayuntamientos, most of them rural and four of them in capitals in which Republicans had been defeated in April.[56] Manuel Cordero and the socialist youth

[51] *La Voz de Galicia* 19, 21 May 1931.
[52] *Boletín de Información Social del Ministerio de Trabajo y Previsión* May 1931.
[53] *ES* 2, 6, 9 May 1931. For a similar bitter reaction see *EC* 12 May 1931; and *Manifiesto de Riaza al pueblo de Brihuega*, May 1931, in RA Leg. 52 no. 15.
[54] Their resolution quoted in B. García Menéndez, *La España Rural*, pp. 276–9.
[55] For the 'provocations' of 10 May see below, p. 277.
[56] Appendix II. See his declaration in *El Sol* 13, 14 May 1931. This number is much greater than that which he admitted in his memoirs: *Así*, pp. 314–15; but obviously

urged Maura 'to dissolve all the Monarchist municipalities', because the May events indicated 'what might happen' if the old caciques continued to rule.[57] But Maura's measure was a compromise which enraged the monarchists, who considered it as a step to republicanize the rural districts, and which was too mild to placate the left. The latter, though recognizing that it guaranteed that in the general elections Monarchists would not be able to triumph in the provinces, opposed Maura's decision not to touch municipalities elected unopposed under Article 29, which provided Monarchists with about a quarter of the total number of councillors in the country.[58]

However, both the fact that Maura did not alter the composition of hundreds of municipalities elected under Article 29, and the evidence of many republican branches opposing new elections in their Ayuntamientos, indicates that, though certainly harmful for the representatives of the old regime, it was far from being a draconian measure against Monarchists. The attitude of the Aznar government towards the result of the elections in rural districts demonstrated that they were aware of the corrupt way in which they were run. The protests received by Maura later were an additional proof. From the province of Murcia came stories about the unrestrained behaviour of *Ciervista* caciques; in Oviedo, Melquiades' agents 'made' the elections in a large number of villages, while in Galicia there was hardly one village in which the agents of Bugallal did not exert pressure on the docile electorate bringing 'total' victories to the Monarchists almost everywhere; so much so that the governor of Orense appealed to Maura to hold new elections in *all* the villages of the province because of the 'growing excitement' of the population over the fact that, under the Republic, they were being ruled as under the Monarchy. There were, however, many places in which Republicans were opposed to the May elections either because they had won in April or because they advocated a better way

smaller than the number of 3000 mentioned in Fernández Almagro, *Historia de la Segunda República Española*, p. 26.

[57] *ES* 5, 12, 14 May 1931.

[58] For monarchists see a furious campaign in *ABC* 21, 23, 24, 26, 28–30 Apr. 1931. For article 29 see *Boletín de Administración Local* 14 May 1931. For the left see *ES* 5, 7 June 1931.

to ensure a Republican majority: their appointment without election. Some also expressed their fear that the caciques might win in May as they had in April because, as Socialist and *Acción Republicana* branches in the province of Granada put it, 'we do not have much time to organize our forces, while the caciques already have a perfect electoral machine'. The relatively small number of protests accepted by Maura (he received about 2,500), indicate, however, that suggestions, like that of the governor of Teruel, to dissolve all the Monarchist municipalities in the province, despite the fact that the elections were not challenged there, were utterly disregarded. On the other hand, a case like that of Santa Elena (Jaén) where Maura insisted on new elections 'because the Ayuntamiento is composed exclusively of old politicians', seems to indicate that vindictiveness against Monarchists was not altogether alien to the minister's policies.[59]

The practice by which *Comisiones Gestoras* (composed exclusively of Republicans and Socialists) were appointed to run the *Diputaciones Provinciales* as well as Ayuntamientos in which the April elections were annulled as corrupt was obviously to substitute the Monarchist caciquismo of April by a Republican caciquismo for the May elections. The Comisiones Gestoras were expected to deal only with urgent administrative questions

[59] Hundreds of telegrams were sent to Maura, either from the governors or from political elements in the villages, concerning these matters. They are collected in AHN. See only selected examples: From Republicans opposing the May elections because they had won: Guadamar del Segura (Alicante) Leg. 31, 18 May 1931 no. 1137; Campillos (Málaga), Leg. 29, 2 May 1931, no. 109; Lorca, Leg. 29, 18 May 1931 no. 1181; Alcudia de Crespins (Valencia) Leg. 29, 16 May 1931 no. 1018; Badalona (Barcelona) Leg. 31, 19 May 1931 no. 2042; Corte Peleas (Badajoz) Leg. 31, 19 Apr. 1931 no. 1861; Berja (Almería) Leg. 31, 7 May 1931 no. 436; Fuente Palmera (Córdoba) Leg. 31, 21 May 1931 no. 1386. From Republicans suggesting their appointment without elections: Satillo Adrade (Avila) Leg. 31, 29 May 1931 no. 2058; Foz (Lugo) Leg. 31, 26 May 1931 no. 1800, here, a similar proposition by 32 Ayuntamientos of Aragón was mentioned. See also *Boletín de Administracion Local* 14 May 1931; The telegram from Granada is in Leg. 31, 16 May 1931 no. 999. For caciquismo in the April elections see: Librilla (Murcia) Leg. 29, 16 Apr. 1931 no. 965; Governor of Orense to Maura Leg. 29, 16 Apr. 1931 no. 915; telegrams from the province of Oviedo, Leg. 29, 24 Apr. 1931, 2, 4, 9, 15 May 1931 no. 1605, 138, 228, 562, 949; Ossorio y Florit to Governor of Málaga Leg. 29, 28 Apr. 1931, a letter relating cases in that province; Canet (Barcelona) Leg. 31, 19 Apr. 1931 no. 1299; Palomares del Campo and Montalvo (Cuenca) Leg. 31, 9 May 1931 no. 574; telegrams from the province of Lugo in Leg. 31, 16, 17 Apr., 11 May 1931, nos. 981, 1005, 661. For the Governor of Teruel, see Leg. 29, 18 May 1931 no. 1172. For Santa Elena see Leg. 47: Maura to Governor of Jaén, 24 May 1931 no. 832.

until either the 'objection' was rejected or admitted by the minister, and in the last resort, until the elections on 31 May were held. But they became the agents of republicanism in the municipalities. They organized demonstrations of loyalty to the new regime; they substituted for street names with a monarchist connotation republican names; they expelled Monarchist activists from the pueblos and they controlled all municipal services.[60] There were even cases in which CG insisted on holding elections in spite of Maura's verdict that the Ayuntamiento elected in April should be restored.[61]

It should, however, be pointed out that the transition from Monarchist to Republican caciquismo was not always smooth. Not all caciques rushed to become Republicans. There were cases in which even the CG could not prevent powerful caciques from exerting pressure on the electorate. There were villages in Granada, Ciudad Real, Burgos, Jaén, Málaga, and Pontevedra where the Republican-Socialists were compelled to retire from the elections because of the unshattered power of Monarchist caciques.[62] These were still able to exercise improper influence on the electorate by offering jobs and by threatening to dismiss workers from their posts. In the province of Huelva, Burgos Mazo personally went from village to village to 'recommend' his men. The results of the elections in some places clearly reflected the continuity of the old caciquista influence. In Noya (La Coruña) the Republicans were unable to gain even one seat, and the *Calvo Sotelistas* and Liberals continued to dominate the Ayuntamiento. A similar trend was noticed in some pueblos of Murcia, Castellón, Alicante, Coruña, Lugo, and Huelva, where the Monarchists managed to have the upper hand. On

---

[60] Maura's circular letter on the CG is in AHN, Leg. 29, 16 Apr. 1931 no. 74. For bitter criticism against the CG and their activities see *La Voz de Galicia* 26 Apr., 21 May 1931; *ED* 18, 21, 29 Apr., 3, 9 May 1931. Tomas Valverde, *Memorias de un Alcalde* pp. 98–101; and AHN Leg. 16: Fernando de los Ríos to Maura 19, 27 May 1931, nos. 1223, 1851.

[61] AHN Leg. 29, 20 May 1931 no. 1292: a telegram from Santapola (Alicante); Leg. 31, 25 May 1931 no. 1685: from the 'Junta electoral' of S. Vicente del Horts (Barcelona) to Maura; *La Voz de Galicia* 29 Apr. 1931 on Coristanco (La Coruña).

[62] AHN Leg. 29: F. de los Ríos to Maura, 30 May 1931 nos. 2154, 2155, 2156 on examples from Jaén and Granada; 30 May 1931 no. 2152: a telegram from Archinoda (Málaga); 30 May 1931 no. 2097: from Mondariz (Pontevedra); Leg. 31, 29 May 1931 no. 2026: Medina Pomar (Burgos); Leg. 31, 31 May 1931 no. 2213: Luciana (C. Real).

the eve of the June elections there were still many Monarchist pueblos (after all there were also thousands in which no new elections were held) in which 'Viva el Rey' and the Monarchist hymn accompanied every official gathering.[63] The major trend, however, was that which led to an almost complete Republican victory, in a proportion of 8 to 1. But it ought to be pointed out that the 'Republican' victory in May like the 'Monarchist' victory of April had caciquista connotations. In both cases the rival was discriminated against, even 'persecuted'. Furthermore, the large 'Republican' majority in May was also the reflection of the influx of 'new' and superficial republicanism in rural Spain. It is highly suspicious to see a village which six weeks before was solidly Monarchist becoming now solidly Republican.[64] There were cases in which Monarchist caciques managed to infiltrate into the CG as Republicans, and Maura had to warn his governors against ex-*Upetistas* and 'undesirables' who joined the CG.[65] It seems that those who voted for the monarchy in April were those who gave now the victory to the Republicans. Republican factions in the pueblos pointed at the recent origin of their rivals. The Republican–Socialist coalition at Coin (Málaga) was presided over by well known caciques, and in Mula (Murcia), the Radical Socialist party was in close contact with the *Ciervistas*. In Galicia, *Bugallalistas* appeared in some places as Republicans, while ex-Upetistas preferred to act as Radicals.[66]

While Maura was worried by the rivalry between 'Republican'

[63] For examples of improper influence of caciques, see ibid. Leg. 31: Companario (Badajoz) 30 May 1931 no. 2110; Dolores (Alicante) 31 May 1931 no. 2209; Motilla de Palancer (Cuenca) 27 May 1931 no. 1829; a telegram from the Agrarian Syndicate in Huelva against Burgos y Mazo, 30 May 1931 no. 2105. For the caciquismo of a Monarchist mayor in Aracena (Huelva) see Leg. 47, 17 May 1931 no. 1076. For continuity reflected in results see Leg. 31: Noya (La Coruña) 31 May 1931 no. 2296; Puerto Lumbreras (Murcia) 1 June 1931 no. 8; Aracena (Huelva) 12 June 1931 no. 881; Azaña to Maura on Viver (Castellón) 2 June 1931 no. 171; Calpe (Alicante) 1 June 1931 no. 59; Mesia (La Coruña) 8 June 1931 no. 556; Puentedeume (La Coruña) 8 June 1931 no. 636; Monforte (Lugo) 31 May 1931 no. 2305; Bolanos (C. Real) 1 June 1931 no. 104. See also OA: Luciano Rodriguez (Carbia, Pontevedra) to Ortega, 31 July 1931. The last statement is based on *ES* 4 June 1931.

[64] Appendix II. See the case of Priego in Valverde, *Memorias de un Alcalde*, pp. 95–111.

[65] AHN Leg. 31: Maura to Governor of Lugo, 20 May 1931 no. 770.

[66] For some cases see ibid: Coin (Málaga) Leg. 29 no. 31, 1 June 1931; Mula. Leg. 29 no. 261, 3 June 1931; Ruavaldeorras and Verín (Orense) Leg. 29 no. 323, 324, 4 June 1931; Cervera del Rio Pisuerga (Palencia) Leg. 29 no. 229, 31 May 1931.

groups on the eve of the elections, the Governor of Tenerife wrote to him explaining the origin of this sudden republican effervescence:

Since there is a great confusion between new political groups ... which are joined by elements of a very doubtful republicanism, I suggest that you should be very careful in investigating their mutual complaints ... There are in this province personal feuds, traditionally rooted, but now reflected in these republican manœuvres.[67]

It is noteworthy, however, that these feuds reflected the crucial political transformation that was taking place in Spain. They represented the growing politicization of the countryside. During the Monarchy, not violent struggles but sheep-like obedience and gentlemanly electoral agreements had been the characteristic features of the silent, politically immobilized rural constituencies.[68] And so 'Republicans' dominated the electoral panorama in May. Even in the recently 'Monarchist' Galicia, the Republicans held the only meetings, while their *Guardia Cívica* (a civilian militia recruited among Republicans and Socialists) patrolled the streets, and the CG provided bands to escort the propagandists from village to village. The atmosphere was increasingly anti-monarchist, and monarchist coalitions preferred in some cases to retire from the elections, thus leaving the field either to pockets of caciquismo which did not go over to republicanism, or to the greater wave of new republicanism, which brought an almost total victory for the Republic. The unequivocal result, therefore, was that by the June elections, Republicans had assured their predominance in hundreds of rural Ayuntamientos by substituting for Monarchist caciquismo their own brand of electoral management.[69]

[67] Ibid. Governor of Tenerife to Maura, 26 May 1931 no. 1777.

[68] See C. Lison-Tolosana, *Belmonte de los Caballeros*, pp. 43–7 describing the sudden political effervescence and divisions in a small village in Aragón, which up to 14 April was politically indifferent. For how the system functioned in the past see J. Varela Ortega, 'Los Amigos Políticos; Funcionamiento del sistema caciquista', *Revista de Occidente* Oct. 1973 no. 127, pp. 45–74.

[69] For Galicia see *La Voz de Galicia* 14, 15, 17, 19–21 May 1931. For monarchists who won in April and retired in May see *El Norte de Castilla* 29 May (on the province of Avila), 2 June (on the 'Albistas' in Medina de Rioseco), and 5 June 1931 (on Monarchists in Toro). For the results of the elections see Appendix II.

3. TOWARDS THE GENERAL ELECTIONS

a. Monarchism in disarray

A general disbandment of the already dissolving monarchist groups took place in the first days after the declaration of the Republic. Prominent leaders like Barón de Viver and Conde de Montseny from Barcelona, the ex-Ministers Hoyos, Estrada, and the Conde de los Andes, aristocrats like Carlos de Borbón and the Marqués de Larios, and the leaders of the UM, all left for voluntary exile. A general mood of pessimism predominated in Monarchist milieux. So much so that the Marqués de Villabragima felt he had to deplore his colleagues' escape as 'unjustified and shameful'. The defenceless position in which they left their ideals by their escape 'is not the most adequate way to safeguard the dignity of their class . . . We must learn how to lose!' Gabriel Maura, though he referred to the new regime as 'the first Republican Dictatorship', recognized that the Monarchy had lost the support of the people and that, rather than through pointless conspiracies, only by a peaceful campaign to regain the national will could it be restored. In these circumstances all that remained for the monarchist press was to express its loyalty to the new regime and to urge it to see in the preservation of order its main task.[70]

As soon as the giddy republicanization of monarchist elements became clear, and the Catholic Angel Herrera threatened to bring an end to political monarchism by absorbing it into *Acción Nacional*, a conservative organization, 'neutral' as far as the form of regime was concerned, a demand for 'a mass monarchist party' was put forward. The separatist and 'communist' tendencies in the country only stressed further the need for such a party.[71] Already there had been plans to give a clandestine and conspiratorial character to the new party. It was suggested that a defamatory campaign be run against the Republic to jeopardize the economic effort of the government

---

[70] For the disbandment see Galindo Herrero, *Los Partidos Monárquicos*, p. 98. For voluntary expatriations see F.O. 371/15773: Colonial Office 11 May 1931 on those who left through Gibraltar. For the UM see *ABC* 22 Apr. 1931; and Acedo Colunga, *Calvo Sotelo* pp. 187–8. See the pessimism reflected in *Mujeres Españolas* 16 Apr. 1931; and in Faustino Albertos' letter to Romanones, 25 Apr. 1931 in RA Leg. 82, no. 14. Villabragima in *LE* 20 Apr. 1931. G. Maura in *ABC* 18 Apr. 1931.

[71] *LE* 25 Apr., 4, 9 May 1931; *ABC* 22, 26 Apr. 1931.

by fomenting the flight of capital, by boycotting its plans of development and by buying as little as possible; that the Republic be boycotted in the international community through influential newspapers in every capital city. This, and the growing rivalries within the San Sebastián coalition, would result in a total discrediting of the Republic. Then, it was believed, power would pass to the mass monarchist party either peacefully or with the support of the army, which would lose confidence in the Republic. If the plan was carried out 'the Republic would not last more than three months'.[72]

After a brief preparatory period, Monarchist leaders met on 10 May, to found a *Círculo Monárquico Independiente*. *ABC* and its director, Luca de Tena, were the leading spirits behind the experiment. The emphasis was therefore put on a refusal to follow *Acción Nacional*'s quest for 'action within the regime'. 'Monarchists should not be counted on' for collaboration with the Republic.[73] The influence of *ABC* was reflected also in the fact that the old figures like Romanones, La Cierva, Bugallal were by-passed. It was a generation of new men, not discredited by their past, which would assume the leadership of the party: F. Santander, Garrido Juaristi, Danvila, the Conde de Gamazo, Antonio Bernabeu, and Arsenio Martínez Campos.[74] In spite of exhortations from King Alfonso not to follow illegal procedures,[75] the Monarchists gathered in the Círculo Monárquico seem to have struck to the conspiratorial plan traced above. Huge sums of money, which they had not been able to raise on the eve of the

---

[72] RA Leg. 63 no. 65: *Breves Consideraciones Acerca del Pasado, del Presente y del Porvenir del Partido Monárquico Español.* See for some examples of anti-republican leaflets: ibid. Leg. 14 no. 14: *Hojas Libres. Segunda epoca* no. 3; Leg. 14 no. 23, *Versos Contra la República.* Alarming gossip was said to be spread by Monarchists, and a picturesque underground Monarchist group called 'Los Cruzados' was alleged to have been discovered, see *ES* 14, 21 May 1931. The flight of capital, however, was not necessarily the direct result of a Monarchist conspiracy; *ES* 19 May 1931 confessed that this was a practice which capitalists in Spain had frequently used since the First World War, including during Primo's Dictatorship, when they believed that their interests were endangered by political changes. See also F.O. 371/15772: a report from the British consul in Barcelona 22 Apr. 1931 reporting on 27 million pesetas transferred to British banks 'as a precautionary measure'.

[73] *ABC* 29 Apr., 7, 9, 10 May 1931.

[74] G. Maura, *Recuerdos* p. 245. He did not attend the meeting because 'the organizers told me that they thought the absence of the ex-ministers preferable'.

[75] *ABC* 5 May 1931. See also MA: 'Letters to Prudencio': Gabriel Maura to Prudencio Rovira, 26 May 1931, on his conversation with the king.

municipal elections, were collected consequently in a matter of weeks, in order to carry out a combined attempt to discredit the Republic and to overthrow it with the help of military elements.[76] Conspiracy was perhaps the only way open to uncompromising Monarchists in the aftermath of the events of 10–11 May. Their demonstrative and arrogant behaviour in the CMI provoked a violent crowd reaction which developed into an attack on *ABC*'s building, and into the festival of the 'burning of convents' on the following day. A violent anti-monarchist campaign was the result. *ABC* and *El Debate* were suspended, the former for about a month. The republican press came out against 'these *Camelots du Roi* with a fascist education', and urged the government 'to be more tough towards the right', and to abandon its initial moderation. Monarchist leaders were arrested regardless of legal procedures, and those who were free were careful not to provoke the extreme left or the government by any open manifestation of monarchist feelings. Gabriel Maura wrote, 'the atmosphere of hatred towards us is unbreathable'. *El Imparcial* summed up accurately the situation when it wrote: 'The Monarchist Party could be now nothing but an incitement to riots, an element of disorder ... because its smallest manifestation as a party was sufficient to arouse in the people the cry of 'The Republic must be defended''.[77]

A monarchist electoral campaign for the June elections was, under such circumstances, virtually non-existent. The old

---

[76] *EC* 16 May 1931; See *El Economista* 16 May 1931 quoting Prieto's allegation that the monarchist plot included 'a financial offensive in order to bring about the collapse of the shares in the stock exchange'. He, therefore, ordered immediately the closure of the stock exchange. See SA Leg. 1304: minute from the Spanish Embassy in Paris, 5 July 1931, on conspiratorial activities of the emigrés in France. See AHN Leg. 16: Governor of Salamanca to Maura 14 May 1931 no. 830 on an alleged conspiracy with military and ecclesiastical elements. See also Hugh Thomas, *The Spanish Civil War*, pp. 39–40.

[77] *EI* 13 May 1931. For the clash in front of the CMI see R. Sánchez Guerra, *Proceso*, pp. 181–4; Maura, *Así*, pp. 241–6. Even the monarchist *LV* 13 May 1931 agreed that the Monarchists behaved provocatively. An eyewitness account: *Estampa* 16 May 1931. For the republican press see *ES* and *EC* 12 May 1931. For the illegal arrest and harassment of Monarchists see the protest of the Bar Association in *Boletín Informativo del Ilustre Colegio de Abogados de Madrid*, Apr. 1931; *The Times* 13 May 1931; and Albiñana, *Prisionero de la República*, pp. 14–18. For the panic among the right see Gil Robles, *No Fué Posible*, p. 63. For Gabriel Maura see his letter to Rovira, 16 May 1931 in MA 'Letters to Prudencio'. See also Silió César, *En Torno a una Revolución*, pp. 170–4 on May as the turning-point in the attitude towards the right.

leaders disbanded their parties. Alba and García Prieto issued statements leaving their followers free to follow other paths; Gabriel Maura left, after the events of May, for Biarritz, 'whose hotels are full of Monarchists'. The Liberals in Catalonia started a process of republicanization, though paying lip-service to Romanones, and those in Madrid were determined to help in the 'defence of the Republic' against extremisms of both right and left. Romanones did not dare to run an electoral campaign in Madrid, preferring to appear in the less excited Guadalajara as an Independent Monarchist. García Prieto who had first thought to put forward his candidature in León abandoned the idea later because of Maura's annihiliation of rural Monarchist municipalities. Only Calvo Sotelo dared to make an electoral platform of both his monarchism and his collaboration with the Dictatorship; but he did it while sitting in Portugal. And when he was finally elected the government refused to guarantee his personal security if he returned to Spain. *ABC* had been preaching, since its reappearance in the first week of June, for electoral abstention. 'The paralysis of our activities, the campaign against our press, the arrest of our colleagues, and the manipulation of the Ayuntamientos' made inevitable such an attitude. The electoral reform of the government abolishing the small electoral districts where old caciquismo could still exert pressure, and limiting the chances of small parties, were also an important factor in *ABC*'s considerations. It was an irony that *La Epoca* and *El Imparcial* were now desperately hoping for a victory of Lerroux and the Republican right as the only guarantee for 'a Republic of order'.[78]

With monarchism in disarray, the values of traditional Spain were to be defended in the June elections by the group of *Acción Nacional*, Agrarian deputies from Castille and León, the Carlists and Basque Nationalists. This obviously reflected the basic difference between the general and the municipal elections.

[78] For Alba and García Prieto see *The Times* 23 May 1931; *El Sol* 21 June 1931. For the Liberals see *LV* 1, 23 May, 6, 21 June 1931; *EI* 12, 14 May 1931. For Romanones see *ABC* 19 June 1931; and RA Leg. 52 no. 26: *Carta que los liberales de Guadalajara Dirigen a Romanones*. The word 'Monarchy' was not even mentioned. For C. Sotelo see his *En Defensa Propia*, pp. 128, 132–3. For *ABC*'s abstentionist campaign see 7, 8 May, 6, 7, 17 June 1931. See also the manifesto of abstention of Monarchist candidates in Avila in *ABC* 12 June 1931; and that of the junta of the CMI in Gutierrez-Ravé, *España en 1931*, p. 189. See finally *LE* 15 June 1931; and *EI* 19 June 1931.

The Monarchy was no longer a topic. The issue was now the defence of Catholicism and tradition against the anti-clericalist policy of the government and against the excessively leftist tendencies of some of its members in social and agrarian matters. But with only regional strongholds in their possession and with an embryonic organization, AN and its allies were not a serious electoral threat to the left.[79]

b. The disintegration of the San Sebastián coalition

The disappearance of an anti-Republican threat obviously made the need to close ranks among Republican less necessary. The first months of the Republic and the subsequent electoral campaign witnessed an accentuation both of the specific character of each of the parties in the San Sebastián coalition and of the ideological gap between them. This stood in striking contrast with the efforts displayed by the members of the coalition after August 1930 to minimize rather than to stress their differences. Moreover, on the eve of the June elections, long before the parliamentary debate on the constitution brought the breach into the open, the electoral alliance of the municipal elections was in total disarray.

The Socialists were now more than ever delighted with the options opened to them by the bourgeois Republic, though the *Besteirista* wing continued to be critical of 'ministerial collaboration'. This enabled them to continue their reformist orientation, and provided their members with a great number of administrative posts. The smooth transition from Monarchy to Republic strengthened their confidence that evolutionary methods and 'legal channels' would bring 'a social content' to the Republic. Although they continued to claim that 'this is not yet our revolution', Socialists were determined to collaborate with the bourgeois Republic, and to be its 'guardian', whether in power or in the opposition, in order to enable it to satisfy, by legislative procedures, the demands of the working class. Serrano Poncela put it in slogan form: 'We must say "Long live the

---

[79] For the origins and development of Acción Nacional, the Carlist movement and Basque nationalism see R.A.H. Robinson, *Origins of Franco's Spain: Right, Republic and Revolution 1931–1936*, pp. 39–40, 44–6, 54–5 and Appendix 2 pp. 415–24 on AN; pp. 46–8, 56 on the Carlists; 48–9, 56 on the Basques; 57–8 on the Agrarians; R.M. Blinkhorn, *Carlism* pp. 51–6 on the electoral campaign of Carlists and Basque Nationalists.

Republic" before we can say "Long live the Socialist Republic"'.
The revolution would have to be carried out in the parliament,
in order to prevent the 'incoherent and undisciplined mob'
from discrediting the new regime in street riots. Manuel
Cordero saw the federal constitution of Germany 'with its
exciting social content', as the desired solution for Spain, while
Largo Caballero strongly advocated a 'legal revolution'. He
assured 'capitalists, employers, and the bourgeoisie' that 'extremism would never take root in Spain'. What would be
established, according to Fernando de los Ríos, was a 'social
and *almost* socialist orientation'.[80]

This line of argument was generally followed by the Socialist
unions, though their declarations reflected a greater eagerness
for immediate material gains. The union of Railway Workers
was impatient to see the nationalization of railways, the
dismissal of soldiers who had been employed in the place of
dismissed workers, and the recognition of the eight-hour day.
But in spite of the fact that Trifón Gómez, their national
secretary, ruled out the question of nationalization, and that
only in July were their last two demands met, the union
maintained its faith in the government 'and in legal means'.
This enabled a rival union sponsored by the CNT to attract
Ugetistas who became disappointed with evolutionary tactics.[81]
Equally disappointed was the union of teachers who opposed
Marcelino Domingo's sympathetic approach to Catalan demands
for bilingual education, and his leniency towards 'reactionary
teachers and inspectors'. They would have preferred a 'radical
reform like that carried out by Azaña in the army'. Yet they
were confident in the final outcome of Republican legislation.
[82] The Theatre and Cinema Employees Union put it in these
terms:

[80] *ES* 16, 22, 26, 30 Apr. 1931. For Besteiristas see Gabriel Mario de Coca, *Anti-
Caballero, Crítica Marxista de la Bolshevización del Partido Socialista (1930–1936)*, pp. 31–2.
ES 24 Apr., 22, 23, 27 May, 2, 4 June 1931 (Serrano Poncela, Cordero, Largo,
Fernando de los Ríos, Besteiro). See also Cordero in his *Los Socialistas*, pp. 93–9. For a
criticism on the reformism of the Socialists during the first stage of the Republic and on
Socialist *enchufismo* see J. Andrade, *La Burocracia*, pp. 241–6; and G. Morón, *La Ruta*, pp.
31–2, 36, 86–110.
[81] *La Unión Ferroviaria* 25 Apr., 10, 25 June, 10 July 1931. For T. Gómez see *ES* 7
May 1931.
[82] *Trabajadores de la Enseñanza* 5 June 1931.

We must not think that we will easily obtain an immediate solution of our problems by the mere fact of the proclamation of the Republic. Our problems will be difinitively solved by a transformation of the capitalist regime ... meanwhile, our duty is to defend the Republic, and our mission is to consolidate it.[83]

The most threatening element in the UGT was the FNTT. Its spectacular growth since the proclamation of the Republic[84] reflected not only the encouragement given to agricultural workers and peasants to join the UGT by the Socialist-sponsored *jurados mixtos,* but also a growing pressure on the Socialists to carry out an agrarian reform.[85] But in spite of alarming symptoms of dissatisfaction among rural workers with the mild agrarian measures of the government,[86] the Socialists were able to lead the FNTT along moderate lines until late 1933.

The moderate features of Spanish socialism were obviously accentuated by the spectacular influx of 'new Socialists'. The UGT which at the beginning of 1931 claimed a membership of 274,000 claimed to have increased in October 1931 by 250 per cent, reaching a figure of 690,436 members. The average increase per week jumped from about 150 until April 1931 to about 1,500 in the weeks following the proclamation of the Republic. There were even days with an average of 2,000 new members. The increase in the party, though lower in absolute terms, was relatively higher. From about 17,590 in June 1930 it jumped to 67,205 members in November 1931, an increase of 380 per cent.[87] Socialist leaders admitted that, though it

---

[83] *Unión de Espectáculos,* Aug. 1931. See also the moderation of May Day petitions of local unions in AHN Leg. 50: 'Peticiones Hechas por las Entidades Obreras el Dia 1 de Mayo de 1931'.

[84] From 275 unions and 36,639 members in June 1930, it reached in April 1932, 2,232 local unions and 308,579 members. See Malefakis, *Agrarian Reform,* p. 292.

[85] F. de los Ríos in *ES* 10 June 1931.

[86] See the case of the province of Jaén in OA: Governor of Jaén to Ortega 23 July 1931. For a more general view see García Menéndez, *La España Rural,* pp. 258–9. The May Day demands of the UGT and PSOE on agrarian matters were, according to *ES* 24 Apr. 1931, 'compatible with any advanced capitalist regime'. The demands are in *BUGT* May 1931.

[87] For the UGT see *BUGT* May, July, Nov., Dec. 1931; and *Almanaque de El Socialista* 1932. E. Santiago claimed that these figures included only those who paid their membership dues. He estimated the real number at 1 million in Nov. 1931. The *Anuario Estadístico* 1931 gave for that period the figure of 958,451 members. For the party see *Almanaque* 1932.

strengthened the political influence of the movement, this sudden influx 'of those who came to us not by conviction, but because of the fashion' seriously endangered the purity of their organization. E. Santiago called them 'the emissaries of the bourgeoisie', while Besteiro claimed that he preferred a qualitative rather than a quantitative increase. In the youth sections of the party, many thought that the newcomers were motivated by a belief that the Socialists were about to assume power, and, therefore, 'posts for councillors and deputies' would be available. The spectacular increase of the CNT—it claimed 600,000 members in June 1931 after having almost disappeared during the Dictatorship—and Largo Caballero's claim that extremist elements were stopped from joining the UGT, might indicate that the bulk of new members came mainly from moderate sectors, including Catholic syndicates.[88]

The CNT's violent campaign, and to a lesser extent that of the small Communist movement, against the bourgeois Republic and its Socialist collaborators as soon as the initial euphoria was over, compelled the Socialists to stress further their identification with moderation.[89]

They responded by using the same old arguments, now further emphasized by the concrete 'achievements' of the Republic. They attacked the extreme left for its unrestrained campaign of agitation and strikes against the Republic. 'The Anarcho-Syndical-Communists are the unconditional collaborators of the most black reaction'. Cordero rejected the attacks on Largo Caballero by claiming that 'from the Ministry of Labour, he is carrying out the social revolution'. 'We', he said,

[88] *BUGT* Nov. 1931 (E. Santiago); *ES* 31 May, 4, 11 June 1931 (Largo, Besteiro, the youth). See also Cordero, *Los Socialistas*, pp. 328–33. According to Caballero there was a week in which 24,000 new members joined in, see Dominique, *Marche, Espagne*, p. 108. See the criticism in Coca, *Anti-Caballero*, pp. 37–9. For Catholics joining the UGT see *Boletín del Sindicato Católico de Tipógrafos y Similares de Madrid* Apr.–Aug. 1931. For the CNT see *SO* 3, 12 June 1931.

[89] *SO* did not stop denigrating the Republic and its Socialist collaborators. For selected references see 8, 14, 26, 28, 30 May, 10, 19 June 1931. See also the *Cenetista* Publication in Madrid, *Vida y Trabajo* 13 June 1931; and also on the hostility to Caballero's legislation see J. Peirats, *Los Anarquistas*, p. 72. For a similar approach by Communists to the bourgeois Republic and its Socialist leaders see: *La Batalla* 23 Apr., 1, 21, 28 May, 11 June 1931; *La Bandera Roja* 6 June 1931; and a highly sarcastic attack on Caballero in *Boletín de la Sociedad de Obreros Encuadernadores de Madrid*, II trimestre 1931. See also *Manifiesto de la Fracción de Estudiantes Comunistas*, in RA Leg. 20 no. 25.

'are revolutionary and conservative at the same time.' Strikes, it was alleged, were unnecessary at a time when workers' representatives governed the country.[90]

Support of the bourgeois Republic as such did not entail loyalty to the San Sebastián alliance. Rather, in their electoral campaign in general and for local electoral purposes, the Socialists strove to stress their differences from their allies, using a radical tone. They demanded that the Republic should be 'filled with the red substance of the European revolutionary vanguard'. Fernando de los Ríos defined this substance as 'a social orientation of the constitution', and in socially turbulent Seville, a Socialist manifesto spoke of the need 'to get rid of . . . those hundreds of latifundistas, caciques, usurers, señoritos'. In some rural districts the Socialists used even more extreme language, similar to that of the CNT, in order to rally ignorant agricultural workers. As far as their relations with other parties of the coalition were concerned, the Socialists continued to stress their circumstantial character, and the fact that they did not make any concession to their bourgeois allies.[91]

In fact, the Socialists were aware of the disintegration of the coalition, and they seemed to welcome it. *El Socialista* pointed out that 'the partial break-up' of the alliance was a fact, and, 'to be sincere', it added, 'we must confess that rather than disturbing us, it flatters us'. It proved that the Socialists were about to struggle for their 'social Republic', and it was, therefore, 'not surprising that the common factors that united us with the revolutionary bourgeoisie have begun to be eroded'.[92] The

---

[90] See *ES* 29–31 May, 6 June 1931 (Ramos Oliveira, Largo, Cordero); E. Santiago, *La UGT* pp. 100–7; Cordero, *Los Socialistas*, p. 308. 1930 was a year of many strikes, but 1931 surpassed it. 734 strikes were recorded in 1931 in comparison with 402 in 1930. During the first four months of 1931 there were an average of 30 strikes per month, but during May–July the figures rose to 140 strikes. Most of them were sponsored by the CNT or by the Communists. See *Anuario Estadístico* 1931; and *Boletín de Información Social del Ministerio de Trabajo y previsión*, July 1931. See some reports of *The Times* on strikes indicating the special role of Communists and Anarcho–Syndicalists: 28–30 May, 6, 9, 12 June 1931.

[91] For 'red' Socialist propaganda see *ES* 23 June 1931; F. de los Ríos in ibid. 26 May 1931; *El Liberal Sevilla*, 19 May 1931; the meeting at Ecija in *ABC, Sevilla* 16 June 1931; the manifesto *Vecinos de Valdenoches* 21 May 1931 in RA Leg. 30; Jiménez de Asua, *Anecdotas*, pp. 17–19; *El Nuevo Evangelio* 4 July 1931. For the circumstantiality see Sanchís Banús in *ES* 20 June 1931; and *El Sol* 27 June 1931.

[92] For the break of the coalition see below, pp. 296–300; and *ES* 27 June 1931. See ibid., also T. Gómez's speech.

Socialists therefore intensified their attacks on the DR as the representative of reactionary bourgeois republicanism least compatible with the final aims of socialism. Maura and Alcalá Zamora were denounced for opening 'the gates of the Republic' to 'Monarchist forces in disarray . . . Liberals . . . Conservatives . . . Jaimistas . . . Jesuits . . .'. If this trend continued, the DR would have to be considered as 'the enemy of the Republic', because it might destroy the 'authenticity of the revolution' by enabling men of the old regime to draw up the new constitution.[93]

The DR was indeed accentuating its conservative nature while the Socialists and left Republicans were demanding a more radical Republic. It absorbed many of the old caciques of the Monarchy and the remnants of its political parties. Santiago Alba exhorted his 'friends' to 'establish cordial friendship with the Republican forces nearest to them'. Subsequently 'the great majority of the Albistas', according to Chapaprieta, joined the Derecha Republicana, because of its 'liberal' and 'evolutionary' principles. Chapaprieta was immediately appointed by Maura and Alcalá Zamora as director of the party's electoral campaign, aimed at 'pushing the Republic towards the right'. He considered the DR as a potential 'mass party' which would create 'half a million or more small property owners in order to solve, once and for all, the social question'. Many of the rural caciques, like the *Ciervistas* in Carabaca (Murcia), who went over to the Republic, now joined the DR as a respectable compromise between their rightism and the fashionable necessity of becoming Republican. Even the pseudo-Republican and Catholic right represented by *El Debate* seemed to be highly interested in the success of the DR. It welcomed the affiliation of ex-Monarchists to the party as likely 'to strengthen it'. This would enable it to become 'a religious and social right'. *El Debate* was interested in maintaining 'good relations' with the DR 'because', as it put it, 'we represent fundamentally the same things'. It therefore urged the DR not to give in to extremists' demands in the coalition. Otherwise the Catholics would be compelled to create a 'genuine right', and the DR would be isolated and attacked by both right and left. Miguel Maura himself seemed to be aware of the importance of *El Debate*'s support. So much so that

[93] *ES* 7, 9, 11, 19 June 1931 (Alvarez Angulo; resolutions of the youth congress).

he proposed that Angel Herrera should harness the Catholic elements represented by *El Debate* and his own personal influence to the DR.[94]

However, it was probably the early discredit of the party among Catholics following the 'burning of convents', the alienation from Maura of many Monarchist councillors who had been dismissed on the eve of the May elections, and the growing prospects of creating a 'genuine right', that brought Herrera to reject Maura's proposition. Both in the crisis of 11 May and in the May elections, Maura had acted as a man of government rather than as a party leader; and his party's alienation from the right seemed to be the result.[95]

The influx of ex-Monarchists into the party and the undemocratic procedure by which Maura and Alcalá Zamora appointed Chapaprieta as 'the election maker' (a term with caciquista connotations used by a Communist newspaper) caused a serious crisis in the party. So much so that the ex-*Albista* Roig y Bergadá who contemplated joining the party, had to go back on his decision because, as he wrote to Alcalá Zamora: 'I could not suspect people proceeding from the dissolved *Izquierda liberal* would be so wildly opposed as members of the party'. The Zaragoza branch of the DR even refused to include the recently joined *Ossoristas* (the following of Ossorio y Gallardo) in its candidature for the general elections, and they had to withdraw; while in Alicante old members of the party made it clear that they would not vote for Chapaprieta.[96]

In the Madrid branch, Torrubiano Ripoll led a group of dissidents into an open split. They denounced the 'Monarchist

[94] *El Norte de Castilla* 19, 23 May 1931 (Alba, Chapaprieta). See also Chapaprieta, *La paz*, p. 151. For the influx of rural caciques into the party see *El Nuevo Evangelio*, 20 June, 4 July 1931. García Menendez, *La España Rural*, p. 250 claims that 60 per cent of the rural caciques joined the DR. For Caravaca see AHN Leg. 16: Governor of Murcia to Maura, 20 May 1931 no. 1322. *ED* 6 June 1931. Maura gave an account of his approach to Angel Herrera to his grandson, J. Romero Maura, who related it to the present writer.

[95] For the alienation of the right by the anti-Catholic measures and by the May elections, see Burgos y Mazo, *De la Republica*, pp. 111, 114; Roig Ibáñez, *La Primera Etapa de la Segunda República Española*, pp. 162–71; Francisco Narbona, *La Quema de Conventos*, pp. 14–15; and MA: Gabriel Maura to Prudencio, 16 May, 25 Oct. 1931.

[96] The Communist organ is *Control* 24 May 1931. Roig y Bergadá in *LV* 31 May 1931. 'Ossoristas' in *EL Sol* 21 June 1931. Ossorio finally found his way into a conservative slate called 'Support for the Republic', see *Estampa* 27 June 1931. For Alicante see *ABC* 19 June 1931.

infiltration' as 'dangerous for the consolidation of the Republic'. Since the junta appointed arbitrarily by Maura and Alcalá Zamora was 'the symbol of the most characteristic feature of the old regime', they appealed to the other Republican Parties not to forge any electoral pact with the official DR, but only 'with us, the old Republicans'. The dissidents started a campaign of defamation against Maura and Alcalá Zamora and the 'Chapadominio' in the party. In their manifestos they pointed out how the DR was ruled autocratically, being the only Republican Party which had never held a democratic assembly since its foundation. They were aware of the isolation of the party among other Republican groups, and they believed that unless a move towards the centre and an end to *caudillismo* were brought about, the DR would remain an anachronistic remnant of the old regime. The conservative line pursued by the party until then, they alleged, did not indicate that there was any difference between the DR and *Acción Nacional*.[97]

Maura was probably right when he referred to the dissidents as a 'minute problem', but he was wrong in underestimating their impact on the future of the party. Their attacks were followed by those of other Republican parties in the coalition; and the DR, which lost the support of many Catholics because of its tacit approval of anti-religious measures, was on the eve of the June elections isolated in the Republican camp.[98]

The DR was probably closer in its ideas to the Radical Party than to any other group of the coalition. Both stood for autonomism rather than separatism, religious freedom combined with respect towards the Church and the religious orders, and a moderate agrarian reform which would create a Conservative Republic of small landowners. But the DR lacked both the 'historical prestige' and the strength of the Radicals. This made it less respectable to other Republicans. Its meetings were violently interrupted by leftist Republicans, and Alcalá Zamora's manifestations of Catholicism were dismissed as 'electoral

[97] *El Sol* 23 May 1931; *La Tierra* 27 May 1931; and the following manifestos in RA Leg. 2 no. 18: *En Apoyo de la República*, 5 June 1931; *Convocatoria a la Primera Asamblea del Partido*, 5 June 1931. See also an open letter of R. Marín del Campo to Chapaprieta in *La Tierra* 3 June 1931. In the elections in Madrid they had a separate slate, see *Candidatura de Pureza Republicana*, and *Bando de Propaganda de la Candidatura de Pureza Republicana*, In HMM A/1686, 1678.
[98] Maura in *El Sol* 28, 29 May 1931.

exhibitionism' by the left. Nor did they convince the Catholic right that the DR was doing enough to curb the efforts of some ministers 'to put us outside the law', as *El Debate* put it. With Chapaprieta leading the electoral campaign of the party, and appealing to 'the conservative classes' to rally for the defence 'of their legitimate moral and material interest', the DR could not hope to draw the sympathy of its colleagues in the coalition, unless it became such a large party that no government could exist without its support. And it was ultimately its failure to create a strong conservative party, rather than its doctrines, which caused the DR to be thrown out of the coalition'.[99] Its failure, however, to absorb the Catholics into a mass conservative republican party was to have fatal consequences for the Republic. Catholics were to feel alienated from the 'sectarian' Republic, and thrown into a position of confrontation rather than collaboration with the Republic.

In fact, for local electoral purposes DR's speakers even coined 'revolutionary' slogans that obviously frightened the right. In Seville, where the revolutionary tension was high and an extreme Republican faction, led by R. Franco and Balbontín, was clamorously campaigning for 'land to the people' and for a revolutionary social Andalucian Republic, the DR committed itself 'not to oppose the legitimate popular aspirations of the Andalucians'. Its local leader, J. Centeno, while confessing publicly that it was a mistake to appoint 'suspect men' as electoral organizers, claimed that his party was as revolutionary as any other, and wanted 'the land to belong to those who work it'. Probably the most leftist speech, delivered at an electoral meeting of the Republican–Socialist coalition in Zamora, was Maura's. He denounced the Catholics as 'cowards', for not defending their churches on the day of the 'burning of convents'. He proclaimed his party's adherence to the principles of separation of Church and state, and of the abolition of latifundios.[1]

[99] For interruption of meetings see *ABC* 24, 26, 27 June 1931 (Alicante, Guadalajara, Ciudad Real). For Alcalá-Zamora's Catholicism see *Catalunya* 15 May 1931; *ED* 16 June 1931. For the programme see Chapaprieta in *EI* 17 June 1931; and Alcalá Zamora's speech in Jaén, *ABC* 23 June 1931.

[1] For Seville see *El Liberal, Sevilla* 4 June 1931, *ABC, Sevilla* 27 June 1931. For the ambiance and Franco's revolutionary activities see Maura in *El Sol* 28 June 1931; and *DSCC* 20 July 1931; E. Vila, *Un Año*, pp. 63–72, 87–99; Balbontín, *La España*, pp. 232–6. See Maura's speech in Zamora in *ABC* 16 June 1931.

But the connections of the party with *Albistas*, with the 'friends' of Burgos Mazo in Huelva, and with Monarchist caciques like those of the ex-Deputy Fernández Jiménez in Córdoba, in addition to its basic conservatism, all led to its becoming anathema among the left. Republican Socialist coalitions denounced the DR as 'an organization not yet liberated from its own monarchist sentiments', which could stymie the 'transformation of Spain in all its aspects'. It is noteworthy that even Melquiades Alvarez's new *Partido Republicano Liberal Demócrata* was not repudiated by Republicans in the same violent terms that the DR's ex-Monarchists were. *El Crisol* claimed that the PRLD was very welcome, because the Republic was its 'natural home', unlike others 'who now join the Republic'. Azaña even negotiated an electoral pact with Melquiades. His electoral propaganda was, however, interrupted by the Socialists in Oviedo.[2]

Lerroux's Radical Party went through a similar process of accentuated rightism, but the undisputed authority of Lerroux and the solid organization of the party avoided any serious crisis. The case of the Santander branch in which some of the members deserted the party as a protest against 'the flirtation with the DR', was an extreme and rare case. In Catalonia, however, because of the *Esquerrista* predominance, Radicals did not always follow Lerroux's moderation, and they made attempts to cope with the revolutionary language of the *Esquerra*. But Lerroux became a refuge for Catholics, bourgeois and capitalists who wanted to safeguard their interests in the new regime. His speeches were a constant assurance to these sectors that the Republic, as far as he was concerned, would incarnate the principles of order, peace and no persecution of the Church.[3]

In his electoral campaign Lerroux presented himself as the champion of moderation and gradualism. His men brought to the provinces the message that as Cesar Puig put it in Alcoy,

[2] For monarchist connections see *ABC, Sevilla* 17, 20 June 1931; and Alba's candidature in Zamora: *El Sol* 18, 19 June 1931. For the coalition's attitude see the articles of Luis Bello and Antonio Espina in *EC* 23, 26 May 1931; and the meeting in Valladolid, *El Norte de Castilla* 25 June 1931; and manifesto of the coalition, *Al Pueblo de Madrid*, 22 June 1931, in HMM A/1680. For the PRLD see *EC* 26 May 1931; and its moderate republican programme in Mariano Cuber, *Melquiades Alvarez*, pp. 112–31.

[3] For Santander see *El Sol* 19 June 1931. For Catalonia, see Solá Cañizares, *El Moviment*, p. 126. For Lerroux see his *Pequeña Historia* pp. 96–7, 106, 108.

'the revolution with barricades in nineteenth-century style is out of date'.[4] He asked for 'discipline' and respect toward religion 'which, after all, is not a tyranny, but a consolation'. The 'social justice' which he asked for should not be achieved through 'vindictive actions'. In Badajoz, he openly appealed to the left 'not to push', while to the right he promised, 'I am a man of order. I am a conservative when faced with anarchism.' His concession to the left was a vague promise that he was 'revolutionary when faced with stagnation'. Against the leftist quest for a social Republic, Lerroux put forward the demand for 'a progressive Republic' supported by the urban and rural middle classes. He agreed that certain reforms in the system of property ownership would have to be introduced, but he emphasized that he would oppose any attempt to suppress 'the bourgeoisie and capitalism'. He also opposed the leftist demand for a dissolution of religious communities, which, he said, should be respected just like the trade unions. He warned his colleagues in the government not to develop sectarian policies, 'because the Republic', he said, 'does not belong only to the Republicans'.[5]

The only sphere in which Lerroux's opinion seemed to coincide with that of both the right and the left in the government was on the Catalan question. They all agreed that Maciá should be prevented from violating the San Sebastián pact, and all of them, in spite of confessions of federalism, were essentially *españolistas*. Lerroux was still the most outstanding representative of *españolismo* and anti-separatism in Catalonia. This was reflected in his capacity to form an electoral coalition there with the ACR, the DR and the Socialists. In Galicia, though not in such a large coalition, the Radicals of Abad Conde played down the extremist autonomist demands, but promised Galicia 'ample concessions'.[6]

Lerroux's new image in the Republic and his peculiar place

---

[4] *El Sol* 16 June 1931.

[5] See Lerroux's speeches in *El Sol* 24, 27, 28 June 1931 (Huesca, Valencia, Cáceres); *ABC* 9, 12, 23 June 1931 (Valencia, Badajoz, Barcelona). For the hopes of small landowners that Lerroux might curb social demagogy see SA, Leg. 1161: Augusto Villalonga to Lerroux, 28 Oct. 1931.

[6] Lerroux's attitude to the Catalan problem in *EI* 9, 25 June 1931. For other parties see *ABC* 16 June 1931 (Azaña); *ES* 10 May, 25 June 1931 (Socialists). For Galicia see *La Voz de Galicia* 20, 27 June 1931.

in the coalition was perhaps reflected, better than in any speech, by the euphoria of the republican moderate press and of monarchist organs. He was acclaimed as 'a great man of government', 'the master of the moment', 'the Spanish Tardieu',[7] and 'many ultra-rightists', and Monarchists, began to join his party. *La Epoca* pointed out with satisfaction that 'the Lerroux of 1931 is not the Lerroux of 1909', and it hopefully believed that he would be the next prime minister. *El Imparcial* claimed that 'even those who are not Republicans would have enthusiastically accepted a dictatorship of Lerroux, if necessary'. Perhaps more indicative than any other judgement on the new phase of Lerroux's image was Calvo Sotelo's statement that 'the defenders of peace and order should fix their attention on the figures of Lerroux and Melquiades'.[8]

The conservatism of the DR and the Radicals was incompatible with the accentuated leftism of the Republican left in the coalition. The Radical Socialists were especially worried with the influx of 'ex-fascists and ex-*Upetistas*' into the rightist parties, though the spectacular increase of the PRRS itself indicated that they also might have been attractive to new Republicans. They called for a firm policy towards monarchists and aristocrats. A simple political revolution was unsatisfactory, and they advocated 'a Republic of producers, an atheistic and anti-clerical regime sustained by a popular army'. The events of May further convinced them that only a radicalization of the Republic, to which the right and centre in the coalition were opposed, could bring to an end the 'conspiracies of reactionaries' against the regime. If the DR tolerated 'this shameful infiltration of monarchists' and insisted on a conservative line, 'the people would have to carry out its own violent revolution'. According to Ayensa, there was even no need to wait for the Constituent Cortes to elaborate a revolutionary

---

[7] Andre Tardieu (1876–1945): French statesman who was the leader of the Right-Centre in the Chamber during the inter-war period.
[8] For the right's euphoria around Lerroux see *El Sol* 23, 24 June 1931; *LE* 15 June 1931; *EL* 19, 25 June 1931; *ED* 16 June 1931. For 'ultra rightists' see *El Sol* 26 June 1931. For loyalty of Monarchists see SA Leg. 1161: José Toral to Lerroux, 9 May 1931; 'Directorio del Partido Liberal de Barcelona' to Lerroux, 15 June 1931. Calvo Sotelo, *En Defensa*, p. 124; Roig Ibáñez, *La Primera Etapa*, pp. 90–3. MA: letter to Prudencio, 25 Oct. 1931. The Anarchist *El Libertario* was suspended for publishing a 'revolutionary' speech by Lerroux from 1906, see *Control* 31 May 1931.

programme, because the plebiscite of April authorized the government to do so. Other members even suggested a reversion to nineteenth-century methods, replacing governors with 'provincial revolutionary juntas'. The Madrid section of the party, under the extremist leadership of Balbontín and Benjumea, asked the government for an immediate disarmament of 'the surviving forces of the old regime', and for the arming 'of the popular forces'. The programme of the PRRS should be carried out immediately by decree.[9]

These views came to a more demonstrative expression in the national assembly of the party, where some delegations urged the government to expel the Jesuits and to confiscate Church property. The representative of Elche exhorted the party to establish closer links with the Communist Party and with the CNT, in order 'to make possible the success of their initiatives'. The most practical motion to be put forward was, however, that of Balbontín who proposed to boycott any electoral alliance with the DR, thus officially bringing to an end the Republican consensus prior to April. 'We cannot unite with the DR and other caciquista organizations which do not follow an ideal, but only their own profit', declared E. Ortega in support of the motion. But the need to preserve the unity of the coalition was imposed by the national leadership of the party. However, the representatives of Seville and Madrid made it clear that they would act according to Balbontín's proposal. Furthermore, the final resolution obligated the party's representatives in the Cortes 'to support ... every principle and orientation which could lead to the promulgation of a social and radical constitution, and to the predominance of leftist forces and governments'.[10] The original *modus vivendi* of the republican

---

[9] The PRRS increased from 5,621 members and 168 branches in May 1931 to 72,815 members and 1,083 branches in May 1932, see *Texto Taquigráfico del Tercer Congreso Nacional Ordinario del PRRS*, pp. 29–40. For 'revolutionary juntas' see ibid. 429. See articles by Radical Socialists and other left Republicans in *NE* 17, 22, 29 Apr., 27 May, 10 June 1931. Ayensa in *El Sol* 9 May 1931. Balbontín in *ES* 22 Apr., 26 May 1931. See also García Menéndez, *La España Rural*, pp. 254–7.

[10] The party congress in *El Sol* 31 May 1931; and *El Liberal Sevilla* 2 June 1931. For the radicalism of the Madrid branch and its campaign against their party colleague, Galarza, who as Director de Seguridad was running the 'policy of repression of the conservative Maura', see *Texto Taquigráfico*, pp. 62–9, and Balbontín, *La España*, pp. 228–32. For the final resolution see SA Leg. 2613: *PRRS. Actitud del Partido ante las Constituyentes*.

coalition subscribed to by the national leaders was to be overwhelmed by this pressure from the rank and file. In its electoral propaganda the PRRS put forward the demand for a radical Republic. 'Social justice' and the 'transformation of the legal conception of property' were proposed. Alvaro de Albornoz even promised, in a gathering at the Murcia bullring, that his party would strive 'to nationalize wealth'. Equally uncompromising was their attitude in regard to education and Church. Albornoz called for a new 'statute of the Church', and his colleague Juan Moreno asked for compulsory secular education. Such a programme, the PRRS realized, could not be carried out by a heterogeneous government in which the moderating influence of the right prevailed. 'Only Republicans should rule' exclaimed Albornoz, not 'Monarchists disguised as Republicans'. Furthermore, the party propagandists maintained that whatever strength the Republican right might gather, 'it had no right' to stymie the revolution. Only a leftist government, according to Albornoz could 'republicanize the Republic'. The Republic, he added, should not be conservative 'because nothing has to be conserved'; as for the Cortes, Marcelino Domingo believed that the Republican right would feel very uncomfortable in it, because it should be 'a convention, a stormy assembly'.[11]

Azaña's *Acción Republicana* pursued a similar leftist line. This organization which did not consider itself as a party, decided by the end of May, after consulting its provincial branches, 'to constitute itself as a party with a leftist orientation'. In a speech in Valencia on 8 June, Azaña put this 'orientation' in violent terms: 'The problem is not the elaboration of a constitution . . . I prefer . . . 300 deputies ready to rise and to fling the thunder of popular anger at those responsible for Spanish tyranny, asking for their heads if necessary.' He maintained that the Republic should be radical or cease to exist. In his electoral propaganda, Azaña made clear his incompatibility with his major ally in *Alianza Republicana*, Lerroux. He warned that he would move even further to the extreme left, and would seek an alliance with the Socialists, as soon as the constitution was

---

[11] For selected extracts of propaganda meetings in the provinces see *El Sol* 16, 21 June 1931; *ABC* 9, 23, 27 June 1931; *LV* 26 May 1931; *El Norte de Castella* 16 June 1931; *El Liberal, Sevilla* 30 May 1931.

elaborated. This would mean separation from Lerroux, who would oppose 'a revolutionary' and 'secular' Republic.[12] In Catalonia the *Esquerra*, supported by the CNT, dominated the scene. This contributed to the creation of an electoral panorama which reflected an obvious fact: the San Sebastián coalition was not transformed into an electoral pact in Catalonia. The CNT explicitly warned its members 'not to vote for Lerroux and the Lliga, or for the Socialists'. Their national congress, rather than adopting an abstentionist position, pointed out their special interest in the Constituent Cortes ('a revolutionary product which was made possible by our help') to which they would like to present a 'minimum programme'. The Republican Parties were not able to present a serious challenge to the Esquerra. The DR was in disarray, many of its members joining the Radicals, and, since their *españolista* propaganda did not differ from that of Lerroux, they joined his slate which included Nicolau d'Olwer from ACR and Alcalá Zamora. ACR in fact did not present any separate candidature. Many of its members had deserted it for the Esquerra, and rather than facing a defeat like that of April, it preferred to scatter its candidates among other slates, including the Lliga's and Lerroux's. Lerroux's candidature, whose declared aim was to fight the social and political extremism of the Esquerra by mobilizing the conservative and capitalist Catalans, was also supported by the Socialists who, lacking any substantial strength in the region, joined what Lerroux called 'a candidature of harmony . . . which would enable us to bring the San Sebastián pact to the Cortes'. But they, as well as other Republicans, opposed his suggestion to invite even the Lliga to his 'slate of harmony'. This seemed to have disappointed the Lliga which sincerely hoped to forge an electoral alliance with Lerroux and the ACR to fight the social extremism of the Esquerra.[13]

The major representatives of the left and the right were, in

[12] For becoming a party see *El Sol* 22 May 1931. Azaña in Maura, *Así*, p. 227; *El Sol* 16, 27 June 1931; *ABC* 9, 16, 23 June 1931; *El Norte de Castilla* 23 June 1931.

[13] For CNT's support see *SO* 2, 24 June 1931. For their attitude to the Cortes see *SO* 25, 26 June 1931. For the DR see Isidre Molas, *Lliga*, pp. 233-5; and *LV* 19 May, 12, 27 June 1931. For ACR see *El* 18 June 1931. For the ACR's decline and virtual dissolution see Bofill i Mates, *Una Política*, pp. 59-61, 73-4, 88-91. For the Socialists and Lerroux's candidature see *LV* 20, 21, 24, 27, 28 June 1930. For the 'slate of concord' and other parties' attitude see SA Leg. 1161: Juan Pich to Lerroux, 13 June 1931.

these circumstances, the Esquerra and the Lliga. The latter, however, was unable to challenge the Esquerra's hegemony. The Lliga accepted the Republic and, on specific Catalan questions, seemed to have admitted that Maciá, 'a highly representative figure' as P. Rahola defined him in a Lliga's meeting, should be left to lead the region, though what the San Sebastián pact promised to the Catalans was far less than what the Aznar government had promised. The main line that the Lliga could still present to the electorate was its defence of religion, family, order, and private property, within the Republic. This could obviously appeal to many bourgeois and essentially non-Republican elements in a Catalonia dominated by social conflicts.[14]

It was precisely an emphasis on social questions and an extreme nationalistic demagogy, unacceptable both to the Lliga and to the Republican–Socialist coalition of Lerroux, which brought to the Esquerra 'an electoral victory without precedent in Catalan politics'.[15] It presented to the electorate a heterogeneous slate of left Republicans, friends of the CNT, Catalanist Socialists, and Nationalists. This slate, according to Maciá's critics, made him a sectarian leftist party leader, rather than the conciliatory president of all the Catalans. His propagandists went from meeting to meeting—and there were days in which ten electoral gatherings were held—stressing the symbolic figure of Maciá and the radical, working-class character of his party. The slogan of 'socialization of land and property' was launched in electoral meetings together with that of a 'nationalist personality'. Maciá appealed to the workers to vote for him because, as he said, 'I am the president of a revolutionary and leftist slate.' The Esquerra's speakers directed their attacks both at the Lliga and at Lerroux's 'candidature of Catalan unity'. Aiguader denounced Lerroux for trying 'to rob us the liberties which we won on 14 April', while the Lliga was caricatured by Companys as 'the last bastion of the Monarchy'.[16]

[14] Lliga, *Historia d'Una Política*, pp. 309–401, and surveys on the Lliga since April in *LV* 10 June 1931; *ED* 9 June 1931; and *EI* 13 June 1931. For P. Rahola and electoral meetings attacking, of course, the Esquerra, see *LV* 16, 27 June 1931.

[15] *LV* 30 June 1931.

[16] For the electoral campaign of the Esquerra see selected accounts in *LV* 22 May, 9, 16, 26, 27 June 1931; *Estampa* 4 July 1931. See also García Venero, *Historia del Nacionalismo Catalan*, pp. 361–2. For Maciá's critics see Solá Cañizares, *El Moviment*, pp. 127–9, 132–4.

The growing differences between the San Sebastián parties were not only reflected in the incoherent programme which they presented to the electorate, but also in an almost total disintegration of the electoral alliance which gave them a victory in April. It should be stressed, therefore, that the San Sebastián coalition had disintegrated at the local level long before it collapsed at the national and parliamentary level on 13 October 1931. This was manifested in the May elections, and was to be further accentuated in the June constituent elections. Very rare were the cases in which all the parties succeeded in creating electoral alliances. In the PRRS a serious crisis had already developed over this question, while the Socialists recommended their branches to join electoral coalitions, 'but this should not be obligatory'.[17]

The most common coalitions were those in which either the DR was dispensed with because of its rightism, or those in which the PRRS refused to take part because of the DR's presence. The case of Toledo reflected the consequent fragmentation of the coalition along lines of left and right. The extreme left (PRRS, Acción Republicana), the right (DR and Radicals), and the Socialists each formed a separate slate. In many cases the reason for the disintegration of the coalition was a struggle over the number of seats allotted to each, rather than doctrinal differences. A fortnight before the elections, *ABC* was rejoicing:

The Republican Socialist coalition is cracking. One has only to read the reports from the provinces. In many of them the 'historical' elements reject those of the right; in others, where moderate tendencies prevail, the Radicals are dispensed with. The Socialists break discipline where they can prevent the inclusion of non-leftist Republicans. Rebellious candidatures are emerging everywhere with the support of their sectarian press which call them 'popular' and 'authentic' in contrast to the 'official' slates.[18]

The DR was obviously dispensed with most frequently.[19] In Valencia the dominant *Partido Republicano Autonomista*, with its

[17] For the Socialists see *BUGT* June 1931.

[18] *ABC* 12 June 1931. See also *ED* 11 June 1931. See AHN Leg. 31: only 115 candidates out of 674 clearly defined as Socialists and Republicans belonged to partial alliances. For the case of Toledo see SA Leg. 1161: Alberto Aguilera y Arjona to Lerroux, 22 June 1931.

[19] J. Beúnza in *ED* 20 June 1931; Alcalá Zamora, *Los Defectos*, pp. 14–15.

Lerrouxista affinities, vetoed any compromise with the DR, on doctrinal grounds. But it also avoided an alliance with the PRRS, because of its reluctance to share a secure victory with other elements. This brought the *Agrupación Valencianista Republicana* to deplore 'the lamentable spectacle' of Republican divisions. In Zaragoza where the Radicals had enough strength to fight alone, they did so, while the other parties rejected the DR because of its 'contacts with Monarchist elements'. A similar approach was noticed in Murcia, Ciudad Real, Guadalajara, Madrid, Albacete, Avila, Valladolid, Bilbao, Las Palmas, and Segovia. In Jaén, the Socialists refused to include Alcalá Zamora in the coalition in spite of exhortations from J. Ortega who offered him his own seat. Ortega's ASR, which now became a political party that prohibited its members from belonging to other factions, was not a member of the San Sebastián coalition, but was courted for electoral pacts more than the DR.[20]

The leftist intransigence of the Radical Socialists was the reason for a breach in a considerable number of coalitions. In spite of the party's congress decision not to harm the governmental coalition by electoral non-collaboration, many provincial branches, that of Madrid included, declared themselves 'autonomous and revolutionary' by refusing to forge alliances with 'non-leftist elements'. In Segovia they almost jeopardized a partial alliance (without the DR of course) by their insistence on including the revolutionary Captain Romero in the slate. But when the DR joined the coalition, as was the case in Palencia, Burgos, and Seville (where the PRRS preferred to make electoral negotiations with the Communists) the Radical–Socialists presented separate candidatures. Nor were their relations with the Radicals always cordial. In Alicante they differed over the number of seats, and in Albacete they were

[20] For Valencia see *El Pueblo* 19 June 1931; and *El Sol* 21 June 1931. For Zaragoza see *ABC* 20 June 1931; and *El Sol* 10 June 1931. For Murcia see *ABC* 14, 21 June 1931. *ABC* 19, 24 June 1931 (C. Real, Guadalajara, Madrid); *ED* 27 June 1931 (Albacete and Avila); *El Norte de Castilla* 13, 25, 26 June 1931 (Segovia and Valladolid); *El Sol* 21 June 1931 (Bilbao). For Las Palmas see AHN Leg. 30: Maura to Guerra del Río, 12 June 1931 No. 323, and Guerra del Río to Maura, 13 June 1931 no. 981. For Jaén see OA: Cruz Salido to Ortega, 26 June 1931. For the politicization of the ASR and its place in coalitions see ibid.: letters from Daniel Camiroaga (Santander) 31 May, 11 June 1931, Gutierrez Bareal (Gijón) 11 June 1931, Julio Bernacer (Alicante) 21 June 1931, Francisco Bohigas (León) 20 June 1931. See also *El Sol* 29 May 1931, *ABC* 19 June 1931 (Ciudad Real).

dispensed with by a powerful coalition of Socialists and the *Lerrouxista*-sponsored *Alianza Republicana.*[21] The Radicals did not seem to have any scruples in choosing their partners. Nevertheless, they tended to dispense with other groups when they thought themselves strong enough to go it alone. Such was the case in Teruel, Huesca, and in Carabanchel where they faced the Socialists with the support of many 'new Republicans'. In Galicia and Andalucía they hoped to profit by separating themselves from regional groups, and by presenting themselves as representatives of a powerful national party. Already at the beginning of May, Martínez Barrios split the *Partido Autonomista Republicano,* whose main bulk was Lerrouxista, and founded the *Izquierda Republicana,* because, as he said, 'in order to bring about the Republic, we needed a coalition of all the Republicans, but in order to consolidate it, it is essential to create mass parties'. In La Coruña, Lugo, and Santiago, the Radicals decided to withdraw from the coalition with the *Federación Republicana Gallega,*(which was represented in the government through the figure of Casares Quiroga), because 'its task ended with the proclamation of the Republic'. To the FRG's claim that this breach was 'a folly', the Radicals responded that 'the republican socialist ideal stands in contradiction to regionalism'. This, and a personal rivalry between Casares Quiroga and the Radical Abad Conde made the alliance impossible. The general pattern of the coalition in Galicia was, therefore, that of separate slates of Alianza Republicana, and occasional coalitions between the FRG and the Socialists. The latter, however, were too weak in Orense to be taken into consideration. In the city of Córdoba where the Radicals, or rather the Lerrouxista sponsored *Partido Autonomista,* were strong enough they fought alone against the Socialists, but in constituencies where the Socialists were stronger, they managed to create a unique coalition which included the DR and the PRRS, against the Socialists.[22]

[21] For the rebellion of provincial branches see *ABC* 12 June 1931, *El Liberal, Sevilla* 2 June 1931; and *El Sol* 18 June 1931. For Palencia and Burgos see *El Norte de Castilla* 21 June 1931. For Segovia see OA: A. Ballesteros to Ortega, 18 June 1931. For Seville see *ABC, Sevilla* 10, 11, 19 June 1931. For Alicante see *ABC* 19 June 1931. For Albacete see *ED* 27 June 1931.

[22] *ABC* 14, 18 June 1931 (Teruel, Huesca); *ES* 19 June (Carabanchel); *El Liberal, Sevilla* 9 May 1931 (Seville); *ED* 27 June 1931 (Córdoba). For Galicia see *La Voz de Galicia* 22, 23 May, 11, 20 21, 23, 24 June 1931; Domingo Quiroga *Quien Es y Adonde*

The breach in the San Sebastián coalition was reflected not only in what can be considered as legitimate differences, but also in mutual harassment and persecutions characteristic of the old regime. In spite of Maura's circular exhorting the governors to be impartial,[23] they acted for their party's interest, and they urged their subordinates to collaborate with them against the rival Republican alliance or party. Where the governor belonged to the PRRS, as in Soria, Alianza Republicana was to realize that 'the caciquismo of the Vizconde de Eza was child's play compared with that of Artigas'. But when, as in Cáceres, the Radical Tuñón de Lara was the governor, it was the Radical Socialists, Socialists and other Republicans who were discriminated against by 'Lerrouxista caciques'. The Radical governor of Huesca led a campaign of harassment against the PRRS in many pueblos, arresting their speakers, and Teruel's governor confessed that in order to get Lerroux's friends elected, he had to quarrel with all the political forces in the region.

It does not seem, however, that Chapaprieta's claim that only the governors of the DR did not intervene in the electoral campaign was true. Martínez Antonio recalled in the Cortes how the governor of Segovia, belonging to that 'monarchist and very reactionary party' used the old systems of harassment against the Republican Socialist coalition. The mayor of Manzanilla (Huelva) warned Maura that if the governor, who was his party colleague, did not refrain from 'launching his Monarchist caciques against the Republican–Socialistic co-alition', 'blood would flow in the streets'; while in Bullas (Murcia) a meeting of the Republican–Socialistic coalition was disrupted by shooting from the DR's club. In Ciudad Real both Socialists and Republicans protested against the DR governor who used the Civil Guard to protect his party's meetings, and who exerted pressure on mayors in electoral matters. In the Catalan provinces where the governors were *Esquerristas*, the Radicals and ACR were obviously the main complainers.[24]

The Socialists who had no governors of their own, were

Va. . .?, pp. 37–41. For the regionalist propaganda of the FRG see its central role in the elaboration of the Galician Statute, *La Voz de Galicia* 27, 31 May, 4, 5, 6, 27 June 1931.

[23] See AHN Leg. 30: circular no. 231, 8 June 1931.

[24] For all the above see *ES* 24 May 1931 (Huesca); AHN Leg. 30: Jaca 25 June 1931

frequently exposed to official discrimination. Such was the case in Huelva where they complained against the DR authorities, supported by Burgos Mazo's ex-caciques, and in Seville where the authorities favoured the CNT for electoral reasons. In the province of Granada, where the Socialists had their separate slate, 'all kinds of pressures' were exerted on behalf of the DR or for the Republican coalition. But Socialists mayors were also active. In Linares the mayor's corrupt procedures meant that 'orderly people dare not go outside their houses'; and in the provinces of Granada and Córdoba Socialist authorities imprisoned elements of the DR on the eve of the elections, in order to obstruct their electoral campaign.[25]

The relations between the San Sebastián parties in the provinces on the eve of the elections were therefore accurately summed up by an observer as 'a war between brothers' and a 'demoralizing competition'.[26]

4. THE AFTERMATH OF THE ELECTIONS : THE SAN SEBAS-TIAN COALITION AS THE ONLY VIABLE SOLUTION.

In spite of a considerable number of incidents and irregularities, the June elections were, according to observers, 'a model of orderliness, and the right of suffrage was successfully guaranteed'. Romanones reckoned that 'a truly admirable mass of voters', had cast its votes for the Republican parties. The new electoral system obviously favoured large parties and coalitions, which only the Republicans possessed; and, by abolishing the small rural electoral districts, had given a severe blow to caciquismo, a virtue recognized by *El Debate,* which was equally aware of

no. 1694; Huesca 28 June 1931 no. 1878, 30 June 1931 no. 1954; Soria 20 June 1931 no. 1381; Plasencia (Cáceres) 24 June 1931 no. 1625; Cáceres 22 June 1931 no. 508; Manzanilla (Huelva) 27 June 1931 no. 1861; Puertollano, Tolloso, Manzanares (all in Ciudad Real) 22, 26, 27 June 1931 nos. 1819, 1523, 1729. For Huelva see also *ES* 10 June 1931. For Teruel see SA Leg. 1161: Governor of Teruel to Lerroux, 4 July 1931. For Martínez Antonio see *DSCC* 20 July 1931. For Chapaprieta, see his *La Paz,* pp. 151–6. For Bullas see AHN Leg. 16: Governor of Murcia to Maura, 28 June 1931. For Catalonia see ibid. Leg 30: Tremp (Lérida) 26 June 1931 no. 1769; Barcelona 27 June 1931 no. 1804; Gerona 19 June 1931 no. 1366.

[25] For the Socialists see ibid: Huelva 28 June 1931 no. 1884; Granada 27, 28 June 1931 nos. 1860, 1917; Linares 26 June 1931 no. 1762; Córdoba 25 June 1931 no. 1691; Leg. 16: President of Socialist centre in Seville to Maura 15 May 1930 no. 928. For Burgos y Mazo's support to the DR see also *ABC* 20 June 1931.

[26] Julio Bernacer to Ortega, 21 June 1931, in OA.

the system's blow to small parties. This, and the fact that the electorate had been asked to decide between left and right republicanism, rather than between Monarchy and Republic, gave victory to the Republican coalition and to the well-organized Radical and Socialist parties. The DR, isolated in the coalition, seems to have been isolated among the non-governmental right as well. *La Epoca*, speaking on behalf of 'the traditional conservative elements', did not mention the DR as the barrier against revolution, but only Lerroux, Largo Caballero, and Prieto. As for the Catholic strongholds in the north, they were represented either by AN or by their own regional, agricultural or nationalist interests. They managed to gather more strength than the DR, which thus was the loser either way. The major victory belonged to the left and the centre, with the Socialists and the Radicals as the biggest parties.[27]

The results of the elections dictated the continuance of the coalition in the government precisely because of the victories of the Radicals and the Socialists. Both knew that a unilateral withdrawal from the government might give the hegemony to the rival. Lerroux's personal victory—he received 133,789 votes in Madrid and was elected in four other capitals—made him the hero of the right. *El Imparcial* acclaimed him as the '*de facto* and *de jure* prime minister'. *El Debate* asked rhetorically: 'How could the people refrain from voting for the man who proclaimed that the Republic belongs to all Spaniards, even to its enemies?' *ABC* wrote of the 'plebiscitary success' of Lerroux as the triumph of the concept of 'law and order'. Ex-Monarchist figures were delighted. Burgos y Mazo put immediately himself and his 'men' at Lerroux's service, the ex-*Romanonista* Luis

[27] For incidents and irregularities see AHN Leg. 30, selected examples: Zalamea Serena (Badajoz) 29 June 1931 no. 1926; Colunga (Oviedo) 30 June 1931 no. 1969; Pontevedra 29 June 1931 no. 1945; Tenerife 30 June 1931 no. 1979; Barcelona 29 June 1931 no. 1920; Ciudad Real 30 June 1931 no. 1984; Lugo 29 June 1931 no. 1951. See also *DSCC* 20, 21, 24 June 1931, Cortes debates on irregularities in León, Salamanca, Lugo, Segovia. For observers see *The Times* 30 June 1931; *The Economist* 4 July 1931; and even *ED* 30 June 1931. For Romanones see his letter to Lorenzo Feliz 30 June 1931 in RA Leg. 2 no. 8. For the electoral law see AHN Leg. 47: Republican Committee of San Sebastián to Maura, 3 May 1931 no. 180; a discussion in J. Linz, 'The Party System of Spain: Past and Future', in Seymour M. Lipset and Stein Rokkan, *Party Systems and Voter Alignments*, pp. 238–9; *ED* 6 May 1931; and *EC* 9 May 1931. For *La Epoca* see 10 June 1931. For the results of the elections see Appendix III.

Massó y Simó referred to him as the saviour of the fatherland, and the ex-Conservative leader of Alicante, Salvador Canals, saluted him with an emotional 'Ave, Alexander!' Lerroux himself responded with great self confidence. 'A great responsibility had been cast on my shoulders'.[28]

This euphoria of the right around the figure of Lerroux alienated him from both the Radical-Socialists and the Socialists. Alvaro de Albornoz pointed at the greater victory of the Socialists and the considerable gains of his own party, as the reason why the next government should be formed by the Socialists and, by dispensing with the Radicals and the DR, would have a leftist tendency. To stress further the necessity of a leftist government, Marcelino Domingo claimed that Maciá's triumph in Catalonia was the consequence of his leftism rather than of his Catalanism, and that Lerroux's defeat there was the result of his rightism rather than of his *españolismo*.[29]

The leftist significance of the elections was also emphasized by the Socialists. For doctrinal and tactical reasons, some Socialists had hoped that their party would not have more than forty deputies in the Cortes so that it should not be compelled to continue in power.[30] But according to Prieto, their victory, greater than that of Lerroux, had closed this option. Now, he said, the Socialists must remain in the coalition, otherwise the right—Lerroux—would predominate. However, in a violent personal attack on Lerroux, he said that his party would refuse to take part in any government presided over by the Radical hero, 'the incarnation of the bourgeoisie', according to *El Socialista*. The country had definitely voted for 'a social and leftist parliament'.[31] However, the national leadership of the party, as well as the majority in its extraordinary congress, opened on 10 July to discuss Socialist participation in the government, though united in its opposition to a Lerroux government, decided to continue in the present governmental coalition, as the only way to prevent a deviation of the

---

[28] *EI* 1 July 1931; *ED, LE* and *ABC* 30 June 1931. For the ex-Monarchist figures see SA Leg. 1161: letters to Lerroux from Burgos y Mazo, 30 June 1931; Luis Massó y Simó, 1 July 1931; Salvador Canals, 1 July 1931. Lerroux in *El Sol* 30 June 1931.

[29] *ABC* 2 July 1931 (Albornoz), 30 June 1931 (Domingo).

[30] *ES* 26 May, 1 July 1931 (Prieto), 30 June 1931 (Besteiro).

[31] *ES* 1, 2, 7 July 1931.

Republic to the right. Even Besteiro, the most characteristic champion of abstentionism, said that this threat left no choice to the Socialists but to remain in the coalition. The final resolution, however, pointed at the rightist menace as well as at previous commitments to stay in the government until the elaboration of a constitution as the essential motives behind the decision.[32]

Though the Socialists ruled out for doctrinal reasons the possibility of an exclusively Socialistic government, neither did the new political balance of power favour such a solution. In a meeting of the *Consejo Nacional de Alianza Republicana*, Radicals, *Acción Republicana*, some Federal deputies and autonomous groups decided to form a parliamentary bloc, which enabled Lerroux to control the largest minority in the Cortes. This was essentially an agreement between Lerroux and Azaña, which the latter accepted after receiving assurances from Lerroux that he would stick to the basic principles of Alianza, rather than pushing to the right. For the time being, it ruled out the possibility of a leftist combination in the government, and it made Lerroux indispensable. He was as opposed to a Socialist government as the Socialists were to a government led by him.[33]

The maintenance of the coalition was also made possible by the defeat of the DR. This meant that it was not strong enough to shift the balance of government in favour of the right. On the other hand, both Maura and Alcalá Zamora were interested in continuing in office, precisely because of their parliamentary weakness, a weakness for which they blamed the abstentionism of the right. Only the fragile balance between left and right in the coalition, a balance which the DR was obviously interested in maintaining, could enable the DR to exercise any influence. Maura therefore called upon the other parties 'to neglect doctrinal and personal discrepancies', in order to maintain the coalition until a constitution was elaborated. On the other

[32] *ES* 30 June, 9, 11 July 1931 (Caballero on behalf of participation; Besteiro and Prieto). A report on the congress in ibid. 11, 12 July 1931; and G. Morón, *La Ruta*, pp. 44–7 emphasizing the traditional collaboration with the bourgeoisie. A similar interpretation was given, of course, by the Communist *Mundo Obrero* 15 July 1931.

[33] For the pact see *EC* 4, 11 July 1931. Azaña stressed in his diary the motive behind the pact: to curb Lerroux's move to the right, see his *Obras* iv, 11, 16, 23. The Socialists were obviously dissatisfied with the emergence of such a strong bloc dominated by Lerroux, see *ES* 12 July 1931.

hand, a government presided over by the leader of the smallest party in the coalition, Alcalá Zamora, was unlikely to alienate either of the two large rival components: the Socialists and the Radicals. Prieto could hardly think 'of a man who could satisfy' the Socialists 'as prime minister' more than Alcalá Zamora.[34] Under these circumstances, the continuation of the San Sebastián coalition in power became not only a fulfilment of previous commitments to stay united, but, for the time being, the only viable solution. And by the end of July the new Cortes passed a motion of confidence in the government.[35]

[34] For Alcalá Zamora's and Maura's resentment against the right's abstention see their respective books, *Los Defectos*, pp. 14–15; and *Así*, p. 321. For their interest in continuing in the coalition see *ABC* 30 June 1931 (A. Zamora), *El Sol* 2 July 1931 (Maura). For Prieto see *ES* 1 July 1931.

[35] *ES* 31 July 1931.

EPILOGUE

The San Sebastián coalition now entered its last phase, and, as the parliamentary debates on the constitution began to deal with sensitive clauses, the government approached its moment of truth. The heterogeneity of the government made impossible any common approach to the constitution.[1] Alcalá Zamora expressed this reality in blunt terms: 'What separates us is all that is fundamental and essential in the constitution'.[2] And even if the government had been able to patch up the differences between ministers, their respective parties in parliament were reluctant to sacrifice their particular views for the sake of governmental unity.[3] There was hardly a substantial issue on which all the parties of the coalition voted together. The Radicals and DR opposed Spain's definition as 'a Republic of workers',[4] whereas on the issue of women's suffrage the Radicals and the Republican left joined forces against the Socialists and DR, who followed the support of the extreme right for women's suffrage.[5] When the right of property was discussed the Republican parties were again divided between left and right, and Besteiro had to warn the Cortes that the failure to create a socially advanced Republic might compel the Socialists to recommend revolutionary methods. This style enraged Alcalá Zamora so much that he publicly warned his colleagues that he might resign.[6] He was obviously isolated further when he found that his moderate proposals for agrarian reform were rejected by the Agricultural Committee in favour of the more radical approach of Socialists and left Republicans.[7]

The Republican right was further isolated by a *rapprochement*

---

[1] This was the view of all the ministers. See *ABC* 10 July 1931 (A. Zamora), 11 July 1931 (M. Domingo), Prieto, *Convulsiones* i, 95–6; Azaña, *Obras* iv, 17.

[2] *DSCC* 17 Sept. 1931.

[3] Azaña, op. cit. 76, 152–5; *ES* 23 Aug. 1931.

[4] *DSCC* 11 Sept. 1931.

[5] *DSCC* 29 Sept. 1931; M. Cordero, *Los Socialistas*, pp. 153–62 on the Socialist view.

[6] Saborit, *Besteiro*, p. 195; *DSCC* 6 Oct. 1931; A. Zamora's 'resignations' became a routine, see Azaña, op. cit. 87, 90.

[7] For the agrarian issue's role in the disintegration of the coalition, see Malefakis, *Agrarian Reform*, pp. 176–85.

between the left Republicans. The Socialists and Radical-Socialists stood for an extreme formula of both separation of state and Church and the dissolution of all religious orders. It is necessary to point out that the Socialists were pushed to adopt an intransigent attitude by the Radical-Socialists' extreme approach to this and other issues. The accentuated leftism of the latter, and their opposition to a Lerroux government, while supporting a governmental alliance with the Socialists, led the Socialists to suggest that there was 'an accidental coincidence' between both parties, a coincidence which might lead to the creation of a 'leftist parliamentary bloc'.[8] The Socialists, who started by being suspicious of the 'reactionary' Azaña–Lerroux pact, contemplated now with satisfaction the disintegration of *Alianza Republicana* thanks to Azaña's growing conviction that the Socialists provided the most solid foundation for a left-bourgeois Republic. He supported their demand that the present Cortes should not be dissolved after the promulgation of the constitution, thus giving a serious blow to Lerroux's hopes of gaining support from the discontent in conservative circles with the constitution in an early general election. He also promised to oppose any Lerroux government, forecasting a governmental alliance with Socialists. The Socialists were now confident that 'Azaña is not so identified with Lerroux as we had previously thought'.[9]

The religious issue was finally chosen by the left to cement its alliance, and by the DR as a flag with which to retire from the coalition. Alcalá Zamora made it clear that an uncompromising solution would result in his resignation in order to lead, from the opposition, a campaign to reform the constitution[10] Azaña took up the challenge in a widely-discussed speech delivered on 13 October, in which he promised his party's support to the

[8] *ES* 25, 30 July, 3, 15 Sept. 1931; Azaña, op. cit. 171. For the leftist programme of collaboration presented by the PRRS see: SA Leg. 2613: *Bases de Colaboración Presentadas por el PRRS a los Gobiernos Azaña y Lerroux.*

[9] For initial suspicions see *ES* 23 July 1931. For the *rapprochement* see Azaña's conversation with Prieto and de los Ríos on 4 August and his attitude to the dissolution of the Cortes in his *Obras* iv, 60–2, 103. See ibid. 68–9 on how Azaña expressed in a cabinet meeting on 7 August his opposition to any government which would not include the Socialists. See also Malefakis, op. cit. 183–4 and R Oliveira, *Historia* iii, 170–3. The Socialists' attitude to new elections is in *ES* 11, 15 Sept. 1931. The last quotation is in ibid. 22 Sept. 1931.

[10] *DSCC* 19 Oct. 1931.

Socialists should they form a new government. His proposals were, however, milder than those of the Socialists, since he asked for the dissolution of the Jesuits, while they proposed the dissolution of all the orders. Nevertheless, he put before them a temptation hard to resist: the Church was to be prohibited from engaging in any educational function. The 'moderation' of his motion, which even Maura and Ossorio recognized, led the Radical-Socialists to abstain from voting, but attracted the support of the Socialists and Radicals.[11] Alcalá Zamora, however, was disappointed. Although he also recognized the relative moderation of the resolution, [12] it was still much more radical than he had expected, since in a cabinet meeting on the previous day only Prieto had adopted an uncompromising line. Prieto later claimed that the rank and file in the parties dictated an intransigent attitude; while Alcalá Zamora, accused the Radicals and Radical-Socialists of supporting extremism as a retaliation against the DR for supporting women's suffrage. Azaña also believed that this was the case. The left seemed to have deliberately collaborated to get rid of the DR.[13]

The resignation of Alcalá Zamora and Maura on 14 October was the culmination of a process of division between right and left in the coalition. The broad basis on which the Republic was to offer the possibility of conciliation to all parties was narrowed as the maintenance of the San Sebastián coalition became 'a task beyond human strength'.[14] The Socialists, tired of 'the influence of the two reactionary ministers' in the government, now agreed with Azaña that 'we have been freed from a nightmare', and that the Republic 'had at last made a definite step towards the left'.[15]

The solution to the crisis was the formation of an Azaña

---

[11] For the debate see DSCC 7, 8 Oct. 1931 (de los Ríos and Albornoz) 13 Oct. 1931 (Azaña's speech); Alvaro de Albornoz, La Política Religiosa de la Republica, pp. 10–32, 40–71. Azaña, Obras iv, 174–81 described how he convinced the constitutional committee to accept his proposition, supported by Maura. See also M. Cordero, Los Socialistas, p. 122; and Alvaro de Albornoz, Al Servicio de la Republica, pp. 94–100. For Ossorio see his Una Posición Conservadora ante la República, pp. 15–16.

[12] Alcalá Zamora, Los Defectos, pp. 89–91.

[13] For the cabinet meeting see Azaña, Obras, iv, 174; Prieto, Palabras, pp. 218–19. For A. Zamora see his Defectos, pp. 12–13. His allegations against the Radicals and Radical-Socialists in ibid. 88–9. This was confirmed by Azaña, op. cit., 159.

[14] Azaña in DSCC 14 Oct. 1931.

[15] Azaña, op. cit. 187; ES 15 Oct. 1931; Cordero, Los Socialistas, p. 128.

cabinet, because of the refusal of Socialists and Radicals to serve in a government presided over by their rival.[16] But the incompatibility between the two major parties compelled Azaña, when he reconstituted his cabinet on 14 December, to dispense with the Radicals, thus further narrowing the coalition. Lerroux could no longer tolerate the dominance of the government by the Socialists, and he definitely moved to the right to fight the leftist Republic. The *bienio Azaña* or the *bienio rojo*, as its opponents nicknamed it, was about to start.[17]

[16] Azaña, op. cit. 183; Lerroux, *Pequeña Historia* pp. 119–21; D. Martínez Barrio, *Los Radicales en la República. Discursos 1932*, pp. 19–20, 46–7.

[17] For the growing incompatibility between Socialists and Radicals in the period between mid-October and mid-December see Malefakis, *Agrarian Reform*, pp. 186–93. Lerroux's attitude is in his *Pequeña Historia*, pp. 34, 125; and Martínez Barrio, op. cit. 47. For the Socialists see Saborit, *Besteiro*, pp. 298–9. For the PRRS' view against Lerroux and on behalf of the Socialists see *Texto Taquigráfico*, pp. 421–8.

APPENDIX I

THE RESULTS OF THE MUNICIPAL ELECTIONS

The final results of the municipal elections have never been published. The Monarchist government capitulated before definite results could come in from the provinces, and the Republican government did not bother to publish them. Furthermore, in the archives of the Ministry of the Interior there is hardly a telegram from the new Republican governors reporting the later results. The whole matter simply seemed irrelevant when the governors, and indeed the minister, were busy with the more substantial issues of establishing the new regime. Nor was the press interested after the proclamation of the Republic.

However, an examination of the reports sent by the governors up to the declaration of the Republic,[1] has made it possible to reconstruct a partial picture of the results, as well as to point out the major trends in electoral behaviour.

The results in most of the provincial capitals indicated an absolute victory for the Republicans.[2] This was obviously the fruit of a period of intensive republican agitation in the major urban centres, in which a new mass of voters, most of them young, was included in the electoral register. Romanones was especially worried about these new elements, 'whose political affiliation is unknown'. Equally disoriented was the governor of Biscay who wrote to Hoyos that he could not predict the electoral behaviour of 16,631 new voters. Hoyos himself confessed that even his allegation, that Saborit had managed to falsify the Madrid register by adding 25,000 fictitious names, fell short of explaining the absolute victory of the Republicans in the capital: 91,898 Republicans against 33,884 Monarchists.[3] Such a disorientation

---

[1] AHN Leg.29–31, in which hundreds of telegrams providing electoral results are kept.

[2] The Republicans achieved a landslide victory in 45 out of 52 capitals. They lost in Avila, Las Palmas (Baleares), Burgos, Cádiz, Lugo, Las Palmas (Canarias); while in Orense there was no decision because of a draw between a Monarchist and a Republican candidate. The summary of the results in the capitals is as follows: 1,037 Republican councillors, 552 Monarchists, 64 Constitutionalists, and 77 unidentified. See AHN Leg.29,30; *ABC; El Liberal Sevilla; La Voz de Galicia*, 14 Apr. 1931.

[3] Romanones in *ABC* 31 Mar. 1931; Hoyos, *Mi Testimonio*, pp. 111–12 (on Biscay), 104–5, 107 (on Madrid).

of both the minister and a governor in electoral matters could hardly be conceived during the 'old regime'. It indicates how completely the Ministry of the Interior had lost control of the electoral machine. Nevertheless, it is obvious that traditional Monarchist dominance in the small pueblos of rural districts remained unshaken. This was fully demonstrated by the results of the elections held on 5 April, under Article 29 of the electoral law, which provided for the automatic election of unopposed candidates. These results, therefore, refer mainly to those pueblos in which Republican organizations were either non-existent, or were too weak to present candidates. One third of the total number—29,804 councillors—were elected in this way. The affiliation of 22,129 councillors, elected by Article 29, was registered in the Ministry of the Interior.[4] It indicates an unequivocal Monarchist victory in a proportion of 8 to 1. It also shows that the data published by the Republican government in *Anuario Estadístico* for 1931,[5] in addition to its failure to provide us with specific party affiliation of the councillors, is also in error by giving victory to the Republicans.[6]

The uncritical approach of J. Linz to the figures published by the *Anuario Estadístico* led him to claim that 'the country was Republican' and to draw the baseless conclusion that Republicans did better in the elections under Article 29 than in the open elections of 12 April. He also claims that the Monarchists did better on the twelfth than on the 5 April. In reality the opposite is true. *Caciquismo* was stronger where Article 29 was applied.[7]

The results of the elections held on 12 April indicated a Monarchist victory in rural Spain; they also prove that the Republicans seriously challenged the Monarchists in the larger villages and towns. They did not, however, always manage to overcome the caciquista predominance of Conservatives in Galicia or of Reformists in Asturias. Out of about 50,000 councillors elected on that day, the results of only some 20,000 seats were registered in the Ministry of the Interior.[8] Whereas on 5

[4] The Minister of the Interior published in his memoirs only the rough affiliation of 15,963 councillors, elected under this article. See Hoyos, op.cit., 183. A reconstruction of the results with the help of AHN Leg.29–31 gives the following picture: 18,041 Monarchist councillors, 2,592 Republicans, 921 Constitutionalists, 215 Traditionalists.

[5] 13,940 Republicans, 887 Socialists, 6,065 Monarchists, 10 Communists, 6,043 others, 2,859 'not available'.

[6] *ES* 9 Apr. 1931 admitted the Republican defeat and pointed at the role of caciquismo in Article 29. *ED* 7 Apr. 1931 was delighted with the results, claiming that it was 'the end of the republican myth'.

[7] J. Linz, *The Party System*, pp. 233–6. His challenge to R. Carr's emphasis (*Spain*, pp. 368–69) on the strength of caciquismo in Art. 29 is, therefore, not supported by evidence.

[8] Hoyos published in his memoirs only the results concerning 12,062 councillors who were elected on 12 April. See his *Mi Testimonio*, p. 183. The results that I was able to

April, the proportion between Monarchists and Republicans was 8 to 1, it now was 2 to 1, though it obviously varied from province to province. The results published by the Republican government in *Anuario Estadístico* for 1931[9] do not show the party affiliations of the elected councillors, and again concede victory to the Republicans. It is unconceivable that the Monarchists, who had 11,000 councillors out of about 20,000 whose affiliation was known on the evening of 14 April, should have reached no more than a total number of 12,970 after the results of some 30,000 more elections had come in.

One might draw a certain consolation from the fact that the final and complete results of the elections were irrelevant to the fall of the Monarchy, because of the government's capitulation before the final results came in. However, the same can not be argued about the results that came in up till the evening of the fourteenth. There is little doubt that Hoyos was constantly briefing his colleagues on the results during the last couple of days of the regime.[10] It is therefore worth presenting the picture the Monarchist government had of the general results on the evening of the fourteenth.[11] This indicated that the Monarchists had in the country as a whole 29,953 councillors and the Republicans only 8,855. The Monarchists had outnumbered the left by a proportion of 3 to 1. Yet the government was determined to give way to the Republicans. The inevitable conclusion is that the government was shocked by its defeat in the capitals and in the big towns, and found no consolation in its numerical victory in rural districts, which represented the routine of local caciquismo, rather than any authentic public opinion.[12] The substantial 'victory' in the

---

reconstruct from AHN Leg.29–31 are the following: 11,000 Monarchists, 5,231 Republicans, 802 Constitutionalists, 1,030 others. The Republicans did much better in towns with a population of more than 6,000 inhabitants than in smaller places. See many examples from the provinces of Seville, Jaén, Badajoz, La Coruña, Lugo, Orense, Cáceres, and Oviedo (a few examples: Utrera, Ecija, Rio Tinto, La Carolina, Ubeda, Villacarrillo, Alconchel, Alburquerque, Jerez de los Caballeros, Santiago, Ferrol, Garrovillas, Hervás, Ribadesella, Parres) in *El Debate*, *ABC de Sevilla*, *El Liberal de Sevilla*, *La Vanguardia de Badajoz* 14 Apr. 1931; and AHN Leg.30.

[9] Results: 20,428 Republicans, 3,926 Socialists, 12,970 Monarchists, 57 Communists, 9,155 others, 4,132 not available.

[10] A number of interim summaries of the results can be found in AHN Legs.29–31.

[11] Results: 29,953 Monarchists, 8,855 Republicans, 1,787 Constitutionalists, 1,322 others. The number of councillors whose affiliation was still unknown in the Ministry of the Interior when the Republic was declared was 38,715.

[12] For an illuminating study on the electoral caciquismo in rural districts in these municipal elections, see J. Tussell Gómez, *Elecciones y vida Politica en Andalucia*, especially pp. 957–60. See also his article 'La Descomposición del Sistema Caciquil Español (1902–1931)' *Revista de Occidente*, no. 127 Oct. 1973, pp. 90–92.

pueblos was not enough to erase the defeat in the capitals, and the Republican gains in the big towns. It is evident that in those places in which public opinion was free to express itself the Monarchy was either defeated or seriously challenged. This dictated to ministers their defeatist attitude, which led to the fall of the Monarchy.

APPENDIX II

RESULTS OF THE MUNICIPAL ELECTIONS
OF MAY 1931

The only official results of the May elections ever published are those
which appeared in the press on 2 June 1931:[1]

Workers	13
Republican–Socialist coalition	1,645
Socialists	674
Derecha Republicana	757
Radical-Socialists	301
Republican–Regionalists	5
Federals	89
Independent Republicans	156
Radicals	208
Agrupación al Servicio de la Republica	15
Agrarian Republicans	91
Partido Republicano Liberal Democrata	84
Alianza Republicana	141
Unión Republicana Autonomista	461
Total Republicans	4,640
Monarchists	201
Gremiales	4
Catholics	47
Juan Marchistas	54
Traditionalists, Nationalists and Jamists	354
Total non Republicans	660

These, however, are partial results. I was able to reconstruct a more
accurate picture, though still not complete,[2] by summing up the
results in the form in which they were sent to the Minister of the

[1] See *ES* and *El Sol* 2 June 1931.

[2] Not in every case did the governors report on the number of Ayuntamientos whose
electoral results they sent. Nor did they always state the results of how many
Ayuntamientos were still unavailable. In both cases, the numbers were, therefore,
probably higher than that recorded in the Ministry of the Interior. It is also noteworthy
that elections took place also in provinces (like Orense, for example) whose governors
did not send any results whatsoever to the Ministry.

Interior by the civil governors.[3] A superficial glance at these figures is sufficient to show how radical was the change introduced by the May elections in those Ayuntamientos in which they were held. They went over to the Republicans. An examination of some specific cases of Monarchist Ayuntamientos which passed almost completely to the Republicans, demonstrates the change.[4] This, however, does not only mean that Republicans who were 'persecuted' in the April elections made a victorious appearance, but also that, either those who 'voted' for the Monarchy in April now voted for the Republicans, or that the Republican caciquismo of the *comisiones gestoras* exerted a decisive influence. Both elections lacked 'purity'.

[3] AHN Leg.29,31 : 7,612 Republicans, 951 non-Republicans.

[4] See for example the cases of Colunga, Villaviciosa, Vegadeo, Pamplona, Valmaseda, Durango, Peñafel, Lugo, Cádiz, Medina de Rioseco, Villa Robledo, Parazona, Caudete and other places in AHN Leg.29–31.

APPENDIX III

THE RESULTS OF THE JUNE ELECTIONS

The elections of 28 June have been adequately studied by scholars.[1] However, although at first sight the results of these elections seem easier to trace than the municipal elections, no attempt has ever been made to organize the available information into a general picture of the party affiliation of the deputies elected in each constituency. And, indeed, one can hardly find two books that agree on the precise composition of the new Cortes.

I have tried to reconstruct a general picture with the help of the archives of the Ministry of the Interior, the *Anuario Estadístico* for 1931, and the press.[2] Since the electoral law provided that the minority seats should be won by at least 20 per cent of the votes in the constituency, twelve seats remained vacant after the first round.[3] The elections held in Lugo on 28 June were later invalidated because of irregularities,[4] and special elections were held there on 23 August.[5]

The composition of the Cortes is shown in Table No. 1. The Socialists were obviously the biggest party, but Lerroux's personal

[1] See J. Linz, *The Party System*, pp. 238–40. J. Becarud, *La Deuxième République Espagnole* 1931–6 (Centre d'étude des Relations Internationales Serie C. Recherche no. 7, October 1962) pp. 37–43 and maps 4–8. For a special reference to Catalonia see Isidre Molas, *Lliga*, i, 217–24, 267–94. For a special study on Madrid see J. Tussell Gomez, *La Segunda República en Madrid, Elecciones y Partidos Políticos* pp. 45–79. For a special study on Barcelona see J. A. Gonzalez Casanova: *Elecciones en Barcelona 1931–1936*, pp. 31–49.

[2] 108 Socialists, 76 Radicals, 50 Radical Socialists, 21 Acción Republicana, 23 Derecha Republicana, 12 Agrupación al Servicio de la República, 10 Federalists, 15 Orga, 33 Esquerra, 2 Republican Liberal Democrats, 12 Independent Republicans, 24 Republican Coalition, 2 Alianza Republicana, 1 Republican Revolutionary Party, 2 Acció Catalana Republicana, 4 Federalist Agrarian Coalition, 10 Independents, 21 Agrarians, 3 Acción Nacional, 4 Basque Nationalists, 9 Basque Navarrese Coalition, 2 Traditionalists, 2 Lliga Regionalista, 2 Monarchists. See *Anuario* 1931; AHN Leg. 30–31; *El Debate, La Voz de Galicia, La Vanguardia, ABC* 30 June 1931.

[3] In the second round held on 12 July the results were; 2 Socialists, 2 Radicals, 2 Acción Republicana, 4 Federalists, 1 Independent Republican, 1 Radical Socialist. See AHN Leg.31; and *Anuario* 1931.

[4] See the debate in *DSSC* 24 July 1931.

[5] The results were 4 Radicals, 4 Derecha Republicana, 1 Agrarian Republican, 1 Federación Republicana Gallega.

achievement, and his ability to maintain Alianza Republicana as a parliamentary bloc, enabled him to create a challenge to Socialist predominance. The non-Republican right, though far from coherent, emerged as a significant factor, stronger than the Republican right. What is evident, however, is that neither the left Republicans not Lerroux, as the champion of Republican conservatism, could by themselves master the parliament. But it is also clear that Acción Republicana's natural home was with the Republican left rather than in a parliamentarian bloc with *Lerrouxismo*; therefore a *rapprochement* between Azaña and both the PSOE and the PRRS would in the future seriously undermine Lerroux's parliamentary position.

TABLE No. 1

THE COMPOSITION OF THE CONSTITUENT CORTES

Republican left
Socialists	117
Radical-Socialists	59
Dissident Federals	3
Partido Republicano Revolucionario	1

Alianza Republicana[1]
Radicals	89
Acción Republicana	27
Non-dissident Federals	11
Independent Republicans	13

Republican right
Derecha Republicana	27
Partido Republicano Liberal Demócrata	2

Regionalist Republicans
Esquerra (including the Unió Socialista de Catalunya)	33
Orga	16
Acció Catalana Republicana	2

Other Republicans
Agrupación al Servicio de la República	12
Agrarian Republicans	1

Non-Republican right
Agrarians	21
Acción Nacional	3
Basque nationalists	4
Basque–Navarrese coalition	9
Traditionalists	2
Lliga	2
Monarchists	2

Independents	14
Total	**470**

[1] This was the composition of Alianza Republicana according to *ES* 28 July 1931.

BIBLIOGRAPHY

I. MANUSCRIPT SOURCES

1. Public Archives

In Salamanca: *Archivo de Salamanca. Jefatura. Servicio Documental. Sección Político-Social.*

In the Archivo Historico Nacional, Madrid: *Sección del Ministerio de Gobernación, Serie A.*

In the Public Record Office, London: *Diplomatic Despatches from Spain,* May 1923–Oct. 1931: F.O. 371/9490, 9493, 10593, 10595, 11096, 11099, 11936, 11939, 11942, 12717, 12719, 13434, 13435, 14164, 14165, 14167, 15040, 15041, 15770–6.

2. Private Papers

Alba Santiago Archive. Uncatalogued. By kind permission of his widow, Madrid.

Maura Antonio Archive. Catalogued. In Fundación Antonio Maura, Madrid.

Maura Gabriel Archive. Uncatalogued. In Fundación Antonio Maura, Madrid.

Ortega y Gasset José Archive. Catalogued according to alphabetic order. By kind permission of his daughter. Madrid.

Romanones Archive. Catalogued. By kind permission of his son, the Marquis of Santo Floro. Madrid.

Unamuno Archive. Catalogued according to alphabetical order. By kind permission of his daughter. Salamanca.

II. PRINTED SOURCES

1. PRIMARY SOURCES

A. Printed Documents

Alianza Republicana, *El 11 de Febrero de 1926* (Madrid, 1926).

Anuario Estadístico de España, 1931, 1932–3, 1963.

Aranzadi Estanislao De, *Repertorio Cronológico de Legislación. 1931* (Madrid, n.d.).

Batllori, M. and Arbeloa V. (eds.), *Archivo Vidal i Barraquer. Iglesia y Estado Durante la Segunda República Española 1931–1936,* vol. i (Monestir Monserrat, 1971).

Boletín de Administración Local, 1931.

BIBLIOGRAPHY   319

Boletín de la Asamblea Nacional, 1928–9.
Boletín de Información Social del Ministerio de Trabajo y Previsión, 1930–1.
Constitució Provisional de la Republica Catalana. Aprovada per l'Assamblea Constituent del Separatism Catalá, Reunida a l'Havana 30 Sept.–2 Oct. *1928*, Havana, 1928.
Cortés–Cavanillas, Julian, *Acta de Acusasión; Epístolas, Documentos, Frases y Diálogos para la Historia de la Segunda República* (Madrid, 1933).
Cuartero, José, *Artículos de don José Cuartero: Homenaje de ABC a su Insigne Redactor* (Madrid, 1947).
Diario de Sesiones de las Cortes Constituyentes, 14 July–14 October 1931.
I Documenti Diplomatici Italiani 7ᵉ Serie 1922–35.
'La Crísis Agraria Andaluza de 1930–1931', *Estudios y Documentos* (Ministerio de Trabajo y Previsión. Dirección General de Acción Social. Madrid, 1931).
Sevilla Diego, Andres, *Constituciones y Otras Leyes y Proyectos de España*, vol. ii (Madrid, 1969).
Texto Taquigráfico del Tercer Congreso Nacional Ordinario del Partido Republicano Radical–Socialista de España Celebrado en Santander durante los dias 28–31 de Mayo y l de Junio de 1932 (Madrid, 1932).

B. *Private Conversations*

With Arturo Soria (member of the FUE's directive junta), Madrid 1972.
With Felisa Unamuno (Unamuno's daughter), Salamanca 1974.

C. *Press*

a. *Spanish National Newspapers*

ABC (Monarchist daily, Madrid), July–Sept. 1923, Jan. 1929–Oct. 1931.
El Crisol (Republican daily, Madrid), Apr. 1931–Oct. 1931.
El Debate (Catholic daily, Madrid), Jan. 1929–Oct. 1931.
El Ejército Español (Military daily, Madrid), editorials July 1923–Oct. 1931.
Ejército y Armada (Military daily, Madrid), editorials July 1923–Oct. 1931.
La Epoca (monarchist Conservative daily, Madrid), Jan. 1929–Oct. 1931.
El Imparcial (monarchist Liberal daily, Madrid), Jan. 1929–Oct. 1931.
El Progreso (Radical-Republican daily, Barcelona), Jan. 1929–Dec. 1930.
El Socialista (Socialist daily, Madrid), July 1923–Oct. 1931.
El Sol (Independent Liberal daily, Madrid), Sept. 1923–Oct. 1931.
Solidaridad Obrera (Anarcho-Syndicalist daily, Barcelona), Oct. 1930–Oct. 1931.

320   BIBLIOGRAPHY

La Vanguardia (monarchist 'españolista', Barcelona), Sept. 1923, Jan. 1929–Oct. 1931.

b. *Regional Newspapers*

ABC, Sevilla (monarchist daily), Mar.–Oct. 1931.
El Liberal, Sevilla (Republican daily), Mar.–Oct. 1931.
El Norte de Castilla, Vallodolid (Albista daily), Mar.–Oct. 1931.
Vanguardia, Badajoz (Republican weekly), Mar.–Apr. 1931.
La Voz de Galicia, La Coruña (Independent daily), Mar.–Oct. 1931.

c. *Collections of other Political Organs*

Agrupación Socialista Madrileña, Secretaría 16 de la Casa del Pueblo, 1929–31.
Alianza, Boletín de Alianza Republicana, 1930.
Almanaque de 'El Socialista', 1931–2.
La Antorcha, Organo del Partido Comunista de España, 1926–7.
La Antorcha, Semanario Comunista, 27 June 1931.
La Bandera Roja, Organo del Partido Comunista de España, June–Sept. 1931.
La Batalla, Semanario Comunista, 1930–1.
El 14 de Abril, Semanario Republicano, May–July 1931.
Catalunya, Periódico Republicano Catalan Españolista, May–June 1931.
La Conquista del Estado, Semanario de Lucha y de Información Política, Mar.–Oct. 1931.
Control, Semanario Comunista, 16–31 May 1931.
El Cruzado Español, 1929–31.
El Defensor del Extrarradio, República y Justicia, 1931 (selected numbers).
España Libre, Paris, Apr.–Oct. 1931.
España Republicana, Organo de la Alianza Republicana de Nueva-York, Apr.–Oct. 1931.
Heraldo de Chamartin, 1930–1.
Izquierda, Diario Republicano, 1931 (selected numbers from August onwards).
La Legión 1 Jan.–9 Apr. 1931.
El Libertario, Semanario Anarquista, 12 May–4 July 1931.
Mundo Obrero, Organo del Partido Comunista de España, 1931 (selected numbers).
Nueva España, 1930–1.
El Nuevo Evangelio, Semanario Republicano, June–July 1931.
El Presidencialista, Organo de la Juventud Republicana Presidencialista de España, 1928–30.
Rebelión!, 1930.
Región, Periódico de Afirmación Monárquica, Alcazar de San Juan, 1930, 1931 (Selected numbers).
República, Semanario de Inteligencia Republicana, 1926 (selected numbers).
Republicano, Organo del Centro Republicano Español, Rosario de Santa Fe, 1927–8.

Unión Patriótica, 1926–30.
Unión Monárquica, 1930–1.
Vida y Trabajo, Semanario de Izquierda, 13–20 June 1931.
d. *Corporative Journals*
Acción Católica de la Mujer, 1930–1.
El Agrario, Organo de la Unión Agraria Provincial, Alicante, 25 Oct., 1 Nov. 1930.
El Arsenal del Predicador, Revista Mensual Dedicada al Clero, May 1929.
Avanti, Revista Decenal Defensora de los Intereses Morales y Materiales de los Empleados, Feb.–May 1931.
Banco de Crédito Local de España, Memoria, 1929, 1930.
Boletín del Banco Urquijo, 1929–31.
Boletín de la Cámara Oficial de Comercio e Industria de Lérida y su Provincia, 1925, 1926, 1929, 1930.
Boletín de la Cámara Oficial de Industria de la Provincia de Madrid, 1923, 1926, 1929, 1931.
Boletín de la Cámara Oficial de Comercio, Industria y Navegación de Málaga, 1929, 1931.
Boletín de la Cámara Oficial de Comercio y Navegación de Barcelona, Memoria, 1931.
Boletín del Colegio Oficial del Secretariado Local de la Provincia de Palencia, 1931.
Boletín Eclesiástico del Arzobispado de Toledo, 1931.
Boletín Informativo del Ilustre Colegio de Abogados de Madrid, 1931.
Boletín Oficial de la Acción Católica Española, 1929.
Boletín Oficial de la Asociación de Agricultores de España, 1929–31.
Boletín Oficial de la Asociación del Arte de Imprimir, November 1931.
Boletín Oficial de la Cámara de Comercio de Madrid, 1923, 1931.
Boletín Oficial de la Cámara de Propiedad Urbana de Madrid, 1931.
Boletín Oficial Eclesiástico del Arzobispado de Burgos, 1931.
Boletín Oficial Eclesiástico del Obispado de Orense, 1931.
Boletín Oficial Eclesiástico del Arzobispado de Sevilla, 1931.
Boletín Oficial del Fenix Agrícola, 1930–1.
Boletín Oficial del Obispado de León, 1931.
Boletín Oficial del Obispado de Madrid–Alcalá, 1931.
Boletín Oficial del Obispado de Vitoria, 1931.
Boletín Oficial de la Sociedad de Obreros Gasistas, Electricistas, Teléfonos, Aguas y Similares de Madrid, 1928 (selected numbers).
Boletín de Precios de la Cooperativa del Clero, December 1930.
Boletín del Sindicato Católico de Tipógrafos y Similares de Madrid, 1928–1931.
Boletín del Sindicato Católico de Tipógrafos y Similares de Madrid, Memoria, 1930.
Boletín de la Sociedad de Obreros Encuadernadores de Madrid, 1931 (selected numbers).

Boletín de la Unión General de Trabajadores, Jan. 1929–Dec. 1931.

C.T.T., Semanario de los Trabajadores de Comunicaciones, 1931 (selected numbers).

El Campesino, Organo Oficioso de la Liga Nacional de Campesinos, 1930–31.

Caridad, Revista Mensual Con Licencia y Censura de la Autoridad Eclesiástica, Mar. 1929.

El Cartero Español, 1931 (selected numbers).

La Ciencia Tomista, 1930–31.

La Cruz de la Parroquia, Alcalá de Henares, 1929–31 (selected numbers).

El Dependiente Español, Organo de la Federación Nacional de Dependientes de Comercio, Industria y Banca, 1928.

El Eco Patronal, 1931.

España Republicana; Agricultura, Industria, Comercio, 1 June–1 Aug. 1931.

España Agraria, 1929, 1931.

España en Africa, 1930–1.

España Comercial, 1928.

Industria, Organo de la Cámara Oficial de Industria de Madrid, 1923–9.

El Magisterio Español, Periódico de Instrucción Pública, Apr.–Oct. 1931.

El Mercantil Patronal, Organo de la Defensa Mercantil Patronal, 1930–1.

Mujeres Españolas, 1930–1.

Mundo Femenino, 1929–31.

Nuestro Programa. Organo de la Dependencia Mercantil de Barcelona, 1930 (selected numbers).

Razón y Fe, 1930–1.

Revista Eclesiástica, 1930–1.

Semana Parroquial. Organo de las Juntas Parroquiales, 1930 (selected numbers).

Somatén, 1930–1.

Trabajadores de la Enseñanza. UGT, ITE, 1931.

La Turbina, March 1929.

La Unión, Revista de las Damas Españolas, 1930–1.

Unión de Espectáculos, Organo de la Federación de la Industria de Espectáculos, 1931.

La Unión Ferroviaria, Organo del Sindicato Nacional Ferroviario, 1929–31.

Unión General de Trabajadores, Semanario, 1926–7.

La Vanguardia Mercantil, Organo de los Obreros de la Administración y Distribución, 1930–1.

e. *Foreign Newspapers*

The Economist, London, Sept. 1923–Oct. 1931.

The Times, London, Sept. 1923–Oct. 1931.

f. *Collections of cuttings*

All major private archives contain collections of cuttings from the

Spanish and foreign press. In addition, the Hemeroteca Municipal de Madrid possesses partial collections of many national and regional newspapers, many of which are referred to in the notes of this book.

g. *Periodicals, Reviews, Novels*

Blanco y Negro, 1929.

Actualidad Española. Revista de Cultura, Arte, Literatura y Espectáculos, 1927.

Ars. Programa de los Espectáculos de S.A.G.E. Palacio de la Musica, 1927–31.

Cartel Político. Periódico Gráfico de Ideas Firmes e Independientes, 27 Feb. 1930.

Colección Novela Política (Madrid 1930, 1931), in Hemeroteca Municipal de Madrid, 364/5.

Colección Novela Roja (Madrid 1931) in Hemeroteca Municipal de Madrid, Carp. 18.

Comentario, Mar. 1930.

Criterio, Revista Semanal de Orientación Política y Literaria, 1930.

El Economista, 1929–31.

El Financiero, Nov. 1930, *Número Extraordinario Dedicado a 1929.*

Estampa, 1929–31.

FRU FRU, A series of pornographic novels in Hemeroteca Municipal de Madrid.

Juventud, Revista Semanal, Alicante 1930.

Komedias y Komediantes, 1930 (selected numbers).

Patria Española, 1930 (selected numbers).

Política, Revista mensual de doctrina y crítica, 1930 (selected numbers).

Radiodifusión, 1932.

Radiotécnica, Barcelona 1929–31.

Radio y Luz, 1931.

Revista de Catalunya. Semanario, 1931.

Tanto, 1930 (selected numbers).

h. *Clandestine Publications, Leaflets and Manifestos*

In Hemeroteca Municipal de Madrid:

A Todos los Compañeros, oficiales, Generales, jefes y Oficiales del Ejército	A/1742
A Todos los Compañeros, oficiales Generales, jefes y Oficiales del Ejército.	A/1743
A los Electores de Asturias. República Cristiana, 14 June 1931.	A/1688
A los Nietos de los Héroes de 1808.	A/1723
Al Pueblo de Madrid, Mar. 1931.	A/1680
Al Cuerpo de Ex-Oficiales del Ejército Español.	A/1745
Al Pueblo de Madrid, 22 June 1931.	A/1679
Al Pueblo de Madrid, Mar. 1931.	A/1679
Bando de Propaganda de la Candidatura de Pureza Republicana.	A/1686
El Bloque Anti-Dinástico. A los Jovenes Obreros y Estudiantes.	A/1679
Candidatura de Pureza Republicana.	A/1678
Contestando a Don Gabriel Maura, 1930.	A/1709

Don Quijote Votando, 8 Apr. 1930.   A/1716
La Gaceta de la Revolución, Jan.–Apr. 1931.
Hoja de Propaganda Republicana, 1930.   A/1684
Hoja de Propaganda Anti-Republicana, 1931   A/1687
Hojas Libres, Hendaye 1927–9.
Los Diez Mandamientos del Elector.   A/1680
Manifiesto Publicado en el Libro 'Alianza Republicana'.   A/1690
Manifiesto Político de los Cristianos.   A/1330
*Manifiesto que la Confederación Regional de Sindicatos Libres del Centro
   de España Dirige a sus Afiliados y a la Opinión en General, Con
   Motivo del 1 de Mayo.*   A/1696
*Manifiesto del Partido Republicano Radical Socialista a la Democracia
   Republicana Española*, Dec. 1930.   A/1674
Manifiesto del Partido Comunista ante las Cortes Constituyentes, 15
   Aug. 1931.   A/1329
Manifiesto del Partido Socialista y Unión General de Trabajadores, 21
   Mar. 1931.   A/1695
El Murcielago (selected numbers).   A/1708, A/1313
El Noticiero de la Huelga Escolar, 29 Jan. 1931.   A/1673
*Noticiero del Lunes (Sobre Sánchez Guerra y el General Primo de
   Rivera).*   A/1711
Nuevos Agravios al Ejército, Hasta Cuando?   A/1744
Obreros Madrileños!
El Partido Comunista de España ante las Elecciones Municipales.   A/1677
*Por la Libertad, Por el Derecho y la Soberanía Nacional (Contra la
   República Instaurada en 1931).*   A/1715
Por qué Hay que Votar Contra los Revolucionarios?   A/1680
Propaganda Electoral de la Candidatura Republicano-Socialista.   A/1637
Propaganda Electoral de 1931.   A/1746
*Propaganda Electoral Contra Aurelio Regulez, Candidato a Concejal
   Por Madrid.*   A/1683
*propaganda Electoral Monárquica ante las Elecciones Municipales en
   Madrid.*   A/1700
Propaganda Electoral en Contra de las Candidaturas Republicanas.   A/1681
Propaganda Electoral de la Candidatura Monárquica.   A/1691
*Propaganda Electoral Republicana Dirigida a los Electores de Canillas,
   Pueblo Nuevo.*   A/1712
El Republicano
Ya Es Tarde (Sobre Sánchez Guerra y la Monarquía).   A/1730

In Romanones Archive;

	Leg.	no.
A la Opinión Nacional.	49	4
A Nuestros Compañeros del Ejército y Al País!, 24 Nov. 1926.	2	36

	Leg.	no.
A Los Trabajadores del Campo!	52	20
A Los Señores Generales, Jefes y Oficiales del Ejército y Armada, 1 Sept. 1924.	63	75
'A Los Hombres Con Verguenza', escrito de Rodrigo Soriano.	54	20
A Los Electores de la Provincia de Guadalajara. Carta Abierta, Oct. 1931.	52	7
A La Asamblea Constituyente de la Segunda Republica Española, 13 July 1931.	2	18
A Los Agricultores de Nuestra Provincia, Alicante, 5 Apr. 1930.	49	21
A España y al Ejército.	2	33
Agricultores Alicantinos. Alicante.	49	21
Al Pueblo de Guadalajara.	49	16
Al Pueblo Saguntino.	75	6
Anónima Dirigida a Sánchez de Toca por el Comité de la Armada con Motivo de la Supresión del Estado Mayor Central.	63	44
Bando de Luis Aizpuru y Mondejar, General en jefe del Ejército de España en Africa, Tetuan 12 Sept. 1924.	75	2
Breves Consideraciones Acerca del Pasado, del Presente y del Porvenir del Partido Monárquico Español	63	65
Briocenses! May 1931.	52	5
Campesinos!	52	20
Carta Circular de la Derecha Republicana, 14 July 1930.	2	25
Carta Circular del Grupo de Ciudadanos "Dios, Patria y Libertad!", Jan. 1927.	53	42
Carta de los Electores de Guadalajara para Designar a Romanones para las Cortes Constituyentes.	52	26
Católicos a Defenderse! Liga de Defensa Católica de Barcelona	28	23
Circular de la Guarnición de Alcoy, 18 Jan. 1926.	63	70
Ciudadanos!	52	29
Ciudadanos!	52	29
Ciudadanos y Trabajadores!	52	29
Compañeros!	20	25
Derecha Liberal Republicana. Una Nota y Una Interviu.	2	18
Derecha Liberal Republicana. Circular, 15 July 1930.	2	18
El Rescate de Riegos de Levante y Almadenes, 25 July 1929.	49	21
En Apoyo de la República. Manifiesto de la Derecha Republicana, 5 June 1931.	2	18
Escrito de Jiménez de Asua Renunciando a la Cátedra de Derecho Penal de la Universidad de Madrid, 24 May 1929.	63	51
Escrito de los Estudiantes en el que Hay que leer Una Linea Sí y Otra No.	63	49

326 BIBLIOGRAPHY

	Leg.	no.
España. Informaciones y Comentarios Actuales, Paris, 18 Nov. 1929.	2	47
Hojas al Viento.	54	15
Hojas Libres. Edición Especial, Oct. 1928.	54	16
Hojas Libres. Extraordinario. Bayonne.	2	48
Hojas Libres. Segunda Epoca. No. 3.	14	14
Ideales del Cuerpo de Artillería.	28	52
Impreso Anónimo Contra el Marqués de Estella.	63	51
Junta Municipal de Madrid de la Derecha Liberal Republicana. Convocatoria a la Primera Asamblea Nacional del Partido, 5 June 1931.	2	18
La Candidatura Agraria y la Vieja Política.	52	29
Las Juntas de Defensa, A los Pocos Lectores de 'La Nación', Aug. 1929.	3	18
Manifiesto de Riaza al Pueblo de Brihuega, May 1931.	52	15
Manifiesto de la Fracción de Estudiantes Comunistas.	20	25
No Vale Badar, Artículo de Pedro Manlleu Sobre Cataluña, July 1931.	74	9
Nota Oficiosa, Ultimas Noticias del Movimiento Escolar, 24 Jan. 1930.	2	44
Noticias Sobre la Toma de Alhucemas.	23	6
Orden General del Dia 30 de Noviembre de 1926 : El General en Jefe Miguel Primo de Rivera.	58	48
Partido Constitucionalista, Manifiesto al País.	28	43
Plebiscito Nacional, Unión Patriótica.	2	28
Poesía de Luis de Tapia con Motivo de la Quema de Conventos.	75	6
Problemas Agrarios, Ante Una Cruzada, Sax, Nov. 1930.	49	4
Reflexiones 6ᵉ Serie.	14	14
Republicano, 1930 (One number).	14	2
Sobre Riegos de Levante, 13 July 1929.	49	21
Unión Patriótica de Sacedón, Al Pueblo! 19 Sept. 1924.	75	6
Vecinos de Valdenoches, 25 May 1931.	30	5
Versos Contra la República.	14	23

In the British Museum:

A Collection of Political Tracts, Attacking the Monarchy 1929–1930   1865 C19(98)

In AHN Leg. 42:

Hermanos! Trabajadores Españoles de Francia!

D. *Memoirs and Accounts of Figures involved in the Events*

AIGUADER, JAIME, *Cataluña y la Revolución* (Madrid, 1932).

ALBA, SANTIAGO, *Para la Historia de España* (artículos publicados en Mayo 1930 por *El Sol*).

—— *Despúes de la Dictadura*. *El Pensamiento Político de Don Santiago Alba* (Valladolid, 1930).

ALBERT DESPUJOL, CARLOS DE, *La Gran Tragedia de España 1931–1939* (Madrid, 1940).

ALBIÑANA, JOSÉ MARÍA, *Prisionero de la República* (Madrid, 1932).

—— *España Bajo la Dictadura Republicana*. *Crónica de un Periodo Putrefacto* (Madrid, 1932).

ALBORNOZ, ALVARO DE, *La Tragedia del Estado Español* (Madrid, 1925).

—— *Intelectuales y Hombres de Acción* (Madrid, 1927).

—— *La Política Religiosa de la República* (Madrid, 1935).

—— *Al Servicio de la República*. *De la Unión Republicana al Frente Popular. Criterios de Gobierno* (Madrid, 1936).

—— *El Partido Republicano* (Madrid, n.d.).

—— *El Temperamento Español, La Democracia y la Libertad* (Barcelona, n.d.).

—— 'El Peligro del Caudillaje en el Régimen Presidencial', in RA. Leg. 54, no. 3.

ALCALÁ-ZAMORA Y TORRES, NICETO, *Los Defectos de la Constitución de 1931* (Madrid, 1936).

ANSALDO, JUAN ANTONIO, *Memoires d'un monarchiste espagnol 1931–1952* (Monaco, 1953).

ARMIÑAN ORIOZOLA, JOSÉ MANUEL and LUIS, *Epistolario del Dictador* (Madrid, 1930).

AUNÓS Y PÉREZ, EDUARDO, *Calvo Sotelo y la Política de su Tiempo (Madrid, 1941)*.

—— *La Reforma Corporativa del Estado* (Madrid, 1935).

—— *La Política Social de la Dictadura* (Madrid, 1944).

AZAÑA Y DIAZ, MANUEL, *Obras Completas* (Mexico, 1966–7).

BALBONTÍN, JOSÉ ANTONIO, *La España de Mi Experiencia (Reminiscencias y Esperanzas de un Español en el Exilio)* (Mexico, 1952).

—— *Romancero del Pueblo Español* (Madrid, 1931).

BALDOMERO, ARGENTE, *La Tregua Aduanera y la Organización de la Paz* (Madrid, 1930).

BERENGUER Y FUSTE, DÁMASO, *De la Dictadura a la República* (Madrid, 1946).

BLASCO IBÁÑEZ, VICENTE, *Alfonso XIII Unmasked. The Military Terror in Spain* (Trans. Leo Ongley, London, 1925).

BOFILL I MATES, JAUME, *Una Política Catalanista* (Barcelona, 1933).

BORBÓN, EULALIA DE, *Memorias* (Barcelona, n.d.).

BULLEJOS, JOSÉ, *La Comintern en España. Recuerdos de Mi Vida* (Mexico, 1972).

BURGOS Y MAZO, MANUEL, *Al Servicio de la Doctrina Constitucional* (Madrid, 1930).
—— *De la República a . . . ?* (Madrid, 1931).
—— *La Dictadura y los Constitucionalistas* 4 vols. (Madrid, 1935).
CALVO SOTELO, JOSÉ, *En Defensa Propia* (Madrid, 1932).
—— *Mis Servicios al Estado. Seis Años de Gestión* (Madrid, 1930).
CAMBÓ, FRANCISCO, *España, Cataluña y la Nueva Constitución* (Buenos Aires, 1929).
—— *Por la Concordia* (Madrid, 1927).
—— *La Valoración de la Peseta* (Madrid, 1929).
—— *Las Dictaduras* (Madrid, 1929).
CAMPALANS, RAFAEL, *Hacia la España de Todos (Palabras Castellanas de Un Diputado por Cataluña)* (Madrid, 1932).
CANALS, SALVADOR, *Spain, the Monarchy and the Constitution* (London, 1925).
CASADO GARCÍA, JOSÉ, *Porqué Condené a los Capitanes Galán y García Hernández?* (Madrid, 1935).
CASTILLO-PUCHÉ, J. L., *Diario Intimo de Alfonso XIII* (Madrid, 1960).
CHAPAPRIETA, JOAQUÍN, *La Paz Fué Posible, Memorias de Un Político* (Barcelona, 1972).
CIERVA Y PEÑAFEL, JUAN DE LA, *Notas de Mi Vida* (Madrid, 1955).
CORDERO, MANUEL, *Los Socialistas y la Revolución* (Madrid, 1932).
CUETO, JUAN, *Cuentos al Nuncio. Sobre Derivaciones Republicanas de los Sucesos de Vera* (Madrid, 1933).
DOMINGO, MARCELINO, *Autocracia y Democracia* (Madrid, 1925).
—— *Que es España?* (Madrid, 1925).
—— *Adonde Va España?* (Madrid, 1930).
—— *Que Espera el Rey?* (Madrid, 1930).
—— *La Escuela en la República. La Obra de Ocho Meses* (Madrid, 1932).
E.T.L., *Por Pueblos y Aldeas. De las Memorias de Un Delegado Gubernativo* (Madrid, 1928).
ESTELRICH, JOAN, *La Questió de les Minories* (Barcelona, 1929).
—— *Catalunya Endins. Un Examen de Consciencia Colectiva en Temps Terbols* (Barcelona, 1930).
—— *El Moment Politic* (Publicacions de la joventut de la Lliga Regionalista. Barcelona. Agost. 1930).
—— *De la Dictadura a la Republica* (Barcelona, 1931).
EZA, VIZCONDE DE, *Mi Responsabilidad en el Desastre de Melilla Como Ministro de la Guerra* (Madrid, 1923).
FINAT ROJAS, HIPOLITO, MARQUÉS DE CARVAJAL, *Cual es el Horizonte Político de España? Reflexiones del Hombre de la Calle* (Madrid, 1929).
FRANCO, RAMÓN, *Madrid Bajo las Bombas* (Madrid, 1931).
—— and RUIZ DE ALDA, *De Palos a Plata* (Madrid, 1926).

GARCÍA BENITEZ, JOSÉ, *Tres Meses de Dictadura Obrero-Ateneísta. Algunas Reflexiones sobre Etica Militar Alrededor del 14 de Abril de 1931. Ideología de los que Hemos Abandonado el Ejército por Decreto del 28 de Abril* (Madrid, 1931).

GIL ROBLES, JOSÉ MARÍA, *No Fué Posible la Paz* (Barcelona, 1968).

GODED, MANUEL, *Marruecos, Las Etapas de la Pacificación* (Madrid, 1932).

GÓMEZ FERNÁNDEZ, RAMIRO, *De la Oposición al Poder. La Dictadura me Honró Encarcelandome* (Madrid, 1930).

GONZÁLEZ LÓPEZ, EMILIO, *El Espiritu Universitario* (Madrid, 1931).

GRACO, MARSÁ, *La Sublevación de Jaca. Relato de Un Rebelde* (Paris, 1931).

GUAL VILLALBI, PEDRO, *Memorias de Un Industrial de Nuestro Tiempo* (Barcelona, 1922).

GUTIERREZ-RAVÉ, JOSÉ, *Yo Fuí Un Joven Maurista (Historia de Un Movimiento de Ciudadanía)* (Madrid, 1946).

HOYOS Y VINENT, JOSÉ MARÍA, *Mi Testimonio* (Madrid, 1962).

HURTADO, AMADEU, *Quaranta Anys d'Advocat. Historia del meu Temps* 3 vols. (Barcelona, 1964).

IBARRURI, DOLORES, *Memoires de la Pasionaria* (trans. Françoise-Marie Rosset. Paris, 1964).

IGLESIA, CELEDONIO DE LA, *La Censura Por Dentro* (Madrid, 1930).

JIMÉNEZ DE ASUA, LUIS, *Juventud. Conferencia de Jiménez de Asua y Réplica de José López-Rey* (Madrid, 1929).

—— *Al Servicio de la Nueva Generación* (Madrid, 1930).

—— *Defensa de Una Rebelión. Informe Ante el Consejo Supremo del Ejército y Marina, Como Mandatorio de D. Casares Santiago Quiroga.* (Madrid, 1931).

—— *Anecdotas de las Constituyentes* (Buenos Aires, 1942).

—— *La Constitución de la Democracia Española y el Problema Regional* (Buenos Aires, 1946).

—— *Política, Figuras, Paisajes* (Madrid, n.d.).

LÓPEZ-REY, JOSÉ, *Los Estudiantes Frente a la Dictadura* (Madrid, 1930).

LARGO CABALLERO, FRANCISCO, *Presente y Futuro de la UGT* (Madrid, 1925).

—— *Mis Recuerdos. Cartas a un Amigo* (Mexico, 1954).

LERROUX, ALEJANDRO, *Al Servicio de la República* (Madrid, 1930).

—— *La Pequeña Historia* (Buenos Aires, 1945).

—— *Mis Memorias* (Madrid, 1963).

—— *Para un Periódico de America. Colaboración o Revolución,* 1929, in Hemeroteca Municipal de Madrid A/1685.

—— *Responsabilidad, Inmunidad, Inpunidad,* in AHN Leg. 45.

LÓPEZ DE OCHOA Y PORTEUNDO E., *De la Dictadura a la República* (Madrid, 1930).

LLIGA CATALANA, *Historia d'una Política. Actuacions i Documents de la Lliga Regionalista 1901-1933* (Barcelona, 1933).

Lucía Lucía, Luis, *En Estas Horas de Transición* (Valencia, 1930).

Marco Miranda, Vicente, *Las Conspiraciones Contra la Dictadura* (Madrid, 1930).

Martí Jara, Enrique, *El Rey y el Pueblo* (Madrid, 1929).

Martínez Barrio, D., *Los Radicales en la República. Discursos 1932.* (Seville, 1933).

Maura Gamazo, Miguel, *Así Cayó Alfonso XIII* (Barcelona, 1962).

Maura Gamazo, Gabriel, *Dolor de España* (Madrid, 1932).

—— *Recuerdos de Mi Vida* (Madrid, n.d.).

Mola Vidal, Emilio, *Obras Completas* (Valladolid, 1940).

Morón, Gabriel, *El Partido Socialista Ante la Realidad Política de España* (Madrid, 1929).

—— *La Ruta del Socialismo en España. Ensayo de Crítica y Táctica Revolucionaria* (Madrid, 1932).

Nadal, Joaquín, *Seis Años con Don Francisco Cambó (1939–1936). Memorias de un Secretario Político* (Barcelona, 1957).

Nin Andrés, *El Proletariado Español Ante la Revolución* (Biblioteca Proletaria, 1931).

Ortega y Gasset, Jóse, *Obras Completas* vol. xi. 'Escritos Politicos II (1922–1933)'. (Madrid, 1969).

Ossorio y Gallardo, Angel, *La Crisis del Sentido Conservador* (Madrid, 1925).

—— *Incompatibilidad. Discurso Pronunciado en el Ateneo de Zaragoza el 4 de Mayo de 1930* (Madrid, 1930).

—— *Una Posición Conservadora Ante la República. Conferencia dada en el Círculo Mercantil el dia 17 de Octubre de 1931* (Madrid, 1931).

—— *El Sedimento de la Lucha*, Vida e Ideas (Madrid, 1933).

—— *La España de Mi Vida* (Buenos Aires, 1941).

—— *Mis Memorias* (Buenos Aires, 1946).

Pemán, José María, *Mis Almuerzos Con Gente Importante* (Barcelona, 1970).

Pérez de Ayala, Ramón, *Escritos Políticos* (Madrid, 1967).

Pestaña, Angel, *Lo Que Aprendi en la Vida* (Madrid, 1934).

Pradera, Victor, *Al Servicio de la Patria. Las Ocasiones Perdidas por la Dictadura* (Madrid, 1930).

Prieto, Indalecio, *Convulsiones de España*, 3 vols. (Mexico, 1967–9).

—— *De Mi Vida, Recuerdos, Estampas, Siluetas, Sombras*, 2 vols. (Mexico, 1968–70).

—— *Palabras al Viento* (Mexico, 1969).

—— *El Momento Político. Discurso en el Ateneo* (25 Apr. 1930), in HMM A/1644.

Primo de Rivera, José Antonio, *Obras Completas* (Madrid, 1942).

——, Miguel, *Intervenciones en la Asamblea Nacional del General Primo de Rivera* (Madrid, 1930).

Queipo de Llano, Gonzalo, *El General Queipo de Llano Perseguido por la Dictadura* (Madrid, 1930).

—— *El Movimiento Reivindicativo de Cuatro Vientos* (Madrid, 1933).

Reparaz, Gonzalo De, *Alfonso XIII y sus Complices. Memorias de Una de las Víctimas 1911–1931* (Madrid, 1931).

Rios, Fernando, de Los, *Escritos Sobre Democracia y Socialismo* (Madrid, 1974).

Roig Ibáñez, Vicente, *La Constitución que Precisa España* (Madrid, 1929).

Romanones, Conde De, *Las Ultimas Horas de Una Monarquía* (Madrid, 1931).

—— *Reflexiones y Recuerdos. Historia de Cuatro Días* (Madrid, 1940).

—— *Notas de Una Vida 1912–1931* (Madrid, 1947).

——. . . *Y Sucedió Así. Aportación Para la Historia* (Madrid, 1947).

—— *Las Responsabilidades Políticas del Antiguo Régimen 1875–1923* (Madrid, n.d.).

Rovira i Virgili, A. *Catalunya i la República* (Barcelona, 1931).

Ruiz de Alda, Julio, *El Viraje del Hidroplano 'Plus Ultra' de Palos a Buenos Aires, Conferencia Pronunciada en el 23 de Abril de 1926, en el Teatro de la Princesa de Madrid* (Madrid, 1926).

Sánchez Guerra, Jóse, *Al Servicio de España, Un Manifiesto y Un Discurso* (Madrid, 1930).

Sánchez Guerra, Rafael, *El Movimiento Revolucionario de Valencia (Relato de un Procesado)* (Madrid, 1930).

—— *Proceso de Un Cambio de Régimen. (Historia y Murmuración)* (Madrid, 1932).

Santiago, Enrique, *La Unión General de Trabajadores Ante la Revolución* (Madrid, 1932).

Solá Cañizares, F. De, *El Moviment Revolucionari a Catalunya. Contribució a la Història de l'Adveniment de la República* (Barcelona, 1932).

Tedeschini, Federico, *Discursos y Cartas sobre Acción Católica Española* (Santiago de Compostela, 1958).

Torrubiano Ripoll, Jaime, *Beatería y Religión. Meditaciones de Un Canonista* (Madrid, 1930).

—— *Rebeldías* (Madrid, 1925).

Unamuno, Miguel De, *De Fuerteventura a Paris* (Paris, 1925).

Valdeiglesias, Marqués De, *1875–1949. La Sociedad Española Vista por el Marqués de Valdeiglesias* (Madrid, 1957).

Vallina, Pedro, *Mis Memorias* (Caracas, 1968).

Valverde, José Tomas, *Memorias de Un Alcalde* (Madrid, 1961).

E. *Contemporary Accounts*

Alcalá Galiano, Alvaro, *The Fall of a Throne* (trans. Stewart Erskine, London, 1933).

ALVAREZ, BASILIO, *Dos Años de Agitación Política (en la Calle)* vol. i. (Alcalá de Henares, 1932).

ANDRADE, JUAN, *La Burocracia Reformista en el Movimiento Obrero* (Madrid, 1935).

ANONYMOUS, *The Spanish Republic* (London, 1933).

ARAQUISTÁIN, LUIS, *El Ocaso de un Régimen* (Madrid, 1930).

ARMIÑAN ORIOZOLA, JOSÉ MANUEL and LUIS, *Francia, el Dictador y el Moro. Páginas Históricas* (ed. Javier Morata, Madrid, 1930).

AYENSA, EMILIO, *'Yo No Merezco ser Ministro del Rey ni Gobernante en España'* (Madrid, 1930).

—— *Del Desastre de Annual a la Presidencia del Consejo* (Madrid, 1930).

—— *Vista de la Causa Seguida Contra el Señor Sánchez Guerra* (Madrid, 1929).

BARANGO-SOLÍS, FERNÁNDO, *Un Movimiento Revolucionario: De los Sucesos de Ciudad Real al Proceso Sánchez Guerra* (Barcelona, 1929).

BENITEZ DE LUGO, FELIX, *Obra Económica, Financiera y Monetaria de la Dictadura* (Madrid, 1930).

BENZO, EDUARDO, *Al Servicio del Ejército* (Madrid, 1931).

BLANCO, CARLOS, *La Dictadura y los Procesos Militares* (Madrid, 1931).

BOTTAI, GIUSEPPE, *Esperienza Corporativa* (Roma, 1929).

BUENO, MANUEL, *España y la Monarquía. Estudio Político* (Madrid, Paris, New York, 1925).

CAMPO, ISIDRO DEL, *Lo Que No Ha Dicho Romanones. Cartas Abiertas al General Primo de Rivera* (Madrid, 1925).

CANALS, SALVADOR, *Apuntes Para la Historia. La Caída de la Monarquía. Problemas de la República. Instalación de Un Régimen* (Madrid, 1931).

CARRION, PASCUAL, *La Reforma Agraria de la Segunda República y la Situación Actual de la Agricultura Española* (Barcelona, 1973).

CASTRO, CRISTOBAL DE, *Al Servicio de los Campesinos. Hombres sin Tierra, Tierra sin Hombres* (Madrid, 1931).

CEBREIROS, NAZARIO, *Las Reformas Militares. Estudio Crítico* (Santander, 1931).

CORTÉS-CAVANILLAS, JULIAN, *La Dictadura y el Dictador, Rasgos Históricos, Políticos y Psicológicos* (Madrid, 1929).

COSTA, JOAQUÍN, *Oligarquía y Caciquismo Como la Forma Actual de Gobierno en España. Urgencia y Modo de Cambiarla* (Madrid, 1902).

DEPARTMENT OF OVERSEAS TRADE, *Economic Conditions in Spain* (London, June 1930, Jan. 1933).

DIAZ-RETG, ENRIQUE, *España Bajo el Nuevo Régimen. Cinco Años de Gobierno Primo de Rivera. 1923 – Septiembre 1928* (Madrid, 1928).

DOMINIQUE, PIERRE, *Marche, Espagne* (Paris, 1931).

ESPERABE DE ARTEAGA, E., *La Universidad de Salamanca de 1923 a 1930. Contestando a Unamuno* (Salamanca, 1930).

FALCÓN, CÉSAR, *Crítica de la Revolución Española (Desde la Dictadura Hasta las Constituyentes)* (Madrid, 1931).

FARFÁN DE LOS GODOS, G. and GONZÁLEZ DE SANTIAGO, *Por los Fueros de la Verdad. Aclaraciones Necesarias Para la Historia de los Sucesos de Valencia* (ed. CIAP. Madrid, 1930).

FITÉ, ELIAS, *Política Republicana. La Obra de Un Partido* (Barcelona, 1924).

FELIX HUERTA, JOSÉ, *Sobre la Dictadura* (Madrid, 1930).

GARCÍA GALLEGO, JERÓNIMO, *Miscelánia Política y Religiosa* (Madrid, 1927).

—— *Necesidad de Cortes Constituyentes. Replicando a 'La Epoca', al 'ABC' y a Significados Hombres Públicos de los Partidos Monárquicos* (Valladolid, 1930).

—— *Por Donde se Sale? El Momento Actual de España* (Madrid, 1930).

GARCÍA MENÉNDEZ, B., *La España Rural. (Hambre de Tierra y Sed de Justicia)* (Madrid, 1931).

GARCITORAL, ALICIO, *La Ruta de Marcelino Domingo* (Madrid, 1930).

Glorias de la Raza, La Voz del Pueblo y el Raid Huelva-Buenos Aires (Madrid, 1926).

GRACO MARSÁ, *Lucha de Clases. (Las Rutas del Proletariado).* (Madrid, 1931).

GRANADA, EDUARDO, *Una Página de la Historia de España Escrita por los Propios Actores. (Sánchez Guerra, Acusado, Procesado y Absuelto). Los Caballeros y la Política* (Barcelona, 1929).

GRIJALBA, ALFONSO DE, *Los Enemigos del Rey. (Al Margen de Una Campaña)* (Madrid, 1924).

GUTIERREZ-RAVÉ, JOSÉ, *España en 1931. Anuario* (Madrid, 1932).

HERNÁNDEZ MIR, FRANCISCO, *Un Crimen de Lesa Patria. La Dictadura Ante la Historia* (Madrid, 1930).

—— *La Dictadura en Marruecos. Al Margen de Una Farsa* (Madrid, 1930).

JOVER MIRÁ, MANUEL, *La España Inmortal* (Madrid, 1930).

LHANDE, PIERRE, 'Le Changement de régime en Espagne', *Études, Revue catholique d'interet général*, Paris, 5 May 1931.

LORENZO, PARDO, *La Confederación del Ebro. Nueva Política Hidráulica* (Madrid, 1930).

MADRID, FRANCESC, *Els Exiliats de la Dictadura. Reportatges i Testimonis* (Barcelona, 1930).

MADRID, FRANCISCO, *El Expediente Picasso* (Barcelona, 1930).

MAGRIÑÁ, FEDERICO DE, *Impresiones Políticas del Momento* (Madrid, 1930).

MARCH, JOSÉ MARÍA, *El Somatén, Su Origen y Su Naturaleza, Su Historia y Organización. La Salvación de España* (Barcelona, 1923).

MARTÍNEZ DE LA RIVA, RAMÓN, *Las Jornadas Triunfales de Un Golpe de Estado* (Barcelona, 1923).

MARTÍNEZ SIERRA, MARÍA, *La Mujer Española Ante la República* (Madrid, 1931).

MASERAS, ALFONS, *La Nostra Gent. Francesc Macià* (Barcelona, n.d.).

MAURA GAMAZO, GABRIEL, *Bosquejo Histórico de la Dictadura* (Madrid, 1930).

MAURA GAMAZO, HONORIO, *Tras el Sentido Común. Reflexiones de un Aprendiz de Político* (Madrid, 1933).

MAURÍN, JOAQUÍN, *Los Hombres de la Dictadura* (Madrid, 1930).

—— *La Revolucion Española. De la Monarquía Absoluta a la Revolución Socialista* (Madrid, 1932).

NAVARRO CANALES, LUIS, *La Cuestión Religiosa en el Anteproyecto Constitucional* (Madrid, 1929).

NEVARES, SISINIO, *El Porqué de la Sindicación Obrera Católica* (Madrid, 1930).

ORTEGA, TEOFILO, *La Política y un Político* (Madrid, 1931).

PEMÁN, JOSÉ MARÍA, *El Hecho y la Idea de la Unión Patriótica* (Madrid, 1929).

PEMARTÍN, JOSÉ, *Los Valores Históricos de la Dictadura Española* (Madrid, 1928).

PÉREZ, DIONISIO, *La Dictadura a traves de sus Notas Oficiosas* (Madrid, 1930).

PERUCHO, ARTUR, *Catalunya Sota la Dictadura (Dades Per a la Historia)* (Badalona, 1930).

Problemas Sociales Candentes. (Publicaciones del 'Grupo de la Democracia Cristiana'. Barcelona, 1930).

QUIROGA RÍOS, DOMINGO, *Ensayo Sobre una Nueva Política Gallega.* (La Coruña, 1931).

—— *Contra los Nuevos Oligarcas. Quien es y Adonde Va Santiago Casares. (Notas para la Biografia de un Político Republicano)* (La Coruña, 1932).

REPARAZ, GONZALO DE, *Los Borbones de España. Historia Patológica de Una Dinastía Degenerada* (Madrid, 1931).

RÉVÉSZ, ANDRÉS, *Frente al Dictador* (Madrid, n.d.).

REVUELTA MARTIN, AGUSTIN, *Ventajas que la Sindicación Católica Reporta a la Clase Agraria* (Leon, 1928).

RICO, PEDRO, *El 'Sport' en España. Amateurs y Profesionales* (Madrid, 1930).

RISCO, VICENTE, *El Problema Político de Galicia* (Madrid, 1930).

RIUMBÁU LAZCANO, MARTIN, *El Levantamiento Militar. Sus Causas y Efectos* (Palma, 1923).

ROIG IBÁÑEZ, VICENTE, *La Primera Etapa de la Segunda República Española* (Valencia, 1932).

RUIMAR, CANDIDO, *Quien Mató a Meco?* (Madrid, 1923).

ROYO VILLANOVA, ANTONIO, *Un Grito Contra el Estatuto* (Madrid, 1932).

SALDAÑA Y GARCÍA, QUINTILIANO, *El Momento de España, Ensayos de Sociología Política* (Madrid, 1929).
—— *Al Servicio de la Justicia. La Orgia Aurea de la Dictadura* (Madrid, 1930).
SAMBLANCAT, ANGEL, *El Aire Podrido, El Ambiente Social de España Durante la Dictadura* (Madrid, 1930).
SÁNCHEZ GUERRA, RAFAEL, *Un Año Histórico. España 1931.* (ed. CIAP. Madrid, 1932).
—— *Dictadura, Indiferencia, República* (Madrid, n.d.).
TARDUCHY, EMILIO, *Psicología del Dictador* 2nd ed. (Madrid, 1930).
TROTSKY LEON, *Escritos Sobre España* (Ruedo Iberico, 1971).
UN ESPAÑOL NEUTRAL, *Réplica al Conde de Romanones Sobre las Responsabilidades del Antiguo Régimen* (Madrid, 1925).
VARELA, BENIGNO, *Cartas de un Aragonés al Rey Alfonso XIII* (Madrid, 1931).
VAZQUEZ CAMPO, ANTONIO, *Hacia la Reforma Constitucional Española* (Madrid, 1929).
VILA, ENRIQUE, *Un Año de Republica en Sevilla (Jornadas de Un Periodista)* (Seville, 1932).
VILLANUEVA, FRANCISCO, *El Momento Constitucional* (Madrid, 1929).
—— *La Dictadura Militar* (Madrid, 1930).
—— *Que Ha Pasado Aqui?* (Madrid, 1930).
—— *No Pasa Nada!* (Madrid, 1931).
XURIGUERA, RAMÓN, *Els Exiliats Acusen* (Badalona, 1930).
YABEN, HILARIO, *Monarquía o Republica?* (Madrid, 1931).
ZARRALUQUI, JULIO and MARSÁ, ANGEL, *Figuras de España. Santiago Alba, El Hombre, El Símbolo* (Madrid, 1930).
ZURANO MUÑOZ, EMILIO, *Hagamos Patria. A España, al Rey, y al Gobierno* (Madrid, 1930).

F. Later Accounts

ARMIÑAN, LUIS DE, *La República . . . Es Esto? Del Retablo Revolucionario* (Madrid, 1933).
AUNÓS Y PEREZ, EDUARDO, *Primo de Rivera Soldado y Gobernante* (Madrid, 1944).
—— *Semblanza Política del General Primo de Rivera* (Madrid, 1947).
AYENSA, EMILIO, *De Teniente-General a Recluso 52. Historia Crítica de Una Vida* (Madrid, 1933).
AYMANI I BAUDINA, *Maciá. Trenta Anys de Política Catalanista. Apunts per a Una Biografía* (Barcelona, 1933).
BUCKLEY, HENRY, *Life and Death of the Spanish Republic* (London, 1940).
CAMBA, JULIO, *Haciendo de República* (Madrid, 1968).
CAPELLA, JACINTO, *La Verdad de Primo de Rivera. Intimidades y Anecdotas del Dictador* (Madrid, 1933).

336 BIBLIOGRAPHY

CIGES, APARICIO, *España Bajo la Dinastía de los Borbones* (Madrid, 1932).

COCA, GABRIEL MARIO DE, *Anti-Caballero. Crítica Marxista de la Bolchevización del Partido Socialista (1930–1936)* (Madrid, 1936).

CORTÉS-CAVANILLAS, JULIAN, *La Caída de Alfonso XIII. Causas y Episodios de Una Revolución* (Madrid, 1932).

—— *Alfonso XIII, Vida, Confesiones y Muerte* (Barcelona, 1966).

—— *Alfonso XIII en el Destierro* (Madrid, n.d.).

CUBER, MARIANO, *Melquiades Alvarez, El Orador, El Hombre. El Político, Sus Ideales. Su Consecuencia. Su Integridad* (Madrid, 1935).

ESPLÁ, CARLOS, *Unamuno, Blasco Ibáñez y Sánchez Guerra en Paris* (Buenos Aires, 1940).

FERNÁNDEZ ALMAGRO, MELCHOR, *Catalanismo y República Española* (Madrid, 1932).

GASCÓN, ANTONIO, *Los Hombres que Trajeron la República. Los Estudiantes.* (Madrid, n.d.).

GAYA PICÓN, JOSÉ, *Los Hombres que Trajeron la República. La Jornada Histórica de Barcelona. Del Centralismo a la Autonomía, Pasando por Unas Horas de República Catalana* (Madrid, n.d.).

GONZÁLEZ RUANO, CÉSAR AND TARDUCHY, EMILIO, *Sanjurjo. (Una Vida Española del Novecientos)* (Madrid, 1933).

GUTIÉRREZ MUÑOZ, F., *España Acusa* (Madrid, 1947).

KARL, MAURICIO, *Asesinos de España. Marxismo, Anarquismo, Masonería* (Madrid, 1935).

MARSÁ BRAGADO, ANTONIO and others, *Libro de Oro del Partido Republicano Radical 1868–1934* (Madrid, 1934).

—— *El Republicanismo Histórico. Homenaje a D. Alejandro Lerroux* (Madrid, 1933).

MILEGO, JULIO, *El General Barrera (de Cataluña al 10 de Agosto)* (Madrid, 1936).

MORAL, JOAQUÍN DEL, *Oligarquía y Enchufismo, Escarceos Críticos Sobre la Actual Política Española* (Madrid, 1933).

OYARZUN, ROMÁN, *La Historia del Carlismo* (Madrid, 1969).

PEERS, ALLISON, *The Spanish Tragedy 1930–1936. Dictatorship, Republic, Chaos* (London, 1936).

PEIRATS, JOSÉ, *La CNT en la Revolución Española* vol. i (Toulouse, 1951).

—— *Los Anarquistas en la Crisis Política Española* (Buenos Aires, 1964).

PICARD-MOCH, GERMAINE and JULES, *L'œuvre d'une revolution. L'Espagne républicaine* (Paris, 1933).

PLÁ, JOSEP, *Madrid, L'Adveniment de la República* (Barcelona, 1933).

PYRENE (pseud.), *Antiespañolismo, Marxistas y Separatistas Contra España* (Zaragoza, 1935).

REQUEJO SAN ROMAN, JESUS, *El Cardenal Segura* (Toledo, 1932).

ROYO VILLANOVA, ANTONIO, *Treinta Años de Política Antiespañola* (Vallodolid, 1940).

SABORIT, ANDRÉS, *Julian Besteiro* (Mexico, 1961).
—— *Asturias y Sus Hombres* (Toulouse, 1964).
SILIÓ, CÉSAR, *En Torno a Una Revolución. Crisis de España. Caída de la Monarquía. La República. La Revolución Socialista* (Madrid, 1933).
TUSQUETS, JUAN, *Origenes de la Revolución Española* (Barcelona, 1932).

2. SECONDARY SOURCES

ACEDO COLUNGA, FELIPE, *José Calvo Sotelo. La Verdad de una Muerte* (Barcelona, 1957).
AGUADO, EMILIANO, *La República, Ultimo Disfraz de la Restauración* (Madrid, 1972).
—— *Don Manuel Azaña Diaz* (Barcelona, 1972).
ALBA, VICTOR, *Histoire des républiques espagnoles* (trans. Louis Parrot. Paris, 1948).
ALFARACHE, JUAN DE, *Berenguer* (Madrid, 1949).
ALTABELLA, JOSÉ, '*El Norte de Castilla*' *en su Marco Periodístico 1854–1965* (Madrid, 1966).
ARMIÑAN, LUIS DE, *Weyler* (Madrid, 1946).
ARRARAS JOAQUÍN, *Franco* (trans. J. Manuel Espinosa. London, 1938).
—— *Historia de la Cruzada Española* vol. i (Madrid, 1939–40).
—— *Historia de la Segunda República Española* vol. i (Madrid, 1969).
AUNÓS Y PÉREZ, EDUARDO, *España en Crisis 1874–1936* (Buenos Aires, 1942).
AZCÁRATE, GUMERSINDO DE, *El Régimen Parlamentario en la Práctica* (Madrid, 1931).
BALCELLS, ALBERTO, *El Sindicalismo en Barcelona 1916–1923* (Barcelona, 1965).
—— *Crisis Económica y Agitación Social en Cataluña 1930–1936* (Barcelona, 1971).
BALLESTEROS Y BERETTA, ANTONIO, *Historia de España y su Influencia en la Historia Universal* vol. viii (Barcelona, 1936).
BECARUD, JEAN, *La Deuxieme république espagnole 1931–1936. Essai d'interpretation* (*Centre d'études des Relations Internationales, Série C.* Recherche no. 7. Oct. 1962).
BEN-AMI, SHLOMO, 'Los Estudiantes Contra el Rey', *Historia-16*, Oct. 1976.
BENAVIDES, LEANDRO, *La Política Económica en la Segunda República* (Madrid, 1972).
BLEIBERG, GERMAN, *Diccionario de Historia de España*, 3 vols. (Madrid, Revista de Occidente 1968).
BLINKHORN, R. M., *Carlism and Crisis in Spain 1931–1939* (Cambridge, 1976).
BORRÁS, TOMAS, *Ramiro Ledesma Ramos* (Madrid, 1971).

BRADEMAS, JOHN, *Anarcosindicalismo y Revolucion en España 1930–1937* (Barcelona, 1974).

BRANDENBERGER ERNA, *Estudios sobre el Cuento Español Contemporáneo* (Madrid, 1973).

BRENAN, GERALD, *The Spanish Labyrinth* (Cambridge, 1964).

BROUÉ, PIERRE and ÉMILE TEMIME, *La Revolution et la guerre d'Espagne* (Paris, 1961).

CARR, RAYMOND, *Spain 1808–1939* (Oxford, 1970).

—— (ed.), *The Republic and the Civil War in Spain* (London, 1971).

CIERVA, RICARDO DE LA, *Historia de la Guerra Civil Española. Antecedentes. Monarquía y República 1898–1936* (Madrid, 1969).

—— *La Historia Perdida del Socialismo Español* (Madrid, 1972).

COMÍN COLOMER, EDUARDO, *Lo que España Debe a la Masonería* (Madrid, 1952).

—— *Historia Secreta de la Segunda República* (Madrid, 1954).

—— *Historia del Partido Comunista de España* vol. i (Madrid, 1965).

—— *Unamuno, Libelista. Sus Campañas Contra Alfonso XIII y la Dictadura* (Coleccion Siglo Ilustrado).

CONELLY ULLMAN, JOAN, *La Semana Trágica. Estudio Sobre las Causas Socioeconómicas del Anticlericalismo en España* (Barcelona, 1972).

CUCO, ALFONS, *El Valencianisme Politic 1874–1936* (Valencia, 1971).

CUESTA GARRIGOS, ILDEFONSO, 'Los Grandes Bancos Españoles. Su evolución (1922–1943)', *Moneda y Crédito* Dec. 1944. no. 11.

DIEZ-NICOLAS, JUAN, *Tamaño, Densidad y Crecimiento de la Población en España 1900–1960* (Madrid, 1971).

DOMINGUEZ, MARTIN, *El Tradicionalismo de Un Republicano* (Seville, 1962).

ESTEBAN-INFANTES, EMILIO, *General Sanjurjo* (Barcelona, 1958).

FERNÁNDEZ ALMAGRO, MELCHOR, *Historia del Reinado de Alfonso XIII* (Barcelona, 1934).

—— *Historia de la República Española 1931–1936* (Madrid, 1940).

FURNEAUX, RUPERT, *Abd-el-Krim* (London, 1967).

GALINDO HERRERO, SANTIAGO, *Los Partidos Monárquicos Bajo la Segunda República* (Madrid, 1954).

GARCÍA VENERO, MAXIMIANO, *Vida de Cambó* (Barcelona, 1952).

—— *Melquiades Alvarez, Historia de Un Liberal* (Madrid, 1954).

—— *Historia de las Internacionales en España* vol. ii (1914–1936) (Madrid, 1957).

—— *Historia de los Movimientos Sindicalistas Españoles (1840–1933)* (Madrid, 1961).

—— *Torcuato Luca de Tena y Alvarez-Ossorio. Una Vida al Servicio de España* (Madrid, 1961).

—— *Santiago Alba, Monárquico de Razón* (Madrid, 1963).

—— *Historia del Nacionalismo Catalan.* vol. ii (Madrid, 1967).
—— *Historia del Nacionalismo Vasco* (Madrid, 1969).
GIRALT, EMILI, ALBERT BALCELLS and JOSEP TERMES, *Los Movimientos Sociales en Cataluña, Valencia y Baleares* (Barcelona, 1970).
GÓMEZ CASAS, JUAN, *Historia del Anarco-Sindicalismo Español* (Madrid, 1968).
GÓMEZ-SANTOS, MARINO, *Vida de Gregorio Marañón* (Madrid, 1971).
GONZÁLEZ CASANOVA, J. A., *Elecciones en Barcelona (1931–1936)* (Barcelona, 1969).
GONZÁLEZ RUANO, CÉSAR, *Miguel Primo de Rivera. La Vida Heroica y Romantica de un General Español* (Madrid, 1935).
—— *El General Primo de Rivera* (Madrid, 1954).
GONZÁLEZ RUIZ, N., *Azaña. Sus Ideas Religiosas, sus Ideas Políticas, el Hombre* (Madrid, 1932).
GUTIERREZ-RAVÉ, JOSÉ, *Gil Robles, Caudillo Frustrado* (Madrid, 1967).
GUZMÁN, EDUARDO DE, *España entre las Dictaduras y la Democracia* (Madrid, 1967).
—— *1930: Historia Política de Un Año Decisivo* (Madrid, 1973).
HENNESSY, C. A. M., *Modern Spain* (Historical Association. London, 1965).
JACKSON, GABRIEL, 'The Azaña Regime in Perspective (Spain 1931–1933)', *American Historical Review* vol. 64 no. 2, Jan. 1959.
—— *The Spanish Republic and the Civil War 1931–1939* (Princeton University Press, 1967).
JATO, DAVID, *La Rebelión de los Estudiantes* (Madrid, 1953).
JOANIQUET, AURELIO, *Alfonso Sala, Conde de Argemí* (Madrid, 1955).
LACOMBA, J. A., *La Crisis Española de 1917* (Madrid, 1970).
LINZ, JUAN, 'The Party System of Spain, Past and Future', in Seymour M. Lipset and Stein Rokkan (eds.), *Party Systems and Voter Alignments* (New York, 1967).
LIPSET, SEYMOUR and PHILIP ALTBACH, *Students in Revolt* (Boston, 1969).
LISÓN-TOLOSANA, C., *Belmonte de los Caballeros. A Sociological Study of a Spanish Town* (Oxford, 1966).
MADARIAGA, SALVADOR DE, *España, Ensayo de Historia Contemporánea* (Buenos Aires, 1964).
MALEFAKIS, EDWARD, *Agrarian Reform and Peasant Revolution in Spain, Origins of the Civil War* (Yale University Press, 1970).
MANUEL, FRANK, *The Politics of Modern Spain* (New York and London, 1938).
MARICHAL, JUAN, *La Vocación de Manuel Azaña* (Madrid, 1968).
MARIÑAS, FRANCISCO JAVIER, *General Varela (De Soldado a General)* (Barcelona, 1956).

340   BIBLIOGRAPHY

Maura, Gabriel and Melchor Fernández Almagro, *Porqué Cayó Alfonso XIII?* (Madrid, 1948).
Miguez, Alberto, *El Pensamiento Filosófico de Julian Besteiro* (Madrid, 1971).
Molas, Isidre, *Lliga Catalana* vol. i (Barcelona, 1972).
Muntanyola, Ramón, *Vidal i Barraquer el Cardenal de la Paz* (Barcelona, 1971).
Narbona, Francisco, *La Quema de Conventos* (Madrid, 1954).
Olmedo Delgado, Antonio and José Cuesta Monereo, *General Queipo de Llano (Aventura y Andacia)* (Barcelona, 1957).
Oñate del Pilar, María, *El Feminismo en la Literatura Española* (Madrid, 1938).
Ordoñez Marquéz, Juan, *La Apostasía de las Masas y la Persecución Religiosa en la Provincia de Huelva 1931–1936* (Madrid, 1968).
Ossorio y Gallardo, Angel, *Vida y Sacrificio de Companys* (Buenos Aires, 1943).
Pabón, Jesus, *Días de Ayer. Historias e Historiadores Contemporáneos* (Barcelona, 1963).
—— *Cambó* vol. ii (Barcelona, 1969).
Payne, G. Stanley, *Falange. A History of Spanish Fascism* (Stanford, 1962).
—— *Politics and the Military in Modern Spain* (Oxford, 1967).
—— *The Spanish Revolution* (London, 1970).
Paz, Abel, *Durruti, Le Peuple en Armes* (Bordeaux, 1972).
Peers, Allison, *Catalonia Infelix* (London, 1937).
Perpiña, Román, *De Estructura Económica y Economía Hispana* (Madrid, 1952).
Petrie, Charles, *King Alfonso XIII and his Age* (London, 1963).
Plá, José, *Historia de la Segunda Republica Española* (Barcelona, 1964).
Preston, Paul, 'Alfonsist Monarchism and the Coming of the Spanish Civil War', *Journal of Contemporary History*, vii, 3–4, July–Oct. 1972.
—— 'The "Moderate" Right and the Undermining of the Second Republic in Spain, 1931–1933', *European Studies Review*, iii, 4, Oct. 1973.
—— (ed.), *Leviatan (Antologia)*, 'Prologo', pp. v–xxix (Madrid, 1976).
Rama, M. Carlos, *La Crisis Española del Siglo XX* (Mexico, 1962).
Ramírez Jiménez, Manuel, *Los Grupos de Presión en la Segunda República Española* (Madrid, 1969).
Ramos Oliveira, Antonio, *Historia de España* vols. ii, iii (Mexico, 1952).
Ratcliff, F. Dillwyn, *Prelude to Franco* (New York, 1957).
Redondo, Gonzalo, *Las Empresas Políticas de Ortega y Gasset* vol. ii (Pamplona, 1970).

ROBINSON, R. A. H., *Origins of Franco's Spain: Right, Republic and Revolution 1931–1936* (Newton Abbot, 1970).

ROMEU ALFARO, FERNANDA, *Las Clases Trabajadoras en España 1898–1930* (Madrid, 1970).

RUIZ GONZÁLEZ, DAVID, *El Movimiento Obrero en Asturias* (Oviedo, 1968).

SÁNCHEZ, JOSÉ, *Reform and Reaction. The Politico-Religious background of the Spanish Civil War* (University of North Carolina Press, 1964).

SEVILLA, ANDRÉS, *Canalejas* (Barcelona, 1956).

SCHOLL, S. H. (ed.), *Historia del Movimiento Obrero Cristiano* (Barcelona, 1964).

SCHULTE, F. HENRY, *The Spanish Press 1470–1966* (University of Illinois Press, Urbana. Chicago, London, 1968).

SECO SERRANO, CARLOS, *Alfonso XIII y la Crisis de la Restauración* (Barcelona, 1969).

—— *Historia de España. Epoca Contemporánea* vol. vi (Barcelona, 1971).

SEDWICK, FRANK, *The Tragedy of Manuel Azaña and the Fate of the Spanish Republic* (Ohio State University Press, 1963).

SFORZA, CARLOS, *European Dictatorships* (London, 1932).

THOMAS, HUGH, *The Spanish Civil War* (London, 1964).

TUÑÓN DE LARA, MANUEL, *La España del Siglo XX* (Paris, 1966).

—— *Historia y Realidad del Poder* (Madrid, 1967).

—— *Medio Siglo de Cultura Española 1885–1936* (Madrid, 1970).

—— *El Movimiento Obrero en la Historia de España* (Madrid, 1972).

—— and MANUEL NUÑEZ DE ARENAS, *Historia del Movimiento Obrero Español* (Barcelona, 1970).

TUSSELL GÓMEZ, JAVIER, *Sociología Electoral de Madrid 1903–1931* (Madrid, 1969).

—— *La Segunda República en Madrid. Elecciones y Partidos Políticos* (Madrid, 1970).

—— 'Elecciones y Vida Política en Andalucía' (unpublished dissertation, Madrid University, 1972).

—— 'La Descomposición del Sistema Caciquil Español (1902–1931)', *Revista de Occidente*, no. 127, Oct. 1973.

VARELA ORTEGA, J., 'Los Amigos Políticos: Funcionamiento del Sistema Caciquista' in *Revista de Occidente*, Oct. 1973, no. 127.

VELARDE FUERTES, *Política Económica de la Dictadura* (Madrid, 1968).

WALTER RICHARD, *Student Politics in Argentina* (New York, 1968).

WOOLMAN, DAVID, *Rebels in the Rif* (Stanford, Calif., 1968).

INDEX